# Behavioral Research

# Behavioral Research

## ASSESSING THE VALIDITY OF RESEARCH FINDINGS IN PSYCHOLOGY

## Paul D. Cherulnik

*Susquehanna University*

**HARPER & ROW, PUBLISHERS, New York**
Cambridge, Philadelphia, San Francisco,
London, Mexico City, São Paulo, Sydney

*1817*

To my Mother and Father

Sponsoring Editor: George A. Middendorf
Project Editor: Pamela Landau
Production Manager: William Lane
Compositor: Com Com Division of Haddon Craftsmen
Printer and Binder: R. R. Donnelley & Sons Company
Art Studio: Fineline, Inc.
Cover Design: Diane Saxe

**BEHAVIORAL RESEARCH**
**Assessing the Validity of Research Findings in Psychology**

Library of Congress Cataloging in Publication Data

Cherulnik, Paul D., 1941–
    Behavioral research.

    Bibliography: p.
    1. Psychological research.    2. Psychology—
Methodology.    I. Title.    [DNLM: 1. Behavioral sciences.
2. Research—Methods.    3. Research design—Standards.
BF 76.5 C523b]
BF76.5.C46    1983        150′.72        82-21354
ISBN 0-06-041258-5

# Contents

## Chapter 8
## Quasi-Experimental Designs 272

## Chapter 9
## Adding up the Score 345

# Preface

When I first got the assignment to teach a course in research methods (Principles of Psychological Research it was called), I was frightened by it. It seemed such a bewildering array of complex, abstract concepts to try to get across to students who, for the most part, weren't planning to become researchers anyway. Glancing through the textbooks that were available for the course did little to calm my fears. They seemed to me to lack any real logical organization. Even worse, they mixed in with discussions of central questions about methodology apparently unrelated topics (from my point of view) such as psychophysics, statistics, and research report writing. Those books weren't going to help me to get organized to teach all those things I had learned over so long a time, from so many sources, without really knowing myself how I had done it.

In the midst of paging through texts, looking for one that would help me and my prospective students, I somehow remembered hearing about a new approach to understanding research methods that had been published several years earlier, first as a chapter in a handbook of methods for educational research (Campbell and Stanley, 1963) and then reprinted by itself as a paperback (Campbell and Stanley, 1966). The fact that I knew one of its authors to be one of our leading thinkers about methodological problems, and the rumors I'd heard about it becoming a kind of underground classic, persuaded me to search for it. When I finally read it, I was impressed more than I had been by anything I'd read about research methods up to that point. The analysis it provided of the strengths and weaknesses of various approaches to doing research was coherent, well organized, and complete. That slim volume of less than 100 pages covered more of the conceptual ground, could be applied to more fields of research, and seemed more logical than I had believed possible. Moreover, I felt I had learned more fundamental truth about research methods in the few hours it took to read that book than I had in the ten years I had studied psychology up to that point. Most important, I believed that the truth could be explained to undergraduate students of psychology.

I finally decided that this was the approach I had to take to teaching the methods course. However, the Campbell and Stanley book was not appropriate as a text for my students. It presumed too much background. There were too few definitions of basic concepts and too few examples for people who hadn't already done considerable background reading in the behavioral sciences. So I wrote an outline of the system Campbell and Stanley had devised, reorganized it a little, added a lot of examples and definitions, and presented it to the students orally and on the classroom blackboards.

Thankfully, they were able to learn a great deal that way, and over the succeeding years my organization, definitions, and examples improved steadily. But the students always felt somewhat uncomfortable without a textbook to carry around with them, which they could consult at their convenience, without waiting for the next class to ask for clarification of a puzzling point or to see where the story went next. I assigned books from time to time that contained bits and pieces of the system I was trying to teach, more than anything else just to give my students and myself the comfort only a textbook can provide. Finally, however, I decided to turn my own notes into a new book. Together with the considerable rethinking that putting it all down formally on paper required, and the helpful suggestions of colleagues who read parts or all of it, the result was the book you are about to read.

Despite my faith in the basic structure of the system we'll be using to understand research methods, I wouldn't want to give you a false sense of security. The issues we will be working to understand are extremely complex. Persons who feel they understand all there is to know about methodology (as the old joke goes) simply fail to comprehend the seriousness of the problems they face. There are many practicing researchers, as the examples you will be reading about should convince you, who haven't got them all straight. There are important questions about behavior for which there are no ready methods of arriving at an acceptable answer. And there are some very vigorous disagreements about how to solve many methodological problems.

The complexity of these problems makes it necessary to be patient in your approach to them. Some of the concepts that have to be understood can only be developed slowly, through repeated explanations and examples. There are no simple definitions that can be extracted. Although there is a glossary of terms at the back of the book the definitions found there can only help to jog your memory, reminding you of examples or bits of the discussions of the concepts. True understanding of the issues can be earned only by reading and thinking about them through the entire course of the book. The greatest strength of the approach we'll be taking is that it is organized as a system. Knowing one part of it increases one's understanding of every other part. At the same time, this makes it impossible to convey a full understanding of a single issue by a concise definition. There are no shortcuts.

Rest assured, however, that your patience will be rewarded. The importance of understanding research methods goes far beyond your studies in psychology or any other behavioral science. I think you'll find, as I have, that it may be even more important as you read newspapers and magazines, or watch the news or other public affairs programs on television. In a very real sense, an understanding of research methods is a guide to thinking, not only about science but also about important questions of many other kinds.

There are many people to whom I owe thanks for helping me in writing this book. I owe Donald Campbell and Julian Stanley a great intellectual debt. They taught me a great deal of what I know about research methods and started me on the way to learning the rest. Much of what I have learned through that inspiration I owe to so many others who have devoted themselves to the analysis of methodological questions. Some of them have been credited for their ideas in the text, but those who have not will have to settle for this anonymous mention. There have also been many collegues who have read sections of drafts of the manuscript. They found many of my errors, but only I can be blamed for the rest.

On a more personal level, there are also many people to whom I am grateful. My wife Beverly has put up with my absences and my moods and has collaborated on the work as well. She has provided love and ideas and clerical help throughout the entire project, and it never would have been finished without her. My parents encouraged me to follow a career of scholarship and I hope that this book, dedicated to them, resolves some of their doubts about the wisdom of that action. Many teachers have inspired me and I would especially like to thank one of them, Ed Hollander, for the confidence he has shown in me over the years. Jack Bevan, who was my boss at the College of Charleston, helped considerably during the period when I did most of the writing there. George Middendorf, my editor at Harper & Row, showed great patience and provided necessary encouragement. His personal wit and charm helped me to open those dreaded envelopes containing criticisms and suggestions from reviewers. And there have been too many others—colleagues, students, and other friends—to thank them all personally. If this book makes a contribution, all these people deserve a share of the credit. I only hope that some of those who read it will someday want to include us in a list like this one.

Paul Cherulnik

# Chapter 1
# Toward an Understanding of Validity

## INTRODUCTION

Those who pursue the study of psychology beyond the introductory level may often be surprised to learn that many of the research findings once presented to them as facts about behavior have been challenged. Advanced courses are often given over, in large part, to the consideration of conflicting theories about various aspects of behavior. And it is rarely possible to choose among these theories on the basis of research findings. Those on each side of an issue seem to be able to muster sufficient supportive evidence to create a standoff.

This condition prevails in all the various subfields of psychology, whether social or developmental or learning. It is also widespread in other behavioral and social sciences, such as sociology and political science, and in such diverse fields as history and philosophy, and even physics and mathematics. It seems to be a rather general rule that the further one progresses in the study of any field, the more one is exposed to uncertainty regarding the true nature of the phenomena with which that field is concerned. Students in an introductory psychology course may learn that reinforcement increases the rate of response, and they may confidently believe that fact for some time. Then, in an advanced course in social psychology, an instructor may present research evidence which seems to prove that some people's behavior is not modified to any substantial degree by reinforcement.

In point of fact, the literature of psychology, and every other scientific discipline, consists of many such inconsistencies. How, then, can one decide among the varying opinions of psychologists, and other scientists, which seem to cloud every issue of importance? One key, it turns out, is a very complex set of principles and techniques that is often referred to as "the scientific method" or "methodology." The purpose of this book is to introduce the reader to some basic principles that make it possible to evaluate the contradictory findings and assertions that plague every scientific discipline.

Unfortunately, it cannot be claimed that a complete resolution to this problem will be effected. One reason is that the approach to be taken here is directed primarily toward research in psychology. That is not to say that the principles which we will consider do not apply to other disciplines as well. But, although they do, the examples that we will use and the issues with which we will deal most fully will be drawn from the literature of psychology. Therefore, they will, inevitably, be most useful in and most directly applicable to understanding the subject matter of that field. As we shall see, one of the complexities of the scientific method is that each field of study presents its own peculiar difficulties of evaluation, in addition to its share of the general problems which cut across disciplinary boundaries. We will see that even within the single discipline of psychology, different research problems may require different research methods in order to cope with their special difficulties. For example, psychological research with human subjects can present problems that are not encountered by psychologists who study the behavior of rats or pigeons.

The study of the scientific method is also complicated by the number of skills that are required to evaluate the findings of research. Many of these lie outside the scope of this book. They include statistics, a substantive knowledge of the phenomenon under investigation, including its literature of past research findings, and general knowledge that has nothing to do per se with either psychology or the scientific method. In addition, the abilities to conceptualize complex problems, and to observe behavior with sensitivity and objectivity are very important, as are such mysterious abilities as creativity and the ability to synthesize.

However, we will be able to make a good start toward being able to understand and evaluate the methods of psychological research. We will stress understanding and evaluating research, rather than doing research, because of its wider importance. Few students of psychology will ever do research themselves. Even those psychologists who are active researchers come into contact with research findings more often as consumers of research findings from professional journals or the popular media. And every consumer, including the consumer of the products of science, needs to be able to evaluate and choose among competing products, which are all offered as the latest and best on the market. It is no less important for a psychologist to buy a good understanding of human behavior than for a driver to buy a good automobile. And science is important not only for the researcher, whose own work depends on an understanding of what has gone before, but also for the average citizen, whose participation in the democratic process depends on an understanding of the world he or she lives in.

The plan of this book has been adapted from a pattern that was laid several years ago by Donald T. Campbell and Julian C. Stanley (1963). The purpose of that plan is to make the basic principles of the scientific method understandable. Its greatest strengths are, paradoxically, its simplicity of structure and the diversity of issues which that simple structure can accommodate. The first four chapters of the book describe the plan and structure and introduce the basic concepts and a framework for organizing them. The remaining chapters evaluate a sample of each of the variety of research methods that can be used to test hypotheses in psychology—and in other disciplines as well. We will also consider some of the methodological issues which are currently being debated most vigorously in psychology.

## A Sample of Psychological Research for Analysis

We will begin by considering an example of contemporary psychological research. This study was not chosen to be representative of the wide range of psychological research. No single study could be. It does, however, introduce some basic concepts, which we will refer to again and again throughout the book. And it demonstrates early on how difficult it can be to decide whether the findings of a particular piece of research can be believed. Most important, this study will help us to define the concept of *validity*, the technical term we will use to represent the complex judgment about the truth of research findings.

Before we go any further, a word about the word "study." There are many ways to categorize the research methods used in psychology. You are probably familiar with many terms already, such as experiment, investigation, study. In Chapter 4, we will look at one scheme for classifying research methods which we feel has certain advantages that recommend its use. Until then, we will use the term "study" to refer to any research, regardless of the methods it employs.

The study in question was performed to test the hypothesis that one's success or failure in performing a task can be affected to a measurable degree by one's initial expectations. That is, it was directed to this question: Is it true that, other things being equal, people who think they will do well on an assigned task will actually outperform those who undertake the same task thinking they are likely to perform poorly? This unpublished study of mine was carried out by a student, Max Zachau, who acted as *experimenter,* the person who actually does the work of performing a study, meeting *subjects* (those whose behavior is studied), giving them instructions, distributing and collecting materials, etc.

To investigate our hypothesis, 48 of approximately 500 male students in various sections of an Introductory Psychology course were selected, simply because they were available during the times that we had chosen to do our study. All students taking the course were required to participate as subjects in research—a common practice about which we will say more later on. Their participation had actually begun several weeks earlier, when they and all their classmates spent the class period answering a number of personality questionnaires. Several faculty members had assembled that set of questionnaires for a variety of research purposes.

The 48 men came to our laboratory, an ordinary room furnished with several tables and chairs, in groups from two to five. The experimenter read a set of instructions which was designed to convince the subjects, first of all, that we could predict their performance on an upcoming task. The experimenter referred to the questionnaires that the subjects had filled out in their classes weeks before, suggesting that some of their answers had been designed to permit us to predict their performance on a task in which we were currently very interested. We gave them no specific reason for our interest.

The task turned out to be solving anagrams—unscrambling scrambled words (e.g., "IFSH" is a simple anagram whose solution is "FISH"). The subjects were told that their participation in our study would help us to find out exactly how well our questions predicted people's performance.

Twenty-four subjects were told that we predicted they would perform the task successfully. The other 24 were told that we predicted they would have great difficulty with the task. The experimenter chose which instructions to give each group of subjects by flipping a coin just before they arrived (until the very end, when the two groups had to be evened out at 24).

These instructions, and the staging that went with them, including the subjects' vague memories of having filled out the questionnaires in class, were our way of creating the feelings about the quality of an upcoming performance, or expectations, to which our hypothesis referred. They were also, of course, total misrepresentations of the truth. To the best of our knowledge, the questionnaire that our subjects had filled out had nothing to do with an ability to solve anagrams. Besides, at that point we had absolutely no idea what their responses to the questions had been.

The next step in our procedure was presented as a warm-up. The subjects were told that because some of them might have solved anagrams before, whereas others had not, we wanted them all to try a sample of ten anagrams before doing the actual experimental task. Then they could all begin the task with at least some experience with anagrams. This was another lie. The real purpose of the warm-up was to strengthen the effect we started to create in the first part of our instructions to them—that is, to produce two groups of subjects who had very different expectations for their performance on the anagrams task.

Months before, a large number of students in a prior semester's Introductory Psychology sections had fulfilled their requirement to participate as subjects in research by solving a large number of anagrams. On the basis of their solutions, we were able to estimate the difficulty of each of those anagrams for the average student. They varied from some that most students could solve quickly to some that almost none of them could solve within a reasonable length of time, and through every point in between those extremes. Using those estimates, we were able to create two lists of ten anagrams that differed greatly in difficulty. These lists were then used in our warm-up, each with the identical 3-minute time limit. Those subjects who had been led to believe by our earlier instructions that they would be successful anagrams solvers received a list of easy anagrams on which to get warmed up. In fact, their average score on that list of ten was 8.63. On the other hand, the subjects who had been told at the outset that we expected them to have difficulty with our anagrams task were given a much more difficult practice list. Their average score turned out to be only 0.55 out of ten. In neither case did we actually tell the subjects what their scores were. One useful feature of anagrams, at least for our purposes in doing this study, is that they are virtually self-scoring. A subject almost always knows when the word he or she has written in the blank space on the answer sheet is a correct word and when it is not. We could be fairly certain that the subjects in one group felt confident that they had done very well in the warm-up, whereas those in the other group knew they had done very poorly.

From that point on, all the subjects were treated alike. First, they were given a list of 25 anagrams to solve—the experimental task we had been building up to. These were chosen from the same pre-tested pool as the two warm-up lists, but from those of moderate difficulty. Each group of subjects was given 6 minutes to complete the task. After their time was up, the experimenter collected their answer sheets and began to "debrief" them. In most studies involving deception, where subjects are lied to about the procedure, the experimenter tries to follow up the subjects' experiences in two ways. First, the subjects are questioned about their perceptions of the information that was given to them. What did they understand it to mean? Did they believe it? Or did they suspect that the true purpose of the study was being hidden from them? If so, what did they think the true purpose was? Our subjects did not admit to being suspicious about the deceptive information they had been given. In the second part of a debriefing, the experimenter tells the whole truth about the study and tries to make certain that the subjects leave without any misconceptions about their abilities or personalities as the result of the deception that was employed. In the case of the present study, our subjects were told that the information given them about their ability to solve anagrams was false, that the warm-up list was rigged to make that false information more plausible to them, and that anagram performance, in any case, is not known to be an indicator of anything important about people's intellects or personalities. They were also told the reason for the deception, the true purpose of the study. Finally, they were asked to keep all this to themselves for a few days until the study was completed.

Now, to the results. Subjects' scores on the anagrams task supported the hypothesis we were testing. Those who had been told, and "shown," that they would do well solved an average of 6.87 of the total of 25 correctly. The group who had been led to believe that they would perform poorly solved only 5.22 out of 25 correctly. This difference, although not that large in absolute terms, is statistically significant. For those unfamiliar with statistics, it means that it is large and consistent enough to satisfy most psychologists that the two groups really performed differently.

## THE LANGUAGE OF ANALYSIS—FACT VERSUS ARTIFACT

Now that we have a concrete example of psychological research upon which to base our discussion, it is time to introduce the basic question with which this book is concerned. Did the difference in performance between our two groups of subjects result from the conditions that we specified in our hypothesis and then tried to create in our laboratory? We know that the two groups performed differently, but was it because they began the task with different expectations for their performance, different feelings about how well they would do?

It is not enough to know whether they performed differently. That *result* is fairly clear, as it is in most studies. We must know why. We are interested primarily, in other words, in the conclusion that we may draw from the comparison between these groups. That is the meaningful *finding* of any research, which is so often controversial!

## Learning the Language

If the difference in performance was actually caused by a difference in the subjects' expectations, then it is a *valid finding* because that was the factor we intended to study. If it was caused by any other difference between the two groups of subjects, any other factor that affected their behavior, then it is an *invalid finding*. In general, a research finding is valid if it correctly attributes the effect that was observed to the factor that caused it. It is the purpose of this book to enable the reader to make the complex series of judgments necessary to decide when that is the case, for this or any other research finding in psychology, if not for the finding of any test of any hypothesis. We begin by restating the question in more general terms, using a specialized vocabulary, or jargon, that psychologists and other scientists have adopted for the purpose of communicating about the scientific method. As you have probably noted, each new term is italicized when it is first introduced. Definitions of all italicized terms are included in the Glossary. But they will also be defined by continued use throughout the book.

We need to analyze a system that consists of two principal elements, the *hypothesis* and some *evidence* that has been produced in order to test it. The hypothesis is a guess about the cause of some phenomenon. It may come from an elaborate theory, from previous research findings, or even from personal observation of the phenomenon in question. In psychology, the phenomenon is usually some form of human behavior; in history, it is usually an event that occurred in the past, and so on. In any case, the hypothesis specifies that some condition produces a measurable effect on the phenomenon, or is one of its causes.

The scientific method is just a systematic way of observing that effect or of providing the evidence for it. The observations, or *data*, are intended to reflect the operation of the causal conditions which are specified in the hypothesis. So, in psychology, research data consist of observations of specific instances of behavior which have occurred under those conditions. A particular set of causal conditions is known as an *independent variable*. The observations of its effect are made on some scale of measurement which is called the *dependent variable*. Thus a researcher chooses to study an independent variable which he or she has reason to believe will affect the occurrence of a dependent variable, some factor which is expected to affect, or be a cause of, some behavior. In our sample study, we chose expectations for performance as our independent variable. The dependent variable upon which its effects were observed was performance on the 25-item anagrams test. The scores on that test constituted our research data.

In our study, as in all research, the causal conditions specified in the hypothesis were studied in an arbitrary form. Through a procedure of our own design, we created a specific version of a more general set of conditions that might act as one cause of the phenomenon in which we were interested. We chose one of many possible ways of studying expectations. The specific causal conditions studied in research are known as *experimental treatments*. We used two, success and failure expectations. Because we produced them ourselves, the procedure is known as an *experimental manipulation*, or a manipulation of the independent variable. But a researcher may also elect to study the effects of causal conditions that occur naturally. In history, for example, an hypothesis might specify a causal relationship between an economic depression and a subsequent war. The historian cannot produce the depression in a laboratory. As we shall soon see, psychologists study naturally occurring phenomena also.

Whether the independent and dependent variables are found in the real world, or are abstractions from natural phenomena that are produced in a laboratory, the data that are collected are used to evaluate the research hypothesis. Those data may indicate that the hypothesis is true or that it is false. In either case, they provide the basis for the research finding, a conclusion that the causal conditions being studied have had the hypothesized effect or that they have not.

To repeat, that finding is valid if the data reflect the operation of those causal conditions alone. We will return to our sample study for an example. There we saw that the subjects' anagram-solving performance was consistent with our hypothesis. The subjects whom we gave expectations for success outperformed those whom we gave expectations for failure. If the scores of the two groups had been reversed, we would have wanted to conclude that higher expectations caused poorer performance. If there had been no difference between their scores, we would have wanted to conclude that expectations had no effect at all on performance. Regardless of the results, our conclusion would have been correct if the performance we observed was caused by the treatments we created. Valid findings are correct conclusions about the causes of research results.

It is the assumption that the independent and dependent variables are linked in a causal relationship that constitutes the critical question with which we have to contend. If the research data that are obtained, the values of the dependent variable, were truly caused by the independent variable that was being studied, then a finding is valid. The research has accomplished what it was intended to. If there is no true causal relationship between the independent and dependent variables, so that the results were not caused by the independent variable, then the finding is invalid.

If a research finding is invalid, it follows that the behavior that was observed must have been caused, to some extent, by some factor other than the independent variable. In that case, any conclusions which are drawn about the hypothesis, which specifies only the effects of the independent variable, are bound to be in error. The influence of an unintended causal factor makes it impossible to determine the separate effect of the independent variable. This is referred to as a *confounding* of the two because their effects cannot be separated. To determine the effect of a single causal factor, the phenomenon must be observed when that factor is present and when it is absent. But all other factors that are capable of exerting a causal influence on the phenomenon must remain constant between those occasions. Any other causal factor that varies at the same time the independent variable does is known as an *extraneous variable* because it is irrelevant to the hypothesis being tested. The invalid finding that results is called an *artifact,* which means that the observations made during the study are attributed erroneously to the operation of the independent variable alone.

Research data must be capable of being attributed correctly to the causal factor being studied. Only then can a valid conclusion be drawn about the truth of the research hypothesis. In order for a research finding to be valid, it must not be subject to alternative explanation. The result of the investigation must not have been influenced by any causal factor other than the independent variable.

An alternative explanation that cannot be ruled out is called a *rival hypothesis,* because it can explain the data as easily as the original research hypothesis can. The aim of the scientific method is to design research which precludes all possible explanations for the eventual results except the one specified in the research hypothesis. We will soon consider many of the possible rival hypotheses that researchers in psychology must rule out, that is, the extraneous variables that must be prevented from influencing the dependent variable, if their findings are to be valid.

## The Complexity of Analysis

We would not want to leave you, even at this early point in our discussion, with a false impression of the magnitude of the task we face. It will undoubtedly become clear to you before long that validity is an ideal that cannot be reached, but only approximated. Two principal reasons for this will be merely stated here to give a framework for what will follow. Each will be considered in much greater detail later.

First, the identification of plausible rival hypotheses is not a finite process. Some rival hypotheses can be identified through a process of applying a set of rules for scientific thought. Others can be identified only on the basis of one's familiarity with the knowledge that previous research has provided about the independent and dependent variables with which one is working. Beyond the question of whether one can ever be aware of all that is known about anything, we must recognize that knowledge is always expanding. Thus, even if one were familiar with everything that was known at the time a particular judgment about validity was made, that judgment might not survive the findings of subsequent research. Realistically, all that can be said is that the more we know about the behavior we are studying and its causes, the better are our chances of producing valid research findings.

In addition, the problem of validity is often oversimplified as a dichotomy between the presence and the absence of plausible rival hypotheses. But even to consider validity as a condition which may exist in varying degrees is to simplify it. The task of the designer or evaluator of scientific research goes beyond having to decide whether research findings are valid or not, or having to choose between findings that are more or less valid. It is necessary to compare findings that permit different alternative explanations to be raised. Such judgments are qualitative rather than quantitative, being based on differences in kind rather than in degree and, as a consequence, are inevitably very difficult.

That is an important point and one that bears repeating. Two or more conflicting findings may each have been produced by methods that failed to rule out all plausible rival hypotheses. But the plausible rival hypotheses that remain may be different for each one. Or in the course of planning to investigate the hypothesis, one may be faced with a choice between two alternative methods, each of which has a different but equally serious flaw. Thus, the choice may not be among findings that are more or less valid. Rather, one may have to decide which kind of invalidity is to be preferred as the least damaging in a particular case.

Fortunately, the task is not hopeless or impossible. It is simply complex. Some tolerance for ambiguity is a useful asset in such an enterprise, but not everything is ambiguous. Every day more is known about the complexities involved, and the ambiguity is reduced that much further. It is only when we seek perfect clarity in a world that is not perfectly clear that we feel despair and futility. At this point in time, at least, we will have to be satisfied with imperfect answers. Those who maintain that science can deal only with perfect knowledge simply need to learn more about the process of doing science, which is just what we are doing now.

## An Illustrative Analysis

Now that we have defined validity in an abstract way, we are going to go back over some of the same ground using our sample study as a concrete frame of reference. Recall that the purpose of that study was to test the *conceptual hypothesis,* the general notion that people's task performance is affected by their expectations of the quality of their performance when they start to work on a task.

The people on whom we tested this hypothesis were 48 male undergraduates who were obligated by a course requirement to help us, and whose schedules happened to be compatible with ours. We divided the 48 randomly into two groups of 24, and presented them with different instructions and experiences that were intended to give them contrasting expectations for their performance on a specific task. Combining the false information about their scores on a questionnaire and their performance on a biased sample of the task they were to perform was our way of manipulating the causal factor, or independent variable, which was specified in our conceptual hypothesis—their expectations.

The task we gave our subjects was to solve anagrams. Their performance on that task constituted the dependent variable for our experiment, the observations or data which we would use to evaluate the truth of our hypothesis. This evaluation was necessarily restricted to the conditions under which the hypothesis was tested, the particular ways we chose to represent the theoretical variables of expectations and performance in our instructions and task. Such a version is called the *research hypothesis* to differentiate it from the more general conceptual hypothesis we started with.

In the context of our study, the question of validity can be stated as follows: Was the superiority of one group's performance over the other's the result of that group's higher or more positive expectations for their own performance? Regardless of what the outcome of the study might have been—either group outperforming the other or the groups performing equally well—in order that the findings be valid the procedure we used should succeed to create the intended expectations in the two groups, and the difference in their performance should be caused by those expectations. All other possible influences on that performance must have affected the two groups equally. If it is really true that expectations influence performance, as the hypothesis maintains, our results should show more positive expectations to be associated with better performance. If it is not true, then the results should show no difference between the two groups' performance. To put it simply, valid research findings reveal the truth.

More specifically, our finding, that a group of subjects who had undergone an experience designed to give them positive expectations for their performance on an upcoming task actually outperformed a group exposed to conditions designed to produce negative expectations, is valid if there is no convincing explanation for the observed difference in their performance other than the difference in expectations. In the next two chapters, we will give concentrated and systematic attention to the possible alternative explanations or rival hypotheses for research results. However, while we still have our sample study in mind, it will be perhaps useful to introduce some examples of rival hypotheses, to whet your appetite, and perhaps to confirm some suspicions you have already, by considering some of the ways in which their findings might have resulted from a causal factor other than the subjects' expectations.

Parenthetically, it might be useful to observe at this point that we typically do not hear much about research that finds that an independent variable failed to have any effect on a dependent variable. Such a study is said to have produced "negative results." Of course, if the hypothesis being tested were found untrue, such a study would not be a failure. However, it would be less informative than one which finds a difference, because it is always possible that the effect of an independent variable was simply not detected because of a poor technique for observing it. Despite the fact that negative results are not widely reported, they can have an important impact on the progress that is made toward answering important questions. They may convince a researcher, and those with whom he or she works, that a particular hypothesis has little promise. Therefore, it should be recognized that negative results can also be invalid, artifacts of the operation of an extraneous variable, in the same way as positive results can. If they should be invalid, which is to say that the findings fail to support a true hypothesis, research may be led away from a fruitful approach, to a series of blind alleys. Because the number of researchers in a given area may be quite small, invalid negative results need not be widely publicized to have a serious harmful effect.

Now let us return to our own "positive" results. Could the difference we found have resulted from the operation of some extraneous variable, a causal factor other than the subjects' expectations for success? Is it possible, for example, that the group of subjects whose superior performance we have attributed to positive expectations came into our study with greater anagram-solving sills than the negative expectations group? The fact that subjects were assigned to the two groups randomly from our initial sample of 48 recruits argues strongly against such an interpretation (the possibility that differences in ability were created solely by chance is taken into account in tests of statistical significance). Is it possible, then, that in the course of the study the two groups of subjects were exposed to different experiences, other than manipulating their expectations, which contributed to their unequal performance? In a laboratory study such as ours, there is very little opportunity for such experiences to take place. The interval between the manipulation of expectations and the test of its effects was just long enough to distribute copies of the anagrams test and to give a few simple instructions. In addition, the laboratory environment was carefully controlled to limit subjects' experiences to those created by the experimenter.

Up to this point, it appears very likely that our findings were valid. As a matter of fact, because our study was typical of much of psychological research, the question of validity might seem to be a minor one. Unfortunately, the picture is not that optimistic. For one thing, the validity of our findings depends on our subjects having believed that the instructions and the rigged warm-up test we gave them really meant that they were likely to do well or poorly on the anagrams task. What if they did not believe? What if their preexisting opinions of their own abilities overrode the few minutes of psychological mumbo jumbo to which we exposed them? Or what if they arrived at our laboratory having learned, from fellow students who had more experience with psychology courses and psychological research than they, that experimenters often lie to subjects and generally are not to be believed? If a sizable number of our subjects held either or both these beliefs, and if they were consequently not convinced by our attempts to deceive them, what could account for their behavior giving the appearance that they had? Some people have argued, as we will see in considerable detail later, that subjects who do not believe what they are told often behave as though they did out of a desire to help the experimenter. Many subjects believe that their role requires them to try to do what the experimenter expects or would like them to do.

In our study, subjects who were not convinced by our deception may have realized that the instructions were intended to influence their behavior in a particular direction, and they may have cooperated with our intent. Given the transparency of our instructions, that understanding might very well have coincided with our hypothesis and produced the data we got in support of it. Thus, in order to accept our findings as valid evidence in support of the hypothesis, we need to rule out the possibility that the data were produced as a conscious effort to help make the study work, instead of by the different beliefs the two groups of subjects held about their likelihood of success on the anagrams task.

We tried in two ways to make sure that this did not happen. First, immediately before the subjects began the anagrams task we asked them to write down, on the back of it, an estimate of the number of anagrams (of the 25) they would be able to solve correctly within the allotted time. In this way, we hoped to be able to assess their expectations in addition to their actual performance. It turned out that the positive-expectations subjects predicted that they would solve significantly more anagrams than the negative-expectations subjects. Second, during an informal group interview at the end of the study, we tried to find out whether subjects believed our instructions or were suspicious of our intent. Based on that assessment, we were forced to conclude that little or no suspicion existed, that our subjects accepted the study as presented. Can we conclude, on the basis of these two additional pieces of information, that suspicion, and an accompanying desire to help the experimenter, do not need to be considered seriously as an alternative explanation for our findings? Or might their suspicion and desire to be helpful have tainted their answers to these questions also? You can make up your own mind at this point, and we will go into the question in considerably more depth later on.

To balance the two apparent strengths of our procedure, that subjects were assigned to the experimental treatments at random and that they experienced only what we wanted them to, let us consider another potential weakness. This one involves the way we chose to study our conceptual hypothesis. That hypothesis stated a causal relationship between two very general concepts—expectations and performance. Our study used very specific representations of these, the results of our deception and the anagrams test. If our results are to be accepted as support for the hypothesis, we need to be assured that those representations are not so atypical that other kinds of expectations and performances are not causally related in the same way.

For example, our conceptual hypothesis might be of great interest to educators. It may mean that the academic achievement of young children is affected by the expectations they have when they enter school. If just believing that they will do well causes some children to do better than those who expect to do poorly, educators would be well advised to try to do something to alter the expectations of children who enter school believing they are destined to fail. Even the best teaching methods might have little positive effect on children who belong to groups within our society who are believed by the population at large to possess poor intellectual skills and who have accepted those beliefs.

But should such remedial action be undertaken on the basis of the results of our study? How confident can we be, on the basis of our very specific test, that the more general hypothesis is true? Are the expectations that young children bring to school with them on the first day like the ones we created in our subjects? Are their tasks in school comparable to the anagrams task we used? Is there a causal relationship between expectations and performance which is the same for white, middle-class college students and for black first-graders in inner-city schools? It is apparent that there are many differences between the specific properties of our study and those of some school situations that we might consider. But are these differences superficial or do they mean that our findings cannot be applied from one case to the other? There is no way to answer that question with absolute certainty. It would increase our confidence in the conceptual hypothesis if we could repeat our study with different combinations of expectancies, tasks, and subject populations. But we could never establish universal generalizability. To some extent, all studies are abstract representations of the reality to which investigators are interested in generalizing.

## FROM THE LABORATORY TO THE REAL WORLD

Perhaps the value of our findings would become clearer if we considered an alternative way of testing the same hypothesis. Even if we were not directly concerned with its relevance in an educational setting, we could test it in one. Six-year-olds entering school for the first time could be used as subjects. It might be wise to sample first-graders from different schools, whose populations represented a wide range of backgrounds. The students' initial expectations for their performance in school would have to be assessed, but with children as young as these, it would be inappropriate to distribute questionnaires. It might be necessary to establish a one-to-one relationship with each child, and then to present the question in the form of a game or story that the child would both pay attention to and understand. Once the assessment of the children's expectations had been accomplished, groups with contrasting positive and negative expectations could be identified for the purpose of future comparison. Measures of their subsequent academic achievement could be obtained from the usual school record of grades and achievement test scores.

How valid would the results of this test of the hypothesis be if it were, in fact, carried out? As we have already implied, it does not really matter for our purposes what those results were; but to keep our discussion as concrete as possible, we will assume that the children with more positive expectations were found to get better grades and higher scores. Let us start roughly at the same place we did in evaluating our laboratory study. It seems fairly obvious that with regard to the initial equivalence of our comparison groups, we have quite a different situation in this hypothetical school study. Rather than created randomly in different groups, the subjects' standing on the independent variable, their expectations, occurred naturally. The fact that the two groups differed naturally in their expectations raises the possibility that they may have differed in other ways as well. In this context, for example, it might be reasonable to speculate that the children with more positive expectations came from families with better educational background and a better financial status. Such families might have provided more educational experiences for their children at a preschool age, which might have resulted in the children's being more confident about such activities. These and other differences would have to be ruled out somehow, either before or after the children were chosen, to make sure that the relative success of the positive expectations group was actually due to their expectations, and not to some other factor such as prior practice or training in the school tasks that served as the dependent measure.

The duration of this study also presents a problem. Because it would take at least several months for reliable measures of the children's achievement in school to be obtained, there is at least a possibility that some event might occur within that period that would affect the children's performance in school. However, for such an event to constitute a plausible rival hypothesis to our own it would have to affect our two groups of subjects differently. Let us consider just one possibility. If our two groups were of different ages so that the positive-expectations group were a few months older, on the average, then the more rapid growth that the older (and the more optimistic) children might undergo in their intellectual and social development could produce, especially if the groups were very large, and sufficient difference in the school performance of the two groups to invalidate our findings. After all, we were interested in the effect of expectations, not intellectual ability or social adjustment. It seems clear that we would have to guard against the possibility that some event with no bearing on our hypothesis could be responsible for our results. The longer the study takes, and the less control we have over the subjects' experiences during that time, the more difficult it is.

Up to this point, our hypothetical study of schoolchildren would seem to present more serious problems of validity than our laboratory study did; it would seem that doing laboratory studies is generally a superior method of doing research. Certainly, the strengths of the laboratory study are not found here. The problem of choosing among alternative methods is not nearly so simple. For example, the issue in the laboratory study of whether or not we had succeeded in producing expectations in our subjects need not concern us here. In the present case, subjects have expectations, and they are real and would presumably be influential in determining their achievement if expectations really do have that effect. In addition, the problem of generalizing to real settings that plagues laboratory findings, which are sometimes based on remote abstractions of real phenomena such as deception-induced perceptions and anagrams tasks, is avoided here. Those who wish to use laboratory findings to understand actual cases outside the laboratory often have difficulty judging where they apply. In studies like this one, what is observed is real and provides, if not a universal finding, at least a view of how one real population functions in its natural environment. The weaknesses of the laboratory study are not found here, either.

The complementarity of the strengths and the weaknesses of these two alternative approaches to testing the same hypothesis will constitute an important theme throughout the book. At this point, at least we have seen one example of how choosing between alternative methods whose strengths and weaknesses are not directly comparable is a critical problem in producing and evaluating research findings. Our laboratory study and the hypothetical school study may have been equally valid or invalid, but with different kinds of flaws and strengths.

This chapter should give you a feeling for the kind of problems we intend to deal with. It would be a mistake to assume that all research problems are exactly like this one, but there is a kind of logic or perspective common to all of them, and this chapter should serve as a first step toward developing your ability to understand and use it. If you are a bit confused or uncertain at this point, that is understandable. This chapter was intended mainly to raise problems. We have the rest of the book to try to solve them.

## REFERENCE

Campbell, D. T., & Stanley, J. C. *Experimental and quasi-experimental designs for research.* Chicago: Rand McNally, 1963.

## SUGGESTED ACTIVITIES

### Study Questions

1. What does it mean to say that research findings are valid?
2. For the laboratory study of the effect of expectations on performance which was described in this chapter:
   What was the hypothesis?
   What were the results?
   What was the finding?
3. If the experimenter's instructions and "warm-up" did not create expectations that caused the difference in the subjects' performance, what might have? What are these alternative possibilities called?
4. How would you characterize the validity of the finding of the laboratory study? In what ways does it seem valid? In what ways does it seem invalid?
5. If the same hypothesis were investigated by comparing the school grades of first-graders who entered school with different expectations for their own performance, how would the validity of those findings compare with those of the laboratory study? What would some possible alternative explanations be for those findings? To what are they alternatives?

# Part I:
# A SYSTEMATIC APPROACH TO THE ASSESSMENT OF VALIDITY

## INTRODUCTION

In the next three chapters, we are going to present the basis for a system that can be used to assess the validity of research findings. Then, throughout most of the rest of the book we will be using that system to evaluate a variety of methods for doing research. The system takes account of a dozen potential extraneous variables. These are the factors that most commonly cast doubt upon the validity of research findings by posing alternative explanations to the investigator's hypothesis. After a few preliminary remarks, you will be introduced to these dozen threats to validity by definitions and examples.

We will consider the 12 in two groups. First, we will deal with eight that can make it difficult to be confident that the observed values of the dependent variable accurately reflect the influence of the independent variable. These, then, are factors that might themselves influence the values of the dependent variable but in which the investigator has no interest. They make it difficult to accurately assess the effects of the hypothesized causal factor that is central to the aim of the investigation.

This difficulty, as we discussed in Chapter 1, can take either of two principal forms. First, it can mask the true effects of the independent variable. This can happen in a case in which the hypothesis is true but some extraneous variable influences the observed values of the dependent variable in a way that is antagonistic to the effect of the independent variable. Thus, despite the fact that the hypothesis is true, the data may reveal no effect or even a markedly different effect from the one hypothesized because they reflect the influence of an extraneous variable as well.

This sort of extraneous variable, the *masking* variety, may, in turn, take either of two different forms. It can be a naturally occurring factor that tends to occur whenever our independent variable occurs, despite the fact that our investigation has not considered it explicitly. Or, it may be a factor that has been produced unintentionally as a result of the procedures that were devised for the purpose of conducting the investigation, and thus bears no natural relationship to the independent variable we are studying. In either case, it is an extraneous variable for the purposes of understanding the true relationship between the independent and dependent variables, and its effects must not be allowed to occur in such a way that they can become confused with those of the independent variable.

An extraneous variable may also have the effect of producing the effect that the hypothesis attributes to the independent variable, when the hypothesis is actually false. Thus the dependent measures may appear to reveal the hypothesized effect of the independent variable when, in fact, those observations have been caused by some other factor instead (as above, either a natural influence on the phenomenon or one introduced by the investigation). In one sense, this kind of *dissimulation* artifact is more damaging than the masking effect. There is a conservative tradition in science that favors errors on the side of omitting true facts from the accepted body of knowledge over errors of admitting untrue facts to it. In this way, it is believed, the rate of growth of knowledge is sacrificed to the cause of truth. Recently, however, investigators who see their findings as having value in their application to pressing human problems have begun to question this conservative view. For them, rejecting a true hypothesis risks needless human suffering. In any case, as we will see over and over again, investigators rarely know enough beforehand about the phenomena they are studying to design their research to favor one kind of artifact over another.

If, in either way, masking or dissimulation, the operation of some extraneous variable causes the observed values of the dependent variable to inaccurately reflect the effect of the independent variable, it is said that the findings lack *internal validity*. This label is applied because the extraneous variables which can produce such an artifact are events or phenomena that occur within the temporal and spatial confines of the research itself. They occur within the time span occupied by the independent and dependent variables, and are an integral part of the investigation. These potential extraneous influences on the dependent variable are called *threats to internal validity*.

The four remaining extraneous variables are concerned with the extent to which a given set of research findings provide general evidence concerning the truth or falsity of the hypothesis. If the findings are attributable to the operation of factors that operate only in conjunction with the particular procedures and representations utilized in the investigation in question, we will say that they lack *external validity*. In that case, the more general conceptual hypothesis is not supported or contradicted to the extent that one could not expect different investigations of it to yield similar evidence.

Research findings may have perfect internal validity, but still may be of little value in answering the question that prompted the investigation in the first place. We may have complete confidence that the observed effect was caused by the independent variable we were studying, but this might hold true only under the specific conditions the investigation in question created or examined. Such findings tell us little or nothing about any external reality.

When research findings are to be used to test a theory, that is, to determine whether it is possible to demonstrate some relationship between independent and dependent variables which is predicted by a theory, a failure to represent external reality may be of little consequence. In such a case, however, the hypothesis ought to be stated in a way that reflects the limited purpose of the research. For the expectations–performance study described in Chapter 1, that statement might be: According to social learning theory, performance CAN be affected by expectations.

When the researcher is concerned about the practical value of the findings, or their generality, then representativeness does become an important issue. Given those concerns, what would be the value of knowing only that a particular set of procedures, used by a specific investigator to study a unique group of subjects or instances of a phenomenon, had an effect on only one measure of a particular behavior? Moreover, our discussion of external validity throughout this book will be based on the presumption that, wherever possible, research ought to be planned so that its potential value is greater than the testing of an abstract theoretical proposition. In other words, features that restrict the generalizability of research findings—known as *threats to external validity*—should be avoided wherever possible.

Perhaps the distinction between internal and external validity can be sharpened by going back to both examples we considered in Chapter 1—the laboratory study of the effect of expectations and the hypothetical investigation of children's achievement in the schools. In evaluating both, we considered two possible alternative explanations for the findings. The first was that the two groups of subjects whose behavior we compared differed to begin with in some way that affected their subsequent standing on the dependent variable but was extraneous to the independent variable. The second was that they were exposed to some influential event, at the same time as or immediately after the independent variable, which was similarly extraneous to the hypothesis and influential in their performance. Both possibilities, an a priori difference between the groups and an exposure to an extraneous event, are potential threats to the internal validity of those and other investigations.

Later in the discussions of both investigations, we considered the possibility that the observed behaviors of the groups we were comparing may have been affected by the subjects' suspicions of the investigator's intent and the subjects' actions as a result. In that case, the findings' relevance to the hypothesis being tested would be limited by the fact that the procedures used to uncover them introduced a biasing effect of their own. In this case, the findings would accurately reflect the effect of the independent variable as it was represented in the particular investigation. However, it would not necessarily reflect the operation of expectations which were studied by some other method or which existed in the real world. This, then, would constitute a threat to the external validity of the research findings.

Another distinction needs to be made before we go further. An extraneous variable can affect the findings of an investigation by modifying the effects of the independent variable in the same way or to the same extent across all the levels or values of that variable. Or it can have different directions and magnitudes of influence on different levels or values of the independent variable. These two variations are sometimes labeled by the statistical terms *main effect* and *interaction,* respectively. These are general terms that can be applied to any case in which two variables or causal factors are operating simultaneously to affect a dependent variable or the phenomenon assessed by it (in this case, the two causal factors are the independent variable and an extraneous variable). In such a case, there are two possibilities. One is that each causal factor may operate on the phenomenon independently of the other. That is, its effect would be in the same direction and of the same magnitude regardless of the effect of the other. The other is that the effects of each causal factor may be changed in direction, in magnitude, or in both as the effects of the other change.

Consider a fairly simple (and nontechnical) hypothetical example. How do the two causal factors of intelligence and socioeconomic status affect children's academic achievement? For the purposes of this example, we will measure intelligence by IQ, socioeconomic status (SES) by family income and parents' occupational levels (roughly speaking, social class), and children's academic achievement by school grades. If the effects of IQ and SES are independent of one another, one might find (to make a reasonable guess) that the higher a child's IQ is, the higher the child's grades are, on the average, regardless of the level of the child's SES. Similarly, the higher the level of the child's SES, the higher the child's grades would be, regardless of what level of intelligence the child might possess. Both these effects, then, the effects of IQ and of SES, are main effects, because each one remains constant as the other changes.

The other possibility is that these two independent variables may affect school children's grades in interaction with one another. Such a case might be described as follows (bear in mind that while these relationships may sound plausible they are strictly hypothetical). The effect of higher IQ might be to produce higher grades for children from higher SES, but IQ might have no effect on the grades of lower-SES children (i.e., lower-SES children at all levels of IQ would earn almost equivalent grades). Similarly, the effect of a higher level of SES, if we look at that factor by itself, might be to produce much higher grades for children whose IQs are relatively high, but only a very slight increase in the grades of lower-IQ children. Each independent variable in this example has different effects on the dependent variable when different levels of the other independent variable are present.

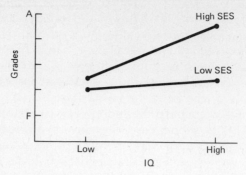

Figure 1-1   IQ has a smaller effect on children's grades when they come from low ES backgrounds.

The main effect and the interaction effect are diagrammed in Figures 1-1 and 1-2. (Note that IQ, in Figure 1-1 and SES, in Figure 2–2 are represented by discrete points, even if the lines connecting the points make it look as if there are gradual increases and decreases across continuous dimensions; the lines are drawn because they make relationships among the points easier to see.)

Of course, this entire discussion has been simplified in that it is possible (common, in fact) for more than two variables to operate in the same causal relationship and for those three or more variables to cause some effect in interaction with one another. For the purpose of trying to get a basic understanding of the threats to internal and external validity, we do not have to go beyond the two-variable case. The rapid increase in complexity that each added variable brings with it becomes clear when you

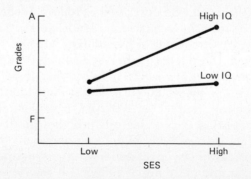

Figure 1-2   SES has a smaller effect on children's grades when their IQs are low.

try to work out the three-variable and the even more complex interactions for yourself.

With this introduction, we will begin to consider a comprehensive list of threats to validity. We will separate the threats to internal and external validity in our discussion because we believe the distinction is an important one. The desirability of maintaining it will become clearer as we go on. We will also provide examples, in each case, of areas of investigation in which such threats are likely to be a problem. Some of these examples will be real and others will be hypothetical, but that distinction is of little importance for our purposes.

## SUGGESTED ACTIVITIES

### Study Questions

1. Define internal validity and external validity. How are they different? In what way are they similar?
2. What are threats to internal validity? How can they mask the true effects of an independent variable? How can they dissimulate true effects? How can they affect research observations as main effects? How can they affect observations in interaction with an independent variable?
3. What was a threat to internal validity in the laboratory study of expectations and performance described in Chapter 1? What was a threat to external validity in that study?
4. How would you compare the importance of internal and external validity? How does that comparison depend on the purposes of the research study being judged?

# Chapter 2
# Potential Threats to
# Internal Validity

In this chapter we will consider eight factors that may operate within an investigation to obscure the true effects of the independent variable. In other words, these are eight extraneous variables that may become confounded with the independent variable. To the extent that one or more of these variables are allowed to threaten the validity of the investigation, the possibility will be raised that the observed experimental effects do not reflect the true effects of the independent variable. In designing an investigation, a high degree of internal validity is assured by eliminating those examples of each of these kinds of threats to internal validity that the existing literature of research findings and the experimenter's understanding of the phenomenon being studied can identify as plausible rival hypotheses. Those variables which the investigator identifies as likely to arise in the course of the investigation as unwanted influences on the dependent variable need to be prevented from operating. The designer of research must attempt to maximize the degree of such *control* and the reader of the research literature must attempt to judge the value of published findings against the control provided by the research design used in producing them.

## EXTRANEOUS EVENTS

In every investigation, some period of time elapses between the onset of the causal factor or independent variable being studied and its effects on the dependent variable. Independent variables are events that necessarily require some period of time to occur and then to take effect. A cause must occur before its effects. But the very existence of this interval can pose a problem for interpreting the findings of an investigation. During that period, it is possible for events other than the independent variable to occur that also have an effect on the dependent variable. These *extraneous events,* should they occur, will prevent the true effects of the independent variable from being reflected accurately in the observations made by the investigator. In other words, the effects of the independent variable and an extraneous event may be confounded so that it is impossible for anyone to determine which has caused what effect on the dependent variable.

Laboratory studies of the sort described in Chapter 1 are typically conducted in such a way that the likelihood of an extraneous event occurring is minimized in two ways. First, the time interval between the occurrence of the causal event produced by the experimenter, the manipulation, and the assessment of its effects is very brief. Although this may be done more often for the purpose of maximizing the impact of that event on the subjects, it also has the effect of minimizing the opportunity for other causal events to occur. In addition to its relatively short duration, such a study generally takes place in an isolated physical environment in which subjects are shielded from events other than those produced for their benefit by the experimenter. Thus, a laboratory environment can provide a great deal of control over what the subjects see and hear during the time it takes to expose them to the experimental treatment and to assess its effect on their behavior. It can restrict subjects' experiences to just those the researcher wants to study.

However, even the laboratory experiment does not completely eliminate the possibility that the findings will be contaminated by the effects of extraneous events. For one thing, human subjects have the disquieting ability (for research purposes, at least) to produce extraneous events for themselves. Human subjects can generate their own experiences—ideas, images, memories, and the like—which can rival the independent variable in their effects on subjects' behavior.

Research in human memory provides one good example of this. Let us say that you wanted to test the hypothesis that forgetting occurs most rapidly immediately after learning, then less rapidly as more time passes. You might think of doing a relatively simple experiment in which subjects are presented with three-letter nonsense syllables one at a time; then varying lengths of time are allowed to pass before they are tested for whether they remember them—say, from zero to 18 seconds in 3-second increments (zero, three, six, etc.).

You hypothesized that the amount forgotten, per second, from the time of exposure to the syllable, would decline as the time interval was lengthened. That is, the 3-second delay group would forget most per second and the 18-second delay group least. At least that is one way of stating the hypothesis. Suppose, however, that you found no differences among the intervals? Would that mean that the hypothesis was false? If you knew that the findings of previous studies suggest very strongly that it should be true, you might be suspicious of these findings. What could be responsible for the discrepancy? One possibility which has been considered by psychologists doing research on human memory is that subjects put to better use the time interval that the experimenter has established for the purpose of having them forget. They may, in fact, spend that time thinking about, or rehearsing, the material they had to memorize, in anticipation of having their recall tested. This might prevent the effects of time from diminishing their memory as much as it otherwise would. To the extent that subjects do this, the dependent variable, their scores on the retention test at the end of the interval would reflect not only the effects of the independent variable, time, to which the hypothesis was addressed, but rather its effects in combination with those of the extraneous event of rehearsal. In order to prevent this, researchers have adopted the technique of providing a task for the subjects to perform during the forgetting interval. This could be any task that would have no direct effect of its own on the material that had been memorized, but which would keep the subjects busy enough to prevent them from rehearsing. One that has been used in the kind of short-term memory study described above is counting backward by 3s or 4s. With the use of such a procedure, only the effects of the independent variable, the passage of time itself, would remain to be reflected in their recall scores. It should be pointed out that some have questioned whether such a procedure can truly prevent rehearsal or fail to directly affect retention of the learned material. The passage of time is a difficult variable to study free of the possibility of the confounding effects of extraneous events.

Another possible extraneous event that may occur even within the relatively strict confines of the laboratory is one that may be introduced unknowingly by the experimenter. Consider the following example. A group of students is serving as research assistants for a study which they are told is intended to investigate the genetic transmission of intelligence. Each one is assigned a number of rats which are to be tested repeatedly over a period of several days in a complex maze. The experimenters are to take each rat from its home cage to the maze, according to a prescribed schedule, to put it into the maze, and to time with a stopwatch its run from a starting point to a finishing point. Half the experimenters are told that their rats have been bred selectively to be "maze-bright" and so should learn the maze very quickly. The other half are told that their rats are "maze-dull" and should learn slowly.

In fact, all the rats have been selected at random from a large colony which has not been bred selectively for maze running at all. But when the experimenters turned in their results the following week, those who believed their rats were maze-bright were found to have recorded faster times for their rats than those who believed their rats were maze dull. How could this have happened? Even when errors in timing are eliminated by using an automated recording system, the difference remains. The student experimenters' reports reveal that those whose rats were labeled maze-bright found their subjects to be more docile, cooperative, and attractive than those who had maze-dull rats. Presumably, experimenters working with "maze-bright" rats enjoyed running them more, and this attitude was transmitted to the rats by the way they were handled, with the result that there was faster learning in the maze by calmer, more contented animals.

An experiment like this one has actually been performed (Rosenthal and Fode, 1963), along with similar experiments with human subjects instead of rats. In many cases, it has been found that experimenters' expectations for their subjects' performance had some effect on that performance. In other words, it appears that experimenters who are aware of the hypothesis they are testing and who know what behavior on the part of their subjects will serve to confirm that hypothesis may unknowingly expose their subjects to an extraneous event. In addition to the instructions and other procedures that they are trained to carry out, experimenters may convey a message, in all likelihood in the form of some kind of subtle nonverbal communication, that causes the subjects to behave in a way that conforms to their expectations.

The resulting difficulty of knowing whether to credit research findings to the independent variable or to the experimenter's unintended influence on the subjects' behavior can be lessened by keeping the experimenter ignorant of the hypothesis. This is often referred to as the use of a *blind experimenter*. However, some recent research has indicated that this alone may not be a sufficient solution to the problem. It seems (Rosenthal, Persinger, Vikan-Kline, and Fode, 1963) that experimenters who are not explicitly informed of the hypothesis may deduce one on their own from the early data that they collect. That is, the performance of their first subjects may suggest a hypothesis to them. To be sure, it is by no means certain that such deductions will be accurate, but even if experimenters influence subjects to conform to an incorrect hypothesis, they will have influenced their behavior in a way that would distort the true effects of the independent variable.

A solution that is even better than using a blind experimenter is using an automated one. If the necessary instructions are tape-recorded by persons who are totally uninformed about the experiment, and other procedures are automated in such a way that contact between subjects and any person who might influence them is kept to an absolute minimum, the likelihood of unintended messages acting as extraneous events will be greatly reduced, if not entirely eliminated.

The difficulties that extraneous events can pose for laboratory studies are much easier to deal with than those which are encountered in other types of research. At the risk of preempting our discussion of prescientific research designs in Chapter 5, let us consider the problems they raise in the study of history as an example. In many cases, over and above their concern with establishing chronologies of events and persons, historians are also engaged in the activity of testing hypotheses. They are interested in finding the answers to such questions as "What caused World War I?" "Why was Ronald Reagan elected President?" or "What was responsible for the migration of American settlers to California in the middle of the nineteenth century?"

The method historians use is quite different from performing a laboratory study in psychology. For one thing, rather than producing the causal events referred to in their hypotheses and then observing their effects on subsequent events, they must start with an important event that has occurred naturally, such as a war, and then look for its antecedent cause. This method has three distinctive properties. First, it is obviously retrospective (psychologists often use the term *post hoc*). This means that one looks for the cause already knowing the effect, which raises the possibility that the search may be biased by one's preconceptions. Beginning to look with a preexisting specific hypothesis about what kinds of factors may have acted as cause may lead one to sift the historical record selectively, with the result that the true cause is discarded as chaff or overlooked entirely.

A second feature of historical investigations, which is dictated by their subject matter, is that they tend to encompass relatively long spans of time. This increases the potential for extraneous events to intrude into the analysis. The number of possible causal events is likely to be extremely large. This in itself increases the possibility that some event other than the true cause will be mistaken for the true cause. Since all the events antecedent to the one whose cause is being sought (the historian's version of the dependent variable) have occurred naturally and are therefore outside the investigator's control, it is difficult to know how the factors that actually did influence the event being studied are to be identified among all the extraneous events around them. A related problem is that of knowing how long any of these events might take to produce the effect being studied. How far back in time need one go in search of causes? Where does the historian stop in the search?

Another characteristic of the phenomena the historians seek to explain that makes it difficult to distinguish causal from extraneous events is that they are global phenomena that are likely to have more than one cause. Laboratory studies in psychology are usually designed to investigate relatively circumscribed fragments of larger phenomena, or phenomena of rather limited scope. In such a case, it makes more sense to try to assess the effects of a single causal factor that can be extremely, if not totally, influential in producing that phenomenon. But the election of a president, or the start of a war, is much less likely to have been caused by a single event. Thus the historian who is trying to find an explanation for such an event among a larger number of possible causes extending over a long period of time needs to consider the possibility that several of these are true causes.

The possibility that extraneous events will influence research findings seems relatively easy to assess in the cases of laboratory experiments and historical investigations. They are not very likely and are relatively easy to prevent in the former, very numerous and much more difficult to deal with in the latter. Between these relatively clear-cut cases, however, lies a very large gray area. One important part of it consists of the investigations called *field studies*, done in real-world settings and concerned with independent variables which are natural events not controlled by the investigator.

The study of the effect of schoolchildren's expectations on their grades, described in Chapter 1, is a good example. Field studies tend to last longer than laboratory experiments, although not nearly so long as many historical events take to unfold (the causes of a war may go back decades). They also permit more control by the investigator, for example, in choosing a relatively specific dependent measure or event to study, like school grades. However, the number of possible causes of such an effect, and the number of surrounding extraneous events, are still great compared to the case of the laboratory study in which subjects can be brought into contact with a single causal event, in the otherwise rather sterile environment of the laboratory, within a fraction of an hour.

We speculated in our earlier discussion of this hypothetical study that children whose expectations were low on entering school might have been from poorer families than were the children entering with high expectations. It is possible that over the course of the several months that would pass in such a study, differences in events to which members of the two groups were exposed, other than their expectations for success, could affect their grades. In that case, attributing differences in their grades to their expectations would be erroneous. There are two such extraneous events that readily come to mind as alternative explanations of the (hypothetical) finding that children with higher expectations make higher grades.

If the children with lower expectations come from poorer families, this information might be conveyed to their teachers by the clothes they wear to school, or even by their speech patterns or their manners. If, as is unfortunately likely, their teachers believed that poorer children were less capable of learning their lessons than, say, middle-class children, those teachers might treat the poorer children with less care and less interest in the classroom. Such treatment could, in itself, have an effect on their grades. Or the very fact that they were poor could mean that they come to school each day without a nourishing breakfast, or even without a nourishing dinner the evening before. If so, their hunger might make it more difficult for them to pay attention in class and do well in their studies.

One could argue that these correlates of poverty are not really extraneous events at all, but, along with expectations, real determinants of young children's school performance. But from the point of view of evaluating a finding that children who bring low expectations with them to school subsequently earn low grades, they are extraneous events. Their occurrence, should the research design fail to rule it out, and should it also be plausible based on existing knowledge that they are related to expectations and grades can be affected by them, means that the effect of expectations on grades may not be what it appears to be. That effect cannot be determined as long as the effect of expectations cannot be separated from the effects of other variables, or causes, such as teachers' behavior and hunger. It is precisely this separation of causal factors that the laboratory study is particularly well suited to accomplish. However, we must not lose track of the problems associated with that approach, which we will deal with, in detail, later on.

As is true of all the threats to validity considered here, the problem of extraneous events will occur again and again throughout this book. For now, just a short concluding statement about it. It would not be possible to chronicle all the possible extraneous events that can threaten the validity of research, or all the settings in which the problem can arise. But by now you should have a good general idea of what the problem is. In our earlier discussion of the expectations–grades study we speculated that the two groups to be compared might differ in more ways than just their expectations; the point was not all that different from the one we made a few paragraphs ago about the likelihood of extraneous events being associated with expectations. The truth is that our delineation of a dozen threats to validity is, as all category systems are, somewhat arbitrary. Although not completely separate, there are enough differences among them to permit different labels to be applied. In this case, if the difference associated with the independent variable is something that happens, like teachers' treatment of their students, we will call it an extraneous event. If it is a characteristic of the subjects themselves, we will talk about the problem of group composition effects (which we will consider a few pages further on). We will run into this problem of overlap again, too, but for the moment, it is more important to recognize the problems than to fit them into any particular set of labels.

## TEMPORAL EFFECTS

Our discussion of extraneous events began with the observation that every investigation extends over some period of time. We showed how this is true of the briefest laboratory experiment, in which the administration of the experimental treatment and the assessment of its effects on the subject's behavior may require only a fraction of an hour, as well as of the historical study that examines events that unfold over a period of years, generations, or even centuries. The passage of time poses yet another threat to the validity of virtually every investigation. It creates the possibility that the subjects or phenomena being studied might be altered with the passage of time by forces that are irrelevant to the independent variable whose effects the investigation was intended to assess. These forces, or extraneous variables, are distinguished from the extraneous events considered above by the fact that they are intrinsic to, or a part of, the subjects or phenomena in question. Extraneous events may be introduced into an investigation by some external agent such as the experimenter or the subject or even a political event. But *temporal effects* are changes in the dependent variable that are bound to occur during the time the investigation takes place as a result of some characteristic that the subjects or phenomena possess naturally. There is no way of stopping them. For this reason, they have also been referred to as effects of *maturation.*

A few examples of temporal effects are in order at this point. I once knew a graduate student who was interested in demonstrating the effect of social reinforcement on young children. In concrete terms, what he eventually did for his dissertation research was to have a number of groups of randomly assigned preschoolers perform an activity while, for each group, an adult experimenter administered a particular kind and amount of social reinforcement (smiles, praise, etc.). The design called for the youngsters to first engage in the activity without any reinforcement to determine their baseline levels of performance (or operant rate), then to be exposed to a particular reinforcement treatment, and, finally, to perform without reinforcement again. This is a commonly used research method that we will consider in detail in Chapter 8. The activity this student chose for his subjects was dropping marbles, one by one, through a hole into a box. It has also been used by other investigators of the behavior of children. As the children worked, an experimenter might smile or say "good" or administer some other reward at predetermined intervals, after a marble was dropped.

The experiment was to test some specific hypotheses about the effects of the types and schedules of reinforcement used on the rates at which the children dropped marbles. The results, unfortunately, were disappointing. For every group of subjects, regardless of the treatment they received, the rate of marble-dropping declined steadily, inexorably, until a very stable low rate was reached. Does this mean that the effects of these social reinforcers, administered according to these schedules, is to lower the rate of response? Are social reinforcers incapable of maintaining behavior? If that were true, it would cause a revolution in psychological theory. More likely, the subjects' rates of response became slower because the attention span of preschoolers is extremely short. Young children naturally lose interest in any activity fairly quickly. By the time the initial baseline period was over, the subjects had had enough of marble-dropping, regardless of what any adult might do to praise them for doing it.

We cannot know the effects of different kinds and schedules of social reinforcement if those effects are combined with the temporal effects of boredom and fatigue. In this particular experiment, the combination of the independent variable and a much more powerful extraneous variable produced the observed behavior. That is, when two variables are confounded like this, their effects are inseparable and it is impossible to reach any conclusion about the separate effects of either one. And findings that cannot be attributed to any cause, much less the independent variable, are invalid.

Another example, this time purely hypothetical, of temporal effects acting as extraneous variables to invalidate the findings of an experiment comes from the verbal learning literature. Let us say you wanted to test the hypothesis that a list of words would be learned more readily if it consisted of groups of words which were related in some way than if there were no such relationships within the list. One could create such a contrast by first writing five simple five-word sentences and then making a list of the words from each sentence so they followed one another in order (i.e., if one read down the list it would make sense), and making another list of the words from the different sentences, but scrambled with one another (no sense). Then, with two randomly assigned groups of subjects, the members of one would be given the ordered list and the members of the other the scrambled list. Both groups would be presented with the same 25 words, but those words would be arranged differently within the lists. It would be hypothesized that the group that was given the ordered list would require fewer trials, would have to go through the list fewer times, to learn all the words in the correct order.

To make the end of this story more interesting, and to make the point we are aiming for, let us say that the experimenter responsible for conducting this experiment decided that it would be easier if the subjects who were to try to learn each list were all tested during the same period of time. The common procedure of having the words printed on 35-mm slides and presented to subjects on a screen using a slide projector makes it possible to test many subjects at the same time if they respond by writing down their answers or in some other way that ensures that they do not disturb one another. In fact, one could easily test as many subjects as would be required for each experimental group at one time. The entire experiment would then require only two sessions to complete. Once this approach was adopted, and the decision made that 2 hours should be allotted for each session, the experimenter set aside two blocks of time for this purpose from her busy schedule. One subsequent Wednesday, the experiment was performed. Thirty subjects learned the ordered list from 10 A.M. until noon and 30 more learned the scrambled list from 1:00 P.M. until 3:00 P.M.

Contrary to the experimental hypotheses, it turned out that the first group, the one that was given the ordered list, took just as long to learn the words in order as the second group, the one that got the scrambled words. This might mean that arranging the words in meaningful combinations does not make them easier to learn, that the hypothesis was mistaken. Or it may mean that some extraneous variable was operating in such a way as to obscure the true effects of the different list arrangements. As you may have already guessed, the fact that the two groups of subjects were tested at different times of day turns out to be a potential key to solving this hypothetical mystery. The subjects who were tested late in the morning, or at least a sizable group of them, may have been distracted from their task of learning the list by the feelings of hunger and the associated restlessness that afflict many of us just before lunchtime, especially when we have had a busy early morning schedule. The afternoon group, then, would have the advantage of feeling fresh and relaxed after their normal lunchtime break as they faced their version of the task. Thus, even if the experimental hypothesis were true, and it was based on a great deal of past theory and research, the predicted effect would fail to emerge because an extraneous temporal effect had worked against the effects of the independent variable.

If one wished to test this hypothesis again, this time eliminating time of day as a possible contaminant of the results, any number of solutions suggest themselves. If the experiment could be automated, the instructions on tape and the slide projector programmed to operate automatically, and if two complete sets of equipment were available, both groups of subjects could be tested at the same time, in different rooms, even next door to one another. Whatever effect the time of day might have on them, it could not affect the two groups differently. Thus, it would pose less of a threat to the validity of the findings. Even so, it would seem to make sense to try to choose a time when subjects could be expected to perform at their normal if not at their optimal levels. Another possibility, besides simultaneous testing, would be to populate each session of the study with an equal number of subjects from the different experimental treatment groups. Although this approach presents some difficulties, perhaps necessitating a separate word-presentation apparatus for each subject, it would eliminate the possibility that the treatments were confounded with any of the environmental attributes of the experimental setting, including time. Further, the more sessions into which the total study could be broken down, the less likely it would be that a significant number of the subjects' performances would be affected by some peculiarity of the time of day or week of which the experimenter is unaware.

Whether one chooses one of these solutions or prefers some other, it seems clear that a premium should be placed not on correcting poor studies but on avoiding them. It is impossible to anticipate the effects of temporal variables like the ones we have been considering in every instance. But if we use methods in which no temporal differences exist between our treatment groups, even if this means giving up shortcuts that could reduce the amount of work or expense involved, we will not have to be clever enough to know in advance what effects all those differences might have. And, of course, the findings of the research which others do will inspire more confidence if their methods meet these criteria.

Although laboratory experiments may be sensitive to the extraneous influence of such temporal variables as the duration of the session or the time of day, investigations that take place over longer periods can be affected by variables that more truly deserve to be called maturational. Suppose that one were interested in comparing the capabilities of men and women for learning higher mathematics. And suppose further that junior high school algebra classes were chosen for that comparison. Because algebra is the first truly complex mathematical system to which most people are exposed, its audience promises to provide the most representative sample of men and women in our society. More complex subjects like calculus may only be attempted by a select, high-aptitude group that has already excelled in earlier math courses. In addition, it would be advantageous in many ways to use such junior high classes rather than attempt to produce a learning task designed especially for the investigation itself. For reasons that we will consider in great detail later, we might reasonably expect to learn more from behavior being performed in the normal course of subjects' lives than from their behavior in the special context of a psychological experiment.

Specifically, then, imagine that the study was carried out in all of the eighth-grade classes in a large school district. This district was chosen because it served a region whose inhabitants constituted a representative sample of Americans, with respect to socioeconomic status, ethnic background, and so on. By restricting the study to a single school district, it would be possible to ensure that all the individuals to be compared had been exposed to a similar course of study. The same textbook would be used throughout the district, and all of the teachers' qualifications would have been judged against a common set of standards. Also, the students' performance could be assessed not only on the basis of the examinations their individual teachers devised for them, but also from their performance on standardized final examinations administered to all of them.

After all the returns are in, at the end of the school year, it turns out that, on the average, the male students have performed better than the female students. It appears that males have more talent for learning higher mathematics, right? Wrong. It turns out that there is at least one other difference between eighth-grade boys and girls besides their grades in algebra (besides that one!). A much larger percentage of girls than boys goes through puberty during the eighth grade. So the girls are more likely to have to deal with a difficult problem of social adjustment at the same time they are trying to cope with algebra. We have been comparing two groups of growing young people whose rates of maturation are different. Despite a great deal of variation within each sex, American women reach sexual maturity, on the average, about a year earlier than American men. And the age period in which we chose to put our study coincides with a time when the groups we wanted to compare typically undergo very different experiences as the result of this maturational difference. As a consequence, our comparison of their abilities in higher mathematics was confounded with that biologically based influence on them. We cannot know for certain whether the difference we found in algebra grades was caused by ability, social adjustment, or both. And, in the event that both factors were operating, it would be impossible to determine how much each one contributed.

In retrospect, it seems that we might have done better had we studied a different age group. At least we could have made an effort to separate the boys and girls into subgroups on the basis of their biological maturity in order to evaluate how that factor influenced their grades. In that way, our comparison would have been made fairer. Or perhaps we should have used a laboratory task after all. A maturation effect like puberty would be less likely to have a noticeable effect on a short-term activity like that than on a course of study in school that lasted a year.

All three of the examples we have considered, the effects of boredom and/or fatigue on preschoolers' marble-dropping, the effects of prelunch hunger and/or restlessness on college students' learning of word lists, and the effects of puberty on young men's and young women's grades in algebra, have several things in common. First, and this is important for defining this class of extraneous variables, in each case the possibility existed that the dependent variable was affected by some natural, inevitable change in the subjects that took place during the time each investigation took place, a change that was irrelevant to the causal factor being investigated. In each case, the subjects' behavior may have changed over time because of a condition inherent in the subjects themselves—the short attention span of preschoolers, the response of college students to food deprivation, and the biological maturation of young women and young men.

All three examples also demonstrated the importance, for controlling these extraneous variables, of having independent knowledge about the subjects one is studying. Since every investigation must have some temporal dimension, the possibility always exists that a temporal variable will become confounded with the independent variable. But this becomes a plausible rival to the experimental hypothesis only when some objective information or logical reason exists to show that the dependent variable is subject to influence from that temporal variable. In other words, the results of the three investigations we have been considering should be distrusted only if we have good reason to believe that marble-dropping would be slowed by inattention or a loss of interest, that word-list learning would suffer as the result of a late-morning slump, or that having to adjust to the onset of sexual maturity would interfere with school performance. It is the plausibility of each of these relationships that casts doubt on the validity of the findings of these studies. Or, to put it another way, it is in those cases in which there is good reason to believe that a temporal variable can produce an extraneous effect that it is most necessary to design an investigation in such a way as to eliminate the possibility of such an effect.

## GROUP COMPOSITION EFFECTS

Many psychological studies are designed to expose two or more separate groups of subjects to contrasting experimental treatments and then to assess the effects of those treatments, and the experiences they create, on the subjects' behavior. In some cases, the individuals are randomly assigned to the groups from a pool of potential subjects. Each individual has the same chance of being assigned to one group as to any other. In this way, the initial comparability of the groups is ensured. Although it is possible, in cases in which relatively small numbers of subjects are involved, for *sampling error* to produce differences between such groups, there are statistical tests that can discount this. But if subjects are not chosen on the basis of any systematic criterion such as sex or age or expectations, any differences that are later observed in their behavior cannot be attributed to some initial difference among them.

Let us look at a concrete example. Someone wants to test the hypothesis that among Chicano high school students a nonverbal test of intelligence would yield higher scores than a traditional test, which depends on the use of the American English language and knowledge of the customs of American culture codified in it. Both tests have been standardized to yield distributions of scores with the same mean and standard deviation. To select a sample on whom to conduct the test, a list of all of the Chicano (Spanish surname) high school students in one county in California is obtained. Six-thousand students are listed in alphabetical order. Then every fiftieth name is chosen, yielding a total sample of 120 students. From a list of these 120, the even numbers (2nd, 4th, etc.) are assigned to the nonverbal test group and the odd numbers (1st, 3rd, etc.) to the traditional test group. A comparison of the test scores of these two groups ultimately reveals that the group given the nonverbal test actually outperformed the group given the traditional test. Because of the method of subject selection employed, we can be confident that this observed difference was not caused by the fact that the individuals in the non-verbal group had superior intelligence, richer families which had provided them with more healthful or intellectually stimulating home environments, or any other initial advantage. Randomization in assigning subjects to groups precludes this.

There are, however, two classes of investigations in which ran-domization cannot be used to ensure the initial equivalence of treat-ment groups. It is in these cases that the problem of extraneous *group composition effects* becomes most acute. One class consists of investi-gation of independent variables that cannot be manipulated by the experimenter. Individual difference variables probably constitute the most common example of this type. Innumerable personality tests have been constructed to measure an almost endless variety of people's beliefs about themselves, significant individuals in their lives, the institutions and values of their society, and too many other things to mention here. Each of these tests was devised because someone thought that a particular set of beliefs would affect the be-havior of those who held it. One of the most popular ways of finding out whether they were right has been the extreme-groups personal-ity experiment, which tests a prediction of a specific behavioral effect of such a trait.

There is a basic pattern for these studies that has been repeated thousands of times. The first step is to administer the test in question to a large number of individuals, then select from this initial group those who scored highest and lowest. The cutoff points for highest and lowest generally depend on how many people are tested and how their scores are distributed, but one might use the top and bot-tom 15% or 20% or 25%. Finally, the two groups of subjects thus chosen are observed in the same experimental situation. A reliable (statistically significant) difference in their behavior in the predicted direction would presumably reflect the influence of the underlying personality trait the test was designed to measure in the first place.

For example, let us say the two groups who received extreme test scores were introverts and extraverts. And let us say we found that introverts were less influential in discussion groups we set up for our study. Was this because they were introverts—people who have less interest in the company of others? Since the introverts and extraverts did not enter the study as equivalent groups (in fact, quite the opposite), this study would have an inherent weakness. The dif-ference in their behavior might have been caused by some differ-ence between them other than the trait we used to classify them. It might have been that their speech was less articulate after years of having very little practice in conversation. It would be impossible to tell whether it was their trait of introversion which made them less effective or the low level of mechanical skill in speaking smoothly. These two things may be related, but they are not the same. If the issue under discussion was equally important to both groups, and if the situation had called for written messages instead of oral ones, there might not have been any difference in the influence introverts and extraverts had in the discussion groups, even if they did differ in their interest in sociable relationships with the other group members.

It is time for a more specific example of this problem. One trait that has been widely investigated in this manner is called "perceived locus of control of reinforcement," or "internal-external control," or "I-E" for short. It concerns, in a more complex way than we will be able to consider here, people's beliefs about the extent to which they have personal control over what happens to them. Extreme scorers on the test used to measure I-E are classified either as internals, those who indicate that they believe they can exercise a great deal of personal control, or externals, those who express the belief that other people and forces such as luck and fate are more influential in determining what happens to them than they are themselves.

Imagine that a group of internals and a group of externals were both placed in a situation in which they could choose either to exercise their own initiative by working at a very difficult task themselves or to put their fate in someone else's hands by letting an expert try it for them—in both cases having some reward hanging in the balance. It would seem predictable that the internals would be more likely to try the task themselves and the externals would be more likely to turn it over to the expert. But if the results of the experiment bore out that prediction, how confident could one be that the difference in the two groups' behavior was caused by the difference in their beliefs about their control over their lives? Let us consider an alternative explanation. What if people who respond to the personality test as internals had some combination of abilities—call it general intelligence or competence or whatever—which in the past had caused them to be highly successful at many of the difficult tasks with which they were faced. Analogously, we could assume that those who responded as externals were people who, by comparison, lacked competence and had behind them a long list of failures. If this analysis were true, it would be just as reasonable to argue that the difference in the two groups' preferences for personal initiative versus expert help was caused by their different records of past success as of their beliefs. In fact, their beliefs may have also resulted from their competence or lack of it.

It might appear that this discussion is an exercise in splitting hairs. Aren't competence and the belief in competence pretty much the same thing? Logically, they are not. It is entirely possible to be highly competent but have little confidence in one's ability, or to have relatively little competence but believe one has a great deal. There are times when the difference between the two can be extremely important. Let us look at a concrete example of such an instance. In the mid-1960s, a presidential commission set out to investigate the basis for the relatively poor academic achievement of children from so-called disadvantaged groups in our society (such as blacks living in poverty in our large urban ghettos). One of the factors they assessed, along with such tangible things as school budgets and teacher qualifications, was the students' beliefs about how influential their own talents and efforts were in their success in school. They found a strong relationship between those beliefs and actual academic achievement (Coleman et al., 1966). Compared to white, middle-class students, the disadvantaged children had, at the same time, poorer grades and beliefs which, in terms of I-E, were more external. (Although this was not really an extreme-groups study, it bears a strong resemblance to one.)

Having interpreted this finding as indicating that the children's beliefs were a major cause of their failure in school (budgets and teachers actually seemed to make much less of a difference), the commission's report suggested that steps might be taken to modify those beliefs in an effort to remedy the failure. But what if the failure was caused by a lack of competence in the skills that are necessary for success in school? If the children's home environments failed to provide such necessary tools as the exposure to adults who speak grammatical English, training in middle-class manners that would elicit approval from middle-class teachers, and positive attitudes toward the value of schooling, those children might be expected to achieve little success in school. Their failure might then lead them to express little confidence in their own ability to cope with the demands of the school environment. They might believe that their fate was in the hands of their teachers and unseen persons responsible for structuring an environment with which they could not cope. Changing those beliefs would not provide them with the skills they needed. Their failure would continue despite new beliefs. In fact, such new beliefs might cause them to blame themselves more for their failure, despite the influence of factors which were, in fact, largely beyond their own control. Not only would they still be failing, but they might also have poorer self-images than they previously had. The influence of an extraneous variable can result in an incorrect interpretation of the findings of an investigation that can ultimately have disastrous consequences.

Human personality traits are not the only causal variables that cannot be manipulated by an investigator. World events, political, social, economic, and natural, can affect people's behavior directly, and they can affect social processes and institutions, which in turn affect behavior. Studying the effects of such events is difficult because such studies are almost always retrospective, depending upon historical records to provide their data. Important events are often not predictable far enough in advance, or their importance is not fully recognized until long after they occur, or they extend over such long periods that it is difficult to collect data immediately after they occur. More important, for the purposes of our present discussion, a study may compare data from a sample of such events (wars, elections, etc.) divided among two or more contrasting classes. The criterion for class membership would be the causal variable being investigated such as the economic situation. These events cannot be chosen randomly from different historical periods or geographic areas or in any other way. Like traits, they simply occur where they do; the experimenter may find them there, but has no control over where they are to be found.

Now, for an example. Let us say we wanted to investigate the hypothesis that presidents from one political party have done a better job of managing the U.S. economy than those from the other major party. In addition to solving practical problems such as finding comparable economic indices across as long a historical period as the twentieth century, we would have to deal with what is perhaps a more fundamental problem. Even if we had comparable measures of the functioning of the economy over that long period, and knew what precise time period each president ought to be held accountable for (there is a troublesome and uncertain time lag between policy decisions and their effects), we would end up comparing two samples of time periods, corresponding to the presidencies of Democrats and Republicans, which we could not be confident were equivalent. If the economic scores of one party's presidents were higher than the other's, how certain could we be that this difference didn't just reflect the fact that the apparently superior party had been in power during periods of more beneficent economic conditions?

Wars, revolutions, important legal decisions, depressions, and all other historical events can be investigated only with this same difficulty. These events happen when they do rather than when we might want them to, and they do not necessarily happen haphazardly. There is a possibility that the dates of Democratic and Republican presidencies bear some systematic relationship to the economic conditions which prevail in the country. Those conditions might be as much as if not more responsible for the records of our presidents as are their programs for the economy. It may be true, for example, that

Democratic presidents have more often been elected after periods of economic decline, and Republican presidents after periods of economic growth. If so, it would hardly be fair to compare the performance of those two groups of presidents. Under these (hypothetical) circumstances, could the Democrats have helped to be associated with more improvement in the economy than the Republicans?

It must be obvious by now that there are serious difficulties in studying the effects of traits or historical events or any causal factor that cannot be produced at will by the investigator. But traits and historical events, among other such variables, may have important effects on behavior. Are we to ignore them because we cannot study them without incurring the risk of extraneous group composition effects? Because those who have done this kind of research are convinced of its value, they have tried to cope with its difficulties. For example, investigators of traits strengthen their case by presenting correlational evidence that the trait in question is independent of other influential traits. Internals and externals have been shown to be comparable in their intelligence and social adjustment, thus eliminating those two variables from the list of potential causes of any observed differences in their behavior. The independence of a trait from other traits is called discriminant validity. It is one test a trait must meet before it is widely investigated.

A very different approach to the problem has been taken by David McClelland (1961). He has studied the effects of people's beliefs in the importance of achievement on economic growth, across very different societies and very broad spans of time, despite the extreme problems of control over group composition variables that such studies present. McClelland simply argues away the question of the comparability of different societies or different historical eras. He maintains that the many potential sources of error in such studies are likely to be random. As a result, their effects are to reduce the apparent strength of relationships rather than to create them where they do not exist. By this reasoning, any support which the findings lend to the experimental hypothesis underestimate its truth.

Neither the evidence for discriminant validity, in the case of traits, nor the logic of McClelland's argument, in the case of complex historical processes, is entirely satisfactory. It is still possible that groups of subjects that differ on one trait also differ in some other important respect. It is impossible to rule out all alternative causes for the observed difference in their behavior. Because there are a limitless number of potential correlates for every trait, there is no such thing as perfect discriminant validity. Getting back to McClelland, it is unclear why different societies or eras cannot be associated with conditions that are related systematically to the causal factor under investigation. For example, natural resources, which are necessary to high levels of economic growth, may not be distributed randomly, but instead may be more abundant in societies that stress achievement more. However, although one must remain sensitive to the possibility that the findings of such studies are invalid, the evidence they provide is in many cases the most trustworthy that can be found.

The problem of extraneous group composition effects may also arise when studies of variables that can be manipulated are carried out in natural settings. There, some contextual conditions may elude the investigator's control. Let us say that an educational psychologist wanted to compare two different methods of teaching mathematics to grade-school students, a traditional approach and one newly derived from a psychological theory about the development of logical thinking, such as Piaget's. In theory, students at the appropriate ages could be selected at random to be taught by one method or the other. Two groups of subjects could be constituted, one to be taught by each method, which were equivalent in all respects, if the groups were large enough for randomization to be effective. In practice, however, such a study would probably have to be carried out in the schools. Assembling groups of children outside school hours, for adequate blocks of time, at regular intervals over a period long enough to do such a test, would be extremely difficult, if not impossible. If the study were to be done in the schools, random assignment of students to special classes established for the purposes of the study might be equally difficult. The school routine might make it necessary for students to remain grouped in their own classes, in their assigned rooms, with their usual teachers.

Even if a school did not assign students to classes on the basis of some systematic criterion, such as their IQ or aptitude, as is done in schools that use "tracking" systems, the administration of the two teaching methods to different intact classes raises some problems. As a result of its past history (i.e., the relationships formed among students and with the teacher, the qualifications and attitudes of the teacher, the teacher's sex, and numerous other factors), each class may develop an identity and an atmosphere that makes it different from every other class. This may be true even if the groups of individual students were comparable when the classes were first constituted. Obviously, if just one class were taught math by each of the two methods to be compared, the achievement of each group of students might be affected by the characteristics of their class as well as by the teaching methods used in it. Regardless of what the results might be, one could not interpret them with any confidence. In any natural setting, then, if it were impossible to assign subjects randomly to groups because of rules imposed by some authority, it would be desirable to use as large a number of intact classes (or prison cell blocks, or mental hospital wards, or whatever units were involved) to ensure that the idiosyncrasies of those units were randomly distributed among the treatment conditions. It should never be taken for granted that intact units are equivalent, even if their members were initially assigned at random. If, in any investigation, individuals cannot be randomly assigned, group composition effects pose a potential threat to the validity of the findings.

## THE INTERACTION OF TEMPORAL AND GROUP COMPOSITION EFFECTS

We have seen how the duration of an investigation can, in itself, pose a threat to the validity of research findings. Extraneous changes in subjects can occur over time as the result of some intrinsic property of those subjects. When subjects have been randomly assigned to treatment groups, some extraneous temporal effects that might occur will have comparable effects in all groups. For example, all subjects may become bored with their task. But when subjects have not been assigned at random, as we have seen in the preceding section, there is the possibility that the treatment groups will differ in their tendency to change in some respect over the course of the investigation. Thus it is possible, when subjects are assigned to treatment groups on any basis other than at random, that different extraneous temporal effects may take place in different treatment groups during the same period of time. When this occurs, it is referred to as the *interaction of temporal and group composition effects,* because the temporal (or maturational) effects that occur within a given treatment group depend upon the composition of that group. In other words, the effects of time vary from one kind of subject to another.

In studies in which treatment groups are not randomly constituted, as we pointed out in the previous section, some investigators have relied upon evidence that the groups are comparable in some important respects. Such evidence places some limits on the likelihood that any comparison between the groups might reflect extraneous group composition variables rather than the pure effects of the independent variable being studied. In the study of traits, this evidence takes the form of discriminant validity. In the study of teaching methods described earlier, it might take the form of evidence that students' scores on math achievement tests were comparable across classes during some period prior to the study. But this technique of determining comparability at the outset of an investigation has only limited utility. It does not deal with the problem of treatment groups differing in ways that can result in different changes over time in the behavior being studied. Let us look at an example.

Suppose that you were called on to do a study of the effectiveness of a Head Start preschool program. Among the goals of the program is the enhancement of scholastic aptitude, the likelihood that the child will do well in school. Thus, your study would have to include an assessment of the scholastic aptitude of children who had been through the program. Their scores would then have to be compared with those of a comparable group of children who had not been through the program. The two groups would have to be composed of children of comparable ages, socioeconomic backgrounds, and intelligence. For example, one would not want to compare poor kids from minority subculture backgrounds who had been exposed to Head Start with upper-middle-class kids who had not. The validity of such a comparison would be threatened by the strong possibility of extraneous group composition effects. One could not be confident that the true effects of the Head Start program were being observed if one group started out far ahead of the other.

In practical terms, then, what could you do? At the beginning of a school year, when the Head Start program was scheduled to begin, you would first have to select one or more Head Start sites at which to study the effects of the program. A list of the children signed up at those sites would contain the subjects in your Head Start treatment group. At the same time, you would have to identify a similar number of children of the same ages, from the same neighborhoods, with similar socioeconomic backgrounds, who were not scheduled to attend Head Start. At this point, you might arrange for the children in both groups to be given intelligence or scholastic aptitude tests to determine their relative standing at the outset of the study. However, in the same way that evidence of discriminant validity is only a limited safeguard against extraneous group composition effects in studies of traits, the assurance of initial comparability in background and intellectual development has only limited value here. The fact is that no matter how similar the groups may be in any other way, they do differ in one respect—one has been signed up for Head Start and the other has not.

One can only speculate about the underlying factors that might be associated with this difference. It may be that children who are enrolled in Head Start have parents who are more concerned about their intellectual development and the risk that they run of doing poorly in school than are the parents of children with similar qualifications for Head Start who have not enrolled them in the program. If this is true, and it seems plausible, one might also speculate that the parents of children enrolled in Head Start might also be more likely to have made other unusual efforts in their children's behalf in the past. Perhaps they were more diligent in supervising their play, reading to them, restricting their television viewing to educational programs, and the like. Therefore, even if the Head Start children were to test out as having the same IQ or aptitude as the non-Head Start group, you might be skeptical about how similar the two groups really were. It might be that the pretest intelligence or aptitude measure failed to detect some real difference, or that the content of the test failed to tap some important dimension of the children's abilities. Further, if the backgrounds of the Head Start children provided them with advantageous treatment of the sort we have speculated about, their resulting superiority might take a form we are unfamiliar with and therefore unlikely to test for in our pursuit of a matching strategy. As we have seen before, such problems seriously limit the potential value of matching.

But what if the Head Start group actually did get higher scores on the pretest? You might still be able to establish two comparable treatment groups by choosing an above-average sample from the non-Head Starters. In this way, you could be sure that the Head Start children were being compared with children outside the program who were their peers in ability. Or could you? Let us suppose that you did indeed find Head Start children to be a superior group in intelligence or aptitude, on average, and therefore chose an above-average non-Head Start group to serve as a standard against which to gauge their progress. In addition to being more intelligent or scholastically better prepared, the Head Start children, perhaps also as a result of their parents' efforts, might also be developing intellectually at a faster rate. This would explain why, as a group, they were ahead of their age-mates who were not enrolled in Head Start. Thus, the two groups of children, those in Head Start and the above-average sample of those not, who were comparable in intelligence or aptitude at the time when the study was to begin, might not be comparable by the time it was scheduled to end one school year later because of their previously determined rates of development, whether or not the Head Start children actually went through the program. In a study that lasts as long as a school year, a maturational effect such as this could conceivably be quite large. Matching is clearly no substitute for random assignment in eliminating group composition effects as threats to validity.

A similar problem with the kind of matching procedure we have been discussing has arisen in connection with studies of the effectiveness of psychotherapy. Such an evaluation is similar in many respects to the evaluation of a Head Start program. To determine how effective a particular program of psychotherapy is, one would have to compare its effects on those who went through it with the improvement, or lack of it, in a comparable group who were not treated during the same period of weeks or months the program lasted. One would not want to compare a group of individuals who sought treatment with a group who had similar problems but did not seek treatment. The first group might have a better prognosis simply by virtue of their concern with seeking help, just as Head Start children might be more likely to improve intellectually simply by virtue of their families' concern with their progress. In both cases, the effectiveness of the program in question might be overestimated by such a comparison. Matching on some predictor of future progress here again runs the risk of either an insensitive or improperly selected criterion or of a difference in maturation rates that would not be reflected in a pretest measure.

An alternative that has been used in studies of therapeutic effectiveness is called the "waiting-list control" procedure. In it, an entire group of individuals who apply for treatment of an appropriate problem or class of problems is divided randomly in two. Half the group is assigned to receive the treatment to be evaluated. The other half is put on a waiting list, to receive the treatment at some time in the future, usually just after the first group's program has ended. The advantage of this procedure is that it permits the comparison of the effects of treatment and lack of treatment in two groups of individuals with similar problems who have shown a similar concern for their future by applying for help. It further makes the two groups as similar as possible by promising both groups eventual acceptance into the program and giving them hope for future relief.

It seems clear that a similar procedure could be used to advantage in studying a Head Start program or any other comparable intervention. It would appear to promise a substantial improvement over attempting to match groups that were known to differ in important ways. However, it should be recognized that its potential for success depends upon its being applied in the way that it is intended. To the extent that the individuals admitted to the program in any such study were those who pursued admittance most aggressively or most intelligently or earliest, one's confidence in the comparability of the group receiving treatment and the group not receiving treatment would be reduced accordingly. Doing research in real-world settings may involve problems the researcher cannot control. In practice, it would not always be possible to use the waiting-list control procedure because the administrator of a preschool, psychotherapy, or other service program may feel that it is unethical or disruptive to modify a first-come first-served policy for the purpose of an evaluation study. And aggressive parents or clients might succeed in influencing an administrator to assign them nonrandomly to the program rather than the waiting list. It is no wonder that questions about the effectiveness of such programs often linger indefinitely, awaiting satisfactory answers.

## OBSERVER EFFECTS

Research in psychology, and in other social sciences, varies widely in the problems it investigates and the methods it uses to do so. But in all of its varied forms it has one common property: It is empirical; it produces objective evidence. And the evidence it produces almost always takes a quantitative form. The dependent variables that are chosen are assessed by some measurement procedure that yields a set of numerical scores or classifies events or people on the basis of some criteria. In some cases these data can be collected in a completely straightforward manner; for example, a study comparing the effects of a number of different schedules or reinforcements on the rate of responding in pigeons. In this case, sophisticated electronic equipment can be used to provide an accurate record of the pigeons' responses, no matter how rapid or numerous they may be. Or consider an investigation of the effects of various incentive-pay plans on worker productivity in an industrial plant. The dependent variable may be the output of workers doing a particular job. Again, automatic recording equipment could provide a completely reliable record of the number of units of a given product completed by each worker and even, in some cases, of the quality of those units.

However, the process of data collection is not always so straightforward. In many cases, an experimenter or technician is required to participate in the measurement process. The task may be perfunctory, such as starting and stopping a timer or assigning numerical values to questionnaire responses on the basis of a predetermined key. Or it may involve making judgments about subjects' behavior or about written records of an historical event by categorizing or rating samples of verbal material, after extensive training in applying a set of criteria. It may, in fact, go to the extreme of very complex and subjective clinical judgments about how much improvement has been made by patients in therapy.

Whenever data are not collected in a completely direct and objective manner, whenever some person is required to exercise judgment in the course of its acquisition, there is a possibility that those data may reflect, in addition to the effects of the independent variable being studied, some systematic bias on the part of the person collecting them. Obviously, this possibility becomes stronger as the measurement process requires greater participation by this person, whom we'll call the observer. But, in every case, even the tabulation of mechanically collected data, the contribution of the observer constitutes a potential threat to the validity of the findings of the investigation. If an observer's judgments are not based on a standard which is applied consistently to all treatment groups, any comparisons among those groups will be invalid. They will be affected by the extraneous influence of *observer effects.*

There are, unfortunately, many research settings in which this problem arises, quite without observers' knowledge that their judgments are biasing the data that they are collecting.

The potential for extraneous observer effects is perhaps best illustrated in some findings reviewed by Robert Rosenthal (1976) concerning the case in which an observer participates in the data collection process to the least extent imaginable, by simply tabulating and tallying numbers that have been recorded automatically. Short of the most sophisticated laboratory arrangement, in which data are fed from counters, timers, and the like directly into an on-line computer for storage and analysis, virtually all research data are subject to at least this much human intervention. In the studies reviewed by Rosenthal, those responsible for handling the data were also aware of the experimental hypothesis, probably a fairly common situation. It was found that about 70% of them made errors in recording observations, and almost two-thirds made computational errors. But more important to this discussion, about three-fourths of all these observers' errors were in the direction of supporting the experimental hypothesis. A few observers made errors that were consistent enough and large enough to bias the findings of an experiment in which they were solely responsible for handling the data. It seems clear that observers as well as experimenters, even those whose role in the data collection process allows the least possible opportunity for their personal judgment to color the data, must be kept blind to the experimental hypothesis. Furthermore, because they can be expected to formulate their own hypotheses as the study progresses, the task should be divided among as many individuals as possible, and each one's work should be checked independently by others to minimize any biasing effect on the findings.

The finding that experimenters make errors in handling data that increase the probability that their experimental hypothesis will be confirmed presumably explains one aspect of the experimenter–bias phenomenon we discussed earlier. At that time, we suggested that automated behavior recording devices would help solve the problem of experimenter bias. Even that precaution is not sufficient to eliminate the problem entirely. Any participation by an experimenter who anticipates the outcome of the research can bias the results. It seems reasonable to expect, then, that if that participation were to consist of making subjective judgments about the behavior being studied—which provided the data—the margin for bias would be increased. For example, in experiments designed to investigate the effects of televised violence on the behavior of children who watch it, the data have often consisted of ratings of the aggressiveness of children during play. In many cases, these ratings seem objective, such as noting the presence or absence of specific behavior on the part of the children being observed. But in these experiments, and in any others that make extensive use of behavior ratings, no matter how well-structured those ratings might appear to be, it is important to take every possible precaution against observer bias. And it is important to recognize the fact that those precautions are unlikely to be fail-safe.

Anticipation of the outcome is not the only possible cause of extraneous observer effects. Let us consider another way in which an observer might bias research results. In this case, we will use as an example a hypothetical laboratory study intended to test the hypothesis that physical attractiveness is a determinant in how rewarding a person is as a partner in social interaction. Two groups of subjects would be selected at random to have "get-acquainted" conversations with attractive and unattractive partners. The members of both groups would all meet the same individual, a confederate of the experimenter. For one group, that person would be made to appear attractive; for the other group, unattractive. This would be accomplished through modifications in the person's clothing, grooming, posture, and the like. Using just one target person would presumably hold constant factors other than attractiveness, such as intelligence, ethnic or other group identification, height, and personality. The subjects would be led to believe, one by one, that the person they met, and whose attractiveness was being manipulated in the experiment, was just another naïve subject. Each pair, one subject and the confederate, would be told that the conversation they were being asked to hold was for the purpose of finding out what kind of topics strangers choose to talk about during an initial encounter. The conversations would be observed through a one-way mirror. Since a one-way mirror rarely looks like a real mirror, the subjects would be told about it and informed that they would be observed. An observer on the other side of the mirror would rate the mood of each naïve subject during the conversation. Rating scales for expressions of happiness, interest, liking, and other positive sentiments would be filled out at specified intervals during the course of each session. It would be expected that subjects who talked with the attractive person would appear happier, more interested, more affectionate, and so on, than those who talked with the unattractive person. Should this result obtain, it would presumably lend support to the notion that more attractive people provide greater rewards for those with whom they interact than do less attractive people. Those who are being rewarded more should appear happier at the time.

This experiment would certainly raise the possibility of observer bias caused by a desire for hypothesis confirmation. Even if an observer were not informed of the hypothesis directly, it might be deduced in the course of observing the same person with a markedly changing appearance interacting with a succession of other people whose reactions are to be rated. This kind of biasing effect might be less likely if different observers each saw only one version of the stimulus person. But let us assume for now that the observer has no hypothesis whatever about the purpose of the experiment or the ultimate use to which the ratings will be put. We will consider an entirely different problem.

For practical reasons, it would be easier to do this experiment in such a way that those subjects who were to meet the attractive confederate would be tested during separate blocks of time from those who were to meet the unattractive confederate. This would avoid the problem of having to change the confederate's appearance from one form to the other every half-hour or so. If 20 subjects were to be tested with each version of the confederate, the unattractive version could be presented on one day and the attractive version the next. Given that this procedure were, in fact, adopted, one would then have to devise a method for having the subjects' behavior observed and rated. We will consider a few alternative arrangements, from the standpoint of their potential for extraneous observer effects.

One person, given enough stamina, could act as observer for all 40 subjects. This would insure that if the observer had an idiosyncratic view of how happy other people look, the ratings of subjects in both treatment conditions would be affected equally. The observer would be scheduled to rate subjects who met the attractive stranger one day and those who met the unattractive stranger the next. Suppose that on the morning of the first day the observer felt eager and highly motivated to do a conscientious job. But as subject after subject was tested, by the time late afternoon rolled around, the task became more and more tedious, boring, and generally unpleasant (these sorts of tasks inevitably prove to be drudgery). While getting ready to leave from home the second day, the thought of having to sit through 20 more sessions gave the observer feelings of panic. But since no substitute had been trained in the event that the observer failed to show up, the observer gave up the thought of calling in sick. As the experiment ran its course, the sessions felt like torture and the second day seemed to last forever.

After the final session was over, the observer's ratings were quickly tabulated and analyzed. On the average, subjects in the second group, tested that day, had been rated significantly less happy than those in the first group. Since those tested on the second day had met an unattractive person, one could assume that the ratings merely confirmed the experimental hypothesis. But the preceding scenario raises another possibility. When subjects in different treatment conditions are run during separate blocks of time, and a single observer makes a contribution to all their data, it is possible for the mood of the observer to interact with the experimental treatments (that is, to affect the different treatment conditions differently) and thus contribute to artifactual findings of differences between them. An unhappy, even hostile, observer might describe any person who came along in negative terms, regardless of behavior. Had the first day's subjects in our present example met the unattractive confederate, and the second day's subjects the attractive one, there might have been evidence supporting the unlikely proposition that attractive people generally cause those with whom they interact to feel worse than unattractive people do.

If one feared that using just one observer would raise the fatigue problem we have described, or if one felt that such an arrangement would make the experimental hypothesis too obvious to the observer, it might seem preferable to use one observer the first day and a different one the second. But what if one of these two happens to be more likely to describe others in positive terms than the other? This could contribute to a finding that the subjects in the two treatment conditions reacted differently when the independent variable, the attractiveness of the confederate, had really had no effect at all on subjects' reactions. Or, if the observer who was prone to overestimate other people's happiness were assigned to rate the subjects who met the unattractive confederate, one might observe no difference in the ratings of the two groups, when the more attractive confederate had, in fact, elicited more positive reactions.

In general, the problem we have been dealing with is that of ensuring that the data which are collected in the course of testing an hypothesis are all the product of the application of the same standard of measurement. This freedom from observer effects is one condition that must be met, along with all the others we have been considering, before one can have confidence that the data reflect the true effects of the independent variable. Many different solutions to the particular problem of extraneous observer effects have been devised. These range widely in complexity. Near one end of the scale is the fairly simple precaution of assigning different portions of the task of recording data, rating behavior, and so on, for each of the treatment groups being compared, to a different observer who has no knowledge of the experimental hypothesis. This should greatly reduce the chances of occurrence of any systematic observer bias that interacted with the treatment conditions. A more complex procedure would require that data or behavior (which might be recorded on videotape) be divided into a large number of small segments. Random samples of these, representing all treatment conditions equally, could then be assigned to a number of different observers who were blind to the experimental hypothesis. The fact that their tasks consisted of such small, unrelated bits would lessen the likelihood of them forming their own hypotheses. And the styles of the observers themselves could be determined later, if their tasks were equivalent, providing a clearer picture of their contribution to the results. Although this latter approach would be relatively costly and cumbersome, it has the advantages of minimizing extraneous observer effects while, at the same time, increasing the investigator's understanding of the contribution of observer effects to the research findings. It would be useful to know, for example, if an hypothesized finding occurred only when the data were treated by observers with a particular style of rating the behavior being studied.

## EFFECTS OF PRETESTING

As we mentioned earlier, in research where groups of human subjects cannot be randomly assigned to treatment conditions, such as investigations of traits or evaluations of educational programs, their comparability is always an issue. In some cases, it is dealt with by measuring relevant characteristics of the groups beforehand, such as abilities, traits, and so on, to rule out some potential extraneous group composition effects. The same procedure may also be followed when subjects are assigned to treatment groups at random. Perhaps because many studies use fairly small numbers of subjects, as few as eight or ten per treatment condition, some investigators are skeptical about the initial equivalence of their treatment groups, despite the fact that subjects have been assigned to them at random. Instead of depending upon random assignment, and just assuming that the groups are equivalent, they test the groups beforehand on any characteristics that seem relevant. A potential advantage of comparing treatment groups empirically in both these cases is that any evidence of nonequivalence that might be obtained can be used to adjust the research findings statistically in a way that eliminates any effects of nonequivalence from the final comparisons among treatment groups. Such procedures are too complex for us to do more than just mention here.

There is still another case in which the initial comparability of treatment groups is important enough to warrant testing subjects beforehand to establish their relative standing empirically. This is when the purpose of the research is to investigate the effects of some causal factor on different types of people, such as the effects of an educational program on students with varying levels of aptitude. In some research, the differences among treatment groups on some characteristic that is presumed to be related to the behavior being investigated actually functions as levels of the independent variable. In this case, the independent variable is sometimes referred to as a blocks or levels variable. In order to establish groups with different amounts of or at different levels of such a variable, such as a trait or an ability, a test is usually given to an available pool of subjects and cutoff points are then established in such a way as to create groups that are approximately equal in size and representative of the desired number of levels. A similar procedure is sometimes followed when an independent variable that is to be manipulated by some experimental procedure is expected on theoretical grounds to have different effects on subjects who possess different amounts of some characteristic. In this way, the effects of that manipulated variable can be determined more precisely by exposing groups of subjects with different levels of the characteristic to it than by observing its effect on random samples of subjects who vary widely on that characteristic.

In an analogous case, subjects' initial levels of some ability might be measured so that the effects of a program or experience that is predicted to affect that ability can be determined more precisely. Knowing where subjects started makes it easier to understand how they have changed.

We will use the term *pretesting* to refer to the case where an instrument that will later be used to measure the dependent variable, or some closely related instrument, is administered to subjects before they are exposed to the independent variable. In research on human subjects with whom direct contact is made, which consists principally of laboratory experiments, the use of a pretest, in and of itself, poses a serious problem for the validity of the research findings. Pretesting can act as an extraneous influence on the dependent variable. It can, in fact, produce two different effects on subjects' behavior that might be reflected in the dependent variable and mistaken for the effects of the independent variable.

The first of these is a *practice effect*. In most cases, practice effects are understood to be improvement in performance that occur as the result of the same test being taken more than once. But, more generally, they are any changes that occur in subjects' scores on any measure or test of behavior that are attributable to that measure having been administered previously. In a test of ability, the increased familiarity with the items after they are first encountered on a pretest could be expected to result in improvement when the test is retaken. But practice in taking a personality test could produce any of a variety of effects. Some of these tests are straightforward enough so that subjects who want to can respond in a way that makes them appear in a positive light. In these cases, experience with taking the test the first time may make such strategic self-presentation easier the second time. Overall, then, there might be a tendency for the scores of a group of subjects to shift in the direction of greater adjustment or praiseworthiness. In a clinical setting, the subjects being tested might be highly motivated to answer honestly. For them, the first testing and the time spent thinking about the questions afterward might produce greater self-insight. Thus the results of a second testing might be a more accurate reflection of the subjects' underlying traits. In general, then, the practice effects of pretesting depend upon the type of instrument or test being used and the motives of those who are tested. But the fact that the pretest is likely to affect subsequent scores, in one of a variety of ways, seems obvious enough.

Practice effects can occur even when the pretest and the measure of the dependent variable are not one and the same instrument. The more similar their content, the greater will be the likelihood and the magnitude of practice effects. But taking one particular intelligence test may enhance a person's later performance on a very different one, if only because one is more anxious during one's first testing experience than during subsequent tests. Taking an aptitude test might affect one's score on a subsequent test of ability if the problems on the two are similar. Moreover, having one's personality evaluated may raise questions of self-enhancement and self-analysis that could affect a person's answers to questions on a subsequent personality test, even if it were quite different in form and content.

But in what way do practice effects pose a threat to the validity of research findings? Suppose that one wanted to test the hypothesis that a special high-protein, high-vitamin diet could increase intelligence. One could select a representative sample of individuals to serve as subjects who would take a standardized IQ test, be placed on the special diet for as long as it would theoretically take to produce its effects, and then be given the test again. Should one observe a large increase in the group's average IQ score from the first testing to the second, one might conclude that the hypothesis was correct. But the validity of this finding would be questionable. The very fact that the subjects took the IQ test twice could be expected to produce an increase in their scores. This extraneous practice effect would be confounded with whatever effect the diet had actually produced. One would have no way of knowing, as a consequence of this confounding of the effects of the independent variable (the diet) and pretesting, whether the diet had increased IQ, decreased IQ, or had had no effect on IQ at all.

As an alternative to that procedure, one could create two randomly assigned groups of subjects and give one group the special diet while the other group makes no change in its normal diet. At the end of the required period, one would measure both groups' IQs. But one might not trust random assignment to create two groups whose levels of intelligence were initially equivalent, especially if the groups were small. By pretesting all of the subjects' IQs initially, one could provide the option of statistically adjusting the results of the postdiet IQ tests for any initial nonequivalence that might be found. As we mentioned above, such precautions are common in psychological research. But what if the normal-diet control group subjects were to become concerned about their performance on the pretest? They might later seek the answers to questions they felt they had not answered adequately, and they might rehearse strategies for attacking those parts of the test that had caught them off-guard the first time ("If only I had . . ."). In this way, they might be able to reduce their anxiety over the possibility that such a challenge might again be presented to them in the future. In fact, both groups of subjects would be equally likely to do these things and, by the end of the test period, their IQ test scores might benefit greatly from them. This could make it difficult to observe any effect of the special diet, even if the hypothesis were correct. In this case as well, the dependent variable would reflect both the effects of the independent variable and the extraneous effects of pretesting that we have described. A finding that the special-diet and normal-diet treatment groups made very similar gains in IQ over the duration of the experiment would not necessarily constitute valid evidence that the hypothesis was incorrect. The beneficial effects of the pretest might have been so great in both groups as to make it impossible to notice any effect of the special diet, or to determine whether it had any effect at all.

A special case of practice effects occurs when a dependent variable is assessed repeatedly in the course of an experiment. This is usually done to map the development of some process induced by the independent variable. An example would be an experiment comparing the intoxicating effects of different kinds of alcoholic beverages. In fact, I myself was once a subject in a study which sought to do exactly that. We subjects were each given one of the common varieties of alcoholic beverage, equated for alcohol content and disguised in fruit juice. It was administered in two doses which were adjusted for our individual body weights. The purpose of this study was to compare the speed and intensity of intoxication associated with the flavorings that make the beverages different (gin from bourbon from scotch, etc.).

One of the ways in which these intoxication effects were assessed was by a perceptual-motor task known as the pursuit rotor. In it, a target revolves on a disk, much like a phonograph record, while the subject tries to maintain contact with the tip of a wand that is hinged to prevent applying any pressure. The plan of the study called for what seemed to be a necessarily large number of repeated testings on the pursuit rotor. First, a pretest was administered to determine the subjects' level of performance while sober. A retest followed each of the two doses of alcoholic beverage. Finally, 2 hours after the second dose, the persistence of the intoxication effect was assessed in a final testing.

Unfortunately for the experimenters, I found out later, my experience was fairly representative. Although there was no doubt that I became intoxicated over the course of the afternoon, it was not reflected in my pursuit rotor performance. Because I had never tried the task before, my pretest performance was very poor. As I gained experience in subsequent testings, my performance improved despite the fact that I was gradually becoming lightheaded. In fact, if one were to take the results of this study at face value, one would have to conclude that highway safety would be improved if all drivers were to drink. It seems more reasonable to assume that performance on the pursuit rotor improves so much with practice that the task is not suitable for use in a study in which repeated assessments are required. One might even suspect, more generally, that the likelihood of performing such a study satisfactorily would depend on the discovery of some task which is proven to have the uncommon ability to resist such practice effects. Or, as we shall see later on, one would have to test the hypothesis without repeated use of the same task.

Besides practice effects, pretesting can also have an effect we call *sensitization.* Sensitization can change the meaning that the experimental treatment and the subsequent assessment of the dependent variable have for the subject from what they would have been without a pretest. It does this by alerting the subject to the research hypothesis and/or that aspect of his or her behavior that is of interest to the experimenter. This is another way in which the comparison of experimental treatments can turn out differently than it would have otherwise as the result of a pretest having been administered.

The vast literature of research on attitude change provides a good example of the threat to validity that is posed by pretest sensitization effects. A large number of studies were done for the purpose of determining what conditions were capable of producing changes in people's attitudes. This question is obviously of great interest to advertisers, politicians, and propagandists, as well as to theoreticians. Among the conditions, or independent variables, that received attention in this research were the characteristics of the perpetrator of an attempt at persuasion (such as attractiveness, expertise, and disinterest), characteristics of the information communicated in that attempt (such as emotional tone and apparent fairness), and characteristics of the target of persuasion (such as sex, intelligence, and initial attitude).

One apparently straightforward method was used in a large proportion of these studies. The researcher would assign subjects at random to a number of groups, assess their attitudes toward a particular issue, provide each group with a different persuasive communication that incorporated a variation of the independent variable, and then reassess their attitudes toward the issue. The comparative effectiveness of the communications could then be determined by comparing the amount of change in the attitudes of the members of the different treatment groups that had been exposed to them, from the pretest to the assessment after that exposure had taken place. This is often referred to as the pretest–posttest method.

Let us consider one hypothetical example in detail. The hypothesis to be investigated is that a communication will produce more attitude change if it comes from a high-prestige source than if it comes from a low-prestige source. Thirty students are selected at random from a pool of several hundred enrolled in an introductory psychology course that requires them to participate. These 30 are then randomly divided into two groups of 15. First, they are asked to indicate their attitudes toward student representation on their university's board of trustees on a 7-point scale. As one might expect, they all respond on the side of the scale that indicates they favor representation. This makes it possible to give them all the same persuasive communication, one that advocates denying students' membership on their universities' boards of trustees.

The communication argues, in an unemotional way, that students are too immature to serve on a university board of trustees, and that they would be placed in conflicts of interest when policies were considered that affected them personally. At the top of the page on which it is reproduced, ostensibly from a newspaper editorial page, is a picture and a short biography of its supposed author. For one group of subjects, a man who appears to be in his middle 30s is described as a past president of the student body at a major university during the student unrest of the 1960s. He is credited with having effected many beneficial changes in university policy in a peaceful manner. Furthermore, it is stated that he subsequently earned a doctorate in higher education administration and currently serves as the youngest president ever of an innovative and prestigious liberal arts college. He is also a consultant to several committees and agencies that make government policy in the area of higher education. For the second group of subjects, the author's picture shows a man in later middle-age who is balding, with a rim of gray hair, and is conservatively dressed. He is identified as the owner of a furniture store in a small rural city. He is a high school graduate whose appointment to their university's board of trustees, it is implied, was because of his high position in one of the major political parties. His accomplishments center around the charitable activities of the several fraternal organizations to which he belongs.

The intent is that these two men are to be seen as high- and low-prestige sources, respectively, for the students being tested. The subjects are given a standard period of time in which to read and consider the "article" and then they are given the 7-point attitude scale again. It is found, as was predicted, that the subjects who think the communication was written by the high-prestige source change their attitudes more in the direction of the arguments in it than do those who think it came from a low-prestige source.

One major problem with interpreting the results of this experiment, notwithstanding the number of times this same basic procedure has been used, is the transparency of its intent. How can subjects fail to realize that the only reason the persuasive communication is being presented to them is to find out how it will influence them to change their attitudes? Thus, what we find out about the effect of a persuasive communication under these circumstances may be relevant only to the case in which the target's attention is drawn to its implications for their susceptibility to persuasion. In this study, for example, it is possible that the subjects' reactions to the persuasive communications were affected by their knowledge of what they had stated as their attitudes on the issue only a few minutes earlier. Might this have been responsible for the fact that it took such an impeccable authority to convince them to change their minds? In the more typical situation in which one reads an article in the newspaper without being concerned with preserving one's prior attitude, would the same effect hold true?

These questions point out that one potential danger of administering a pretest is that it may sensitize subjects to the independent variable manipulation that follows. Their reactions to that experience may then be different from what they would have been had the pretest not been given. The pretest makes it more difficult to conceal the true purpose of the experiment. It has occurred to some investigators of attitude change, for example, that a persuasive communication would best be presented so subtly that its true purpose was camouflaged, such as in a newspaper editorial. The administration of a pretest makes that already difficult task even more difficult.

It may have already occurred to you, and we have actually implied as much, that extraneous pretesting effects are not that difficult to prevent. In many ways, the outstanding feature of this particular problem is that it is encountered so frequently in the research literature despite the fact that the performance of many of the studies would actually be made less difficult by avoiding the pretesting. We will consider two ways in which the possibility of extraneous pretesting effects, both practice and sensitization, can be averted—eliminating the pretest and disguising it.

When subjects are assigned to experimental treatment conditions at random, no pretest is needed and, usually, none should be administered. It is clearly preferable to set the size of one's samples at a level where randomization can be trusted to produce equivalence, making it possible to omit the pretest, rather than risk extraneous pretesting effects and compromise the validity of one's findings. There is no good reason to believe that groups of 15 or 20 that have been constituted randomly should differ in intelligence, or in their attitudes toward student representation on a university's board of trustees, or in any other important respect for that matter. Any possibility that nonequivalence will exist despite random assignment can and should be left to the eventual statistical treatment of the data, where the investigator can decide what an acceptable risk of such a sampling error would be. It goes without saying, then, that existing findings produced by the pretest-posttest method must be accepted at face value only in those cases in which one is confident that they are not artifacts of a sensitization effect.

When subjects are not assigned to experimental treatment groups at random, the possibility of extraneous group composition effects cannot be ruled out on the basis of a pretest or on any other evidence that the groups are comparable in some characteristic believed to be a factor in determining the behavior being investigated. The use of a pretest to establish comparability has only very limited value. In some cases, there may be a key trait that previous research has indicated may differ among the nonrandomly chosen groups and that has also been shown to be an important cause of the behavior on which the groups are to be compared. With such a highly plausible rival hypothesis, evidence of comparability would be more useful. However, extraneous pretesting effects need not necessarily be risked in order to obtain it. Evidence of comparability may also be available from an indirect source, thus avoiding the necessity of direct pretesting and its undesirable consequences. For example, if the subjects were nonequivalent groups of college students, and if intelligence were the trait in question, the needed information might be found in the students' records. The results of IQ tests taken much earlier in their lives, or scores on standardized aptitude tests that have been shown to be highly correlated with intelligence test scores, could take the place of an IQ pretest. This alternative is not always available, especially when the privacy of students' records is rightfully protected. However, when it is available, its advantages over direct pretesting need to be recognized.

In those cases in which the need for a direct pretest is greatest (i.e., nonrandom assignment plus a clear danger of an extraneous group composition effect plus a lack of any indirect source of data about comparability), the likelihood of extraneous pretesting effects can still be reduced by attempting to dissociate the pretest from the remainder of the study. In some cases, it is possible to administer the pretest long before the study itself, weeks or even months ahead. If that is not possible and if, for example, subjects must be pretested for their attitudes toward some issue, the attitude scale can be embedded among numerous scales dealing with irrelevant issues. Either delay or distraction might serve to lessen at least the likelihood that subjects' responses on a pretest will affect their responses to the experimental manipulation or the dependent measure to follow. Our confidence in the findings of such a study should increase accordingly.

If it is necessary to obtain data from groups of subjects on numerous occasions in order to assess some progressive phenomenon such as gradual intoxication, one can also take steps to reduce the likelihood of pretesting effects—in this case practice effects. If enough random groups of subjects were induced to undergo the intoxication process, data bearing on each key point could be collected from different subjects. This would eliminate the situation in which each successive assessment of a given state in a single group of subjects can, in itself, affect each subsequent assessment. Alternatively, one might use a number of different, but related, tasks for the same group of subjects at different points in the study.

In sum, extraneous pretesting effects are a serious threat to validity because of their prevalence, but in most cases they are relatively easy to eliminate. Direct pretesting is only rarely necessary. When it is, every effort should be made to minimize its effects. In most cases, however, researchers must simply practice abstinence in the use of pretests.

## EFFECTS OF SAMPLE ATTRITION

What if you wanted to test the hypothesis that people's IQ scores will predict their accomplishments in life? You might identify, at the earliest possible age, perhaps 3 years or so, groups of children with extremely high, moderate, and extremely low IQs. You could then follow these individuals' accomplishments over a long period, perhaps as long as 40 years, through intermittent follow-up contacts. This should cover a period of their lives when they are striving for important personal and occupational goals. You could assess their achievement in school, their adjustment to adolescence, their eventual choice of occupations, their success in marriage and in other personal relationships, or any of countless other accomplishments in which you might be interested. Such a plan is called a longitudinal design, because it studies the same individuals through an extended period.

In the course of such a study, one would expect to lose contact with some of the initial sample of subjects. Some people would move without leaving forwarding addresses, some would tire of repeatedly reporting their activities, and some even die during such a long period. The three IQ groups being compared might suffer similar rates of attrition and the individuals who were lost from the groups might be a random sample of those who began the study. If this were true, your only problem would be to keep the rate of attrition down far enough, or to start with large enough groups of subjects, so that enough people would remain to permit making the necessary comparisons along the way.

Attrition, however, could pose a threat to the validity of those comparisons if it were selective. If attrition were greater in some groups than in others, or if those who were lost were somehow systematically different from those who continued, the true effects of IQ could be distorted. We will call such an occurrence an extraneous effect of *sample attrition.* Using our IQ study as an example, let us see how such an effect might occur.

If our hypothesis were in fact true, then subjects with higher IQs could be expected to be more successful in school, to be more likely to go on to higher education, to earn relatively high incomes, to enter professions or other prestigious occupations in greater numbers, and perhaps even to live happier and longer lives. Any or all these factors could lead to a lower rate of attrition among subjects with higher IQs. They might be easier to locate through their schools or employers and their names and addresses found more easily in telephone books, lists of property owners, or of members of professional societies, or other similar sources. They might also be more willing to report their current financial or occupational status if requested. They might be more likely to establish long-term residence in their communities and to have long and stable careers. And their health, both physical and mental, might be better, and their longevity greater.

If the fact that lower IQ was associated with greater attrition were to go unnoticed and the comparisons required in the study were made only of those subjects with whom contact was maintained, then it would follow that those comparisons might underestimate the true effects of IQ. Records for those with lower IQs who would have shown the least accomplishment and thus would have provided the strongest evidence in support of the hypothesis would be missing disproportionately from the comparisons. Attrition would be greatest in the low IQ group and least in the high IQ group, and those lost from any group would be those with the lowest IQs and the least accomplishments. The individuals who were left in the moderate or the low IQ group would be those whose records of accomplishment were better than what the records of the whole group would have been had the group remained intact, and less different from those of the high IQ group than they would have been.

Not only is selective attrition a problem in long-term studies like the one just considered, but also in many laboratory experiments in psychology that require subjects to return for several sessions. This may be because the subjects' task is too long or strenuous to complete in a single session. It may also be because the data that are to be collected early in the research need to be analyzed and evaluated before the materials and procedures required for subsequent stages can be planned. In any event, some attrition of subjects is as possible in this sort of research as in a longitudinal study. The rate of attrition would depend upon such factors as the kind of subjects being studied, the demands placed on them by the experiment, and the length of time the experiment continued. But the important point is that if attrition were selective, so that the lost subjects were different in some way from those who continued, the validity of the research findings would be threatened.

Let us see how that might happen in a hypothetical case. This case is a study of the process of habituation to electric shock. The intent is to determine whether someone will get used to electric shocks faster if they are spaced close together or if the same shocks are spaced farther apart. It is hypothesized, on the basis of some obscure theory of synaptic transmission in the brain, that habituation will be faster when the shocks are spaced close together or, in other words, when the intershock interval is short.

Because many people find electric shock extremely discomfiting, and because many series of shocks are required to obtain reliable records of the subjects' physiological and psychological reactions, our hypothetical study is broken up into six brief sessions to be carried out over three weeks. The subjects are 40 volunteers from undergraduate psychology courses who are paid $3 per session. They are randomly divided between the two experimental treatments. All are to receive the same number, intensity, and duration of shocks during each session, but one group will receive a rest period of 2 seconds after each shock and the other 2 minutes. Specifically, it is predicted that when the intershock interval is 2 seconds, the magnitude of subjects' reactions to the shock will decrease more rapidly across the series they receive within each session than will the magnitude of the reactions of subjects who get 2 minutes' rest between shocks.

It seems almost inevitable, as we stated at the outset, that some subjects will drop out of the experiment along the way. Some will find that it demands more of their time than they had anticipated, others will be faced unexpectedly with a competing activity during the same time they had promised to give to the experiment, and still others will honestly find the experiment too unpleasant an experience if given a choice. Suppose that at the end of the experiment, 18 subjects in the 2-second interval group and 12 in the 2-minute interval group had gone through the entire series of six sessions. An examination of the data collected from these 30 subjects shows that the 2-second interval group habituated to the shock slightly faster than the 2-minute group, but that the difference was not great enough or consistent enough across subjects to be statistically significant. Would you be ready to give up on the experimental hypothesis and the theory it was drawn from?

If we assume for a moment that our hypothesis is correct, then we would expect each of the experimental sessions to be more painful and trying for subjects in the 2-minute interval group. This could explain why more subjects dropped out of that group than the 2-second group. Furthermore, one might suspect that the subjects who dropped out of either group were those who had the most unpleasant time. It is possible, then, that the true effects of the intershock interval on habituation were underestimated by comparing the surviving subjects in the two treatment groups. If the subjects who would have shown the greatest detrimental effects of long intershock intervals were those who dropped out of the 2-minute group, that comparison would have included only the subjects who habituated fastest in the 2-minute group. That would minimize the difference between the two groups.

In both studies we have considered so far, it may be possible to determine whether extraneous effects of attrition have occurred. One can utilize the early data which are collected for comparing subjects who dropped out along the way with those who did not. If there is no difference between the two in their early patterns, one might have more confidence that attrition was not selective. On the other hand, such a study typically lasts as long as it does because the behavior of interest can only be observed over that long a period. Consequently, comparisons based on fragmentary returns have only limited value. Another source of information about selective attrition is the rate at which subjects drop out of different treatment groups. Differences in attrition rates suggest the possibility that attrition is somehow related to the behavior being studied. The fact that more subjects are lost from a group that was hypothesized to have less rewarding experiences, or to experience more pain, makes one doubt that attrition has occurred in a random fashion. Thus differential rates of attrition are a useful sign that extraneous attrition effects may have occurred. In any case, it seems clear that research methods that raise the possibility of attrition should be chosen with the danger of extraneous attrition effects in mind.

This latter point is especially important for research in which attrition occurs but no early returns are available. Consider an experiment in physiological psychology designed to compare the effects of lesions (deliberate destruction of tissue) in different parts of the brain on the eating behavior of rats. Suppose that two groups of rats are established, one to receive lesions in one area of the brain and one to receive lesions in another area. These lesions are created by a procedure which includes neurosurgery. A portion of the skull is removed and an electrode, or thin piece of wire, is inserted so that its tip lies in the desired area of the brain. Then an electrical current is passed through it to destroy the brain cells in that area. After the surgery, the animals need some time to recover physically. A comparison is then made of the two groups' eating behavior to evaluate the effects of the lesions.

But some of the rats may fail to survive the surgery. This is another form of attrition, one which suggests why attrition has sometimes been referred to as *experimental mortality*. In any case, if the animals who fail to survive are not representative of the initial group, the validity of the findings is questioned. If those that die are different in some way from those who survive, any comparison of the survivors could be mistaken as evidence for the effect of the lesions when it also reflects the effects of the surgery. In such a case, differential attrition rates may provide the only clue to the occurrence of such an extraneous effect. It might mean, for example, that the groups' behavior was different because they contained rats with different characteristics after more of the weaker animals in one group failed to survive the surgery because it involved an area of the brain that is more vulnerable to the trauma of surgery.

Perhaps even more important is that such a case points out the danger that attrition itself can pose for the validity of research findings. It is not always possible to determine after the fact whether attrition has been selective or not. Even when the rates of attrition are identical, different types of subjects may have been lost from different treatment groups. In fact, it is rarely possible to determine whether attrition has been selective with any certainty. As is true of all threats to validity, prevention is the only trustworthy cure. If prevention is impossible, some objective means of comparing dropouts with nondropouts should be included in the study whenever possible.

Finally, there is a variation of attrition called *retrospective attrition.* For reasons considered in detail later, social scientists are becoming increasingly interested in methods of testing hypotheses that do not require making direct contact with the targets of their research. One reason is that some questions of great social significance can be answered only in this way. Suppose that you were interested in learning what factors are responsible for people committing suicide. You might think that their religious beliefs could be one important factor, helping to determine the significance they attached to suicide, the meaning it had for them personally. More specifically, you might be willing to predict that because Catholics believe that suicide is a mortal sin, there would be fewer suicides among Catholics than among Protestants or Jews.

Perhaps the only reasonable way of testing your hypothesis would be to use public records. These are one source of what is called, more generally, *archival data.* Some records which are kept for very different purposes can be very useful in testing research hypotheses. It would be possible to find official records of suicides in a city or county office building or, for a wider area, from some state or federal government agency. Let us assume from those records that you could determine the religious affiliation of each suicide victim. By comparing the total number of suicides from each religious group with the size of that group in the area covered by the records, you could then determine whether Catholics did, in fact, have a lower suicide rate.

But does the public record contain all the actual instances of suicide? Could some of the cases have been lost? Some deaths may have been classified as accidental although they were, in fact, caused by suicide. The cases of people who decide to commit suicide by driving their cars into trees would be one example. But there may be no good reason to believe that such cases would be lost disproportionately from the different religious groups. If they were not, attrition would not really affect the comparison you want to make.

But what if there were selective attrition? What if more cases of suicide among Catholics were listed as accidental or natural deaths than were suicides among Protestants or Jews? This could happen if the families and friends of Catholic suicide victims wanted to avert the censure of their church. Those who found the body might conceal evidence or persuade a family doctor to certify that the death was due to natural causes or an accident. Thus, the finding from the public record that the suicide rate is lower among Catholics, and the conclusion that religious beliefs are an important determinant of suicide, could be invalid. Although archival records have some very real advantages as sources of data, one needs to consider carefully that they may be selectively incomplete. Retrospective attrition, unlike attrition in cases in which subjects are contacted directly, may be completely unknown to the investigator. No one knows how many cases were present to begin with, so that these "subjects" vanish without leaving a trace.

## STATISTICAL REGRESSION EFFECTS

Imagine that you have just administered a measuring instrument to assess the behavior of a very large randomly selected group of people, or rats, or any other kind of subjects. You will get a distribution of scores for those subjects that ranges from very high scores to very low. Now imagine that you could administer the same instrument to the same individuals without their second scores being affected at all by the first—in other words, without any pretesting effect. If the instrument is applied directly to the subjects, rather than simply measuring their walking speed without their knowledge, for example, this is unlikely to be true. But, for the moment, let us deal with the purely hypothetical case in which the second set of scores is uncontaminated by the first.

First, identify the subjects who got the highest and the lowest scores on the first testing, let us say those in the upper and the lower 10% of the distribution. These may be the best or worst, or just the most extreme such as fascists and radicals. Then determine the average score for each of these two groups of subjects on the first testing. Now find the scores for the same individuals on the second testing—not the top and bottom 10% of the second testing, but the same people who were in the top and bottom 10% on the first. Compute the means for the two groups on that second occasion. Finally, compare the mean scores for the same two groups of individuals between the first testing and the second. You will find that the means for both groups, the high and the low, on the second testing are closer to the mean for the entire sample (which should be the same on both occasions) than they were the first time. Both groups, on the average, become less extreme. The people who were in the upper 10% on the first testing, as a group, get lower scores the second time they are tested, and some of them are no longer in the upper 10%. The lower 10% on the first testing get higher scores, on the average, the second time around, and do not all remain in the lower 10%. This phenomenon is called *statistical regression,* or *regression toward the mean.*

You might be wondering why it happened. In any group of extremely high or extremely low scorers on any behavioral measure, there are some individuals whose extreme scores were caused partly by transitory conditions. To use the vernacular, these are people who have had, for them, unusually good days and bad days. Their "true" scores—hypothetical scores which reflect perfectly accurately their standing on the characteristic the test was designed to measure— might have been just moderately high or moderately low except for some unusual conditions that existed at the time.

Certainly, we have all had the experience, at least once, of taking a test when we were either well, alert, sharp, and lucky, or when we were ill, tired, "out of it," and unlucky. That test might have been measuring our knowledge of a subject that we actually knew moderately poorly or moderately well. The way we felt that day may have influenced our performance, causing our scores to be even further toward the end of the distribution for which we were already headed, either high or low. If that were so, then we could have ended up as an extremely high or low scorer when our knowledge of the subject matter warranted our score being less extreme. If we would have taken the same test again, even the following day, assuming that we had no memory of having taken it the first time, chances are that our second score would have been less extreme, a truer indication of how mediocre our knowledge actually was.

In any really large group of people (or rats, for that matter) whose behavior is being assessed in any way, on any occasion, some individuals are going to have good and bad days. Some of those having good days will have true scores no better than moderately high. They may, however, end up with extremely high scores on this occasion. If tested on a subsequent occasion, their scores will probably be lower. Because their true scores are only moderately high, the odds are against them getting another extremely high score. Those who have a bad day, and whose true scores are moderately low, may, analogously, end up with extremely low scores. In following the same line of argument, if they are retested, their scores should be higher. Thus, when the entire group of subjects is retested, the groups who were high and low the first time should be less high or low, even assuming that no practice effect occurs.

**Table 2-1.** A MODEL OF STATISTICAL REGRESSION

| SUBJECT NO. | FIRST SCORE | SUBJECT NO. | SECOND SCORE |
|---|---|---|---|
| 10 | 50 | 25 | 50 |
| 9 | 49 | 5 | 49 |
| 25 | 49 | 12 | 49 |
| 33 | 48 | 9 | 48 |
| 37 | 47 | 10 | 47 |
| 20 | 45 | 42 | 45 |
| 48 | 44 | 26 | 44 |
| 5 | 44 | 20 | 44 |
| 8 | 43 | 8 | 43 |
| 42 | 42 | 37 | 42 |
| 26 | 42 | 48 | 42 |
| 1 | 42 | 1 | 42 |
| 29 | 40 | 29 | 40 |
| 12 | 40 | 33 | 40 |
| 6 | 39 | 31 | 39 |
| 47 | 38 | 6 | 38 |
| 17 | 38 | 47 | 38 |
| 31 | 38 | 17 | 38 |
| 21 | 37 | 50 | 37 |
| 35 | 37 | 21 | 37 |
| 11 | 37 | 11 | 37 |
| 50 | 36 | 43 | 36 |
| 45 | 35 | 19 | 35 |
| 34 | 35 | 15 | 35 |
| 40 | 34 | 35 | 34 |
| 43 | 33 | 3 | 33 |
| 3 | 32 | 34 | 32 |
| 32 | 32 | 40 | 32 |
| 49 | 32 | 49 | 32 |
| 23 | 32 | 23 | 32 |
| 44 | 32 | 45 | 32 |
| 19 | 31 | 32 | 31 |
| 7 | 31 | 44 | 31 |
| 4 | 31 | 4 | 31 |
| 15 | 29 | 7 | 29 |
| 13 | 29 | 36 | 29 |
| 36 | 28 | 30 | 28 |
| 14 | 28 | 38 | 28 |
| 30 | 28 | 18 | 28 |
| 38 | 27 | 13 | 27 |
| 18 | 26 | 14 | 26 |
| 24 | 26 | 41 | 26 |
| 40 | 25 | 24 | 25 |
| 2 | 24 | 40 | 24 |
| 39 | 22 | 28 | 22 |
| 27 | 19 | 27 | 19 |
| 16 | 19 | 2 | 19 |
| 41 | 16 | 16 | 16 |
| 28 | 12 | 22 | 12 |
| 22 | 11 | 39 | 11 |

NOTE: The "high group" average was 48.6 on the first testing and 45.4 on the second. The "low group" averaged 15.4 on the first, then 19.0 on the second. The overall group average was 33.68 on both occasions.

Table 2-1 shows how this might happen on a reduced scale. It includes the scores of 50 individuals, numbered 1 to 50. They all take the same 50-item multiple-choice test twice (the second time with no memory of the first). The top 10% of the class on the first testing consists of the five individuals numbered 10, 9, 25, 33, and 37. Their average score on the first test is 48.6. On the second testing, they are not all in the top 10% again. Two do worse (individuals 37 and 33). Presumably, their scores the first time were due in part to their having a good day. Because they take the test the second time under more normal conditions, their scores go down. The average for the group that was the top 10% the first time also goes down, from 48.6 to 45.4, as a result. Two of the bottom 10% on the first go-around (subjects numbered 27, 16, 41, 28, and 22) do better the second time. Presumably because they do not have another bad day, numbers 41 and 28 get higher scores and the group's average goes up from 15.4 to 19.0. Thus the averages for the two groups of individuals whose scores were at the top and bottom of the distribution on the first testing are closer to the overall group average of 33.68 on the second testing.

Some of the subjects having good or bad days on any particular occasion will obviously not end up in either the top or bottom 10%. For example, someone whose true score is precisely at the average for the whole group but has a good day may end up with a score only slightly above average. But among the top 10% we are more likely to find people who have had good days than people who have had bad days. And among the bottom 10%, we are more likely to find people who have had bad days than good days. It is obvious that the highest scorers could not have been feeling too unwell, and the lowest scorers could not have been too lucky. Therefore, the true scores of the highest scorers are likely to be lower than their actual scores, and the true scores of the lowest scorers are likely to be higher than their actual scores, rather than the other way around.

Now let us take the argument one step further. Let us say that the large group of subjects is first tested on one instrument and is then given a different measure, but one highly correlated with the first. That is, scores on the second measure can be predicted with great accuracy from scores on the first, to such a degree that, for all practical purposes, one could discover how a person would score on both by giving them either one; two standard tests of intelligence, for example. It follows that those who got the very highest and the very lowest scores on one would also get the very highest and the lowest scores on the other. However, statistical regression would occur here, too, with the result that the highest and lowest groups' average scores on the second test would be less extremely high and low than expected from their scores on the first. The temporary conditions which caused some members of those very high and low groups to score as they did on the first measure would not likely be present again to affect their scores on the other measure in the same way.

Take the two different but highly correlated IQ tests as an example. Or take the two parallel multiple-choice tests, which cover the same material but contain questions worded in alternative forms. In both cases, across large numbers of subjects, the scores each made on one measure would have the same relative magnitude as their scores on the other. If, however, they took both in succession, again discounting practice effects, the groups of the very highest and lowest scorers on one would have mean scores closer to the overall group average on the other. This same effect—statistical regression—would occur for any pair of highly correlated measures in the same way as it would for successive administrations of the same measure.

We can now look at some of the implications of statistical regression for the validity of research findings. We have already considered some examples of research in which subjects were not assigned to experimental treatment conditions at random. When contrasting groups of subjects are to be compared, they may be chosen on the basis of their extreme scores on some instrument. They may then be exposed to a common experimental treatment in order to compare its effects on individuals who are as different as they are. What if the effects of that treatment were to be assessed by readministering the same instrument that was used to screen the subjects initially, or some highly correlated instrument such as an alternative form of the screening instrument? This kind of "before–after" design is very common. One would expect the average scores of extremely high- and low-scoring groups to come closer to the overall mean on the second testing due to statistical regression. If this were not taken into account, those regression effects would be confounded with the experimental treatment effects; therefore, valid conclusions could not be drawn about either. Let us look at a specific but hypothetical example of this problem.

In recent years, there has been considerable interest across this country about the effects of school desegregation on students' academic achievement. Some have hypothesized that although desegregation may be beneficial for the less capable students who are introduced into an integrated classroom, it may "hold back" the progress made by their most capable classmates. Let us consider one way in which this hypothesis might be tested.

First, we would need to find a newly desegregated school. Then as students arrived in the fall, before classes actually began, we could administer a standardized achievement test to all of them. Their scores would tell us how well they had been progressing in school relative to their age and grade peers across the country. On the basis of this test, we would choose the highest and lowest achievers to serve as our comparison groups. The "experimental treatment" would consist of the experience of attending an integrated school— one that might have a greater range of student abilities than the students' previous schools, among other things. At the end of the school year, the students would be given another standardized achievement test, perhaps a parallel form of the one they had taken the previous fall. By comparing their scores at the end of the year (again, relative to their peers around the country) with those at the beginning, the two groups' rates of progress during the school year could be determined.

Let us suppose that our subjects' scores on that second testing showed that the poorer students had improved more over the year than the better students. Given the nature of the test we used, this would mean that the poorer group had benefited from desegregation because their rate of progress in school had accelerated. But the better group had suffered as a result of desegregation because their rate of progress had slowed. Or is this really what it would mean? Statistical regression could produce the same effects. Even if there had been absolutely no influence of desegregation in the interval between the two testings, one would expect that the average of the low group would have increased and the average of the high group decreased. Desegregation might have added to this effect, or detracted from it, or made no difference at all in the students' performance in school. Because there is the possibility that extraneous effects of regression took place at the same time, the actual effects of desegregation, the causal factor of interest, is indeterminate.

One way of controlling for the effects of statistical regression would be to compare the gains and losses in achievement of students whose school had been desegregated with those of students whose school had not been desegregated. Let us assume that you could find a school that seemed comparable to the desegregated school in most important respects, but was still segregated. In actuality, it might be necessary to locate two such schools, one predominantly black and one predominantly white, to permit meaningful comparisons. The highest and lowest achievers in the segregated schools could be identified at the beginning of the school year, and their achievement reassessed at the end. Then you would be able to compare the changes that occurred during the school year without desegregation with the changes accompanying desegregation. Because statistical regression effects should have been the same in both cases, whatever difference you find must reflect only the effects of desegregation.

There is a more common kind of research problem in which subjects are assigned to treatment groups on the basis of extreme scores on a screening instrument. That is sometimes called experimental personality research. Although we've discussed it once before, we start with a capsule description of the extreme-groups design for personality research. First, someone usually gets the idea that people vary along some dimension that has important implications for their behavior. Such a dimension is often called a personality trait. Then some means of assessing where people stand on that dimension is developed, most often a questionnaire that can be used to test large groups of subjects quickly and economically. Finally, the notion that this trait is an important determinant of people's behavior is tested empirically. The hypothesis predicts that individuals who differ along the trait dimension will behave differently in a specific situation. That hypothesis is tested by first identifying individuals who score extremely high and extremely low on the trait measure, exposing them to the situation in the form of an experimental treatment, and comparing their subsequent behavior. During the past ten years or so, this same basic procedure has served as a model for many hundreds or even thousands of studies aimed at evaluating personality traits.

Consider the example of a personality trait called need for achievement, or "nAch" for short. To keep this discussion brief, we will define nAch simply as caring about whether or not one does well in any activity one attempts. Each person supposedly feels a characteristic amount of concern about the quality of his or her performance that is relatively constant across everything he or she does. This level of concern is usually measured by having an individual write stories about pictures. The pictures depict settings that are relevant to achievement, such as a classroom and an office, but their content is otherwise very ambiguous. No particular event can be seen taking place. This is called a projective measure because it is assumed that the subjects' stories about what might be happening will reflect their own concerns about achievement, projected onto the neutral background of the picture.

Our hypothesis about nAch is concerned with its relationship to the amount and quality of effort a person will extend in a particular achievement situation. Specifically, we will predict in our hypothetical study that the success of a salesperson who calls on industrial accounts for a manufacturer of cleaning supplies will depend upon his or her level of nAch. We will begin our test by screening a large number of applicants for such sales positions with the test of nAch. The highest and lowest scorers, in numbers sufficient to fill the available positions, will be hired and their success evaluated. We should be able to obtain from their employers accurate records of the number of calls they make and the amount of merchandise they sell. We can then compare the performance of the high and low nAch groups.

But what if a salesperson's level of nAch does turn out to be closely related to the amount of success he or she achieves? This would mean that for a large group of randomly selected salespeople, measures of nAch and productivity would be highly correlated. But groups of these salespeople selected for their extremely high and low nAch scores would not achieve productivity scores that were correspondingly high and low. That is because their true nAch scores were not as high or low as our single estimate of them. Because of the effect of statistical regression, then, some of the high and low nAch salespeople would achieve levels of productivity more consistent with their true, less extreme nAch scores. It follows that in our study the differences we found between our extreme groups would underestimate the actual effects of nAch because they would also reflect the contradictory effects of statistical regression. Thus, we might conclude mistakenly that the hypothesis was not supported because the effects of nAch were partially hidden by the extraneous effects of statistical regression.

In our first example of the regression problem, regarding the effects of school desegregation, we suggested using a control-group procedure as a remedy. In the present case, however, that would require that the salespeople's success be assessed without the effects of nAch being reflected in the measurements. That is obviously an impossibility. There are, however, alternative means of coping with the problem. These alternatives would also be applicable in any other case in which the same variable is used for screening the subjects and for evaluating their response to the experimental treatment. Furthermore, they all require the abandonment of the extreme-groups design.

One possibility is to screen subjects and then divide them into several comparison groups, representing many different levels along the trait dimension. Instead of only one group of extremely high scorers and one group of extremely low scorers, moderately high and low scorers and groups close to the population mean would also be compared. Alternatively, one could divide the screened subjects into just their upper and lower halves, a procedure known as a "median split." Both procedures would yield evidence of the degree to which the effect of the experimental treatment depends upon the trait that is uncontaminated by the effects of statistical regression. In the first case, the effects of regression among extreme scorers would be less likely to be misleading because moderately high and low scorers would show the relationship uncontaminated by the effects of regression. It is only the most extreme scorers, whose true scores are likely to be closer to the mean because they cannot get any further away, for whom regression effects are a problem. In the second case, extreme scorers would constitute such a small part of their group that the group mean should not be affected significantly by the regression effects reflected in their scores.

Yet another alternative would be to use an undifferentiated random sample of subjects. Both their standing on the trait in question and their response to the experimental treatment would be assessed and the relationship between the two sets of scores would be expressed as a correlation coefficient. One advantage of this procedure, along with the multiple-levels procedure considered above, is that it gives a more complete indication of the relationship. For example, the relationship might be nonlinear, so that the effect of the trait on the subjects' behavior varies with the actual level of the trait. That is, extreme levels of the trait might have a different effect from less extreme levels. Such relationships are fairly common, but they would not be discovered by comparing two extreme groups. That method would not show the true form of the relationship, whereas the alternative approaches could. And, of course, the advantage of the correlational approach is that statistical regression effects will not obscure the relationship in a random sample that contains individuals at every level along the trait dimension.

Still, it may seem to some that the use of any of these alternative procedures sacrifices some valuable features of the extreme-groups procedure. It appears to have been widely believed, judging by the popularity of the extreme-groups method, that the effect of a subject characteristic can be seen the most clearly—and with a minimum number of subjects having to be exposed to the experimental treatment—by comparing two extreme groups. Many may also have felt that the correlational method yields a more ambiguous answer because no mean scores of comparison groups are presented. The extreme-groups comparison, in short, seems to best indicate the magnitude of the effect. But its advantages are all illusory. Because of the possibility of statistical regression effects, the extreme-groups method may not only fail to give a clearer picture of what is going on, but it may also actually give a false or invalid one.

## SOME CONCLUDING NOTES

In this chapter we have considered eight potential threats to the internal validity of research findings. Each is a kind of extraneous variable, a potential influence on the behavior being studied, which is not included in the plans of the researcher. As such, its effects on the dependent variable are mixed in with or confounded with those of the independent variable and threaten the validity of conclusions drawn about its effects. These eight, however, are not the only possible threats to internal validity, merely the ones we know enough about at this point to be concerned about. And they are not mutually exclusive categories. There may be a very fine line between calling a particular threat an extraneous event and calling it a temporal effect. But because we will be considering all these potential threats whenever we evaluate the validity of a proposed research design or a research finding, this problem of classification is not of major importance. In short, this classification scheme, like most other classification schemes, is merely an arbitrary way of organizing a body of information. In itself, it has little ultimate significance for understanding the concepts. It just makes them easier to think about and to write about.

A second point that needs to be made here is one that we have already made more than once. But it is important enough to repeat and elaborate. Not all extraneous variables can or need to be eliminated from an investigation. They cannot all be kept from affecting the phenomenon being studied. The concept of experimental control is often stated in a way that implies that every variable except the one being studied is absolutely prevented from exerting any influence on the dependent variable. This, however, is not true. Many variables, such as individual differences among subjects, are always capable of influencing the dependent variable. But they are not all serious threats to the validity of an investigation. Some have random effects, so that each experimental treatment reflects them equally, as when subjects are assigned to treatments at random. This creates variability or diversity of behavior within each treatment group, but it does not affect the comparisons among groups.

If, however, an extraneous variable has a nonrandom effect, as when subjects are not assigned at random, it may change the relative standing of the treatment groups. Such an effect must be prevented whenever possible, and we have considered ways of doing this and will be considering many more. But, as we have seen already and will see again later, not even all systematic effects of extraneous variables can be eliminated from every research design. Sometimes the nature of the phenomenon makes that impossible. The researcher may have no control over when or to whom an event may occur. In such an instance, the effects of a potential threat to validity can only be discounted. That is, the research findings must be evaluated cautiously, in the light of the possibility that such extraneous effects have occurred. In doing so, we must depend on existing empirical evidence about the relationship between the extraneous variable and the phenomenon being studied. If there is known to be a strong relationship, then the threat provides a highly *plausible rival hypothesis* and very little faith can be placed in the findings. If there is no known relationship, then the threat has little plausibility and the findings can be relied upon heavily in spite of the imperfection in the research design.

Take the example of a study of the effects of two different teaching methods by which children learn to read. If the investigator could not assign subjects at random to be taught by the two methods, the possibility would exist that an extraneous subject characteristic might affect the performance of the two groups in addition to the methods by which they were taught. If the two groups differed in IQ and the high IQ group did better, then the hypothesis that the method used to teach them produced their superiority would be rivaled by the hypothesis that their higher IQ was responsible. This rival hypothesis would be highly plausible because we know that IQ is related to reading performance. But if the group that did better was taller, this would not suggest a plausible rival hypothesis in the absence of convincing evidence that height is related to reading performance.

In our consideration of threats to internal validity throughout this chapter, we have made use of specific examples of research problems to illustrate our definitions of important concepts. A point needs to be made about those examples. Although they were hypothetical, many were based upon actual investigations that have been published. There are two reasons why credit was not given to the original investigators. First, although it was necessary to be critical of many of them, they share the criticism with many other similar studies and therefore do not deserve to be singled out. Second, it was usually impossible to do justice to the original studies in our descriptions of them. We had to oversimplify their details in order to make our points clearly.

Our simplified presentations of those sample research projects may possibly have caused some problems for the reader. We hope that you noticed that in several cases studies that were presented to illustrate one problem also suffered from one or more other flaws. In every case, our discussion stuck strictly to the single threat to validity with which we were dealing at the time. We wanted to keep the definition of each variety of threat to validity clear of any discussion of others. We will present that kind of exhaustive analysis of research designs shortly, but only after all the basic concepts have been introduced one by one.

One final point. In discussing the effects of extraneous variables by examples, some confusion might exist about the direction of their effects. In some examples, extraneous variables masked or obscured the true effects of the independent variable. They raised the possibility that a true experimental hypothesis would be abandoned on the basis of invalid findings that no effect was observed. In other cases, extraneous variables dissimulated or produced differences between treatment groups of the kind predicted by the experimental hypothesis. These differences could have been mistaken for the effects of an independent variable that actually had no such effect. Thus a false hypothesis appeared to receive empirical support. In still other examples, extraneous variables masked by producing effects opposite to those predicted, suggesting incorrectly that the experimental hypothesis was not only false, but also that it should have been stated in reverse. All three outcomes are, in fact, possible. The existence of a plausible rival hypothesis means that, regardless of the effect observed, the true effect of the independent variable might have been in the direction predicted, in the opposite direction, or nothing at all. That is the real extent of the danger of confounding between the independent variable and an extraneous variable. It makes it impossible to know what effect the independent variable actually did have, because its effect was mixed with that of the extraneous variable.

## REFERENCES

Coleman, J., Campbell, E., Hobson, C., McPartland, J., Mood, A., Weinfield, F., & York, R. *Equality of educational opportunity.* Wash., D.C.: U.S. Government Printing Office, 1966.

McClelland, D. C. *The achieving society.* New York: The Free Press, 1961.

Rosenthal, R. *Experimenter effects in behavioral research* New York: Irvington, 1976.

Rosenthal, R., & Fode, K. L. The effect of experimenter bias on the performance of the albino rat. *Behavioral Science,* 1963, *8,* 183–189.

Rosenthal, R., Persinger, G. W., Vikan-Kline, L., & Fode, K. L. The effect of early data returns on data subsequently obtained by outcome-biased experimenters. *Sociometry,* 1963, *26,* 487–498.

## SUGGESTED ACTIVITIES

### Study Questions

1. How can extraneous events threaten the internal validity of research findings? Give some examples. Can you think of any examples of your own from courses you have taken or any other source? (This is a good exercise for all the questions that follow here and throughout the book.)

   What are the characteristics of research studies in which extraneous events pose the greatest threat to validity?

2. How can temporal effects become confounded with the effects of an independent variable? What are some examples? How could the studies you chose as examples be altered to increase their internal validity?
3. What are group composition effects? Give some examples of how they can threaten the validity of research findings. What is the only way of making certain that this threat has been eliminated?
4. What is meant by the interaction of temporal and group composition effects? How does this extraneous effect complicate the evaluation of any therapeutic program? Can you explain why matching is not always as good a way of eliminating extraneous group composition effects as it seems?
5. How can researchers affect the observations they make in their studies? How do those effects hinder the interpretation of the research results? What are the best solutions to this problem? How can less radical steps be taken to lessen the threat to validity?
6. How does the administration of a pretest threaten the validity of research findings? Describe examples of both practice effects and sensitization effects of pretests. What can be done to lessen the threats they pose to the validity of research findings?
7. How can sample attrition produce effects that cloud the interpretation of the effects of the independent variable? What is the difference between sample attrition that poses a threat to validity and sample attrition that does not? In what sorts of studies are these effects most likely? What can be done about them?
8. What is statistical regression? How does it affect the interpretation of research results? How can it be eliminated as a threat to validity?
9. What makes a rival hypothesis plausible? Why should we take only plausible rival hypotheses seriously in judging the validity of research findings?
10. Can you identify the characteristics of research studies that minimize threats to internal validity? What rules would you follow to produce research findings which were as internally valid as possible? If you had to go so far as to state one general principle which could be used to guide the production of internally valid research findings, what would it be? (Do not be surprised if this sort of abstraction does not come easily now. You have enough opportunities to think about these questions and to check out your current impressions of the answers as we continue on.)

# Chapter 3
# Potential Threats to
# External Validity

## OVERVIEW

There is another set of problems in interpreting research findings. In this chapter we shall examine these threats to *external validity,* that is, the generalizing of research findings beyond the specific context in which they were produced. All research conducted to test a hypothesis must be placed in a specific context of independent and dependent variables, subjects, instructions, and the like selected from a variety of alternatives. But if the results occur only in that specific combination of circumstances, their value is extremely limited. The aim of any piece of research is to understand a large class of events similar to the specific example chosen for examination. To the extent that it is representative of such a class or category, it has high external validity. Threats to external validity, then, are the ways in which a specific research setting fails to be representative of other settings, especially those outside laboratories and other testing locations.

Even if research findings have high internal validity (a big "if," as we have already seen) so that we can be confident in tracing subjects' behavior directly to the causal factors specified in our hypothesis (the independent variables)—even if we have succeeded in eliminating all threats to internal validity (those extraneous causal factors that might be mistaken for our independent variables)—our findings would have little value if they could not be generalized to a large proportion of the variety of settings to which our hypothesis could be applied. What is implied in most hypotheses of the form, "*X* causes *Y*," is the more general and more important version, "*X* causes *Y* whenever and wherever the two come together."

We are considering internal and external validity separately for two reasons. One is to make it easier to deal with a great deal of information. Psychologists who study human learning have found that it is easier to process information if they can divide it up into more manageable "chunks." Internal and external validity are two such chunks. Another reason is historical. Not too many years ago, discussions of the validity of research findings began and ended with threats to internal validity. Although some recognition was given to the problems we will discuss in this chapter, not too much thought had been given to them, probably because they were not believed to be as important. That belief might be related to the assumption that internal validity can be absolute, the outcome of the perfect research design, whereas external validity is of necessity less than perfect. Of course, we can never represent all possible settings by one specific example. As a practical matter, however, this distinction lacks force because perfect internal validity is only very slightly more likely than perfect external validity, if at all.

Recently, both our knowledge of threats to external validity and estimates of their importance have increased greatly. In fact, it seems clear that although it may be convenient to separate threats to validity into two categories, they are all really different aspects of the same underlying problem. In both cases we are dealing with the same basic question of what research findings mean—more specifically, of how research results bear on the hypothesis being tested. The increased attention to the problem of external validity should not weaken efforts toward assuring the internal validity of research findings, or the concern of anyone about the internal validity of findings we read about. Now that there is a growing awareness of this other side to the problem of validity, however, we can see that internal validity is only a part of the problem. Having reviewed the complex nature of the internal validity problem, you can probably appreciate the reluctance of some researchers to accept that idea. Perhaps the argument that external validity is a less important problem can be traced, at least in part, to their frustration at having this additional burden thrust upon them.

## INTRODUCTION

Most research begins with a hypothesis. At the outset, at least, that hypothesis is usually a very general statement about some form of behavior. "Expectations affect performance." "Frustration causes aggression." "Behavior is performed, or not, depending on the environmental events contingent upon it." "The lecture method of teaching is inferior to classroom discussion." Despite all the research which psychologists have done, or maybe because of it, there seems to be no shortage of opinions. They are not all as general as the examples above, although the more general ones often seem to be the most important and interesting; but they are all too general to be investigated as they are.

In order to find an answer to one's question, one must begin by making it more specific. The subjects, human or otherwise, whose behavior is to be studied must be selected. The events to which they will have to react must be chosen. What kind of expectations or frustrations will they experience? What specific procedures will be used to create them? And what particular aspects of the subjects' behavior will be observed to assess their effects? How will that behavior be measured and quantified? In what specific locations will all of this take place? These questions must be answered as the research takes form. When they are, the original conceptual hypothesis will have been transformed into a completely specified research hypothesis. Otherwise, no one would know how to proceed to collect data.

There is no choice but to test a specific research hypothesis. Conceptual hypotheses cannot be tested. No individual piece of research, no conceivable long-term program of research for that matter, could determine whether everyone's expectations were a causal factor in every possible sort of performance. Or whether every possible source of frustration caused an increase in every form of aggression on every individual's part. Or . . . you get the picture. To answer any question, to test any hypothesis, we need to "particularize" it—to put it into a specific form we can work with.

Chapter 1 describes one possible form in which to test the hypothesis about expectations and performance. A specific group of college students was placed in a specific situation in which their expectations for the outcome of their performance of a specific task were manipulated in a specific way; that performance was finally measured by a specific test. While reading about that study, you may have asked yourself a series of questions about why all its objectives were not accomplished differently. Why use college students as subjects? Why choose anagrams as the task for subjects to perform? And so on.

In fact, there are a very large number, perhaps even an infinite number, of possible combinations of all those factors that could reasonably be used in place of the combination actually used. The same would be true of every research study. As a consequence, for every research finding we can ask: If the particular ways in which the hypothesis was investigated were altered, if the study had attacked the question differently, would the findings be the same?

The importance of this question lies in the nature of the general question or conceptual hypothesis with which a study begins. Most researchers, and most consumers of research findings as well, are more interested in the general questions that stimulate research than in the specific details of the research study itself. Researchers aim to discover general laws about behavior through their particularized research studies. Positive expectations enhance performance. Frustration leads to aggression. Classroom discussion facilitates learning in school. All consumers want to use a research finding to predict behavior in a particular setting that has a practical importance—on their job, in their home, and so on—or even in their own laboratory with a different group of subjects and a somewhat modified procedure. It is very unlikely that the setting of interest to any consumer would be identical to one in which a given research finding was obtained.

Both researchers and consumers, then, need to be able to generalize the findings of research beyond the particulars of the study in which they were produced. The question of generalizability is one of external validity. Beyond asking simply why a given set of particulars was chosen, we need to ask whether it is reasonable to expect that the particular response of a particular group of research subjects to a particular set of research procedures represents a more general pattern. Would a different version of the hypothesized response by a different group of individuals to a different version of the hypothetical situation follow that same pattern? Does the research simulation accurately portray the reality outside? Are the particulars of the research study representative of the variety of individual cases in which the hypothesized relationship could occur? These are all questions about the external validity of research findings.

Of course, this question is one of degree, notwithstanding the ways in which it is worded above. One would not expect identical findings under different circumstances. A change in any feature of the setting would produce some change in the behavior being observed. But would there be a change in the form of the relationship between cause and behavior? The point, then, is to choose a set of particulars that permits the greatest possible degree of generalizability of the eventual findings. Or from the consumer's point of view, to base one's predictions for the particular setting in which one is interested on the findings that promise to be most generalizable.

Even if a particular research study succeeds completely in overcoming the potential threats to the internal validity of its findings, so that, for example, it could be maintained that in our particular test of the expectations-performance hypothesis no causal factors other than expectations could have been responsible for the variations in performance we observed (and absolute certainty is not attainable in practice), some vital questions would still remain. Would we observe the same relationship if we studied a different kind of performance—chess, basketball, selling real estate? What if we studied older or younger or more intelligent or less cooperative subjects? What if the people we did study were unaware that we were interested in evaluating their performance? Research findings that do not depend on the particulars of the setting in which they were obtained have external validity. To be more accurate, again, to the degree that we can expect the same phenomenon to occur under different conditions that still represent the conceptual hypothesis, our findings then have external validity. Our concern in this chapter will be with the most important factors that threaten to limit the generalizability of research findings—the threats to external validity.

Thus one difference between the problems of internal and external validity is that logically the latter can be solved only to a partial extent. By randomly assigning subjects to our different comparison groups, we can effectively rule out the possibility that a difference in the groups' behavior was caused by some preexisting difference between the subjects. We can never be certain that a finding observed in a particular group of subjects would hold true for people in general or any other particular group of people under similar conditions. In fact, all the research that psychologists have done documenting individual differences suggests that they would not. Because all research must be conducted in particular settings, we can never produce a research finding in a way that ensures that it can be generalized to any possible set of conditions. There will always be potential peculiarities of people, tasks, and settings that could produce a different relationship between expectations and performance than what we observed in our research study.

What we need to do, then, is to minimize the limitations of our findings. In order to do that, we need first to be aware of the potential problems. We also need to remember that the situation is far from hopeless. There are two particularly encouraging facts. First, if we want our findings to pertain to any particular group of subjects, or activity, or setting, we need only approximate those in our research, rather than attempting to study conditions with universal applicability. This is the case especially in applied research. Second, if we do seek to establish a universal relationship, one which would hold true under any imaginable combination of circumstances, then we need not try to do this within a single research study. Instead, we could use the cumulative findings of a series of studies, in which the same conceptual hypothesis is tested under a variety of conditions, to give us more confidence in the generalizability of our findings.

In this chapter, we will be considering several factors which constitute threats to the external validity of research findings. These factors set the limits for the generalizability of our findings. Of course, this is not intended to be an exhaustive survey or the only kind of organization that could be imposed on this information, but merely those examples to which so far research students have paid the greatest attention. The recent growth of interest in the problem of external validity will inevitably alter our thinking about it in the future.

## THREATS TO EXTERNAL VALIDITY

### Nonrepresentative Sampling

Few research hypotheses specify the organisms to which they apply. Depending on the particular behavior, it is usually understood that either all organisms or all human beings can be expected to behave as described by the hypothesis. However, no hypotheses are tested by examining, or even sampling, all organisms or all human beings. This gap between the hypothesis and its test raises the question of how far one can generalize results based on the particular subjects tested. If those subjects are not representative of other organisms to which those findings are generalized, then the findings will not apply. In other words, the findings will lack external validity.

Two principal criteria, singly and in combination, are used in selecting research subjects. The first is biological. Experimenters choose subjects who are capable of performing the behavior in question, preferably in a way that is easily controlled and evaluated. Second, they choose subjects that are convenient for them. Consequently, some have characterized psychology as the study of the college sophomore, others as the study of the albino rat. Psychological research has been concentrated in few species and in a homogeneous segment of the world's human population. This fact underscores the need to consider whether research findings can be generalized from the narrow range of subjects whose behavior was actually observed to the much broader constituency to which the hypothesis is directed. Do we learn the effects of an independent variable in some general sense for all people or all animals? Do we learn about the behavior of a small group of subjects which may not be representative of any others?

It is not possible to represent all living beings in any single research study or program of studies. But failure to do so does not mean that the findings of research cannot be generalized beyond the subjects actually studied. The question we need to consider is whether or not others in general or some particular group would respond in the same way as the research subjects did. If the research sample is not representative, that is, if the subjects' behavior cannot be generalized, it is because some specific characteristic of the subjects was responsible for their behavior in the circumstances under which they were observed. Others who do not share that characteristic would respond differently under the same circumstances. In other words, the others' behavior would be described by a different relationship between the independent variable and the dependent variable—that is, a different hypothesis. Only in that case would *nonrepresentative sampling* constitute a threat to the validity of the research findings.

There can be little doubt that there is variation among human beings in a long list of characteristics that affect their behavior. There is, in fact, a separate and very large branch of psychology devoted to the study of those individual differences or personality traits. At the same time, the field of comparative psychology has produced its own vast literature describing the variations in behavior across species. In the face of these large bodies of knowledge, do general hypotheses, which place no limits on the range of organisms or people to which they apply, make any sense? Should not every hypothesis include a clause stating that the effects it describes depend on the organism involved?

There are those who argue vigorously that behavior can and should be explained by principles that are so basic, so fundamental, that they apply to every member of every species. This argument advocates research aimed at the discovery of universal laws of behavior which would be analogous to Newton's laws of thermodynamics, Einstein's relativity principle, and the like. On the other side of this question are those who maintain that the differences among species, as well as the genetic and environmental differences within species, produce a range of response in any setting which must be addressed. According to this latter view, any generalization about behavior must be qualified to some degree to reflect the contribution of the organism itself to the behavior in question.

This is far too broad a question to be resolved in this part of the chapter. Fortunately, it is possible to consider it in a form that is more directly relevant to our present concerns and much more manageable at the same time. We will be presenting some research findings and some special kinds of subjects that demonstrate strongly that generality is a serious problem. In this way, we will be able to gain some perspective on the scope of the problem. Our modest goal is to become sensitive to the presence of the threat posed by nonrepresentative sampling. When we plan a research study or read a report of one, we need to ask ourselves how restricted the findings are to the limited group of subjects that was studied. Specifically, is some other group of organisms in whose behavior we are interested likely to behave similarly under the same conditions?

One of the most troubling aspects of this issue lies in the area of cross-species generality. Considerable research that psychologists have done during the past century or so has used nonhuman subjects. The study of learning and motivation in particular has relied heavily on rats and pigeons, along with lesser numbers of dogs, monkeys, and other assorted species. But the intent of these studies was not to test hypotheses about pigeons, dogs, or any other such individual species. In fact, most investigators who have expressed an interest in a particular species have singled out the human species. And most consumers of behavioral research have human behavior in mind. But when we wish to predict the behavior of one species on the basis of research findings produced with a different species, we must face the issue of generalizability. Any differences between two species in characteristics that can influence the behavior being studied can threaten the validity of our predictions.

There are many reasons for using nonhuman subjects in research. Laboratory animals are convenient, at hand 24 hours a day. Some of the most popular species are also chosen or bred to be docile and economically caged and fed. Animals can be treated in ways which are essential to research procedures but inapplicable to human subjects. They can be starved, altered surgically, drugged, and so on. There are long traditions of using particular species in particular kinds of studies—pigeons for operant conditioning, rats to run mazes, dogs in avoidance learning. As a result, there are readymade apparatus, research procedures, and publication outlets supervised by established researchers who expect to see reports of studies resembling those done in the past. For these and other reasons, researchers have often used nonhuman subjects as analogues of human beings. They have assumed that their research findings, based on observations of the members of some nonhuman species, would apply to human behavior. Neither they nor their readers had any true interest in the behavior of the albino rat. But is their assumption tenable? Can we generalize from the behavior of nonhuman species to that of humans?

As an example of the difficulties involved in generalizing across species, we will consider the most interesting and important case—generalizing to human behavior from findings from research with nonhuman subjects. To make it even more interesting, we will consider a research finding that is among the most accepted in both psychology and outside the field. Innumerable studies, most of which have used rats and pigeons as subjects, have yielded the generalization that if an organism makes a response that is followed by the satisfaction of one of that organism's needs, that response will occur more frequently in the future under similar conditions than it did before. The fact that this finding is labeled the Law of Effect suggests the generality with which it is assumed to apply. Its reliability for rats and pigeons has been established beyond any reasonable doubt, and some evidence shows that it operates in other species as well, including humans. But does human behavior generally follow this same pattern? (The statement above is an amalgam of the concepts of reward and reinforcement, somewhere between Skinner's position and Thorndike's, but it does represent the most commonly understood version of this generalization.)

A series of recent studies by Edward Deci and his colleagues (Deci, 1975) suggests that the relationship between need satisfaction and response rate may differ for humans. To summarize their findings very briefly, human subjects who engage in an activity that they find enjoyable may actually be discouraged from pursuing it when rewards such as money are made contingent upon the quality and/or quantity of their performance. Their participation in the activity actually declines after they have been rewarded, as compared with subjects who pursued their activities without ever being rewarded, getting no more than whatever pleasure they derived from it.

Assuming that no comparable effect of reward would be observed in any other species, why does human behavior seem to follow somewhat different rules? In short, it appears to result from a difference between humans and other species. Humans are capable of believing that they should be free to do what they like. They are capable of feeling resentment at the control which others can exert on their behavior by being able to provide valuable rewards at their discretion, according to their criteria. All this is not to say that facts about the behavior of other species cannot tell us anything about human behavior. It is to say, however, that they must be generalized cautiously, recognizing that there are differences among species that limit the generalizability of research findings from one to another. For the example we have been considering, it is not that the principles of reinforcement developed through research on rats and pigeons do not hold at all for humans; rather it is that humans are apparently different enough from rats and pigeons in relevant respects that make it necessary to qualify those principles before successful application to humans is possible.

There are also important differences within our own species which can lead to varying responses to identical stimulus conditions. A mountain of research evidence, commonly called personality research, documents the behavioral correlates of many of those individual differences. This raises the question of whether the behavior of subjects in a particular research sample is representative of all people. If any characteristic is distributed differently in a research study sample from some group of people to whom the research results are to be applied, that application is suspect.

Many of the subjects in psychological research are American college students enrolled in introductory courses in psychology, which is attributable largely to the fact that many of the researchers are teachers of psychology in American colleges. But whatever the reasons, research findings in psychology have traditionally been based disproportionately on subjects who constitute a very limited segment of the human population. To begin with, most people, unlike most of our research subjects, are not American. Many critics of psychological research have claimed that its findings constitute a study of just one of the world's many cultures. In most respects, no one definitely knows whether the generalizations that have been found in studies of American subjects hold true for people of other cultures as well.

In addition, because college attendance is still much more likely for white, middle-class Americans, even the American culture is poorly represented. Ethnic minorities and low-income groups are certainly underrepresented. Furthermore, regardless of their social background, college students fail to represent all the levels of intellectual ability, interests, or almost any other characteristic one could mention that are found in the population at large. A very obscure example may indicate the scope and some of the subtlety of this problem.

The story began when social psychologist Eliot Aronson and his colleagues reported a fascinating study of interpersonal perception. By means of a series of comparable tape recordings of staged interviews, their subjects were exposed to a male stranger who was identified by his behavior as either competent or incompetent. Near the end of this taped introduction, the subjects heard the stranger spill a cup of coffee on himself, an accident described by the researchers as a pratfall. The results of this study consisted of comparing how four equivalent groups of subjects evaluated the four versions of the tape-recorded stranger—the competent and the incompetent versions who suffered the pratfall and the competent and the incompetent versions who did not. The subjects' ratings showed that the competent stranger was liked better if he suffered a pratfall, whereas the unfortunate version of the incompetent stranger was liked less than his neater counterpart.

This interesting finding attracted other investigators who felt they could shed more light on its origins. Unfortunately, subsequent modified versions of the original study failed to produce the original findings. Subjects in those later studies consistently judged the incompetent stranger more harshly when a pratfall spoiled the end of his interview, but the more interesting finding—that a pratfall made the competent stranger more attractive—could not be reproduced. Aronson eventually participated in a successful effort to reconcile the discrepancy between his original findings and the later ones (Helmreich, Aronson, and Lefan, 1970).

It turned out that a pratfall had a favorable influence on the ratings of a competent stranger only when the subjects who made the ratings had an average level of self-esteem. Aronson's original research sample was composed of a homogeneous group of college students with average levels of self-esteem, whereas the samples in later studies included high- and low-self esteem subjects whose ratings of the competent pratfall victim were less favorable. Without going into the intricate reasoning applied to those research findings, they do point out one of the possible problems of using college students as subjects. Because many social groups within our society are underrepresented in the college population, samples of college students can be extremely homogeneous. One must suspect that people who represent the extremes of any dimension, whether age or intelligence or self-esteem or any other dimension, are less likely to be found in the college population than in the larger culture from which it is drawn. The studies that we have just looked at show that relationships between causes and behaviors do not always take the same form for those extreme individuals as for more average people.

Other examples of nonrepresentative sampling of human subjects are especially relevant here because of the way in which research with human subjects is often carried out. Because it is common practice to offer college students a small incentive to encourage them to volunteer as research subjects, the resulting studies are performed more often on students who wish to be subjects than on those who do not. Frequently, students participate in several different experiments over the span of the one or two semesters of their "Psych 101" course.

Unfortunately, there is evidence that both volunteer and experienced subjects behave differently in a variety of settings from nonvolunteer and naïve subjects in their first research study. One apparent reason for this is that the tendency to try to do what seems to be expected by the experimenter in a research situation is greater in volunteer subjects distinguished by their cooperativeness and in those who have had past experience as subjects that make them better at interpreting what is happening to them. When researchers rely on deception to create an influence on subjects' behavior, an increased willingness to help the researcher and a greater sophistication about research in general are especially likely to influence the subjects' behavior. There is some reason to believe, therefore, that the findings of research studies using volunteer and experienced subjects might not be able to be generalized to the considerable numbers of naïve and nonvolunteer individuals. This is especially troublesome because research reports rarely describe their subjects in these terms.

Another troublesome practice, which is not as common as using volunteer or experienced subjects, is that of pretesting. As we saw in Chapter 2, some investigators attempt to reassure themselves (unnecessarily in most cases) about the comparability of groups of human subjects to be exposed to different conditions by administering some instrument at the outset of their study. In addition to the effects of pretesting that we discussed then, there is one that is relevant to the issue of sampling. A pretest may provide subjects with a clue to the purpose of the research study. This, in turn, may increase the possibility that the subjects will manage their behavior in attempting to make it fit the research hypothesis. Because the pretest is likely to be aimed at a behavior of interest in the study, so that the same measure or one closely related is administered later to assess the effects of the independent variable, pretested subjects may become sensitized to the surveillance of some particular behavior of theirs that is being conducted by the researcher. Therefore, one could not safely expect that pretested subjects would react to the conditions being studied in the same way as naïve individuals who had not been similarly alerted.

Now that we have discussed volunteering and pretesting in the abstract, we can look at an empirical study that provides a concrete example of their effects. Ralph Rosnow, a pioneer in many of the issues we are now considering, and Jerry Suls have provided this look at these biasing factors in action (Rosnow and Suls, 1970). They used an experimental situation which was once quite popular among social psychologists studying attitude change. In it, subjects' attitudes toward some issue are first assessed—the pretest. Then randomly selected groups are exposed to different forms of a written message containing arguments on the same issue in a particular (and often unpopular) direction. Finally, the subjects' attitudes are assessed again, usually by the same questionnaire or rating scale used for the pretest. Although the original attitude change studies were designed to compare the persuasive impact of different kinds of messages on the subjects' various attitudes toward a variety of issues, Rosnow and Suls had a very different interest.

They varied two characteristics of the subjects themselves. First, half the subjects had volunteered for the study and half had not. If you are wondering how nonvolunteers can end up serving as subjects, it goes something like this. The researcher enters a classroom and makes a plea for students to volunteer as research subjects. Those students who wish to sign up do so. Later, nonvolunteers from the same class are contacted personally and persuaded to participate. Rosnow and Suls's groups of volunteers and nonvolunteers were both subsequently divided in half. One-half received an attitude pretest in the usual manner, and the other half did not. Then all subjects received the same persuasive message, followed by the same final measure of their attitudes toward the issue in the pretest and in that message.

As you might have suspected already, the attitudes that subjects expressed at the end depended both on whether they had volunteered to be in the study and whether they had been pretested. Among the volunteers, the pretested subjects seemed to have been influenced more by the persuasive message than those who had not been pretested. In other words, pretested volunteers expressed attitudes more closely in line with those expressed in the message they read. Among the nonvolunteers, pretesting had the opposite effect, resulting in less apparent attitude change. In line with the arguments about volunteering and pretesting we presented earlier, the results of this study can be explained as follows. Volunteers, who had wanted to help the researcher out from the start, expressed attitudes that they thought would further the purposes of the study when the pretest made those purposes clearer to them. Nonvolunteers, who may have been unhappy about being recruited into the study, an activity they probably tried to avoid whenever possible, worked against the researcher's apparent purpose when they were tipped off by the pretest, or just paid less attention to the message.

Volunteers and nonvolunteers have different motives. Pretested and unpretested subjects have different information about the study itself. People who differ in these ways apparently cannot be expected to respond to the research situation in the same way. More importantly, if one wants to predict how someone would respond to a persuasive communication under natural conditions, the behavior of volunteers or nonvolunteers as defined in the Rosnow and Suls study and of pretested subjects is a poor guide. In an attitude change study in which subjects were pretested, the message being studied would be cast in an unusual light. Contrary to the researcher's intent and the best interests of the study, subjects would be informed unintentionally of the true purpose of that message. It seems from what you have just read that the information (as researchers have assumed all along and for which reason they usually go to great lengths to conceal the true purposes of their studies from their subjects) can have the effect of engaging strategies for controlling the behavior being studied—the subjects' expression of their attitudes.

It is undoubtedly clear to you at this point that the representativeness of a research sample is an important determinant of the value of research findings. There are, however, those who disagree. In fact, there are two ways in which the issue of the representativeness of research subjects fails to be addressed. Some argue that differences from subject to subject, whether across species or within the same species, are unimportant. For them, demonstrations of differences in the behavior of different groups reflect only variations in the same fundamental processes; they show differences in what organisms do, but not in how they do it. According to this view, basic processes underlie all these different-looking forms of behavior. Even more dangerous is the practice of ignoring representative sampling as an issue altogether. Many researchers seem to fall into this group. A glaring example of their attitude is reflected in data describing the participation of women as research subjects.

The subject samples tested in research studies of social behavior, which have been published in prominent psychological journals, contain disproportionately few women. This occurs in spite of the fact that an entire research literature is devoted to sex differences that leaves little room to doubt that men and women can respond differently to standard situations to which both are exposed. It is difficult to imagine the reason. In fact, it seems impractical for such a large part of the college population to be thus ignored. Perhaps the researchers conducting these studies felt that using both male and female subjects would complicate whatever relationship they wanted to study. (I have certainly had that feeling myself.) It is exactly that sort of complication which we have been examining.

## Reactivity in the Research Setting

The common requirement of every form of research, in every discipline, is measuring some phenomenon. In psychology, that process is referred to as the assessment of the dependent variable. For a long time, before the formal establishment of psychology in fact, it has been recognized that whenever a measurement procedure is applied to any phenomenon, some alteration of that phenomenon is possible. Heisenberg, a physicist, referred to this problem as one of uncertainty. One can never know the true state of a phenomenon, he maintained, because the act of determining its state may cause it to be altered. In psychology, this problem is labeled *reactivity*. A measurement procedure is considered to be reactive if its application distorts the phenomenon being measured.

A simple example of this general problem is the procedure for measuring the temperature of a liquid. First, we need to imagine that the liquid has a true temperature. Second, we need to imagine that we have a measuring instrument, a thermometer, which can provide a perfectly accurate assessment of the temperature of any substance with which it comes into contact. If we chose to measure the temperature of our liquid by inserting our thermometer, we could be certain that the reading we obtained was not the true temperature. Introducing the thermometer into the liquid would alter its temperature unless the assessment was instantaneous or the temperatures of the thermometer and the liquid were identical (neither a very likely possibility).

The measurement error introduced by a thermometer can be overcome rather straightforwardly in one of two ways. If it could operate almost instantaneously or if its mass were extremely small relative to that of the substance it was to measure, measurement error could be minimized. These technological solutions to the reactivity problem occur, in fact, in modern temperature-sensing devices. If they were not available, however, one could keep the thermometer in a constant state prior to its being used in each of the series of measurements required and applied in a strictly standardized manner. If every measurement made with the thermometer were affected to the same degree, any comparisons made with them, based on relative temperatures of different substances, would be accurate.

Unfortunately, behavioral researchers face a more complex problem, especially when they study human subjects in laboratory settings. It is this extreme case of the reactivity problem on which we will focus in this chapter. Put most simply, the problem is that the human subject in the laboratory setting is aware that his or her behavior is under the scrutiny of the researcher—that it is being evaluated in some way. This realization brings into play a complex pattern of ideas, perceptions, and motives that threaten to prevent the generalization of research findings to behavior in nonlaboratory settings in which unaffected humans respond naturally and spontaneously to the events taking place around them. We will be examining examples of how behavior unique to the laboratory setting has been conceptualized and studied, and at the characteristics of measurement procedures that make them more or less reactive.

The principal reason for the special problems of reactivity that affect the measurement of human behavior in the laboratory is the reflexive nature of the subject. A beaker of liquid is a passive subject. It simply reflects the conditions that exist around it. It does not initiate any action on its own which might alter its surrounding environment. Thus it can be described as having a nonreflexive relationship with that environment. A human subject is quite different in this respect. Whatever events take place around the human subject, whether those created intentionally by a researcher so that their effects on the subject can be studied, or other events, undergo active interpretation by the subject. The human subject can initiate action that alters the meaning and even the substance of surrounding conditions. The researcher who chooses to study humans must contend with the fact that the behavior taking place in the laboratory is the product of both the impact of the conditions imposed on the subject and the conditions imposed reflexively by the subject.

There have been many attempts to understand the role played by the human research subject. Efforts to substantiate these explanations and to choose among them through research have not produced much in the way of conclusive evidence. However, the possibility remains that any or all of them may describe accurately the ways in which human subjects respond in the laboratory. For that reason, we will review them briefly.

The first was proposed by Martin Orne (1962). According to Orne, because subjects are in a laboratory they understand that their role in research is to behave in ways that will confirm the researcher's hypothesis and thus maximize the value of the research findings. Rather than responding directly to the incomplete and often misleading information provided by the experimenter, as the researcher intends, they search for clues to the true purpose of the research and respond to those they find, whether they are correct or not. According to this reasoning, laboratory research findings are often based on subjects' attempts to mimic the behavior predicted by the research hypothesis rather than "natural" responses to the situations researchers intend to study.

Rosenberg (1969) has analyzed subject behavior quite differently. He focuses on subjects' evaluation apprehension, or concern about the credit that their behavior will reflect on them. In this view, subjects are expected to try to perform as effectively as possible, to succeed at the tasks with which they are confronted during the research, or, in general, to make themselves look as good as possible.

These two views, Orne's and Rosenberg's, are not perfectly compatible. If the researcher's hypothesis is that the conditions under which subjects are performing will cause them to perform inadequately, then subjects who are motivated to cooperate will not try as hard to succeed as those who are motivated to achieve a positive evaluation. But, whichever motive prevails, and this might vary across subjects and across specific research settings, both explanations have something very important in common. Subjects' behavior, in response to the conditions the researcher created for study, would not be a valid guide to the behavior of individuals who were not research subjects, but who were exposed to similar conditions while going about their everyday lives in a variety of natural settings. Thus the research findings would have very limited external validity, being able to be generalized only to people who find themselves in reactive arrangements, knowing their behavior is being studied.

There is yet another way of conceiving subjects' responses to laboratory settings, perhaps an alternative to the first two or simply a third strategy used at different times by different people. In this view, research subjects are cast into a passive and subordinate position in their relationship with the researcher. They are told what to do, they are given much less than complete and accurate information about the purposes and procedures of the research, and whatever they are permitted to do must be fitted into the rigid mold of response alternatives provided for them. These subjects are confronted with a "director" who is usually older than they, has higher status in the academic society to which they both belong, possesses technical information beyond their understanding, and often has command over sophisticated equipment that is to be applied to them. Thus a research subject is responding under a set of conditions which exists in only limited parts of the world outside the laboratory. In this role, the subject may be expected to behave in ways that are not characteristic of individuals in more autonomous roles who have greater freedom of expression and action, who see themselves as having more control over what happens to them, and who do not have to look to others so much for guidance and approval. Again, to the extent that all or even any of this is true, laboratory research findings may apply only to the behavior of people who face the situation being investigated in subordinate, helpless roles comparable to that of the research subject.

Roger Brown, a social psychologist, has written about a "universal norm" that governs interaction between individuals of unequal status. By his account, many behaviors in such interactions, including forms of address, touching, and gaze, are used differently by the two parties involved. The superior uses the behaviors appropriate to interaction between intimates—familiar forms of address, frequent gaze and touching, and the like. The inferior uses forms appropriate to interactions between strangers. This is another way of saying that the subject role may limit the behavior observed in the laboratory to those of a formal or public variety. This would preclude generalizing the findings to settings in which private, informal behaviors take place.

In addition to these and other conjectures, reasonable as they may be, about research subjects' behavior, we can also look at some examples of research that demonstrate both directly and indirectly the reactivity of laboratory experimental arrangements for human subjects.

Robert Wicklund (1975) and a number of his associates have studied a phenomenon that has an indirect but nonetheless very important bearing on this issue. They call the phenomenon objective self-awareness (OSA)—quite literally, the awareness of oneself as an object that can be perceived by others. A major premise of their work is that one behaves differently when one's perception of the situation is that of an actor, directed outward at the persons and objects around oneself, than when one is conscious of the status one has in others' eyes—that of an object observed, judged, evaluated, and the like. If this is true, then the possibility that the role of a research subject increases one's level of OSA threatens the generalizability of research findings to settings in which people function as actors, with their attention directed more toward their environment and less toward themselves.

There is extensive evidence for the premise stated above, but space permits only one simple example. In one of their prototype studies, Wicklund and his colleagues gave subjects a test. Afterward, they told them that their performance was poor—that they had failed to do as well as the average of a group of students like themselves. In fact, however, this evaluation had nothing to do with their actual performance. Finally, the subjects were asked to complete a questionnaire. That questionnaire was a measure of self-esteem, the level of esteem in which a person holds oneself. At the time, all subjects were seated alone at a table in a small room. However, half of them were seated in such a position that a large mirror, seeming to have been left in a certain corner of the room, reflected their image. The other half of the larger research sample were seated so that the same mirror, in approximately the same location, was outside their line of sight. Those who could see themselves in the mirror received a lower score for self-esteem based on their questionnaire responses. It seems that the mirror increased their OSA and this magnified the effect of their failure on the prior test. When they were forced to become aware of themselves as objects that others evaluate, their own self-esteem was lowered.

When I read the results of Wicklund's research, and especially this particular study, I was myself engaged in research. In the process of studying nonverbal behavior, I had adopted a means of observing subjects' facial expressions that was and still is quite popular. My subjects were seated in a room across from a large sheet of partially silvered glass through which they could be observed from an adjoining room. When that room was brightly lit and the adjoining room was dark, the glass served as a "one-way mirror"—from the subjects' side it was a mirror and from the other side an almost clear pane of glass.

My attention during that research was on the view that the glass afforded of the subjects. Like others who have used this device for some time (I would suspect), I paid no attention to the fact that my subjects, although they were prevented from seeing the observers in the adjoining room, could see their own images whenever they looked toward the "mirror." Wicklund's research suggests that this was a very serious oversight on my part. One-way mirrors are used to withhold from subjects the fact that their behavior is being observed because it is recognized that this knowledge would cause their behavior to be less natural, that is, less like the behavior of non-subjects. But the mirror itself probably has the same effect. Worse yet, the typical experiment probably has many features which produce high OSA and unnatural behavior, mirror or no. And even worse, the fact that the one-way mirror is so popular a device suggests that many researchers lack sensitivity to the problem of reactivity.

An interesting example of the influence of demand characteristics on the behavior of research subjects comes from the study of a phenomenon called verbal operant conditioning. Studies in this area follow variations of a common procedure. An experimenter elicits a sample of speech from a subject—in a conversation, an interview, or some other way. During this period, the experimenter is careful not to respond in any way while the subject is speaking. The frequency with which some component of that speech (e.g., plural nouns, or pronouns, or adjectives) occurs is calculated. Then another speech sample is obtained, but this time the experimenter responds to the chosen component of that speech by nodding his or her head and saying "uh-huh" in a way that indicates interest in or approval of what is being said (or some similar combination of responses). After the second speech sample has been taken, the frequency of occurrence of the speech component in question is reassessed. In some cases, there are further episodes during which the experimenter's response may be alternately withdrawn and reintroduced.

What has been found, typically, in studies of this type is that a component of the subject's speech is emitted more frequently when it is followed by a response by the experimenter that indicates inter-

est, approval, or something of that sort. Those involved in the research refer to the experimenter's response as reinforcement, hence
the term verbal operant conditioning. But there has been disagree-
ment among researchers about whether subjects who undergo this
procedure are aware of the contingency between their words and
the experimenter's responses. If they were, it has been argued, it
would be unclear whether their behavior changed because of the
given reinforcement or because they had discovered the experimenter's purpose and decided to cooperate in fulfilling it.

In the cause of discovering whether subjects are aware of this
information, postexperimental interviews have been used. The results have been mixed. Some have found that conditioning takes
place only when subjects are aware, others have not. Fortunately,
an investigator named Monte Page (1972) has taken this problem one
step further. He first applied a traditional verbal operant conditioning procedure. Then he asked his subjects to make the experimenter
make the reinforcing response (saying "good") during each of their
subsequent utterances. All the subjects who had previously shown
the conditioning effect were able to do so. They were also revealed
in the subsequent interview to be aware of the hypothesis (able to
state it). Of the subjects who had not shown the conditioning effect
prior to being asked to get the experimenter to say "good," some
were able to do so and others were not. All those who could were
later determined to be aware of the hypothesis. Those who could not
were not. Page concluded that verbal operant conditioning was a
pure artifact of demand characteristics. Only subjects aware of the
hypothesis show the effect. In other words, the "effect" consists
purely of consciously providing the experimenter with the words he
or she is known to be trying to reinforce.

Another example of potential reactivity in research is found in
the longitudinal method used by developmental psychologists. In
Chapter 2, we considered one drawback of longitudinal research—
the selective loss of subjects over time which distorts comparisons
among the groups being studied. Unfortunately, this method, which
promises to yield such fascinating data, has another potential flaw as
well. It can be extremely reactive.

Let us focus on a recent concrete example. During the early
1970s, a group of developmental researchers led by Burton White
conducted a longitudinal study of the development of children during the first 3 years of life (White, 1975). Their general aim was to
identify those factors in the early experience of children that were
responsible for the development of effective functioning by age 3.
To that end, they adopted the longitudinal method used many years
ago by Terman (1925) in his study of the lives of highly intelligent

individuals and by others since then. They observed their subjects at regular intervals throughout their first 3 years of life. The children's parents agreed to have trained observers visit their homes to observe the conditions under which the children lived and to assess their behavior.

One question that is raised by this procedure, as employed by White and elsewhere, concerns the reactivity of the setting in which the required observations were made. Because of the children's extreme youth, one need not be so concerned about the self-consciousness of the research subjects or their response to the special role requirements that subjects face in their interactions with researchers. But, interestingly enough, the basic problem of reactivity remains. In fact, the problem appears in an especially virulent form. One is forced to ask whether the first 3 years in the life of a child participating as a research subject in the White study were comparable to the life of a child outside the study. To what extent did the parents' conceptions of their roles in the study, of the purposes of the research, of the perceptiveness of the trained observers, and so on, influence their efforts to rear their children? Beyond that, one might ask whether such parents might view the responsibility of child rearing differently as a result of the constant evaluation of their performance during the study.

There is the general danger, in this and in any longitudinal study, of reactivity. When one, or one's child, is the target of a long-term investigation consisting of repeated observations by a trained student of behavior, it is difficult to act as one would in other circumstances. Did Terman's "geniuses" see themselves as special because of the attention lavished on them, combined with what they must have learned about their special talents? Did the parents of the children who were observed by White and his colleagues feel a special responsibility to provide an orderly or progressive home environment for the observers' benefit? If the research arrangements were reactive, altering the subjects' behavior in these ways, how generalizable are the research findings? Might Terman's subjects actually have led more productive lives as a consequence of their participation in his study? Or might the preschoolers in the White study have been reared differently if the research assistant had not visited them?

Beyond the question of whether participation in a longitudinal study influences subjects' behavior is the question of whether the findings of such studies can be generalized to individuals leading more private lives. Although an affirmative answer to the first question might generally imply an affirmative answer to the second, this is not necessarily so. That depends on the objectives of the study. It seems certain that the repeated direct observations that longitudinal studies typically entail would inevitably make the behavior observed more socially desirable and less deviant simply because it was public. But one major finding of the White study was that children whose parents gave them more physical freedom of movement around the home, more opportunity to explore their environment for themselves outside the playpen, or any other restraining device, eventually became more capable 3-year-olds. No matter how much parents in the study primped or fussed to make a good appearance for the observers, this finding could not have been produced in the process When all the participants in a longitudinal study are subject to the same reactive arrangements, comparisons between different groups among them would seem to remain valid. Terman's reports of the accomplishments of highly intelligent individuals, on the other hand, are of dubious value in understanding the lives of such individuals who are outside the glare of the researcher's spotlight.

Fortunately, many clear avenues can be pursued by researchers who are concerned with generalizing their findings beyond a reactive research setting. To begin with, the use of animal subjects, despite its numerous drawbacks, has the potential advantage of lessened reactivity. It is possible to automate research with animals to the point where observations place few if any restrictions on the animals' behavior. Although the behavior must take place within the confines of some piece of research apparatus, we will deal with the implications of that requirement later. In any event, it is unlikely that any of the self-conscious strategies employed by human subjects in a laboratory setting can be expected of their nonhuman counterparts. Surely, reactivity, if it exists, is a less difficult problem in the study of animals as opposed to human subjects.

However, even research with human subjects can be conducted in ways that alleviate the problem of reactivity to some degree. One of the foremost possibilities is to move the research from the reactive arrangements of the laboratory to settings outside that are referred to variously as "the field," or "natural settings," or "the real world." Subjects in field research, who encounter some situation created by a researcher for their benefit in a public place, or who react to a naturally occurring situation whose effects the researcher is monitoring, are unaware of their status as subjects. As a result, it seems reasonable to expect that their behavior would be free of self-consciousness, the motives associated with the role of subject, or any of the other consequences of reactive arrangements. Thus it could be generalized with greater confidence to nonsubjects.

To achieve this benefit, some researchers have attempted to create conditions in the laboratory that are designed to minimize reactivity. One popular example might be called the waiting room ploy. In it, subjects are enrolled to participate in a fictitious study. Any title sounding like a scientific psychological enterprise will do. When subjects arrive, individually or in groups, depending on the true purposes of the study, they are told that the "experiment" is not ready for them yet and are directed to a waiting room where they can stay until a prior subject leaves, or the apparatus is made ready, or whatever story is chosen.

The real study takes place in that waiting room. In some cases, a confederate of the experimenter acts out a scene to which the subjects must react. A tape-recorded scene in an adjacent room can act as the same kind of stimulus. The possibilities are endless. Or the study could be as simple as one that was conducted by two social psychologists, Coutts and Schneider (1975). They simply observed the interaction between two subjects in a waiting room to determine whether people look at one another less when they are strangers in a public place than when they know one another and their interaction is "focused" on some common task or concern. Although subjects in a waiting room are still subjects, their concern for the implications of their behavior and their suspicions of the events that transpire in the waiting room before the experiment begins may be lessened so that their behavior would be more natural and more spontaneous and the findings of the study more generalizable than would happen in a more traditional laboratory setting. When the research permits its use, this technique may provide a useful antidote to reactivity. The ethical implications of this sort of deception, however, bear further scrutiny.

One advantage of much field research lies in the use of less obtrusive means of observing subjects' behavior. In place of the questionnaires, the electrodes attached to various parts of the body, or the obvious (or the suspected) observation mirror, microphone, or camera often found in the laboratory, field studies typically incorporate less reactive alternatives. Unobtrusive observation can be accomplished through using observers or instruments located at some distance from the subject or camouflaged among the realistic accoutrements of a public place. Like the waiting room ploy, some of this advantage can be captured in a laboratory setting. If the subject's response can be assessed through nonverbal behavior rather than direct responses to researcher's questions, the opportunity for the subject to disguise or dissimulate can be reduced. The subject is less sure of the direction of the researcher's scrutiny and less capable of tailoring the responses to fit some conscious strategy. For example, one subject's liking for another could be assessed through the amount of gaze directed toward the other or through the closeness with which the other is approached during interaction. Or the degree to which black and white students on a college campus disregard race in interacting with one another could be assessed through observing seating patterns in the classroom. These unobtrusive measures, as well as others, increase the possibility that the subjects' behavior represents their spontaneous responses to the conditions being studied and that the research findings are not only applicable to responses made under reactive conditions.

A more elaborate means of studying behavior in the laboratory while minimizing subjects' awareness of their participation in the research, and the problems associated with reactivity, was devised by social psychologist Stuart Cook (1971). He tested the hypothesis that highly prejudiced individuals would become more favorable toward blacks if they had extended contact with a black person under conditions in which that person's status was high and the interaction between the two took place in a cooperative context. Cook managed to avoid testing subjects either in a setting that they perceived as a laboratory or in a natural setting where the course of the relationship and interactions between the two could not be manipulated.

A sample of highly prejudiced subjects was found among female college students in the Atlanta, Georgia, area who volunteered to take a test battery for pay in response to ads they saw on their campuses. Amid the battery was a measure of racial prejudice. These women were later recruited for part-time clerical jobs. There was no apparent connection between the agency that conducted the initial testing and the personnel office on their own campus that offered them work weeks afterward. Those who took the job found themselves working with a black woman and her white subordinate. The work setting, including the activities and behavior of her fellow workers, constituted the laboratory for Cook's study. The part-time women workers were his subjects. Their experience followed a research design and their behavior was monitored closely by the experimenters. Weeks after ending this combination of temporary employment and a social–psychological research study, the subjects fulfilled their prior commitment by taking a second test battery from the same agency as they had the first. Their attitudes toward blacks were then measured again.

Cook found that when highly prejudiced white women had extended contact with a black woman whom they could respect, under conditions which produced predominantly friendly, cooperative interaction between the two, their prejudice was greatly reduced. But the way he found that was at least as important as what he found, because it allows us to rule out the possibility that the subjects' reactions to the experience they had was atypical of those that would occur when people do not know they are subjects, that they are being studied by a psychologist, and that the events that occur have been designed specifically for an evaluation of their responses to them. We can place more confidence in the findings, because it is likely that the subjects in this study responded spontaneously and naturally to the conditions created for their benefit and their responses were assessed very unobtrusively. Yet, the researcher retained enough control over the situation to allow continuous and precise observation of the subjects' behavior.

In conclusion, then, to the extent that the behavior of research subjects is self-conscious, that it is influenced by its perceived significance for the researcher's unknown purposes (influences that do not operate outside the research setting in which the behavior in question usually takes place and needs to be understood), the generalizability of the research findings is limited.

## Nonrepresentative Research Context

To many, the gist of "the scientific method" is contained in a statement something like the following: We study the effect of one or more variables while holding the others constant. To a certain degree, this basic goal of what is really just one type of scientific method, the experimental method, can be accomplished by eliminating some of those "other" variables. Laboratory settings are, therefore, typically much less complex than those outside. For the rest of those other variables, it is sufficient to expose all subjects to the same context, whereas some of them receive one variation of the independent variable(s) and others receive different variations.

The wide agreement on the generalizations above reflects insensitivity to the external validity problem. Those generalizations are a fair recipe for assuring the internal validity of research findings (just fair because, as we saw in Chapter 2, there is more to holding all other variables constant than meets the eye of the casual observer). But even if all subjects, regardless of the treatment they receive, respond in precisely the same surrounding context, the nature of that context is an extremely important determinant of the value of the research findings produced in it. Comparing the effects of two or more sets of conditions in a particular context has little meaning if the comparison cannot reasonably be expected to hold true in other contexts as well. Unfortunately, there are good reasons to suspect that this is often not so.

Several characteristics of a *research context* may affect the outcome of the comparisons that are made within it. For convenience we separate them into two categories. The first contains the immediate details of the *research setting* itself. These are the features that the researcher builds into the research procedures intentionally. Primarily, these consist of the particular means of manipulating the independent variable(s) (instructions, props, people), the task that is presented to the subjects (what they are asked to do during the period of observation), and the means of assessing the subjects' behavior (questionnaires, instruments, observers) which are applied. These particulars of the research setting represent the researcher's operational definitions of the conceptual hypothesis—the operations which carry out the intent of the hypothesis. Although the research may be addressed to concepts, general classes of causal factors, and behaviors, it must concern itself with particulars. Subjects must be asked to do something specific, under a specific set of conditions, and specific aspects of their behavior must be selected for monitoring. This inescapable process of particularization opens all research findings to the question of whether they would have been obtained under a different set of particular circumstances.

There is also a second, broader kind of context in which research findings are produced. This context is much less the choice of the researcher involved and may not even be apparent to the researcher, the subjects, or the consumer of the research findings. It is the *socio-historical context* in which the research is carried out. Research must take place not only within a particular setting, but also within a particular culture at a particular time in the world's history. This broader context also constitutes a potential limitation on the generalizability of the research findings. One must be concerned about the possibility that any given research finding would not have been obtained if the study had been carried out among the members of a different culture or at a different point in time.

Like the other potential threats to external validity, these two types of research context are unavoidable. Research cannot be done in no context at all or in every imaginable context. Yet this does not mean that the context can be safely ignored when evaluating research findings. On the contrary, as we will see in the following examples, one can judge research findings only in light of the context in which they were produced.

First, let us examine a few examples of the ways in which the particulars of research—the immediate setting in which research findings are discovered—may limit the generalizability of those findings. As formerly throughout our discussions, we will not present innumerable examples. The purpose of the examples is simply to clarify and to bolster the general point that the immediate setting is influential.

Each of the causal factors specified in a conceptual hypothesis needs to be operationalized as an independent variable in the eventual research study. The particular form that an operationalization takes depends on the criteria that the researcher applies. The researcher may choose a form because it promises to have the greatest impact on the subjects or because it is the easiest to administer to the subjects. In any event, it is important to consider the possibility that the response to the particular form chosen would not be obtained with alternative forms.

Almost 20 years ago, Stanley Milgram (1963) performed a well-known experiment on the causes of obedience. In it he created a complex situation in which verbal instructions, a person acting the role of an authoritative scientist, a second individual who was a potential target of electric shock, and a whole series of props were combined in various ways designed to produce varying levels of obedience in naïve research subjects. That obedience took the form of delivering (apparent) electric shocks to the victim provided by the researcher. One of the most prominent findings of that study was that, across the varying experimental conditions employed, the level of obedience manifested by the subjects was very high. That is, the subjects were willing to punish the target person severely.

This study was criticized both on the grounds that the deceptive treatment of the subjects was unethical and that it was too likely that subjects did not actually obey the authority figure in the experiment but simply responded to the demand characteristics of the experiment. One alternative to the manipulation of authority used by Milgram, which was suggested repeatedly as a remedy for both those faults, is the use of a technique referred to as role playing (see Chapter 8 for a clarification of the error in that reference). That would consist of a description of a hypothetical set of conditions to the subjects and a request that they predict what their response to those conditions would be. In fact, Milgram had followed exactly such a procedure before doing his experiment and it had yielded quite different results. Subjects reported much less willingness to obey the person in authority than subjects in the later experiment actually displayed. Thus two alternative means of creating the conditions Milgram wanted to study produced startlingly different findings.

I had my own experience with a mundane form of this same problem a few years ago. A colleague, Martin Sherman, and I set out to demonstrate that a popular personality questionnaire (Rotter's Internal-External Control Scale) was susceptible to faking and that, in fact, subjects who were inclined to present themselves in a favorable light through their answers to the questionnaire would alter their responses consistently in the same direction. We decided that such a demonstration could be accomplished by providing a comparison between the subjects' responses under conditions that varied in their perceived importance of a favorable self-presentation—our independent variable.

To that end, we developed two sets of instructions to serve as our means of manipulating that perception. We scheduled two groups of about 30 Introductory Psychology students, with each one to receive one set of instructions. One group was told that we were in the process of constructing a new instrument to measure a personality trait. They were asked to complete the questionnaire anonymously so that we could determine simply the average and the range of the scores of students on that campus. In other words, we asked them, in nontechnical terms, to serve as part of the standardization group for that test. These instructions were designed to minimize the perceived value of favorable self-presentation.

The second group completed the questionnaire after hearing instructions that were designed to create a much greater desire to present themselves favorably. The questionnaire was (mis-) represented to them as an established test of mental health. We told them that the purpose of the study they were participating in was to determine whether diagnoses based on this "test" were consistent with people's perceptions of their own condition. They were led to believe that after they had taken the test and we had evaluated their responses they would return to comment on the results as judges of themselves. For that purpose, they had to sign their names on their answer sheets.

Our research hypothesis, then, was that the group that answered anonymously for the purpose of standardizing the test would score differently, more honestly, and less in the socially desirable direction than the group who signed their names and expected to be questioned about their scores later. We found no difference at all between the two groups. Other, less obstinate, researchers might have concluded that increased motivation for favorable self-presentation had no effect on the scores on this particular questionnaire. We decided that our manipulation was at fault. We repeated the experiment with two changes in the way we tried to manipulate motivation for favorable self-presentation. First, we tested subjects one at a time to increase the impact of the instructions on them. Second, for the same reason, we actually scheduled those in the high motivation group for appointments to return for their expected consultations before they took the test. This time we found a large difference in the average scores of our two groups of subjects, thus supporting our hypothesis (Cherulnik and Sherman, 1976). Different, although similar, ways of manipulating the same independent variables resulted in very different findings.

It may seem that the chance of success of a particular manipulation procedure is a rather mystical process. How can one anticipate in advance what results will be produced by which alternative procedure? How can one determine which of a number of alternatives is best? Or how can one know whether a reported finding would have occurred if the manipulation used had been (even slightly) different? In this regard, one technique that can be useful is called the manipulation check. In general, it involves collecting information about the effects of a particular manipulation administered on subjects. Every manipulation is intended to create some specific effect—a belief, an emotional state, a desire to engage in some activity, whatever. If subjects are asked to reveal what they believe or feel or want to do, or whatever, then the value of the manipulation can be determined and alternative manipulations can be compared. It is even possible, and indeed desirable, to do this outside the research study itself with groups of subjects who are merely exposed to the manipulation and are then administered the manipulation check. It is rarely safe to merely assume that alternative manipulations of the same independent variable are equivalent or that any of them produce an effect that is truly representative of the causal factor that was specified in the conceptual hypothesis that gave rise to the research study.

The second particular part of the research study which we will consider is the activity in which subjects are asked to engage—often called the task. Perhaps more than any other part of a research study, this part is likely to be taken for granted and its contribution to the findings overlooked. To assess the effects of the causal factor being investigated, subjects need to be doing "something" at the time. As is true of other aspects of a particular research setting, the task is rarely specified in the conceptual hypothesis. In fact, that hypothesis implies by exclusion that some aspect of the performance of any task would be affected by any version of the causal factor in question.

One of the most interesting aspects of the lack of attention paid to these mundane aspects of the research setting is that they are themselves the causal factors of interest in other research studies. Differences among tasks can be the principal focus of research. One classic example should clarify this point fairly quickly. One traditionally popular question in psychological research concerns the effect of arousal on performance. One of the most popular answers to that question is the Yerkes-Dodson Law. This determined that it is misleading to talk about the effect of arousal on task performance without specifying the task that is being performed. If that task is one on which the subject has had extensive practice so that he or she is prepared to make all the right moves with great facility, higher levels of arousal will produce correspondingly better performance all the way to the normal upper limits of arousal. If, however, the task is new or confusing to the subject, if it is still being learned, so that there are incorrect responses competing strongly with the correct ones, increases in arousal at the lower levels will improve performance, but increases at the higher levels will cause performance to deteriorate.

This finding has both specific and general relevance to the point in question. Specifically, if a research study concerns a causal factor in behavior that might involve altered levels of arousal, its effect will surely depend on the activity that is in progress while it operates. More generally, it points out that it is not safe to assume that a research finding which reports the effect of a causal factor on subjects engaged in one particular activity can be generalized to any other activity. We do not know, from observing performance on a single task, the nature of a general relationship between arousal and performance. Other tasks might be affected similarly or, as we now know, they may not.

An excellent example of the more subtle forms that this problem can take in the area of animal learning is provided in a recent review by David Olton (1979) of research on maze learning in rats. When early investigators trained rats to follow a single path in a complex maze, they found that the rats' efficiency improved over long series of trials. Those early reports emphasized the apparent inflexibility or stereotyping of the rats' performance. Support was even claimed for behavioristic learning theories that stressed the chaining together of simple responses on the basis that the rats ran those mazes like machines, running straight into walls if the maze's original path was altered after they had had extensive experience. More recently, however, different kinds of mazes have been used that demonstrate, on the contrary, flexibility in behavior. For example, when a rat learns to approach the goal box in a maze from three different directions, it follows a new path straight to the goal in over 80% of cases on its very first attempt. This is anything but stereotyped behavior—in fact, it is being used to construct theories of cognitive processes ("thinking") in animals. For our purposes, what the rat does, and even the general theories about behavior based on the research results, depend on what the rat is asked to do. The rat's solution to the problem of finding its way through a maze is not always the same. It cannot be described by a general law of behavior. Instead, different generalizations are needed to describe different kinds of performances in different kinds of mazes. This fact should be kept in mind by anyone who is tempted to extend the findings of one research study to a context that is very different from the one in which they were produced.

Another choice that a researcher must make in planning a study is that among the alternative measures of the subjects' behavior. It is true in this case, again, that there are different aspects to the problem. If the research hypothesis is correct, so that the conditions to which subjects are exposed can be expected to affect the behavior they are asked to display, this can be observed only if the procedures chosen to measure the predicted effects are sensitive to them. One cannot expect to measure a change in reaction time with a kitchen clock. The effects of subjects' expectations on their performance will not be revealed in a test consisting of two simple anagrams. All subjects, whatever their expectations, would be sure to get both right.

A more difficult problem in research with human subjects concerns their willingness to admit their true reactions. If the researcher chooses a measure of behavior which provides the subjects with the opportunity to describe their reactions as they would like to, it is possible that a true hypothesis will not be verified. We rarely learn of occurrences like these because it is impossible, after the fact, to know whether the effect failed to take place or whether it was obscured by the subjects' censored reports. We have already considered some instructive examples of such response biases in our discussion of the reactivity which is characteristic of laboratory research with human subjects.

As a general rule, then, it needs to be recognized that the conditions under which subjects are studied, the activities in which they engage, and the measures used to gauge their reaction all play some role in determining the findings of a research study. Therefore, an important issue in determining the value of any finding concerns the range of contexts to which it can be generalized. Whether one is interested in ensuring the range of generality of a finding or its applicability to one particular context, the choice of a research context must be made with an eye toward that goal. And if one seeks to use the findings of a research study, the same factors must be weighed in judging their value.

Apart from the aspects of the research context considered above, which apply in every case, there is a related problem that is much less widely found. There are occasions when the effects of varied conditions on a particular behavior are assessed by exposing one group of subjects to each of the conditions under investigation. We will be considering this sort of study in a later chapter, but for now it is sufficient to note that it is quite popular in studies of the effects of reinforcement on animal learning and in certain areas of research with human subjects. In the latter case, at least, it poses problems. When a human subject is exposed to a series of research conditions, or treatments, the effects of each in the series depends on those preceding it. That is, the first treatment provides a part of the context in which the second has its effect, the first and second provide a context for the third, and so on. Although it is common practice to take the order of the treatments into account, as we will see later, this does not entirely eliminate the problem that this multiple-treatment interference can cause. It is extremely difficult to use this sort of sequential procedure with human subjects, even when very good reasons exist, without creating problems in interpreting the effects of each treatment in the context of the others.

Now that we have seen how the particular context of a research study can limit the interpretation of its findings, we need to consider a broader, more subtle, and more troublesome issue. First, it has been pointed out in recent years, especially by the social psychologist Kenneth Gergen (1973), that every research finding is limited by the historical period and the social context in which it is produced. What is not really clear as of now is the extent of that limitation. There are innumerable studies in the psychological literature that may be called normative. They describe what a group of subjects does in response to a particular situation or a particular set of stimulus conditions—how many of them conformed, how many nonsense syllables each one of them learned on the average, how many trials it took them on the average to learn an avoidance response, or the like. The results of many, if not all, of these studies could be expected to differ somewhat if they were carried out in what Gergen calls a different sociohistorical context—in other words, in a different place at a different time. The personal histories of the subjects, or even the natural histories of their entire species, might be different. As a result, their behavior could be expected to be different as well.

There have been many studies whose primary purpose was to compare human subjects from different cultures. As one might suspect, it is not difficult to demonstrate differences in behavior between people whose entire lifetimes have been spent in very different surroundings—whose languages, points of view, experiences, and beliefs are all very different. They have different abilities, different personalities, different responses to almost any situation in which they might be observed, at least on a superficial level. It seems almost unnecessary to document Gergen's thesis at this level, but there are so many interesting examples that at least two cannot be resisted.

Numerous psychologists have been interested in the formation of emotional ties between parents and children. Perhaps because these strong bonds have been accorded a major role in shaping the behavior of adult persons, the conditions under which they are formed have long been of interest. But how long? How many of those who have investigated this problem, the research psychologists in this modern age, have considered the possibility that the phenomenon itself, which seems so important and so universal to us, might not even exist at some other time and place?

The work of the historian Laurence Stone (1977) indicates that we should consider that possibility, and others like it, very carefully. In his study of the historical changes in family relationships in early modern England, the 1400s through the 1600s, by using the remains of the public and private records of the time, marriage licenses, birth certificates, published writings, private diaries, and the like, Stone has found that the strong parent–child bonds that we take for granted hardly existed then (if at all). During the fifteenth century, when the rate of infant mortality was very high, parents' feelings for their children were rather casual and distant by today's standards. By way of illustration, Stone mentions that the French philosopher Montaigne, in one of his writings, indicated that he was unsure of the number of children that had been born to his wife and himself. By the seventeenth century, when improvements in sanitation had extended the life span and greatly reduced infant mortality, parents' bonds with their children were close, like those that exist today. We need to recognize that what we study today is not as permanent as it seems. It has not been here forever, or in some other places at all, and its future is problematic.

On a simpler level, consider the social psychological research on conformity sparked by the work of Solomon Asch (1956). Although there has been a great deal of sophisticated inquiry into the determinants of conformity, one of the findings that has impressed readers most has been the sheer amount of conformity that a simple laboratory procedure can produce. When Asch had a group of confederates give an incorrect answer to a simple perceptual problem, a naïve subject responding after the confederates was influenced to give that same obviously incorrect answer an average of about one-third of the time. When Stanley Milgram put Norwegian subjects into a similar situation, the observed rate of conformity was much higher (Milgram, 1961). A further comparison showed that French subjects conformed less than did Norwegians. Milgram attributed these differences between cultures to the training that children receive which may stress independence more in one culture and cohesiveness or conformity more in another.

That these facts about human behavior depend on the particular time and place in which they are investigated has disturbed some researchers more than others. Some have argued that it is irrelevant to the business of testing hypotheses, which occupies most researchers. They maintain that the variability in behavior across history and culture leaves the relationships between behavior and its basic causes intact—that it is unimportant how much conformity occurs in the Asch-type experiment. What is important, according to this line of argument, is what causes people to conform—what factors can be shown to increase or decrease the level of conformity. These relationships, it is argued, do not change with time or place. The basic underlying processes that explain behavior are common to all peoples.

The validity of this argument depends upon one's conception of "basic underlying processes." Throughout the history of modern scientific psychology, there has been considerable support for the notion that all the behavior we observe is a manifestation of biochemical events that hold the promise of providing, eventually, their best explanation. At the biochemical level, we are all the same and may always have been. Differences of time, place, and even species may be unimportant, and the apparent differences in behavior associated with these merely superficial.

Whether the reductionist argument is true or false, only some psychological research is concerned directly with such basic processes. At the level at which behavior is usually, almost always, studied, the distinction between basic and superficial levels is less clear. For example, in Milgram's cross-cultural investigation of conformity, he found not only differences in the sheer amount of conformity, but also differences in the way that various aspects of the conformity situation affected the amount of conformity observed. When subjects could respond privately, so that the other members of the "group" could not learn how they answered, the amount of conformity was reduced more than twice as much among French subjects as among Norwegian. To put this another way, it may very well be that a test of the hypothesis that conformity in the kind of situation studied by Asch and Milgram is greater when subjects must respond publicly than when their responses are not made available to the others present would be confirmed if the study were performed in France but not if it were performed in Norway. One can only imagine the result if the study had been performed in fifteenth-century England.

So influential is the sociohistorical context that Gergen has gone so far as to claim that any hypothesis could be confirmed (or disconfirmed) at some time in some place. Some of his critics remain unconvinced. Although we cannot settle this issue here, we will pursue it again near the end of this chapter. However, it does seem fairly clear at this point that context is an important problem in psychological research. Any claim for positive or negative evidence for a particular hypothesis needs to be qualified, by the writer or the reader, by specifying the context in which it was discovered. Both the particular details of the research procedure and the broader sociohistorical context in which the study was carried out influence research findings and thus limit their generality.

A variety of means are available to the researcher for maximizing the generality of findings beyond the research context. To the extent that a relationship between some causal factor and some behavior can be demonstrated in a variety of research contexts, with different combinations of independent variable manipulations, tasks, and dependent variable forms, the estimate of its generality can be more generous. Similarly, to the extent that a finding survives scrutiny across time and across cultures, it can be assumed to be general rather than specific to any single set of contextual circumstances. Either of these questions can be addressed in a single, complex research study or in a series of separate studies in different contexts.

If the investigation of a causal relationship across contexts results in variable findings, then we have gained evidence that the causal factor involved interacts with, or has a different effect depending on, contextual variables. Systematic investigations of this sort can identify precisely the contextual variables involved, resulting in more limited generalizations of the form: Causal factor A has the effect of "blank" in context 1, but no effect in context 2 and the reverse effect in context 3, and so on. In fact, some would argue that most behaviors have several contributing causes, making this kind of compound generalization their only accurate explanation.

Having said that, we should point out that there is some difference of opinion on this subject. Some researchers have argued that the knowledge we gain from the total of all the investigations of any causal factor is greater if the procedures used in those separate studies are as similar as possible. Among other things, this provides us with information about the reliability of a research finding— whether or not it recurs when the same procedures are repeated at another time. It also makes investigations of different aspects of a single phenomenon comparable, so that their findings can be combined more easily. But on the other side of the issue are those who argue that such a "standardization" of research procedures promises to produce very precise information about relationships between causal factors and behaviors that may occur under such limited sets of circumstances, or in such unique contexts, that any knowledge about them, however precise or reliable, has little value. This is especially true of a finding discovered in a laboratory setting which may have no counterpart anywhere else. If diversified procedures are used in different studies, we obtain more widely useful knowledge and relationships which are reported in ways that are more realistically limited by the specific contextual variables that produce variations.

Even if the specific effects of context are not known, a research finding can and should (although this is certainly not the rule in practice) be stated in a form that indicates the potential limitations on its generality. For example, one scholarly publication, the *Journal of Social Psychology,* requires its authors to state explicitly that any finding based on the observation of subjects from a particular culture be reported as being specific to that culture. In most other cases, such limitations are not made explicit. Other kinds rarely are in any journal. But readers, like you, who are aware of the importance of the research context, can read the appropriate qualifications into any finding. When, and this happens too, insufficient information about the context is given, one is safer in assuming the worst—that the finding may have such limited generality that it is worthless.

Finally, there may be a more subtle consequence of the effects of research context. The features of a particular context may obscure a relationship between some causal factor and some behavior that exists in other, even in most other, contexts. Thus the traditional practice of choosing one particular research context for investigating a hypothesized relationship, and choosing with little regard for the representativeness of the context versus other possible contexts, may prevent verifying generally true hypotheses as well as appearing to verify generally false ones. To state the problem more moderately, before we move on to the next section, no particular research context can serve as a proving ground for a finding of considerable generality. Consistent with that, no research finding should be interpreted or applied generally without giving careful consideration to the specific context or contexts in which it was observed.

## Ecological Validity

The general principle that the generalizability of research results is limited by the context in which they are produced has a more specific and especially interesting corollary. In fact, it is interesting and important enough to warrant its own separate discussion. In addition to considering the overall breadth of populations and contexts to which research findings can be generalized, we need to consider whether the particular relationship between some behavior and one of its possible causes has an existence beyond the research study itself, that is, in nature, and whether, if it is real in that sense, it is observed in a context in which it can be expected to take the same form as it does in its natural context. A research finding that describes a natural relationship based on observations made in an adequate simulation of its natural context is said to have *ecological validity.*

These concerns are raised whenever a researcher creates a setting in which to test a hypothesis. This is more obviously relevant in the case of laboratory studies in which subjects may encounter a situation that does not resemble, even superficially, anything in their own experience, and that may be defined, for human subjects, as a different world—that of the psychological laboratory. But even a field study must create a particular context in the choice of the stimuli presented to the subjects and/or of the aspects of subjects' behavior that are observed, which may have no real counterpart elsewhere.

The first, most basic of these concerns is about the degree to which the causal relationship being studied is representative of some chain of events that occurs in nature. In some research studies, there is a direct concern with simulating, usually by producing a simplified, manageable version of some real phenomenon. However, to accommodate the traditions of procedure, apparatus, and even research species, this goal may be met in such a way that the resulting situation bears little resemblance to the phenomenon of interest. In such a case, we must ask whether it is, indeed, the same phenomenon. In other cases, the research problem arises out of purely theoretical aims. A particular theory might be supported by a finding that some event produced a particular change in some specified behavior. It is entirely possible, in those cases, that the cause-and-effect relationship being studied exists nowhere in nature at all. Its only reason for being may be to provide a test of the theory. Regardless of its origins, if a research study pertains to some causal factor and behavior which have no counterpart elsewhere, the findings are said to lack ecological validity.

Even if the phenomenon being studied is real, or a successful simulation of some real phenomenon, it may be studied in a context in which it does not occur in nature. In that event, there is reason to suspect that the relationship that is observed might be different from that which occurs in the natural context of the behavior in question. If the context in which the research findings are obtained is not representative enough of that natural context to assure that the observed relationship is the same relationship that holds true in nature, then those findings are also limited in ecological validity.

The problem of ecological validity occupies an unusual position among the threats to external validity in two respects. First, rather than demanding the broadest possible generalizability of research findings, a specific criterion is posited. Second, rather than asking about representativeness for all people or procedures or cultures, or whatever, it is asking about representativeness of reality, of some specific behavior or context for behavior which can be found in nature, the so-called real world. It is even more unusual in the fact that there is room for considerable debate about its merits. That is the reason that this section is headed "ecological validity" rather than "lack of ecological validity." Although one could argue about the severity of the threats posed by the other limits on external validity, or the possible remedies for them, some would argue that to strive for ecologically valid research findings is not necessary at all. For example, it was pointed out in Chapter 1, and implied only a few paragraphs ago, that theories may be tested in research settings which lack ecological validity altogether. Is there any reason to strive for ecological validity in such a case, or to criticize the resulting research findings for their lack of it? We will return to this question after we have seen some examples of the lack of ecological validity. By then, we will have a fuller, more concrete perspective from which to consider the question. Perhaps by then you will even have anticipated some of the other arguments against ecological validity.

One of the most important discussions of ecological validity in recent years has centered around the phenomenon called classical conditioning. This example shows the generality of the problem, across species and behaviors, and also the depth of it, extending to one of the fundamental building blocks of psychological knowledge.

If you can recall your introductory course in psychology, you'll recognize the following description of Pavlov's famous studies of classical conditioning. A bell is rung, powdered food is sprayed into a hungry dog's mouth, and the dog salivates. This sequence is repeated many times, a precise time interval being maintained between the sound of the bell and the delivery of the food. At that point, if the bell is rung but no food follows, the dog is still observed to salivate, although not quite as much as it had after receiving food. In more technical terms, pairing a "neutral stimulus" (the bell) with an "unconditioned stimulus," abbreviated US, (the food), results in the bell becoming a "conditioned stimulus" (CS) for the "conditioned response" (CR), a somewhat diminished form of the "unconditioned" salivation response (UR). Moreover, research evidence portrays classical conditioning as a gradual process. The more times the bell and food are paired, the more saliva flows in response to the bell alone. And the more times the bell is rung without the subsequent delivery of food, the less saliva flows each time. Without the "reinforcement" of the food, the gradually acquired conditioned response gradually extinguishes or disappears.

There can be little doubt that classical conditioning occurs in the way that Pavlov originally described it. Experiments like his have produced similar findings for a variety of responses and a variety of species of subjects. The effect is general enough that pairing a bell with a puff of air directed at the eye of a human subject produces a conditioned eyeblink response. But recent research has cast considerable doubt on the relevance of such findings for behavior that occurs naturally, outside the classical conditioning experiment. Would any neutral stimulus that appeared repeatedly at about the same time as a natural sequence of US and UR gradually acquire the capacity to elicit that response, or some CR variant of it, itself? And would this effect wear off or extinguish after that previously neutral CS had been encountered repeatedly without the "reinforcement" of the US?

The manner in which the principles of classical conditioning are usually described, even as "laws" of behavior in some cases, might make those questions seem unnecessary. But an intriguing series of studies by John Garcia and his colleagues (see Seligman and Hager, 1972, for a review) have shown not only that they are necessary, but also that the answers to them are "no." As it turns out, the outcome of the classical conditioning procedure depends on the total context, the particular combination of species, stimuli, and responses in which it is applied. Certain pairings of neutral and unconditioned stimuli lead to the acquisition of a conditioned response and some do not. And when classical conditioning does take place, the process is not necessarily gradual. Nor does it gradually reverse itself afterward. Even more important, for our current discussion, the determining factor in all of this is the natural history of the organism. More specifically, it is the correspondence, or lack of correspondence, between the sequence of events that makes up the classical conditioning procedure and the experiences that the members of the particular species to which that organism belongs have in their natural environment.

Let us backtrack now and look at some of Garcia's findings. Using rats as subjects, he found that pairing a compound stimulus consisting of a bright light and a loud noise with an electric shock would result in the light–noise stimulus alone becoming capable of eliciting a response similar to that which was elicited originally only by the shock—a reflexive startle response. If a substance such as quinine, which has a strong, unpleasant taste, was placed repeatedly in rats' mouths just before a chemical which induces nausea was delivered directly to the animals' stomachs, the foul-tasting substance acquired the capacity to cause some of the symptoms of nausea, such as stomach contractions. So far, two examples are to be added to the long list of demonstrations of classical conditioning.

However, when the light–sound stimulus was paired with the nausea-inducing chemical, and when the taste of quinine was paired with the electric shock, the findings were quite different and, to some, quite unexpected as well. At the time Garcia performed these studies, there was a widespread belief that Pavlov's descriptions of the behavior of his dogs could be applied to the behavior of any animal for whom any initially neutral stimulus was paired with any other stimulus which was capable of eliciting some reflexive (unconditioned) response. But Garcia's rats never did show signs of nausea when the light–sound stimulus was presented alone. And they never were startled by the bad taste of quinine alone. In short, there was no evidence of classical conditioning for these particular CS–US pairings. Where no limits to the generality of classical conditioning had previously been recognized, Garcia found that there were limits after all. Moreover, there was a pattern to those limits.

One way of stating Garcia's findings is that classical conditioning occurs for some combinations of organism, neutral stimulus, and US–UR reflex, but not for others. One possible explanation for those mixed, even contradictory findings, has been supplied by Seligman and Hager (1972). It is based on a concept they call "biological preparedness." The gist of their argument is that the natural history, or evolutionary history, of each species makes the association of some combinations of neutral stimulus and US–UR reflex especially likely to result in classical conditioning (the neutral stimulus becoming a CS), other combinations especially less likely to produce that effect, and still other combinations neither, or moderately likely or unlikely, depending on how one looks at it. In other words, the progress of classical conditioning depends on the degree to which a particular species is biologically, or evolutionarily, prepared to associate a particular neutral stimulus with a particular reflexive response.

Some examples will help to make their point clear. If you think for a moment about the experiences in the real life of a real rat that would correspond loosely to the electrical shock psychologists use in their research, you might imagine the poor rodent being snatched up off the ground by an owl's powerful talon, or perhaps being struck by a rock thrown by a mischievious child. What would the animal's response be? The general excitement we call a startle reflex? An attempt to get away from the offending stimulus? I suppose that would depend on the force of the attack. What natural stimulus might have preceded that sort of painful experience in the wild? The sight and sound (at the last instant) of the swooping owl? The sound of the child stepping on a dry twig or grunting with the exertion of the throw? Whether or not these are successful attempts at understanding a rat's life, there would be some occasions when a "shock" would be experienced soon after some distinctive sight or sound or combination of the two. That is simply because of the nature of the usual causes of such shocks. And if the pairing of that initially neutral (meaningless?) pattern of light and/or sound with the dangerous event that follows caused the effect called classical conditioning, the animal might, in the future, be better able to protect itself. It might begin to move, even flee, before the actual strike occurred, when the sight and/or sound of its perpetrator was first noticed.

Seligman and Hager go so far as to argue that there are combinations of stimuli that have so much significance for an animal in its natural environment that the animal is prepared to associate them immediately. In such cases, a single pairing of CS and US can produce a classical conditioning effect. Moreover, they argue, that effect can be so strong that the bond will never weaken, no matter how many times the CS is encountered alone or how much time has passed since the first pairing took place. This is because that particular association has such great importance for the survival of the animal. And that, in turn, is because of the way the animal's behavior and its natural environment fit together. The taste of food and an illness caused by that food is such a pair of stimuli. If the animal were not biologically prepared to make a connection between the two quickly and permanently, its future survival would be jeopardized. On the other hand, there are combinations of stimuli such as a taste and a "shock" or a combination of a loud noise and bright light and nausea that have no significance for a rat in its natural environment. Therefore, the animal is biologically unprepared to make the association between these pairs. In fact, to do so would be a "mistake." It would lead to ineffective behavior on the animal's part—for example, ducking behind a bush after nibbling on some awful-tasting plant instead of spitting it out.

Garcia's work and Seligman and Hager's analysis of it demonstrate the importance of ecological validity in interpreting research findings. In contrast to pairs of stimuli such as taste and nausea, which are especially likely in the rat's natural environment, and pairs of stimuli such as noise and nausea that are especially unlikely, the pairs of stimuli chosen for study in research into classical conditioning tend to fall somewhere in between. That is because they are not chosen for their representativeness of the animal's natural behavior in its natural context. They have no meaning for the animal, no place in its natural history. Instead, they are chosen because they conform to laboratory traditions, including the apparatus which has been developed over the years; or, as in Pavlov's case, for an entirely different kind of research which produced unexpected results. The connections which develop between the arbitrary pairs of stimuli that result are described by laws of behavior that apply only to those laboratory phenomena, but not to the real experiences animals have in their day-to-day lives. The gradual development of the conditioned response, and its gradual extinction, occur only in arbitrary laboratory experiences. In the animals' natural environment, conditioning is either instantaneous and permanent or it is impossible.

If Garcia's studies of classical conditioning and Seligman and Hager's biological preparedness explanation for their findings are applicable to other areas of research, much of what we know about behavior may apply only to unreal problems created for subjects in psychological laboratories, and not to the real behavior which goes on outside. This analysis is diametrically opposed to the viewpoint that has prevailed for most of the history of scientific psychology. It had been assumed that one of the great strengths of laboratory research lies in its very arbitrariness and the artificiality of the conditions under which it is conducted. If behavior is predictable in such an antiseptic climate, it must be even more so when the dramatic forces of nature act to shape it. The single abstract laboratory situation can thus simulate a great variety of real situations efficiently. And so on. But if we want to understand real behavior in real situations, can we really depend upon laboratory results, or the findings of any study in which behavior is in a context that is not designed to represent that reality?

Rarely has any threat to validity been exposed so clearly and documented so fully as the limited ecological validity of traditional studies of classical conditioning. Our remaining examples will show increasingly less strength in that direction. The first comes from the study of organizational decision-making. In the early 1960s, a graduate student at M.I.T. named Stoner (1961) designed a study of the effects of group discussion on the willingness of business decision-makers to take risks. At the core of his study were a series of hypothetical problems which individuals or groups could solve.

Each problem described a dilemma, or difficult decision, faced by a fictitious person. For example, an executive employed by a large corporation is offered a job by a new firm. This man has a comfortable income and good prospects for permanent employment at his present position. However, there is little likelihood that his status or income will improve much in the future; he has risen about as far as he can in the organization. The job he has been offered, on the other hand, offers competitive terms with his present ones, but the promise of much greater things in the future. If he moves to the new company, and the venture succeeds, he stands to achieve much higher status and financial rewards than his present and, seemingly, permanent ones. But there is a risk, should he decide to move, that the new business will fail. In that event, he will have lost the security and not inconsiderable rewards of his present position, presumably forever. How is this man to decide? Or how is an individual research subject, or a group of subjects, to decide for him?

Stoner's subjects read each case description, or dilemma, and then read a series of alternative solutions or responses to it. For each problem, the alternatives were phrased in terms of the amount of risk the hypothetical protagonist should be willing to accept in order to choose the problematic but potentially more rewarding alternative. Put another way, the subject is asked to decide, either individually or as the member of a group, how much of a risk is warranted by the promise of the more attractive but less secure alternative. With our present example, the choices range from 10% that the new company will succeed, with all its attendant benefits for the executive, to 30%, to 50%, to 70% to 90%. In other words, a subject can "advise" the person to move if there is one chance in ten of success, to take a large risk, to make the move only if success is 90% certain, to take only a small risk, or some alternative between those extremes. The problem also presents one other alternative that states that the person should not move, no matter what the risk.

Stoner first made use of these problems in a rather simple study which drew considerable attention. He first had business administration students respond to the series of problems as individuals. For each problem, then, he determined the level of risk each subject was willing to take. Then he grouped the subjects together randomly and asked them to discuss each problem and reach agreement on the best course of action. It was the finding of this study that proved so interesting to students of the decision-making process. For most of the problems, the decisions made by the groups were riskier than the average of the decisions previously made by the members of those groups as individuals. This phenomenon became known as the "risky shift." For most of the decade following Stoner's original study, investigators in many different locations worked to discover the cause of this difference between group and individual decisions. Why are people willing to take greater risks in groups than they are as individuals?

In the course of those many follow-up studies, it was made clear that Stoner's observations were reliable. They were reproduced repeatedly in studies which varied the characteristics of the decision-makers, the nature of the group discussion, and other aspects of the process in attempts to choose among a variety of explanations that were proposed. However, at a somewhat later date, a very different line of research began that was also aimed at understanding decision-making in groups. These studies were not bound together in the way that studies of the risky shift were. They were not based on the same materials or designed to test the same hypothesis. But what they did have in common was that their findings relate to the question of the tendency of decision-making groups to make risky decisions.

Because these studies are very different from one another, they need to be described individually. And for reasons of space, those descriptions will be very brief. Chris Argyris (1969) conducted one of them, a large-scale study of decision processes in groups. Instead of randomly constituted groups of students, he studied existing boards, committees and organizations in government, industry, and the academic world; such as corporate boards of directors, university boards of trustees, and government agency administrators. Observers sat in on their meetings as they discussed the normal problems of their organizations. On the basis of the system by which Argyris categorized their actions, it can be determined that the decisions made by these groups were characterized, for the most part, by a tendency to avoid taking risks. If any description fits, it is one of excessive caution, bound by past actions or traditions.

A social psychologist, Irving Janis (1972), has also studied group decision-making. Rather than observing the process directly, he chose to use historical records, first-hand accounts by participants in momentous government policy decisions such as the decision to sponsor the Bay of Pigs invasion of Cuba and the decision to establish the Marshall Plan to aid in rebuilding Europe after World War II. Although his data came from unusual sources, and they were analyzed somewhat more subjectively than is the custom in psychology, it is Janis's conclusions that are most important to this discussion. He found that the quality of many important group decisions suffered from the unwillingness of participants to risk stating unconventional or unpopular points of view. In fact, Janis has argued, based upon these findings, that there is a general tendency for group discussion to inhibit participants' presentation of new, innovative, risky courses of action to the group. He has also argued that outside the context of a group, individuals can and do generate such innovative solutions to problems, although they are unwilling to expose them to the scrutiny of others. This is in marked contrast to a theory advanced to explain the risky shift findings, which assumes that those who advocate extreme positions in a group discussion are encouraged to do so by the admiration other group members show for their adventurousness. Both Argyris's and Janis's findings have in common the point that the group decision-making process focuses participants' attention on their personal relationships with other group members and fosters conservative action by the group.

The last link in this chain of studies is much more directly comparable to the risky shift research. A team of researchers headed by Clark McCauley (1973) approached racetrack patrons immediately after they had placed a $2 "win" bet. They placed these bettors in groups of three and offered to buy each one a $2 win ticket if all three could agree to bet on a single horse. Needless to say, the groups were able to reach a decision. Then the odds on the horse each group agreed to bet on with the researcher's money were compared with the average odds on the three horses they had bet on individually immediately before. There was a clear tendency for the groups of bettors to choose horses with lower odds—that is, to make less risky or more conservative decisions—than the members of those groups did when acting as individuals. Their decisions were actually more risky when their own money was at stake than when the researcher's was.

It seems clear that the studies performed by Argyris, Janis, and McCauley all yielded findings that contradict the findings of the risky shift research. One possible explanation centers on the fact that the groups who participated in the risky shift studies made decisions that had no bearing at all on their own well-being. However, the members of real decision-making groups have a direct selfish interest in the quality of the decisions they reach. Subjects discussing Stoner's "choice dilemmas" do not stand to suffer at all if they suggest a risky course of action that brings ruin to the person who actually faces the problem. Furthermore, it seems clear that outside the confines of research, real members of real decision-making bodies tend to have a selfish interest in the outcome of their deliberations. Their jobs, the value of their stock, or at the very least their reputations ride on the decisions their groups make. It could be for these reasons that they are hesitant to take large risks, that they seek the comfort of traditional solutions to the problems at hand, and that they fear assuming responsibility for influencing the group decision. Moreover, the decision makers in Argyris's and Janis's studies were members of groups who met regularly over extensive periods and whose members were drawn from the staffs of single organizations. Therefore, the relationships among the group members, as well as the consequences of the group's decisions, were likely to be with the participants for a long time afterward.

One way of choosing between the conflicting findings of these two groups of studies is on the basis of their ecological validity. The risky shift studies placed an unnatural form of group decision-making in an unnatural context. The decisions made in the studies which showed that groups tend to be more conservative than individuals were more like the decisions made by real decision-making groups. And those decisions were made in the same natural contexts. Finally, one could conclude that the findings of risky shift studies do not generalize to true group decision-making, because the decisions they studied and the contexts in which they were studied were not representative. In other words, those findings lack ecological validity.

Our final example is completely in the form of an argument. In his recent book, *Cognition and Reality,* Ulrich Neisser (1976) has criticized traditional research in the area of human learning. Many years ago, Herman Ebbinghaus began a tradition of studying human memory, which still exerts a profound influence on that field. He invented nonsense syllables as material for the subjects' learning tasks (Ebbinghaus himself was the only subject in most of his research). This eliminated past experience with meaningful material such as words from intruding into the subjects' performance. The nonsense syllables were presented one at a time, one pair at a time, or in some arrangement in which the pace of the presentation could be controlled very precisely. The subject learned the material simply because the researcher required it.

Neisser points out that every feature of the traditional human learning or memory study is obviously different from the learning or memory tasks people face in their everyday lives. The material in the research study is meaningless or disconnected or broken down into small parts or all those things. The natural material is meaningful, connected, and encountered in much larger pieces, if not as a complete entity. The research material is presented at the researcher's pace, whereas the natural material is absorbed at the reader's own pace. The research subject has no good personal reason for performing the task, whereas the reader in nature wants or needs to learn or to remember. These are not Neisser's exact words, but that is the point of his argument. There is altogether too great a possibility that research findings about human learning and memory are based on procedures that misrepresent crucial features of the natural learning or memory task and the context in which that task is performed. Those procedures and the apparatus used in carrying them out make research efficient and easy to understand. But the value of the findings is threatened by their lack of ecological validity. The findings may give us a misleading picture of the behavior we want to understand.

In all our examples, we have seen the creation of frameworks within which behavior can be studied. In each case, the features of the real behaviors and the natural contexts of those behaviors to which the original conceptual hypotheses were directed were represented in ways that resulted in research findings whose applicability to real behavior was questionable at best, and unquestionably misleading at worst. How can the ecological validity of research findings be maximized? One of the most obvious ways is to investigate real phenomena. The more that research is based on observations made in natural settings, and the less that the researcher intrudes into the setting or constrains the behavior that takes place there, creates the task to which subjects respond, directs the subjects' behavior, or selects from that behavior so that it fits what happens into some measuring device or technique, the more likely will the behavior that is observed and the findings of the research being undertaken represent real behavior in its natural context. The field is simply more real than the laboratory.

At the same time, two reservations to the statement above must be pointed out. First, conducting research in the field does not guarantee the ecological validity of its findings. One real setting is not necessarily representative of a wide range of other real settings. Thus, even the findings of a field study could have only limited ecological validity. Furthermore, the selectivity that is inherent in a researcher choosing which aspects of a real behavior to attend to, and a form into which observations of the chosen aspects are to be fit, can also reduce the ecological validity of the findings of field research. Second, the fact that research is conducted in a laboratory, in a setting that does not resemble the real world in its superficial appearance, does not guarantee that the findings of that research will not have ecological validity. It is possible to represent the essential features of a real behavior in its natural context in the abstract form of a laboratory setting.

If it is not so simple as laboratory versus field, how can we know whether research findings have sufficient ecological validity? As is so often the case, the answer is one that is painful to accept. If research findings have applicability to a real behavior as it occurs in its natural setting, then it should be possible to make predictions about that real behavior based on the findings of research that has been addressed to it. In fact, if predictions about real behavior in its natural contexts are unimportant, when research is directed solely toward testing a theory about behavior, then ecological validity fades as an issue. But when it is an issue, the proof is in the pudding. If research findings map onto the real world accurately, then one can be assured that the behavior that was studied and the contexts in which the research was performed were representative of the natural behavior in its natural context. Any researcher who plans to test the ecological validity of his or her findings in this way is likely to pay close attention to the representativeness of research procedures, and the problem of ecological validity is likely to be minimized.

The prescriptions offered above are not as clear-cut as they might be, but, then, neither is the problem of ecological validity. Perhaps even more than the other threats to external validity, it is difficult to quantify and to cope with. It is also distinct from all the other threats to validity in that it is not always a handicap for research findings to lack ecological validity. Or so some have argued. I first encountered this argument at a meeting of social psychologists. Paul

Rosenkrantz, of Holy Cross College, was a participant in one of the panel discussions at that meeting. Although I forget the exact context of his remarks, the point was that psychological research can and ought to be directed not just to understanding behavior that occurs naturally around us, but also to possible alternatives to that behavior. Many natural behaviors, including those elicited by the traditional sex roles that were discussed at that meeting, pose problems for individuals and for the society at large. In some cases, it is possible to envision alternative forms of behavior that might have fewer drawbacks and more benefits, but which do not occur spontaneously in nature. Or they may not occur often or widely enough to make careful study of them feasible. In such an event, one of the great strengths of the scientific method can be utilized. Artificial conditions can be created, either in the laboratory or even in a natural setting, which will cause subjects to perform the behavior in question. That may be the only way in which that behavior can be evaluated.

This problem of investigating rare or even nonexistent behaviors has been stated in other terms as well. One current school of thought among critics of research methods is called the dialectical approach. For every behavior or relationship between a behavior and its causes, there is possible an opposite response to the situation or causal relationship. When one describes the naturally occurring behavior or relationship, or the most common form of it, it is argued, one endorses at the same time its appropriateness and rules out alternative possibilities.

Research findings inform the readers about the nature of the universe. This leaves the impression that what happens in nature is inevitable, and that it is good at least in the sense it was meant to happen. But racism is no more natural than brotherhood. It simply reflects the existence of one set of conditions, perhaps economic or political, that are conducive to it. To create the necessary conditions for brotherhood, by studying the rare or even hypothetical behaviors involved, one does no disservice to reality. The dialectical alternative is real in the sense that it is the rest of the picture of the behavior that may occur in our world. It even does occur, although more rarely and less conspicuously. And in some ways, it is more important to understand the rare or hypothetical than the real; it gives true perspective to what we can see with our own eyes. We know that behavior does "change" over time and across cultures. Research findings that reflect only the current state of a single culture mislead us about the true nature of behavior. By studying behavior that is not produced by real events, we can understand better the causes of real behavior. As Rosenkrantz speculated several years ago, science can emphasize ecological validity to the extent that if a scientist studying gravity dropped 100 balls and one of them did not fall, the research report would mention only the overwhelming consistency of the 99 that did. But the ball that did not fall might tell us much more about gravity than the 99 that did. Although research findings certainly do not maximize ecological validity as a general rule, the point that the most interesting and useful behaviors can be ignored in the effort to achieve ecological validity is an important one.

There is one final point that needs to be made, at the risk of having you jerk your head back in the other direction too quickly. One of the ways in which we can evaluate the ecological validity of psychological research, albeit indirectly, is by cataloging the topics which the research addresses. There are many important natural behaviors, I would argue, to which researchers have paid disproportionately little attention. Sexual behavior stands out as an obvious example. In reading a social psychology textbook chapter addressed to that topic, I was struck by the fact that the research cited was concentrated in such areas as responses to erotic stimuli and the effects that viewing nudity has on aggression and other behaviors. Nowhere in that chapter did I find an examination of sexual behavior itself—the intimate stimulation of one partner by another. Although I cannot document it, I feel that this small example points up a much larger issue. Psychologists have traditionally been committed to research methods which require the direct observation of behavior. We watch subjects act or we ask them about their actions or feelings after they have been exposed to some situation which we have created or, at least, which we have monitored as it occurred naturally. In any case, the use of such methods is restricted for the most part to behaviors that take place in public places or what subjects are willing to expose to us. We cannot, ordinarily, gain access to the most intimate, and perhaps most important, acts which social norms define as private or intimate or inappropriate for inspection by a third party. Only methods that utilize indirect observations, such as those included in literature or the other arts, or those revealed indirectly by public records of their outcomes (medical treatment and drug prescriptions, births and deaths, marriages and divorces, and the like), can allow us to pursue the causes of such intimate behaviors. It is only through such approaches that the research literature of psychology as a whole will be able to fill in the gaps in knowledge which threaten its overall ecological validity.

## CONCLUSION

Although we have considered four categories of threats to external validity separately—nonrepresentative sampling, reactivity, nonrepresentative research context, and ecological validity—in all four cases we have seen variations on one common theme. In each case, the general issue is how well the key functional features of some behavior-environment relationship are represented in the more or less cryptic form of a research study. In every research study, the combination or pattern of the subjects who are acting, their feelings about their actions, and the features of their environment to which they are responding differs from their counterparts in the context in which the behavior occurs naturally. But it is this latter natural form of the behavior that must be understood. Therefore, the possibility that the obvious differences between the research context and the natural context could produce differences in the behavior, or in the relationships between the behavior and the causal factors whose effects need to be understood makes the use of the research results, as a guide for understanding the natural behavior, problematic. Put in the words we have been using up to now, the research results may not be generalizable to the natural forms of the behavior.

Without external validity, even research findings with perfect internal validity, which leave no question about the effects of the causal factors in the research context, have limited practical or theoretical value. No one has any use for information about the causes of behavior that occurs only in one idiosyncratic, artificial setting. Nor is there any use for a theory that holds only for such a limited form of behavior. Research findings must be representative of a meaningful variety of naturally occurring behaviors in their natural contexts. The broader the generalizability of the results, the greater their external validity and the greater, all other things being equal, their overall value.

However, the threats to external validity can never be eliminated entirely. No sample of research subjects can be representative of all the organisms to which the research results might apply. Even a series of studies, each utilizing different kinds of subjects, cannot assure such generalizability. And the same might be said of the procedures and contexts that are represented in any study or series of studies. There will always be the issue of generalizing from one context to another. Every behavior is performed by a variety of organisms in an endless variety of contexts. It is impossible to investigate each of these organisms and contexts or their combinations directly. External validity can be perfect only if the research context is a perfect analogue of each of the contexts in which the behavior needs to be understood.

In addition to this general problem of the comparability of research contexts with contexts to which research results might be generalized, there is an even more difficult problem. If we can assume, for a moment, that a hypothesized relationship between some causal factor and some behavior does, in fact, exist—without qualification or exception—producing research findings that support the hypothesis depends on creating a research context which permits the hypothesized relationship to be observed.

The causal factor being studied must be represented by a stimulus which is chosen or created so that it elicits the behavior in question. That stimulus must appear in a context that is free of other stimuli that would interfere with its effects on the behavior, either by masking or augmenting them. Also, a measuring instrument must be applied to the behavior that is sensitive to the effects of the stimulus that represents the hypothesized causal factor. All these choices influence the likelihood that a true causal relationship will be confirmed by the findings of a particular research study. What one finds in the research depends not only on what is really "out there," but also on how and where one looks for it.

Recent research into the phenomenon of autonomic conditioning illustrates both this problem and its relationship to the broader problem of generalizability of research findings (see Obrist, Black, Brener, and DiCara, 1974, for review of this area). In the middle 1960s, Neal Miller and others working in his laboratory reported a remarkable research finding. They found that rats were able to reduce their heart rates by about 20% when reinforced for doing so by electrical stimulation of the brain or the avoidance of shock. The rats were tested while under the influence of curare. This procedure was used to rule out the possibility that the reinforcement merely affected some muscle activity, which then only secondarily affected the animals' heart rates. Thus, it could be reported that activities controlled by the autonomic nervous system, previously known as the involuntary nervous system, could be brought under direct voluntary control.

These findings were extremely important for two reasons. First, they led to a new conception of the relationship between visceral and somatomotor processes—for one thing, the notion of voluntariness seemed like an oversimplification in light of these new findings. Second, these findings sparked the development of a variety of so-called biofeedback treatments for human medical and psychological problems such as hypertension, migraine headaches, and chronic pain. However, as investigators around the country began to follow up on the initial reports from Miller's laboratory, a funny thing happened to the original findings—they could not be reproduced. Even the researchers who produced them in the first place could not do it again. According to one review of the total effort, there was a steady, very regular decline in the magnitude of the observed effect during the five years following the first studies.

In laboratories all over the country, the scientists involved in the study of autonomic conditioning made an intensive effort to discover the cause of this apparent shrinkage in the phenomenon. Although their efforts met with very little concrete success, they developed several hypotheses about it. One suggested that changes (technological improvements really) in the procedures used to maintain the curarized rats by artificial respiration were responsible. Another focused on changes in the design of the respirators themselves. Some proponents of these first two hypotheses claimed that in the early experiments, a lack of sophistication about the artificial respiration procedure resulted in the animals developing extremely high initial heart rates. Against these baseline figures, the reduction that resulted from the conditioning procedure was artificially large. Still another hypothesis was based on the variations in the process of manufacturing the curare compound used in the early experiments. Unfortunately, no progress was made toward determining whether an unusual batch of the drug had been used in just those experiments. Miller himself believed that improvements in the conditions under which the rats were used as subjects in these experiments might have produced a different strain with a lower level of emotionality. Like all the other hypotheses, this one was never substantiated.

Ironically, it now appears that curarization, the factor common to most of the presumed causes of the difficulties in reproducing the original findings, never did serve its intended purpose of ruling out any involvement of somatomotor processes in heart rate changes. But, regardless of their cause, what is the significance of these events? If it is true that the magnitude of the research finding of heart rate conditioning depends on the particular context in which the experiment is conducted, what does this say about the original hypothesis? Are the developments in theories about the nervous system and in therapeutic techniques tainted by the lack of dependability of the research findings? In this case, it seems possible that the alterations in the original findings do not mean that the findings were not real, that is, a product of some fortuitous set of circumstances that occurred in the original experiments but not afterward or elsewhere, but merely that the particular experiments in which those findings were obtained could not be repeated. In any case, only the magnitude of the findings changed. The effect never disappeared completely or changed direction. That may be why it has been possible to use the original findings as a base for further progress in theory, research, and application, even while they were changing.

The experiences of those investigating the voluntary control of visceral responses is not unique or even unusual in psychology or in other sciences. Failures to replicate research results, inconsistencies from one laboratory to another or from one time to another even in the same laboratory, and conflicts among experimental findings in general are common. These inconsistencies reflect two intrinsic properties of research. One is that the context in which a hypothesis is tested influences the findings. Different contexts produce different outcomes. Another is that a research study produces only an estimate of what exists in reality. The accuracy of that estimate depends on the extent to which all the threats to validity we have discussed in these last two chapters are ruled out. But no matter how successfully that has been done, a measurement is still only an estimate. Some error is bound to intrude.

At this point, it might be useful to go back over some of the ground we covered earlier, aided by the fuller perspective provided more recently by the additional information. Now that we have discussed the threats to both internal and external validity and been introduced to some of the ways of reducing or even eliminating them from research findings, we need to see how they are related. First, it is often said that increasing either internal or external validity, guarding against the problems that threaten one of them, is bound to have a negative effect on the other. It would not be surprising if your reading up to this point had already given you at least a slight suspicion of that. To give just one brief example, one can increase external validity, other things being equal, by conducting research in the field. For one thing, this can have the effect of decreasing reactivity. For another, it can put the behavior being studied into a context more similar to one that occurs in nature and thus increase the generalizability of the research findings to the natural forms of that behavior. In other words, the ecological validity of research findings can be increased in this way. At the same time, however, it is more difficult to safeguard research findings against some of the threats to internal validity in a field setting. It is also more difficult to know, much less to eliminate, the influence of extraneous events, group composition effects, and other threats to internal validity. This does not mean, however, that internal and external validity are inherently antagonistic to one another. Although the simplistic approaches to each of them contributes to that impression, innovations like Cook's method of studying the reduction of prejudice demonstrate that both internal and external validity can be increased at the same time, by the same procedure, even if this is not usually the case. The problem is soluble, but not easily. The conflict is not inevitable, just common.

The very act of discussing the relationship between internal and external validity implies that they are two separate problems. The way the presentation in this book, and in others, is organized reinforces that impression. Of course, it is not accurate. Any threat to the validity of a research result makes the interpretation of that result ambiguous. To say that the validity of the research finding is threatened means that there is some doubt about what it means. As we have seen, there are many kinds of doubts. Dividing them up into the two categories of internal and external validity is more for convenience than anything else. Given our limited knowledge of these problems, it is easier to think about one group of them at a time than all of them at the same time. In the same way, listing the threats to validity under separate category labels disguises the fact that they are not independent of one another. They are related. Some problems transcend the arbitrary barriers of these separate categories and can be placed in just one only by ignoring their relationship to other categories. Again, it is a matter of simplifying complex matters in the hopes of making them easier to understand. We just need to keep in mind what it is that we are actually doing. In the same vein, do not be misled into thinking that we have considered all the possible threats to validity. These are only the ones that have been most widely recognized up to now.

Another question we considered earlier bears a brief repetition here. That involves the relative importance of internal and external validity. This is not really a very meaningful question. Research findings cannot have external validity if they do not also have internal validity. We cannot generalize findings correctly to anything if they are simply artifacts produced by the unintended influence of unrecognized causal factors within the research setting. By the same token, what sense does it make to claim that a research finding has internal validity if that means only that it provides a clear understanding of some behavior which occurs only under the unique set of conditions in which it was studied, or which is unlike any real behavior in which organisms engage spontaneously in their natural environments?

To end this chapter and this section, we need to point out the extent of the silver lining among all the dark clouds we have been exploring for so long. There have been hopeful signs sprinkled throughout, to be sure, but because we have been looking at problems primarily, one could easily become pessimistic about the state of behavioral research, or even about its future prospects. But there is an important difference between skepticism and pessimism that needs to be recognized here. You should be skeptical about research findings because they are fraught with problems, but not pessimistic because there is great promise that those problems can be solved. And even though research findings may be difficult to evaluate, they provide essential information. This is a good time to look at some of the reasons we can be optimistic, although perhaps cautiously, about the future of behavioral research.

The first of these hopeful signs is one we have considered before. A rival hypothesis that exists for a research finding poses a danger only if that rival hypothesis is a plausible one. For example, regardless of the composition of the sample of research subjects on whose behavior a finding is based, there are bound to be other organisms who differ from them in some way. That by itself is no reason for despair. We only have a strong reason to doubt the applicability of research findings if the difference between the research sample and the group to which we want to generalize the findings is one we know to be relevant to the behavior in question. No matter what the particular threat to validity is, the same general argument applies. The existence of logical alternatives to the hypothesis being tested is not in itself a compelling reason for discounting a research finding. If, however, there is some evidence or a respectable theory which supports the plausibility of that alternative, then we may not be able to place much confidence in the findings of the research study that fails to rule it out.

There is another point that is closely related to that first one. Scientists are trained to be conservative in their work. That means that they accept new research findings only after they are satisfied that they are subject to no alternative explanations. In their effort to rule out all possible artifacts, scientists tend to be the first to discover the existence of rival hypotheses and to indicate the ambiguity in research findings. Unfortunately, this analysis is often misinterpreted by people who merely read about scientific research. Those readers often assume that the research in question has no value, that it brings the truth no closer than it was before. In addition, politicians and others who formulate public policy often capitalize on this situation to justify taking courses of action which are based, in reality, on their own selfish interests. They can tell the public, who are probably already familiar with the tentative way in which research findings are presented, that scientists are never sure of or in agreement about anything. However, because there are alternative explanations for research findings, it does not mean that those findings are worthless. Unless the evidence for the alternative is as strong as the evidence for the original hypothesis, the research findings in question are certainly better than no objective evidence at all. And they are clearly superior to total ignorance or to someone's desire for political gain or personal profit.

Another positive point, which has been stressed by many defenders of research methods in psychology, involves the distinction, which we also considered earlier, between normative research studies and tests of hypotheses about the basic processes underlying behavior. Even if the behavior of one group of subjects differs from the behavior of another group, for example, it is still possible that both groups' behavior follows the same basic rule. Children may respond more strongly to candy and bankers to money—a normative difference—but both groups might still be behaving in ways that result in pleasurable outcomes; that is, the same basic principle of reinforcement may underlie the behavior of both groups. Unfortunately, the distinction between normative findings, what certain subjects do under certain conditions, and basic processes, the mechanisms underlying their behavior, is not always clear. Consider a study performed by social psychologists Bibb Latane and James Dabbs (1975) as an example. They compared the amount of help given to men and women who dropped an armload of books in an elevator. They made that comparison in several locations around the United States. Women received more help overall, but the difference was clearly greater in the South than in the Midwest or the Northeast. Does this mean that there are different norms for this kind of helping behavior in different regions of our country, or did the behavior of the three groups of subjects follow different rules? Cases like this one seem to fall in one of those all-too-common gray areas that make all our rules difficult to apply. In any case, however, we clearly need to be more concerned about the consistency of evidence for the operation of basic processes than we do about the consistency of normative findings.

Another reason for optimism about our research methods has been pointed out by two researchers who have collaborated frequently to analyze psychological research. Robert Rosenthal and Ralph Rosnow (1969) have described what might be called the natural history of a threat to the validity of research findings. At first, the problem goes unrecognized. The research findings affected are in error. Once it has been discovered, it becomes a problem for researchers to solve. They need to develop research methods to eliminate it in order to do their work. Finally, the threat to validity becomes the topic of systematic research in its own right. Interest develops in how experimenters' expectancies affect their subjects' behavior or in how people from different cultures respond to perceptual illusions. Two lessons may be drawn from this sequence of events. First, many problems have, in fact, been recognized and dealt with, although some more satisfactorily than others. Even if a perfect scientific method were possible, it would take time. It would also require a continuing commitment to research. No problems will ever be solved if researchers throw up their hands and abandon a very fruitful way of answering important questions. In addition to this promise for the future, a great deal has already been learned about behavior in the course of studying the research process which is, after all, a form of behavior itself.

Finally, we need to keep threats to validity in their proper perspective. The fact that a research study fails to rule out all the possible threats to the validity of its findings does not mean that it has failed. As we will see in the coming chapters, every method for doing research, called a research design, has its weaknesses as well as its strengths. Therefore, the task of the researcher need not be seen as either the production of a perfect research study or a completely unambiguous research finding. Rather, it can only be to design the best possible research study that will provide the least ambiguous answer to a particular question. Many people, including researchers, have believed mistakenly that the scientific method is a foolproof formula for producing the absolute truth. This belief has had a number of unfortunate consequences. It has led some to assume that any means of applying the scientific method, any research design, is bound to produce a valid outcome. We have seen already how untrue that is. It has also produced a lack of tolerance for the ambiguities that are inherent in the research process and an unjustified lack of confidence in scientific research findings. If a flaw is apparent in a particular research study, if even an implausible rival hypothesis suggests itself, those who hold these rigid beliefs assume that the researcher must have been incompetent and could have produced a flawless result if only the scientific method had been applied correctly. Instead of facing up to the problems involved and attempting to resolve them— instead of trying to perfect research methods in a systematic manner—many have simply totally rejected methods that are viewed as presenting problems of interpretation or research findings that appear to have less than perfect validity. If we have learned nothing else, it is that this approach is wrong. Every research finding has some chance of being an incorrect answer to the question being studied. The job of the scientist is to reduce that chance to the absolute minimum. That will be enough to guarantee the value of that finding among answers generated by other approaches.

As we consider the possible designs for research, in the following chapters, and the strengths and weaknesses of each, bear in mind that we are learning not only about the problems of interpreting research findings, but also about the promise of methods that can be used to learn the answers to important questions about behavior. We will see that it is possible to match the potential of a research design to the requirements of the hypothesis that one wishes to test. In the process, we will be introduced to an exciting possibility which a rigid true-or-false approach to research methods precludes. A hypothesis can be put to a series of tests by a variety of research designs which have complementary strengths and weaknesses. In this way, we can get closer to the truth than any single research study ever could.

## REFERENCES

Argyris, C. The incompleteness of social-psychological theory: Examples from small groups, cognitive consistency, and attribution research. *American Psychologist*, 1969, *24*, 893–900.

Asch, S. E. Studies of independence and conformity: A minority of one against a unanimous majority. *Psychological Monographs,* 1956, *70* (Whole No. 416).

Cherulnik, P. D., & Sherman, M. F. The expression of belief in internal control as a strategic response. *Journal of Social Psychology*, 1976, *99*, 299–300.

Cook, S. W. *The effect of unintended racial contact upon racial interaction and attitude change.* Washington, D.C.: U.S. Office of Education, Bureau of Research, 1971.

Coutts, L. M., & Schneider, F. W.. Visual behavior in an unfocused interaction as a function of sex and distance. *Journal of Experimental Social Psychology,* 1975, *11,* 64–77.

Deci, E. L. *Intrinsic motivation.* New York: Plenum, 1975.

Gergen, K. J. Social psychology as history. *Journal of Personality and Social Psychology,* 1973, *26,* 309–320.

Helmreich, R., Aronson, E., & Lefan, J. To err is humanizing—sometimes: Effects of self-esteem, competence, and a pratfall on interpersonal attraction. *Journal of Personality and Social Psychology,* 1970, *16,* 259–264.

Janis, I. L. *Victims of groupthink.* Boston: Houghton Mifflin, 1972.

Latane, B., & Dabbs, J. M. Sex, group size, and helping in three cities. *Sociometry,* 1975, *38,* 180–194.

McCauley, C., Stitt, C. L., Woods, K., & Lipton, D. Group shift to caution at the racetrack. *Journal of Experimental Social Psychology,* 1973, *9,* 80–86.

Milgram, S. Nationality and conformity. *Scientific American,* 1961, *205*(6), 45–51.

Milgram, S. Behavioral study of obedience. *Journal of Abnormal and Social Psychology,* 1963, *67,* 371–378.

Neisser, U. *Cognition and Reality.* San Francisco: Freeman, 1976.

Obrist, P. A., Block, A. H., Brener, J., & DiCara, L. V. (Eds.). *Cardiovascular psychophysiology.* Chicago: Aldine, 1974.

Olton, D. S. Mazes, maps, and memory. *American Psychologist,* 1979, *34,* 583–596.

Orne, M. T. On the social psychology of the psychological experiment: With particular reference to demand characteristics and their implications. *American Psychologist,* 1962, *17,* 776–783.

Page, M. M. Demand characteristics and the verbal operant conditioning experiment. *Journal of Personality and Social Psychology,* 1972, *23,* 372–378.

Rosenberg, M. J. The conditions and consequences of evaluation apprehension. In R. Rosenthal and R. Rosnow (Eds.), *Artifact in behavioral research.* New York: Academic Press, 1969. Pp. 280–349.

Rosenthal, R. & Rosnow, R. L. (Eds.) *Artifact in behavioral research.* New York: Academic Press, 1969.

Rosnow, R. L., & Suls, J. Reactive effects of pretesting in attitude research. *Journal of Personality and Social Psychology,* 1970, *15,* 338–343.

Seligman, M. E., & Hager, J. L. Biological boundaries of learning: The sauce-Bernaise syndrome. *Psychology Today,* 1972, *6*(3), 59–61; 84–87.

Stone, L. *The family, sex and marriage: England 1500–1800.* New York: Harper & Row, 1977.

Stoner, J. A. F. *A comparison of individual and group decisions involving risk.* Unpublished master's thesis, School of Industrial Management, M.I.T., 1961.

Terman, L. M. *Genetic studies of genius,* Vol 1. Stanford, CA: Stanford University Press, 1925.

White, B. L. *The first three years of life.* Englewood Cliffs, N.J.: Prentice-Hall, 1975.

Wicklund, R. A. Objective self-awareness. In L. Berkowitz (Ed.), *Advances in experimental social psychology,* Vol. 9. New York: Academic Press, 1975.

## SUGGESTED ACTIVITIES

### Study Questions

1. What is external validity? Why can threats to external validity never be eliminated completely? In what sense must all research studies be specific rather than general?
2. How can nonrepresentative sampling threaten the validity of research findings? How could researchers' choices of subjects be altered to reduce the threat? Which kinds of research are most vulnerable to the threat of nonrepresentative sampling? Which are least vulnerable? What arguments would you use to justify the continued use of animals in research aimed at understanding human behavior?
3. How does subjects' knowledge that they are being studied affect their behavior? In what sense does this restrict the generalizability of the research findings based on that behavior? How can research be carried out free from reactivity? In cases in which absolute freedom from reactivity is not possible, how can one determine the extent to which research findings are limited by the reactive arrangements under which they are produced?
4. How is the generalizability of research findings limited, inevitably, by the context in which the research takes place (both the context provided by

the research setting itself and the sociocultural context within which the research takes place)? How can generalizability across settings be maximized?

5. What does it mean when we say that research findings have ecological validity? Distinguish between findings for which ecological validity is a major issue and findings for which it is a less important issue. What kinds of research are likely to produce findings with the greatest ecological validity?

# Part II
# DESIGNS FOR
# RESEARCH

# Chapter 4
# Systematic Evaluation of Research Designs: The Validity Scorecard

## INTRODUCTION

Every research study is a comparison between what happens under one set of conditions and what happens under another (or a number of others). In psychology, it is behavior that is compared across different conditions as it occurs in the presence of different events. A research study is usually based on a conceptual hypothesis that predicts the effects of those conditions or events on a particular behavior. But that effect can be evaluated only by comparing the behavior which occurs under that specified condition with behavior that occurs under different conditions.

In the simplest case, we could compare behavior that followed the event specified in the hypothesis with behavior that was not preceded by that particular event. Comparison would be the only way to learn whether the form of the behavior that was observed was influenced by the event in question. For example, take the hypothesis that varied stimulation early in life promotes intellectual development. A test of the hypothesis would clearly require that some organisms be reared in environments containing varied stimulation, and that their intellectual development be assessed at some "later" point. But no conclusion could be drawn about the effects of early stimulation on their intellectual development unless they were compared with other organisms reared under different conditions. In order to evaluate the hypothesis, it is necessary to learn more than the fact that high intellect is associated with varied early stimulation. It might also be associated with uniform early stimulation. This issue is just the small tip of a much larger, more general iceberg. What we learn from any research study about the conceptual hypothesis depends upon the particular comparisons we make.

What must happen, then, in constructing a test of the conceptual hypothesis is another step in the process of translating the general statement made in the conceptual hypothesis into the particular question known as the research hypothesis. A plan must be developed that specifies the comparisons to be made in the research study, including descriptions of the subjects to be compared and the sequences of events to which each group of subjects is to be exposed. This plan is called the *research design.* The use of a particular research design represents the selection of just one of a number of possible alternative tests of the conceptual hypothesis. More than selecting the specific techniques and procedures which are to be used (instructions, apparatus, instruments to measure behavior, etc.), the research design determines the basic form of the research study—more what is to be done than how. That point should become clear in the chapters ahead.

To further illustrate the concept of a research design and the ways in which choices are made among alternative designs, let us return again to the example we considered in Chapter 1. The conceptual hypothesis that expectations affect performance was tested by comparing two groups of subjects who were selected at random. An attempt was made to influence their expectations in performing a specific task in different directions. One group was given instructions designed to lead them to expect to do well on that task. The second was led to believe they would do poorly. The research hypothesis, then, predicted that the first group would perform better on the task than would the second. That is a description of the basic research design, the plan which specifies who will be compared and how. In Chapter 1, we also considered an alternative research design for testing the same conceptual hypothesis. According to that plan, two groups of children entering school who had positive and negative expectations for their academic performance were to be identified. Then their actual performance was to be compared. As we saw then, the choice of groups to be compared makes an important difference in the kinds of conclusions, or findings, which can be drawn from the results of the study. We saw that different comparisons, different research designs, produced results whose interpretation raised different kinds of questions.

Knowing what we do now, we could say that the conclusions drawn from the results produced by these alternative research designs—the findings of these two research studies—are vulnerable to different threats to their validity. Their results are open to different kinds of alternative explanations or rival hypotheses. But the research designs and the threats to validity considered in Chapter 1 just happened to be relevant to that particular hypothesis. In the last two chapters, we have acquainted ourselves more systematically with the important factors which affect the validity of research findings. Now it is time to make use of that knowledge. In the next several chapters, we will consider how the role played by each of those threats to validity depends on the particular research design that is chosen for testing a conceptual hypothesis. As we continue, of course, we will be learning about the variety of available research designs. We will also learn that a researcher's choice among the designs is limited by the very nature of the question that needs to be answered. He or she may not be able to choose among all the possible designs for research, but only among a subset of designs which are appropriate to the conceptual hypothesis. But at that point, in which the available alternatives have been identified, how is the choice to be made and how is the interpretation of the research results affected by that choice?

Those are the principal questions to which this book is addressed. Our attention has been focused so far on learning a vocabulary that we can use to discuss the components of the research process and the ways in which that process can be evaluated. Now we are going to put together all of what we have learned in order to evaluate the research designs used to study behavior. And we are going to go about that task systematically. For every research design we consider, we will estimate how serious a problem is posed by each of the 12 threats to validity we learned about in Chapters 2 and 3. The outcome of our evaluations will be recorded graphically on the *Validity Scorecard.* But before we reach that point, we need to learn how to use a set of symbols which can be used to portray research designs efficiently. In the process, we will also be able to gain a preliminary view of three categories of research designs we will be evaluating in the next three chapters. Ten basic symbols enable us to represent all the research designs we will be considering. In order to introduce and define them, together with some of their variations, we will need to consider the basic types of research designs.

## SYMBOLS FOR REPRESENTING RESEARCH DESIGNS

Each of the research designs we will learn about will contain plans for one or more groups of subjects. I realize that we have already seen that it is difficult to draw any conclusions about a single group of subjects. However, to introduce the topic of research designs, we are going to be looking at some designs, called "preexperimental," that contain just one group of subjects. Although these designs are not used much in psychology, there are questions that can only be answered by observing a single group of subjects. By evaluating the answers provided by these designs we will have a better appreciation of the answers provided by the more sophisticated designs to come later. Ironically, we will eventually return to some more complex single-group designs that can be powerful tools for psychological research.

In every design we will be considering, whether one group of subjects is being studied or 12, the treatment of each group is represented by a separate line or row of symbols. Thus the row is really our first symbol. It tells us that all the operations described on the row refer to the same specific group of subjects. The way that those operations are arranged is itself important. As we go along each row, from left to right, we are following the temporal sequence of the events that are experienced by the group of subjects involved. The first event is represented by the first symbol in the row, and so on.

So far, then, each row in a symbolic representation of a design is allotted to a separate group of subjects and each event planned for those subjects is represented by a symbol. The order of those symbols along the row, from left to right, represents the time sequence of those events. The operation represented by a symbol which is farther to the left in the row occurs earlier. In addition, if there is more than one group included in a design, each row will begin with the letter G and the groups will be numbered from the top row to the bottom by adding subscripts to the Gs. From the top of a multigroup design to the bottom, the rows will begin with $G_1$, $G_2$, and so on, so that we can refer to Group 1, Group 2, and so on, when we describe what is going on.

Now it is time to introduce the symbols we are going to use for the two important classes of events to which research subjects are exposed in every research study. We introduced these events, in the form of the independent and dependent variables, in Chapter 1. First, in every study subjects are exposed to some event which is supposed to represent the causal factor referred to in the hypothesis. When it is an event created by the researcher, this is usually referred to as the experimental treatment (even though, as we will see a little later, not all such studies are experiments). But whatever it is called, we use the symbol X to represent this kind of event. In some multi-group designs, different groups of subjects are exposed to different kinds of events. For example, it is often necessary to compare different strengths or intensities of an event that is hypothesized to influence subjects' behavior. In many classic studies of motivation, animal subjects were deprived of food for varying lengths of time, such as 0, 4, 8, 12, 24, and 48 hours. These deprivation conditions represent quantitative variations of a single independent variable or experimental treatment. These studies (or one aspect of them at least) compared their effects on the animals' behavior. We use subscripts to identify variations such as that. In the simplest case, two contrasting treatments could be represented by the symbols $X_1$ and $X_2$. Or we might want to use more descriptive subscripts, in specific cases, to make the different variations of a treatment easier to identify. The treatments in the motivation study alluded to above could be symbolized as $X_0$, $X_4$, $X_8$, $X_{12}$, $X_{24}$, and $X_{48}$. Our old standby, the laboratory study which was performed to determine the effects of expectations on performance, contained two treatments. The sequences of events which were intended to produce expectations of success and failure in that study might be represented by the symbols $X_S$ and $X_F$, respectively.

In addition to the experimental treatment that is expected to have an effect on their behavior, every group of research subjects is exposed to an event that is designed to measure the effects of that treatment. That measurement operation, which could consist of subjects' performance on a task or their responses to a questionnaire or even the public record of their divorces, to give just a few examples, is represented by the symbol O. We can also use subscripts to differentiate between the dependent measures that are administered to different groups of subjects within a single research design. Ordinarily, although different groups of subjects in a study are exposed to different treatments (Xs), all are subjected to the same assessment of their behavior (the hypothesis predicts the effects of different conditions on a single behavior). The use of subscripts for the dependent measures, then, is not to denote different events, but to keep track of the scores for the different groups of subjects. When we have occasion to refer to the effects of different treatments or to compare the behavior of different groups of subjects, it will be helpful to label the measurement operations applied to those groups, after the different treatments. We can then use expressions such as $O_1$ versus $O_2$ or $O_2 > O_1$, rather than having to say "the performance of Group 1 versus the performance of Group 2," or "the effects of $X_1$ versus the effects of $X_2$," and so on. We can also use letters as subscripts as we did for the study of expectations and performance. In that way, the anagram task performance of the group of subjects who received the success treatment $(X_S)$ could be symbolized $O_S$, and the performance of those receiving the failure treatment $(X_F)$ could be symbolized $O_F$.

We have been describing treatments and measures of their effects, our X's and O's, as experiences to which subjects are exposed. It should be pointed out, however, that our descriptions of research designs are made from the point of view of the researcher. In some studies, such as those concerned with the influence of naturally occurring events on behavior, the assessment of the effects of the events in question may be made on the basis of public records. For example, to pick up on one of our earlier examples of dependent measures, one might study the effects of a change in the divorce laws on the rate of divorce within a particular state. In such a case, O is not a measurement operation that is applied directly to the subjects involved. They would have no conscious experience of their behavior being measured by the researcher. In fact, in this particular example, they might have no conscious experience, either, of the event, the change in the divorce law, whose effect on their behavior was being studied. In fact, it is conceivable that many such events could affect people's behavior without them ever noticing, in the midst of the rest of their busy lives, that they have occurred. Even with laboratory studies, it is not always clear that subjects are aware of the events that are most important to the researcher. Many researchers go to great lengths to disguise the treatments that they administer to their subjects, and some undoubtedly succeed. Subjects may know that they have performed poorly on a task provided by the researcher, but they may be unaware that a negative expectation for their future performance has been created in the process. Subjects in laboratory studies may also be unaware that some particular aspect of their behavior is being monitored, even if they feel generally self-conscious about being put on the spot as research subjects. In any case, it is not really important whether these hypothetical examples are correct. The point that would be useful to remember is that the treatments of subjects and the measurements made of their behavior, which make up the most important parts of the research design, do not represent the research subjects' experiences during a study. Rather, they are those events on which the researcher's attention is focused because they are parts of the hypothesis that the study is designed to test. They may or may not be important parts of the subjects' lives.

We have already considered the case in which comparisons are made among groups of subjects who receive different versions of a particular treatment. There are also cases in which the effects of a treatment are compared with the behavior that occurs in the absence of that treatment. In some of those cases, the comparison between the treatment and no treatment is truly a comparison between a group of subjects who have had a particular experience (that created by the treatment) and a group who have had no experience at all. This would be especially likely in studies of naturally occurring phenomena. For example, one might compare the rate of divorce following passage of a no-fault divorce law in one state with the rate in the same state before that event took place, or with the rate in a second state that had made no change in a law that was comparable to the law that the first state started with. These would be comparisons (we will see how problematic they can be later) between an event and no event or between a treatment and no treatment. In these cases, the group given the treatment would have the symbol X in their row at the appropriate point (time) and the group given no treatment would have a blank space at that same point, to indicate that nothing was to happen to them while the other group was receiving their treatment.

However, in other studies, more likely to be among those in which the events are created by the researcher, the situation can be quite different. As an example, take a study designed to test the hypothesis that the likelihood an individual will engage in aggressive behavior is increased by exposure to an act of aggression committed by another person. One way of testing this hypothesis is in a laboratory study in which a group of subjects is shown a film where an aggressive act takes place (X), such as an assault by a vicious hoodlum on a defenseless victim, and then are given an opportunity to display aggression themselves (O). They could simply be compared with another group of subjects who were merely put into the situation where there was an opportunity to aggress. If it were found, however, that their level of aggressive behavior was higher, it would be difficult to know precisely why. Was it merely the fact that the extra time they spent in the laboratory made them more comfortable about being subjects, or that they had seen an exciting film? The comparison would be sharpened considerably by creating a different kind of experience for the group of subjects who were not supposed to observe aggression. If what happened to them was much more like what happened to the other group, except for the fact that they did not observe an aggressive act, we could be more certain that any difference that was observed in the amount of aggression in the two groups was attributable to the specific fact that one had observed an aggressive act and the other had not. The "other" group could be shown a film of a circus acrobat performing a series of exciting stunts on a high wire. If we used the symbol X, even with some subscript, to represent this experience, it might be misinterpreted to mean that these subjects were shown a different kind of aggressive act than the assault episode shown to the other group or a film intended to inhibit aggression. In order to denote the special purpose of these subjects' experience, in cases like this one we use the symbol (C). It stands for *control treatment,* distinguished both from no treatment (a blank space in the row designating the experiences of a group of subjects) and from a version of the treatment given to other groups (X, with or without some subscript). The parentheses with the symbol *(C)* indicate that subjects have not been exposed to anything that is expected to influence the particular aspect of their behavior being studied. It is a nontreatment in that respect, even though it is a real experience in its own right. The value of the symbol (C) and the distinctions it implies will become clearer later when we actually use it in specific cases.

Next, we need to consider how the subjects are chosen for those groups. There are two general methods of assigning subjects to groups, to which we have already been introduced earlier in the book. One is random assignment. In this method, the subjects for two or more groups in a research design are selected from a larger pool of potential subjects in some nonsystematic manner. Its purpose is to ensure that every potential subject in the larger pool is as likely to be chosen for any one treatment group as for any other. (The subjects for any treatment group are chosen blindly from the pool, picked out of a hat, so to speak.) The groups that are created through the process of random assignment are called *equivalent groups* because they should be alike in every respect. If a group of subjects in a research design is to be constituted by random assignment, the first symbol, at the far left end of its row, will be an R. We will see in Chapter 6 that research designs which use this method of subject selection exclusively are called Experimental Designs. Most laboratory studies and field studies in which all the events are under the researcher's control use random assignment. For reasons we will consider later, it is the method of choice for creating treatment groups, which means it should be used whenever possible.

The alternative to random selection is to select subjects for each treatment group because they meet some selection criterion. In some studies, the goal is to compare the behavior of different types of subjects. The treatment groups in such a study are composed of subjects who have different characteristics—levels of anxiety, ages, genders, socioeconomic levels, and so on. In other cases, different treatments must be administered to groups of subjects that have been created by some agent other than the researcher. We have already seen that if one wished to compare the effectiveness of various methods for teaching algebra to high school students, it might be necessary to use an existing class of students as the treatment group for each method. Many school administrators would resist having students assigned to classes at random for the purposes of a research study. Finally, if one wanted to compare subjects who experience a variety of naturally occurring events, such as natural disasters, environments with different levels of population density, or systems of parental discipline, one would need to compare groups that had been created (had a common experience) for some purpose other than that of the researcher. Groups of subjects that have been created by some systematic process are called parallel groups (later we will introduce the term "comparable groups"). In our notation system, they are designated by a dashed line between two rows in a research design. That is, if two groups that are to be compared were not selected by the process of random assignment, the rows that describe the events they are to experience in the study are separated by a dashed line (--------).

Research designs containing parallel groups are known as Quasi-Experimental Designs. Some of the quasi-experimental designs that we will be evaluating contain both parallel groups and, within them, smaller groups composed of subjects assigned to them at random. Thus, both dashed lines and Rs are used to represent the various groups in these complex designs.

Our last symbol is used in the special case in which different groups are tested with different sets of materials. As we saw in the previous chapter, there are cases in which the effect of some condition on subjects' performance may depend on the precise form of the task presented to them. In such a case, it can be useful to include different samples of materials which represent the various forms the task might take. When such a sampling of materials is an integral part of the research design, the various samples of materials are represented for each group of subjects by the capital letter M and a lowercase-letter subscript—$M_a$, $M_b$, $M_c$, and so on. The limited applicability of this designation will become obvious when we get to the designs in which it is needed.

To review, we have introduced a total of 10 symbols that we can use to represent all the basic aspects of research designs. Table 4.1 lists and defines all 10 in the order in which they were introduced. Each symbol denotes a part of the plan a researcher makes for evaluating the hypothesis being investigated. This system of notation is used in the next three chapters to represent the 12 basic research designs we will be evaluating. Those 12 do not represent all the research studies that could be done (even with the variations which will be described for some of them), but types of studies in which

**Table 4-1**  A NOTATION SYSTEM FOR RESEARCH DESIGNS

| SYMBOL | MEANING |
|---|---|
| 1. ROW of symbols $(G_n)$ | A specific group of subjects; in multigroup designs, groups will be identified by G and a numerical (ordinal) subscript. |
| 2. ORDER of symbols | The temporal sequence of events to be experienced by the group of subjects from left to right along the row. |
| 3. $G$ | Group of subjects. |
| 4. X ($X_{subscript}$) | A treatment (event, experience) to which subjects are exposed whose effects are to be determined. |
| 5. O ($O_{subscript}$) | A measurement of subjects' behavior; the criterion used to evaluate the effects of X. |
| 6. Blank space in row | No treatment. |
| 7. (C) | An event to which subjects are exposed, which consists of the extraneous features of X; to sharpen the evaluation of the effects of X. |
| 8. R(R′) | Subjects are randomly assigned to this group; successive rows preceded by R represent equivalent groups of subjects. |
| 9. ----- | Groups separated by a dashed line are not created by random assignment of subjects; they are parallel groups. |
| 10. M | A sample of materials employed to evaluate the effects of X on a group of subjects. |

each could have an endless number of specific variations based on it. In discussing the general designs and their specific variations, it will be useful to have our shorthand system of notation so that we can quickly sketch out the comparisons included in each one.

## KEEPING SCORE FOR THREATS TO VALIDITY

In addition to describing research designs, we will evaluate each one on the basis of the 12 criteria that were introduced in Chapters 2 and 3. The vulnerability of each of the research designs to each of the potential threats to internal and external validity is estimated.

A summary of the discussion of each design is made on a form called
the validity scorecard. An example of this form is shown in Table 4-2.
Below the symbolic representation of the research design, on each
line a symbol represents the estimate of the extent to which the design is vulnerable to the particular threat to validity named on that
line. If the design is free of that threat, a plus (+) is entered. If the
design is clearly vulnerable to that threat, a minus (−) is entered.
If that threat is a possible source of concern, a question mark (?) is
used. Finally, if the threat has no relevance to the design, that line
is left blank.

Question marks and blanks are obviously more problematic than
pluses and minuses, but we will have a better idea of what they mean
after we have explored some specific examples of analyzing designs.
Another source of ambiguity is in interpreting the total pattern of
symbols that appears under a particular design. Unfortunately, there
is no quick and dirty way of quantifying a design's overall freedom
from threats to validity—so many points for a plus, so many subtracted for a minus, and so on. In each case it will depend on the purpose for which the design is being used (the hypothesis), the
particular threat to validity that is involved, and other factors as well.
But, if you are patient, you should find, by the time we have finished
going over all the designs, that the pattern of symbols makes some

**Table 4-2**  THE VALIDITY SCORECARD

Example: The Static-Group Comparison Design

$$G_1 \underline{\ X \ \_ \_ \_ \ O}$$
$$G_2 \qquad\quad O$$

| THREATS TO VALIDITY | STATUS |
|---|---|
| INTERNAL | |
| 1. Extraneous events | + |
| 2. Temporal effects | ? |
| 3. Group composition effects | − |
| 4. The interaction of temporal and group composition effects | − |
| 5. Observer effects | + |
| 6. Effects of pretesting | + |
| 7. Effects of sample attrition | − |
| 8. Statistical regression effects | + |
| EXTERNAL | |
| 9. Nonrepresentative sampling | − |
| 10. Reactivity in the research setting | |
| 11. Nonrepresentative research context | |
| 12. Ecological validity | |

SOURCE: D.T. Campbell, J.C. Stanley. "Experimental and quasi-experimental designs
for research." *Review of Educational Research,* 1966, p. 48. Copyright 1966, American Educational Research Association, Washington, D.C.

overall sense. The particular pattern of strengths and weaknesses of each design—how definite they are and what kind they are—will be clear to you almost at first glance. That incentive should make you eager enough to get on with it, so let us look at the first group of research designs, the Preexperimental Designs, in the next chapter.

## SUGGESTED ACTIVITIES

### Exercise

Practice using the system of symbols introduced in this chapter to diagram actual research studies. Probably the best way to do this is to go to your school's library and choose a sample of recent psychological journals. It might be more interesting if you picked one recent issue from each of three or four journals representing different areas of research—learning, physiological, social, and so on.

Next, you should probably go through their tables of contents to select research studies whose titles interest you. You should need to read only the method section of each article, although reading the introduction might give you a better grasp of the study you are dealing with.

Finally, once you understand what was done you can use the symbols to describe the research design. Keep your work so that later, when different types of research designs are described, you can match your diagrams for this activity with those general types.

# Chapter 5
# Preexperimental Designs

## INTRODUCTION

The first group of three research designs we are going to consider are called *Preexperimental Designs.* They carry that inglorious name because they either lack comparison groups altogether or include only inadequate provisions for making comparisons. We have already seen how difficult it is to evaluate the effects of a suspected causal factor without comparing the reactions of those exposed to it with those of some other group. As we continue, it will become increasingly clear that the value of any research that tests a hypothesis depends to a great extent on which comparison group is chosen. So, why should we consider these preexperimental designs at all? They exist, in part, because this principle is not universally recognized. And even when it is recognized, as is true of any ideal, it is not always easily followed.

There are disciplines, including some concerned with the study of behavior, which have traditionally used research designs that do not include provisions for appropriate comparisons. (We will see shortly that these disciplines and phenomena tend to go together.) They deal with complex phenomena, such as wars and technological revolutions or unusual adult personalities, which occur very infrequently or even in what appear to be unique forms. Even though one might suspect some event to be the cause of such a phenomenon, it would be difficult to test that hypothesis by making systematic comparisons. To do that, one would have to observe other instances of the phenomenon (or, at the very least, something like it) that were not preceded by that event, or which were preceded by variations of it (like stronger or weaker versions) to see if the phenomenon came out differently. If we lack such cases, because they are too few and far between and their antecedents are too unpredictable, the appropriate comparisons are impossible.

As you might already have suspected, preexperimental designs are rarely used in behavioral research, but they are included in our discussions for three very important reasons. First, they will help us begin to understand a fundamental truth about the research process—that the nature of the question being investigated exerts a strong determining influence on the way in which the answer is sought. Second, these designs will acquaint us with the work of some of the important and interesting scholars who use them, as well as with the kinds of questions they try to answer. At the same time, we might gain some insight into the many important questions that people try to answer in their everyday lives that present these same difficulties of analysis. We all want to know, at one time or another, what causes a war or a recession or a friend's seemingly constant bad temper. Few of us are able to do formal research on these questions, but in just trying to understand what is happening around us we follow similar courses of investigation to those laid out in formal research designs. And even those of us whose principal interest is in the formal process of doing behavioral research do not test as many hypotheses or work in as wide a range of fields as we are interested in. In fact, in some ways it is more important to be able to evaluate the arguments we hear and read every day than to be able to design formal tests of scientific hypotheses. By the time we finish our survey of behavioral research methods, you might even agree with me that there may even be an inverse relationship between the importance of a question and the degree of certainty with which it can be answered.

Finally, and most important, we will be able to use our discussion of prescientific designs as a springboard for our consideration of more sophisticated designs that can provide behavioral researchers with much better alternatives to apply to their hypotheses. By examining the specific weaknesses of prescientific designs, we will gain an appreciation of just what makes the alternatives better. Our first step in learning to design a good way of answering a question will be to learn to recognize a poor way.

## PREEXPERIMENTAL DESIGN 1—THE ONE-SHOT CASE STUDY

| X | O |
|---|---|

As you can see from the symbolic representation of Design P-1 above, this first research design consists of just two elements—a single instance of a causal event and the assessment of its effects on just one group of recipients. These are the two most basic components of any research effort, a suspected cause and a likely indicator of its effect—the minimum requirements to test a hypothesis. They are found here in their simplest form. For example, there is no measure of the behavior in question (0) before X occurred. This leaves open the troublesome possibility that the observed behavior had looked that way before X ever occurred, possibly because of some earlier event. Nor is there any measure of that behavior under different circumstances. How can we be sure that the behavior that was observed following X was not really a characteristic trait of this particular sample, independent of the events occurring around them? Or that any sample we studied might not always behave that way, not because of X or any other specific events but because it is the nature of whatever sort of "beast" we happen to be looking at?

If one were planning a study to determine the effects of X on O, then, why would one use Design P-1? The simple answer is that one would not. But, not all studies can be planned in a way that would permit including all the helpful features that Design P-1 lacks. In many cases, interest in the effects of X develops long after it has occurred. Many events in people's lives and in nations' histories seem important only in the light of the events that follow them. Still, if there is some way of tracing their effects, it may be possible to test hypotheses about their effects, albeit in a primitive way. In cases like these, where the perspective is necessarily historical, there may be no satisfactory alternative. At any rate, Design P-1 is actually applied in a number of hypothesis-testing disciplines. We will begin our evaluation of it by looking at examples of two of its more prominent applications. After we see those concrete examples of some of the most important problems associated with its use, we will conduct a more systematic analysis.

We begin with an example from the psychological study of individual behavior, the case study method. We will go back to its origins for our example, one of Freud's "classic" cases, the case of Dora. Like other examples from Freud's time and our own, clinical case studies are attempts to account for the behavior of an individual that is defined as pathological. The investigator is usually that individual's therapist, who is searching for the cause of that problem behavior. It is a characteristic of the after-the-fact studies that use Design P-1 that although the hypothesis puts X before O, because the cause must precede the effect, the actual investigation begins with the observation of O and proceeds backward in time toward the discovery of X.

In the case of Dora the behavior of interest was a complex syndrome consisting of such "symptoms" as migraine headaches, breathing difficulties, loss of voice, and, especially, persistent and uncontrollable coughing. Brought to Freud by Dora's father for treatment at age 18 she was to become one of the most famous cases of one of Freud's most interesting varieties of neuroses—hysteria. To say that Freud diagnosed Dora's symptoms as hysteria is to begin at the end of our story, for that represents Freud's conclusion about the cause of her behavior based on a long process of investigation—his "research findings." Using the basic tools of psychoanalytic "research," free association, dream interpretation, and the like, Freud searched for evidence of an underlying causal event. The conclusion that Dora was an hysteric indicates very clearly that he did not find that cause in a physical disorder like tuberculosis or emphysema but in a psychological one.

Freud discovered that Dora believed that her father had had an affair with a close family friend and neighbor. It allegedly occurred when Dora was 12 years old and coincided with the onset of her symptoms. She felt rejected by both her parents afterward and sought consolation with the woman's husband, someone she had always felt very close to. But she interpreted his response as an attempt to seduce her. All this was interpreted quite differently by Freud, with the help of Dora's father, in light of his very elaborate theory of psychosexual development. At the risk of doing Freud a grave injustice, we will limit ourselves to his conclusions. As Dora's sexuality awakened, he reasoned, she began to have feelings toward men which she had already learned were socially unacceptable. Therefore (at least within the framework of Freud's theory), she substituted fantasy for action. Her true feelings of sexual desire for her father, similar feelings for the fatherly friend of the family, and jealously toward the man's wife were so threatening that they were translated, through various "defense mechanisms," into the fantasized affair and rejection and seduction. The physical symptoms that developed along with the fantasies helped keep the true feelings from coming to the surface and cast Dora into a more sympathetic role among her loved ones.

So ran Freud's conclusions, followed by lengthy and unsuccessful attempts to treat Dora by bringing her true feelings into the open. According to a prominent contemporary personality theorist, Salvatore Maddi (1974), who has studied this case, Freud's analysis was biased and inaccurate. Maddi maintains that Dora's version of the events which took place among her family and friends was probably the correct one. She was, in fact, rejected, deceived, and seduced. Freud was misled by the assertions of those adults who wanted to cover up the truth, and also by his own theory and attitudes toward sex and toward women. In fact, Maddi asserts that Dora's recovery was slowed by the disbelief and mistreatment she experienced at the hands of Freud. Only when her realistic view prevailed over the fabrications or fantasies of Freud and the others involved did she make progress toward regaining her health.

Whether Freud was correct, or Maddi, it seems clear that the method each of them used to arrive at their own interpretation falls far short of providing a trustworthy answer to the question of what caused Dora's problems. An intrinsic problem in this sort of inquiry is that the hypothesis and its test tend to be one and the same idea. The investigator starts with the behavior and searches backward in time for a likely cause. As the example of Dora shows quite dramatically, the search is likely to end when the investigator comes across an event that fits into one of his or her preconceived notions about how such behaviors typically come about.

This kind of retrospective search for X raises other problems as well. One of them is illustrated by the following example from one of the other disciplines in which the method symbolized by Design P-1 is often used, the study of history. In this case, the events and behaviors concern nations, or at least the groups of people who lead them, rather than individuals, but the approach and the problems with it are analogous.

For roughly half a decade, beginning in December 1941, the United States and Japan fought a bloody and destructive war, part of the even larger conflict known as World War II. This war between the United States and Japan was a very significant event in the lives of most ordinary Americans as well as for historians. It is not surprising that both groups searched for a cause or an explanation for it. It may be slightly surprising that most of them came to agree that one overwhelming event deserved to be identified as "the" cause. That event was the Japanese naval air attack on the American naval base at Pearl Harbor in the Hawaiian Islands on December 7, 1941.

Although many probably realized that the attack on Pearl Harbor must have had causes of its own, there were good reasons to identify it as the cause of the war. It immediately preceded the U.S.

Declaration of War against Japan and, as we will see repeatedly, one of the most important indications of cause and effect is the order and closeness in time in which events occur. Political leaders cited Pearl Harbor as their reason for supporting war and therefore abandoning a longstanding U.S. policy of isolation from international conflict. Finally, it must have made sense to many that a war of such proportions would have been triggered by a brutal unwarranted act of aggression.

I shared these beliefs, because of the reading in American history which I had done as a student, the conventional wisdom I had acquired from my parents and others, and the sense it all seemed to make, until I had occasion, in a graduate seminar in International Conflict, to study the events leading up to the attack on Pearl Harbor. In my reading I was surprised to learn that some historians, and some government officials and diplomats who had been involved in the contacts between the Japanese and U.S. governments before Pearl Harbor, saw the Japanese attack as much less important and as more of an effect than a cause of the subsequent war.

Again, in the cause of brevity I will have to give a very sketchy picture of their new point. The Japanese had for some time felt that Western interests (the Americans, British, Dutch, and others) had taken advantage of them in trade relationships with nations in Asia, especially those in Southeast Asia. Under a moderate government they tried from 1939 to 1941 to negotiate a fairer deal, particularly with the United States. All the while, more militant factions in Japan warned that drastic military action would have to be taken soon before Japan's economy weakened to the point where she would be helpless before the West. The U.S. government was aware of all this and of a Japanese contingency plan to launch a preemptive military strike to give her some breathing space against the economic and political squeeze being applied to her by the Western powers in Asia.

The argument continues that President Franklin D. Roosevelt, his Secretary of State Cordell Hull, and other U.S. officials chose to frustrate the Japanese government so that the militant faction would gain the upper hand. They did so primarily to break the isolationist foreign policy under which they had been prevented from going to the aid of Great Britain in her struggle with Germany. If a war with Japan could be justified on the basis of military aggression on her part, the freedom to resist Nazi aggression in Europe would come along with it. Unfortunately, the Japanese attack was expected to be directed against targets in Southeast Asia, especially the British naval base at Singapore, not at Pearl Harbor.

Luckily, we do not have to choose between the rival explanations for the war. What is important is that there is a good reason why many Americans, historians as well as ordinary citizens, failed to consider this latter possibility. Most of the facts upon which that explanation is based were, as one might expect, concealed by those involved in the alleged conspiracy. Those who were willing, even eager, to make those facts known waited until those they held responsible had died. By then, almost everyone else had written the history and made up their minds.

There is a very important general point to be made here. The research for historical causes is more likely to turn up some facts than others. Not all facts are equally accessible. Thus, a choice among alternative hypotheses or explanations might often be made on the basis of just a fragment of the total range of evidence which might be evaluated. And the part that is missing might not have been simply lost somewhere along the way. There might be a gap that was created intentionally by the principals to the events being studied. Presidents and adulterous fathers of neurotic girls may both have reasons for keeping secret the causes of distressing events for which they might be held responsible.

Thus, we have seen how Design P-1 is used in some formal disciplines. In these cases researchers go to great lengths to amass as much of the relevant evidence as they can, and they learn a great deal. They are also as serious as they can be about making valid judgments about the causes of the phenomena they study. But the highly critical descriptions of their work that you read above are inevitable. These are not isolated examples, but are typical of the deficiencies in this approach to the search for cause-and-effect relationships.

Outside the research in formal disciplines like psychology and history, we are all constantly faced with similar important questions as we try to understand the world around us. We have to answer some of these questions for ourselves, and we have to evaluate answers that others provide for us. Was the president responsible for a deterioration in the economic or international situation which occurred during his term of office (and should we support his bid for reelection)? Is a defendant in a highly publicized murder trial guilty? If so, why did he or she do it?

The difficulty in answering questions like these is reflected in the great differences in opinion that arise so often. One authority may claim that the demands of modern society have destroyed the institution of the family, whereas another blames moral decay. People on different sides of the family or of the political fence come to very different conclusions about who or what was the cause. These partisan disputes are not unheard of among scientists who use more advanced methods, but they are certainly rarer and more likely to be resolved. That is because the fault lies not with the ability or dedication or intentions of the person making the decision as much as with the methods used in attempting to answer the question. Let us look at Design P-1 more closely now, by applying to it our criteria for validity one at a time. It may seem like an unnecessary exercise in kicking a research design when it is down, but we are trying to become more familiar with the threats to validity and with the design features associated with them and this design will certainly give us an opportunity to do that. You can follow along in Table 5-1 through the following discussion.

Extraneous events are a serious threat to causal inferences drawn from this design. Even the most thorough history of a case is no guarantee that the true cause of O will be discovered. One problem is that the events that are potential causes of O are distributed very widely over both time and space. It is hard to know whether the cause is a fast-acting and a unitary one which must have come soon before O, as when an assassination causes a revolution, or whether it is a longstanding condition made up of many discrete events scattered in time and location, as when social injustice is the cause of a revolution. It is difficult to know how far back to look or how fine a time perspective to employ. All these problems are aggravated when the phenomenon one is trying to explain is as global as a war or someone's personality. Such phenomena are really aggregates of many simpler events or behaviors and therefore must have many interacting causes.

Temporal effects are also a special problem because of the scope of the phenomena to which Design P-1 is usually applied. Over long periods of time, in a person's life or a nation's history, there are influential cycles of development. A child matures as a natural, biological matter of course. A nation's economy changes as the fossil fuels which supported an intensive industrial phase are exhausted. Against these extensive backdrops, discrete events are occurring continually. These may be mistaken for the causes of changes following the larger cycles because they stand out for their uniqueness as the figures against the more diffuse ground of cyclical change. A president's economic policies may thus be singled out as the cause of an economic downturn, which is, in reality, just a part of the inevitable cycle of preindustrial to industrial to postindustrial economy within a particular nation. But discrete events that take place fairly quickly are easier to see than a long-term trend. The owner of an ocean front home is more likely to blame the dredging of a nearby harbor for the erosion of his property than a geological cycle of sand movement that takes hundreds of years to complete.

Group composition is also a problem in Design P-1, although in a very peculiar way. Because only one "group" or case is involved,

**Table 5-1**  THE VALIDITY SCORECARD: PREEXPERIMENTAL DESIGNS

| | INTERNAL VALIDITY | | | | | | | | | EXTERNAL VALIDITY | | | |
|---|---|---|---|---|---|---|---|---|---|---|---|---|---|
| | EXTRANEOUS EVENTS | TEMPORAL EFFECTS | GROUP COMPOSITION EFFECTS | TEMPORAL X GROUP COMPOSITION EFFECTS | OBSERVER EFFECTS | EFFECTS OF PRETESTING | EFFECTS OF SAMPLE ATTRITION | STATISTICAL REGRESSION EFFECTS | | NONREPRESENTATIVE SAMPLING | REACTIVITY OF THE RESEARCH CONTEXT | NONREPRESENTATIVE RESEARCH CONTEXT | LACK OF ECOLOGICAL VALIDITY |
| P-1: ONE-SHOT CASE STUDY $X$  $O$ | – | – | – | – | – | + | – | – | | – | | | |
| P-2: ONE-GROUP PRETEST-POSTTEST DESIGN $O_1$  $X$  $O_2$ | – | – | + | – | – | ? | + | ? | | – | ? | | |
| P-3: STATIC-GROUP COMPARISON DESIGN $\dfrac{G_1\ X\ O_1}{G_2 - O_2}$ | + | – | – | – | + | + | – | + | | – | ? | | |

SOURCE: D. T. Campbell & J. C. Stanley. "Experimental and quasi-experimental designs for research." *Review of Educational Research*, p. 40. Copyright 1966, American Educational Research Association, Washington, D.C.

there is obviously no problem in the usual sense of comparing unlike actors. But because the design is usually applied to a unique set of events—one person's neurosis, a particular war, or one specific corporation—there is the possibility that a cause is being sought for something that looks like an event, but which is really a permanent characteristic of the actor's being observed. In other words, an event which might be singled out as the cause of O, although it really had nothing to do with it because that particular behavior had always been that way. Does it make sense to point to televised portrayals of aggression as the cause for the violence in our society? Have not human societies, including ours, had violence as a permanent feature, television and other specific developments notwithstanding?

In a similar vein, a unique person or government can undergo its own peculiar cycles of change that can be mistaken for the effects of specific causal events. Even if it is possible to show that a property of that particular case has not always been around, it is possible that it has been evolving all the time independent of any specific event one might wish to name as its cause. Particular forms of urban violence may be fairly new to our society, but they might be a product of a long-term process of urbanization, which caused a shift in the form of violence, rather than the development of a particular kind of TV programming.

Observer effects are another problem that stands out as a serious byproduct of the manner in which Design P-1 is employed. The search through any historical record is bound to be selective. There is no end to the archives of materials that might conceivably bear on the question. The historian's search for documents and the psychoanalyst's search through a patient's memory have to be guided by preconceptions about what is relevant and where it is likely to be found. There is altogether too much latitude for bias to magnify the apparent importance of one event and to deny the real importance of another. Maddi makes this a central point in his criticism of Freud's analysis of Dora. Freud found just what he was looking for, as some patriotic American historians certainly did in their investigations of the events which drew the United States and Japan into conflict in 1941.

We will finish discussing the important threats to internal validity in Design P-1 by skipping to the effects of sample attrition. We have already discussed the way this problem can jeopardize conclusions drawn from studies using Design P-1 in our consideration of historical analyses of the war between the United States and Japan. Because studies using Design P-1 often use archival records as the source of their observations, the possibility of selective loss of cases from those records must be considered. Unfortunately, it is usually impossible to tell where gaps exist in the record. Thus, the nature of the missing material cannot even be guessed at. Some historians credited the passivity of slaves for the survival of the institution of slavery because the records they examined overstated the contentment of slaves and understated their active resistance. This was no accident, but part of the effort of slave owners to avoid revolution or abolition for their own selfish interests.

The two remaining threats to internal validity are not very likely to be applicable to studies based on Design P-1. Direct testing, whether repeated or not, is not likely to be employed in such a study; rather, as we have seen, existing records of behavior are typically used. Patients in psychoanalysis may change their responses as they become more sophisticated about the whole process, but that is a very special, atypical case. Statistical regression effects are unlikely to be relevant to such a study either. Even if an extreme case is selected for study, it is likely to be selected on the basis of many factors which contribute to its unique identity, not a single extreme test score that could overestimate its uniqueness.

But the uniqueness of the persons, international events, and other cases, which are likely to be selected for study using Design P-1, does raise a serious problem for the external validity of the findings. Even if it could be determined that a particular causal event was responsible for the phenomenon to be accounted for, all the problems we have considered so far having been overcome, how much confidence could we have that the same relationship would obtain in another case? For example, even if some historians' conclusion that the Great Depression of the late 1920s and early 1930s caused the rise and acceptance of Naziism in Germany could be trusted completely (a very big "if," indeed), would one want to predict a drastic swing to the political right in other countries, even Western industrialized ones, at the same historical point as a consequence of similar economic circumstances? Although it may be true that the depression in the United States was not quite as severe as the one in Germany, the political result here seems to have been the opposite. In reality, this probably means that the cause of Naziism in Germany was not just the depression.

We will see later that comparing the effect of different amounts of X is one powerful way of telling what the relationship between X and O really is. But for now it points out the difficulty of generalizing conclusions from case studies across a variety of different cases. In part, at least, this difficulty stems from a property of "cases" which we have discussed repeatedly already. They are so complex—a person or a nation, for example—that it is difficult to establish comparability among them. For instance, even though the United States and

Germany may have been at about the same point in the world's history when the Great Depression struck in the 1920s, they may have been at very different points in their own, unique histories. And, whatever caused Dora's psychosomatic problems, it would be reckless to expect the same event to have the same consequences for another, uniquely different individual. In fact, both Naziism and Dora were attractive cases to study precisely because they had so few parallels with most other political and psychological phenomena. What we know about them can thus be expected to have little potential for generality.

Other restrictions on the generality of research findings also apply to some applications of Design P-1. When case studies are based on archival records of real human activities, there need be little fear that the observations do not represent a realistic form of the phenomenon in question. But participants in psychiatric cases and historical events may have concerns about being observed. A psychotherapy client (or therapist) may well be under some of the same constraints as the subject in a laboratory study. There may be motives to tell what others want or expect to hear, or to hide what one fears would lead to rejection. The extent to which such motives influence the observations included in a case study determines the validity of the conclusions that may be drawn from it. An examination of the historical record of the conflict between the U.S. and Japanese governments which led up to the attack on Pearl Harbor shows another form of reactivity. Participants in historical events are sometimes self-conscious about the possible scrutiny of their actions by future researchers.

It should be clear at this point that Design P-1 is of very little use in drawing causal inferences about behavior. Its main utility is as a good example of what can go wrong. Even those who test hypotheses about past events under the most difficult circumstances can usually do better, as we will see. Design P-1 does, however, have one important use. At the earliest stages of research on any question, a researcher must make some very important decisions that will have a lasting influence on what follows. The choice of hypotheses to be tested is foremost among these decisions. Even the most complete and sophisticated knowledge about research methods is of little consequence if it is applied toward testing a hypothesis that misses the truly important aspects of the phenomenon, or that postulates a nonexistent relationship. To many researchers, this early stage seems the most difficult to cope with. They see no reliable rules to follow. The whole process of generating fruitful hypotheses seems mysterious to them. One reason is that they spend too little time actually looking at the phenomenon they want to study before formulating their hypotheses. Case studies like those described by Design P-1 are one way to take a good look before making guesses about cause-and-effect relationships. The detail that such studies generate can be put to better use in this exploratory, hypotheses-generating phase of research than in the advanced hypotheses-testing phase. The conclusions drawn from such studies are more deserving of the status of hypotheses than of causal inferences. Many earlier critics of behavioral research have suggested quite correctly that we concentrate more of our resources in exploratory studies.

Once we have formulated our hypotheses, how do we give them an adequate test? We know by now that Design P-1 is not the answer. Actually, there is no one answer, but we are now started on the path toward understanding the question and some of the answers to it. The next two preexperimental designs begin that process, each by demonstrating how one of the important flaws in Design P-1 can be corrected. From there, it is on to more problems and more solutions. Unfortunately, as too often seems to be the case, there will always be more of the former than of the latter.

## PREEXPERIMENTAL DESIGN 2—THE ONE-GROUP PRETEST-POSTTEST DESIGN

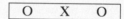

In this section, we will see how the addition of a single element to Design P-1—a measure of the behavior being studied before the suspected causal event took place—can alter the status of the research findings. But before we make a detailed analysis of the strengths and weaknesses of Design P-2, let us examine how it has been and can be used.

We will start with an actual example from the emerging area known as environmental psychology. At the 1980 annual meeting of the Environmental Design Research Association, Glen Shippee (1980) reported the results of a research study which was conducted using Design P-2. His goal was to evaluate the effects of a one-day workshop on energy conservation and local policymaking on energy problems. Fifty-seven government officials, labor leaders, and ordinary citizens attended the workshop. Shippee was interested specifically in how their participation affected their feelings of "learned helplessness." In other words, he felt it was reasonable to expect that the information they received from experts during the workshop, and the opportunity to work on energy problems with the help of others, would diminish any feelings they might have of being incapable of coping with the energy problem.

To test that hypothesis, Shippee administered a questionnaire to the participants before the conference began and again at its conclusion. A comparison of the feelings expressed before and after the conference revealed stronger (although not too much stronger) feelings of helplessness after than before. This is clearly the opposite of what might have been expected by the sponsors of the conference, the participants, and the researcher. Shippee chose to explain it as the result of the workshop's lack of attention to concrete plans for action to solve energy problems. A whole day of discussion of the many problems that exist, he reasoned, might have simply increased the feelings of helplessness that had existed previously. After all, each of the participants must have learned from colleagues about new facets of the problem he or she had not previously encountered. And each one's frustration and pessimism over his or her own failures may have been strengthened by others' descriptions of similar experiences.

The fact that Shippee tested the workshop participants both before and after the event permits us to rule out some alternative explanations that plagued our attempts to understand the findings of studies using Design P-1. We know that the expressed feelings of the participants after the workshop were not merely what they would have said all along, workshop or no. In other words, we can rule out group composition as an explanation. We are also in a position to determine whether any of the subjects dropped out of the study along the way and, if so, whether they were systematically different, at least in their initial expressed feelings of helplessness from those who remained. Of course, the limited duration of the workshop and the fact that the participants can all be identified and kept track of makes sample attrition very unlikely, but the availability of $O_1$ measures is a comforting safeguard.

Unfortunately, the advantages conferred by the pretest $O_1$ are gained at the expense of raising yet another alternative explanation for the findings. The experience of completing the preworkshop questionnaire might have influenced the subjects' responses to the questionnaire that followed the workshop in expressing stronger feelings of helplessness. Perhaps answering the pretest questions themselves increased the subjects' awareness of the depth of their despair about solving the problems caused by energy shortages and costs, and perhaps also made them aware of problems they had not even recognized before. Or they may have come to feel, while completing the pretest questionnaire, that those responsible for conducting the workshop were interested in how helpless they felt. This may have caused them to view the postworkshop questionnaire as an opportunity to inform "Washington" of their desperate need for help in solving their problems. Although none of these speculations can be supported, the use of repeated testing in this study makes each of them, and others as well, worth being concerned about while drawing conclusions about the effects of the workshop.

In addition to formal evaluation studies like the one above, there are innumerable informal ones which follow the pattern of Design P-2. One prominent example is the efforts of psychotherapists and administrators of mental health programs to evaluate the effectiveness of the services they provide. Each new client is first evaluated, and sometimes diagnosed, on the basis of standardized tests and interviews. Then a treatment of some sort is administered. Although it may be tailored to the client's individual problem, each therapist probably also contributes some aspects of a personal style to the treatment. It may last a short while or for years. After it is completed, the client's behavior is assessed again, although often not as formally as it was before admission to the treatment.

If the client is better off after the treatment than before, by whatever criteria the evaluator chooses to apply, it will probably be concluded that the treatment was effective. Again, however, there are alternative explanations for the observed change in the client's behavior—so many, in fact, that we will consider just a few.

The single most disturbing possibility is that the change was the result of an ongoing process that began before the therapy and probably continued afterward. In short, the therapy itself may have had no effect at all. It may simply have coincided with a temporal effect known as spontaneous remission. It has been shown, in fact, in better evaluation studies than the one I described above (which we will consider in Chapter 8), that some people with emotional problems do improve without treatment—as quickly and as frequently, according to some, as people with similar problems who receive formal treatment. Perhaps they solve their own problems—as they try to do when they seek formal treatment in the first place. Or perhaps the cause of their problem just goes away or affects them less as it fades further into the past. Whatever actually does happen, it is impossible to rule out temporal effects when a study is conducted with Design P-2.

Another serious potential problem with this "outcome evaluation" study is the introduction of observer bias. If one observer rates clients before treatment and a second observer rates them after treatment, the difference between $O_1$ and $O_2$ might just reflect different standards applied to clients' behavior by different observers. If the same observer rates clients before and after, perhaps he or she applies different criteria to the two sets of measures being compared. This might be especially difficult to avoid if the observer is also the therapist, with a strong belief in the effectiveness of the treatment being used and a strong need to feel that the client is being helped.

A final problem in interpreting an observed change in behavior in such a study is the possibility that any number of events other than the therapy—extraneous events, in other words—could have been responsible for it. The fact that most therapy programs are likely to last at least several weeks or months and the fact that clients are beyond the therapist or evaluator's view for all but a few hours during those weeks or months provides ample opportunity for their emotional well-being to be affected by forces other than those applied during the therapy itself. Clients may seek help from friends, clergy, or even other mental health professionals at the same time. Their commitment to the therapy program being evaluated might carry over into other avenues of self-help whose effects are combined with or even substituted for the effects of the therapy.

There are additional weaknesses to Design P-2, which we will touch on later. It should be pointed out here, however, that the problems discussed above apply equally to similar evaluations of the activities of other helping professionals, including those in medicine and remedial education. At the same time, the design is not without its strengths. Our discussion of group composition effects and sample attrition in the energy workshop evaluation example applies equally well to this case. We know that the clients were not well emotionally all the time and that the ones assessed at the end were not only the least troubled ones of the group that started out in the program.

Finally, the approach represented by Design P-1 is also popular in lay people's attempts to answer their questions about the causes of important everyday phenomena. When someone concludes that a change in the nation's economic situation (from $O_1$ to $O_2$) was caused by the policies of a newly elected president (X), they are using the results of an informal Design P-2 study. The notion that a serious foreign policy failure can improve the public's opinion of a president—John F. Kennedy's popularity rose after the Bay of Pigs fiasco and Jimmy Carter's popularity rose after the taking of American hostages in Iran—is a similar sort of conclusion. In all these cases, there tends to be too little attention paid to alternative explanations. Trends that occur independently of the specific events claimed to be their causes, extraneous events that are overlooked by observers and biased judgments by those who have a vested interest in blaming a particular event or person, all pose serious threats to the validity of the outcomes of such "studies."

Now that we have an idea of how Design P-2 is used and some of its most important shortcomings (as well as its principal asset in comparison with Design P-1—the elimination of group composition and sample attrition effects as alternative explanations for the findings), we will take a closer look at its standing on each of our criteria. Follow along closely with Table 5-1 because this time we will not proceed strictly in order.

To begin on a positive note, introducing an assessment of the phenomenon under study before the supposed causal event takes place has the effect of eliminating two potential threats to internal validity. Whether a group of subjects is tested directly before being introduced to X or whether some historical record contains data that can be used to assess the phenomenon during the period before X occurred (we will see later that these two alternatives are far from equivalent in some respects), this information has great value. First, it rules out group composition effects as an alternative explanation for the observations made following X. A difference between $O_1$ and $O_2$ shows clearly that the subjects or groups being studied were not "that way" all along. Their relatively stable characteristics would have affected both the pre-X and the post-X observations equally. Second, the pre-X measure makes it possible to rule out sample attrition as a possible rival hypothesis. It provides a record of any loss of participants and allows the researcher to determine whether the loss changes the character of those being studied from the pre-X to the post-X period. If those who are lost can be shown to be a representative portion of the initial group by comparing their pretest scores with those who remain, a difference between $O_1$ and $O_2$ cannot be explained by the attrition. If those lost are not representative, the $O_1$-$O_2$ difference will not be accepted as unequivocal evidence of an effect of X. Thus, attrition may cause the study to turn out to have little value, but it will not invalidate its findings.

Despite these two improvements over Design P-1, Design P-2 still has several difficult problems. To begin with, it shares with Design P-1 its susceptibility to both extraneous events and temporal effects as alternative explanations, in this case for any observed difference between $O_1$ and $O_2$. Both designs tend to be used to study naturally occurring phenomena that take place over long periods of time, during which those being studied are also being exposed to a great variety of experiences other than the one (X) being considered by the researcher as a likely cause. Both factors increase the possibilities for extraneous events (i.e., events other than X) to influence the phenomenon. Therapy patients are subject to many influences other than the therapy itself over the months or years during which they are treated because they continue to spend most of their lives outside the treatment setting. Similarly, any change in the rate of inflation takes place over such a long period and in the context of so many other influences that the effect of one president's policies is difficult to determine. In both cases, we know what happens over time, but we do not know why. Temporal effects are a problem for exactly the same reasons. Long-term processes of change can affect the behavior of a person or a nation's economy, but a researcher whose attention is focused on a particular event that occurs during the period of change can view it as the cause.

When Design P-2 is applied to more short-term and more isolated phenomena, the problems of extraneous events and temporal effects are less serious. The study of the effects of an energy workshop described above is a good example. The assessment of the participants' attitudes took place over a span of time and within a context that restricted greatly the number of influential events to which they could have been exposed. In the same way, temporal effects that developed over longer periods than the 24-hour time frame of the study, such as changes in personality or the nation's economy or the weather, could not have affected the behavior being studied. There are still possibilities that a relatively short-term and isolated study will be plagued with these problems—a critical incident can occur in someone's life or in world affairs, a person can become bored or tired in a matter of hours, or a natural disaster or even a violent change in the weather can occur. But these are clearly less numerous and less likely to be overlooked than are long-term background processes.

Interestingly, studies that follow a natural phenomenon over a long period also have their own advantages. Pretesting is less likely to affect the phenomenon being studied. Measures are less likely to be applied directly to the subjects being studied and more likely to come from existing records. And a pretest will probably have less of an effect on subsequent measurements if the time interval between the two is great. Subjects are less likely to remember their earlier responses to a questionnaire, for example. In short-term studies in more isolated, artificial settings, repeated testing poses a greater danger. Any test administered under those conditions is likely to be noticed, to engage the interest of subjects, and to raise concerns about what it and their responses to it imply. The energy workshop evaluation is a clear-cut example of such a case.

To skip a little to the problems of external validity, administering a pretest increases the likelihood that subjects will form their own hypotheses about the purposes of the study and that they will adopt strategies to guide their behavior whose effects could be mistaken for those of X. In other words, it increases the reactivity of the research setting. Archival studies are free from this threat, but many other studies, even those conducted under fairly naturalistic conditions, may not be. For example, therapy patients may learn to say what their therapists want them to say, what will make them appear as though they are benefiting from their treatment, as they are questioned repeatedly and see the reactions to their answers. Participants in a weight control program may improve more because they are being watched by other participants and the program leaders than because of any unique feature of the program itself such as the diet which is advocated. In these cases, one could argue that the presence of the observer is an integral part of the program, but few therapists or "diet doctors" would admit that the content of their programs was irrelevant. If the effect of the content is the target of the evaluation, the reactivity of the test must be minimized by separating the program from the assessment of its effects.

Even though group composition effects per se are ruled out by comparing each subject before and after X—a procedure sometimes referred to as using each subject as his or her own control—two related problems remain. The internal validity of the findings of a study carried out with P-2 is threatened by possible interactions between group composition and temporal effects. A change in behavior that is peculiar to the particular group being studied could be attributed mistakenly to X. Those who seek help in psychotherapy may be more likely to change for the better spontaneously (for some reason other than the therapy itself) than others who need help just as badly but do not actually enroll in a treatment program. Similarly, poor children who actually get into a Head Start program may be on the road to success, with or without the program itself, because their parents care enough about them to give them many different kinds of help.

The fact that only one group is included, and that is usually a unique intact group rather than one sampled randomly from a diverse population, also limits the generalizability of the findings of a Design P-2 study. It raises the possibility of nonrepresentative sampling. Even if one could be certain that X was responsible for an observed difference between $O_1$ and $O_2$, it is not clear that the effect would be observed in other groups exposed to X. This would be an interaction between group composition and the effect of X which could not be seen in a study of a single group. The fact that this particular group is also pretested raises the further possibility that X might have the observed effect only when those exposed to it were alerted, by a direct pretest, to someone's interest in that effect!

A final threat to internal validity lies in the possibility of observer effects. The fact that the observer in a Design P-2 study is often also the person applying the treatment being evaluated raises very clearly the possibility that the phenomenon is being evaluated differently before and after the occurrence of X. We discussed earlier the possibility that a therapist might interpret the same patient behavior as healthier after therapy than before because improvement is expected and even needed by the therapist. There are also more subtle ways in which the criteria for judging the phenomenon in question can change between two repeated assessments. If the person responsible for those assessments makes the pre-X batch all at one time and the post-X batch all at another time, any change in that person's state of health or psychological condition, including interest, energy level, or mood, could produce an illusory $O_1$-$O_2$ difference. If subjects are evaluated before X in one place and after X in a different place, their behavior may appear different even though X has had no effect upon it—because the change in setting has affected it. Therapy patients may be evaluated first in an interview with a stranger and later in a therapy session with a trusted friend, as their relationship with their therapist changes. All these potential biases are more difficult to cope with in a naturalistic study in which behavior must be evaluated in the course of events like psychotherapy or professional activities that cannot be tampered with than in a more artificial setting where conditions can be arranged to insure equivalent judgments before and after X—observers who are unfamiliar with the purpose of the study or who rate disconnected samples of behavior on video tape, for example.

Finally, the two remaining issues of generalizability, the representativeness of the research context and the ecological validity of the findings, apply less to all preexperimental studies than to those to be considered later. First, these studies tend to take place in natural settings, in realistic, complex contexts. Second, many are studies of unique cases whose findings do not have to be generalized much beyond the instances that are actually observed. Finally, the internal validity of these findings is so limited that the question of where they apply becomes almost meaningless.

## PREEXPERIMENTAL DESIGN 3—THE STATIC-GROUP COMPARISON DESIGN

$$
\begin{array}{ll}
G_1 X & O_1 \\
\hline
G_2 & O_2
\end{array}
$$

The static-group comparison design evaluates the effect of X by comparing measures made at one point in time of a group exposed to X and a second group who have not been exposed to X. A very important feature of this design, indicated by the dashed line separating the two groups in the preceding diagram, is that the researcher does not determine which group is exposed to X. That exposure is the product of some natural circumstance or pattern of events in which the recipients of X themselves may play an important role. Their characteristics or their own decisions may be a determining factor in their being exposed to X. This makes a very big difference in interpreting the comparison between the two groups' behavior. Unfortunately, it can be more difficult to determine when this is the case than it may appear on the surface.

We will start with a true example of a Design P-3 research study. It was planned and carried out by a friend and former undergraduate student of mine, Bob Evans, as an independent study project (Evans, 1979). He was interested, first of all, in people's feelings about death—in particular, in how their fears cause them to avoid thinking about the subject and how their failure to confront their feelings may contribute to perpetuating those fears. Accordingly, he decided to compare college students who had participated in informal group discussions of death, which focused on their feelings and especially their fears, with similar students who had not participated in such discussions. He expected that the students who had discussed their own fears about death openly and heard other students express their feelings as well would feel less fearful afterward. Bob's reasoning seemed to be based on a kind of Freudian analysis, centered around the concepts of repression and catharsis.

The procedure for the study was fairly simple. A group therapy room at the college counseling center was reserved for convenient one-hour periods. Students who were passing time around the campus, especially those Bob knew, were approached with a request for their assistance in a student independent study project in psychology and a brief description of what would be required of them. Sixteen groups from three to seven students each (77 in all) eventually participated in discussions that were loosely organized around a standard set of questions about death and dying (for example, "If you had a choice, what kind of death would you prefer"?), each accompanied by a variety of alternative answers. Bob Evans presided over each session, participating as little as he could beyond raising the questions and encouraging his subjects to participate in the discussions. At the end of each session, the subjects were asked to fill out questionnaires—standardized measures of their anxiety about death, their overall level of anxiety at that point in time (state anxiety), and their typical level of anxiety in all types of situations (trait anxiety).

During roughly the same period of time, other students were solicited for the comparison group. Eighty-five students who were similar to those who participated in the group discussions of death, in the ratio of men and women, in age, and in other obvious characteristics, simply filled out the three anxiety questionnaires. These students were obtained from classes whose instructors asked for volunteers to help Bob out with his study.

The results were much as Bob expected. Students who had been in the discussion groups scored lower on the death anxiety and the state anxiety questionnaires than those who had only filled out the questionnaires. Bob concluded that his hypothesis had been correct—that after the discussions of death and dying, participants had fewer fears about death and even less anxiety overall. Unfortunately, his research design permits other explanations for the differences that were observed.

The most troublesome explanation is that the two groups of subjects would have been just as different if the discussions had never been held. Remember that the students who took part in the discussions knowingly volunteered to do so. They agreed to participate knowing that they would be subjects in a psychological study in which their behavior would be observed, and aware that they would be asked to face questions about death and to discuss their feelings about the subject. On the other hand, the students who made up the comparison group merely agreed to fill out some questionnaires. The fact that members of the two groups faced such different hurdles, passed such different tests in a way, in order to become subjects in the study, leads one to suspect that those two groups might have been composed of different kinds of people. Students who were unwilling to deal with the subject of death may have not agreed to participate in the discussions, but may have had no objection to merely filling out questionnaires. In that case, the discussion groups would have been composed from the beginning of people who were less anxious about death. The questionnaire items about death may even have made some of the comparison group subjects more anxious than the discussions made the select group who took part in them. Thus, the results of the study may not inform us about the effects of discussions of death and dying as much as about the kinds of people who are willing to take part in them, in general, and the selection of subjects for the two groups compared in this study in particular. The subjects who participated in the group discussions may have been less anxious from the start (a group composition artifact). Or they may have reacted to the discussions positively because they were especially receptive to them (a nonrepresentative finding caused by the interaction of group composition with the discussion treatment).

The problem created for Design P-3 by nonequivalent group composition can be even more subtle and dangerous than the previous example indicates. Consider a hypothetical study to test the hypothesis that victims of heart attack will be less likely to suffer recurrent attacks if they engage in a prescribed exercise program as part of their recovery. Patients could be matched by age, sex, and other relevant background characteristics as well as on medical criteria such as the severity of the damage to their hearts. From each matched pair, one patient could be assigned at random to the exercise program and one could be assigned to a nonexercise regimen of follow-up treatment. This procedure would seem to ensure that any subsequent differences between the exercise and nonexercise patients in the occurrence of second heart attacks would be attributable clearly to the beneficial effects of the exercise.

But anyone who has embarked on a new regular program of vigorous exercise knows that his or her life changed in more ways than the exercise itself. People who start jogging, for example, experience changes in their eating habits, their sleep patterns, their toilet habits, and more. Thus the two groups which might be identical when the study begins, except for their commitment to an exercise program, quickly diverge in many other ways as well. They eat differently, sleep differently, even work and make love differently, and, perhaps most importantly, feel different about themselves. If we find that the "exercise group" has a lower rate of subsequent heart attacks and a higher rate of survival if a second attack occurs, how do we explain it? Was the exercise program the cause of those differences? Or was it one of the other secondary changes brought about by the exercise program or some combination of all the differences which eventually emerge between the two groups?

The plan of this study appears to create two groups of subjects that are equated by random assignment except for the single difference to be evaluated. But in reality that single difference created by the researcher is soon accompanied by other differences that emerge over time. The emerging changes in the exercise group may be thought of as an interaction between group composition and temporal effects, but their principal importance is in the ways in which they produce nonequivalence between the exercise group and the comparison group who is not assigned to an exercise program. As our whole discussion of Design P-3 should make very clear, comparing nonequivalent groups is a very risky, very confusing business.

The difficulties inherent in Design P-3 are very apparent in the cases in which lay people use it to answer important everyday questions for themselves. Almost all of us have had the experience of living in a city or state where some new program is being advocated. It may be no-fault auto insurance or an end to the 55 mile-per-hour speed limit or minimum competency examinations for high school students. Whatever the program, those who are faced with making a decision based on the facts, about whether to support or oppose it, often encounter a difficult problem. One of the most common sources of data upon which such a decision can be based comes in the form of a Design P-3 comparison between cities or states which already have the program and those which do not. But if the economic conditions or highway safety records or crime rates are different in those two groups of places, is it because one group has that program and the other does not? Or was there some difference between the two groups to begin with? Is that why the programs came to be different and why the "statistics" did, too? For example, is no-fault insurance more likely to be adopted in states where people are better educated and more concerned about automobile safety? If it is, then a superior safety record in those states may be the result of that education and concern rather than the insurance program. In other words, the safety difference would have existed even if the idea of no-fault insurance had never been born.

It is probably clear by now that group composition effects are a very serious threat to the validity of Design P-3 findings. In such a study, we compare two or more groups which are exposed to different events, not because we determined that they should be but because they chose to be or because they possessed some characteristic which caused them to be. If their behavior is found to be different, there is no way of knowing whether the hypothesized events to which they were exposed were responsible or whether the groups had been different all along. We have also seen already that group composition can interact with temporal effects to make groups that were equivalent at the outset of a study different by the end of it.

There are other problems in interpreting Design P-3 findings as well. Sample attrition is one of the most serious of them. It is especially troublesome in studies that compare persons or institutions that are subjected to different programs or run by different methods. If such evaluations of the effects of a program are carried out using Design P-3, in which a comparison is made only after the program (or after it has been in effect for a certain period), there is no way of knowing whether the group receiving the program being evaluated has lost some of the members or what kind of members have been lost. It is probably safe to assume, however, that the individuals who are undergoing any program (psychotherapy, weight control, management training, etc.) at a given point are more likely to be those who agree with the program's goals and feel they are benefiting from the program than those who disagree with it or get poor results from it. Every program suffers attrition, and it is likely to be selective, concentrated more among the program's failures than its successes. As a consequence, there is likely to be a systematic difference between the two groups, those in the program and those not, when they are compared. Thus, systematic sample attrition is ultimately responsible for a group composition effect.

Another way of looking at the same problem is as an interaction between group composition and the effect of the program or treatment. At the end of a program, or after an extended period of operation, any assessment of the participation is likely to be generalizable only to the select group that would continue in the program for that length of time. The program might have very different effects (e.g., less impressive benefits) on those who were less appreciative of it.

Comparing nonequivalent groups at a single point in time also raises the possibility that systematic changes over time will be mistaken for effects of the hypothesized causal event. Cyclical changes may differ between groups, producing an eventual difference in their behavior. Even if the comparison group is chosen for its similarity to the group exposed to X, the lack of random assignment to the two groups makes different changes over time a possibility that cannot be ruled out. Our example of the evaluation of the effects of exercise on cardiac patients was a special case (where the changes were triggered by the treatment itself) of this problem.

One final potential problem for interpreting Design P-3 findings exists only when the treatment and the measures are applied directly to human subjects. In those cases, reactivity in the research setting can limit the generalizability of the findings to cooperative subjects who are aware that their behavior is being studied. The study of the effects of group discussions of death and dying raises this problem quite clearly. Students who participated in the discussions may very well have realized that the experimenter's intent was to break down their fears about death. They may have responded, then, by minimizing their actual fears on the questionnaires they filled out afterward. Thus, their relatively low anxiety scores may have reflected their motives to be good subjects rather than the alleviation of their anxiety through confrontation of the dreaded subject.

Although Design P-3 findings are obviously difficult to interpret, they do have their advantages. The availability of a comparison group, even though it may not be equivalent to the group exposed to X, adds considerably to the meaning of the findings. If both groups are open to the effects of events other than X, then those events cannot act as extraneous events whose effects are mistaken for those of X. Automobile safety, for example, may be affected by numerous economic and social factors in addition to the legal speed limit, but states with different speed limits should all be affected by them. If they are, then none of those factors could explain a difference associated with the speed limit. Of course, any non-X events which affect one group more than the other would limit the internal validity of the findings. Local events with the cities or states, like weaker traffic law enforcement in non-55-mile-per-hour states, would qualify as extraneous events.

The availability of comparison data also makes observer effects less likely. If it can be ensured that both sets of measures, $O_1$ and $O_2$, are judged by the same criteria, then this limitation of their meaningfulness can be eliminated. To the extent that $O_1$ and $O_2$ are simultaneous, the same judgments and record-keeping procedures are more likely to be applied to both. When public records and objective questionnaires provide the data, the elimination of observer bias is made even easier. These data can even be gathered by experimenters who are unaware of the hypothesis being tested or the group to which the observations belong.

Because each group in Design P-3 is tested only once (if they are tested directly at all), no pretesting effects are possible. This lack of repeated testing also eliminates one potential source of reactivity in the research setting. A pretest is often an aid to cooperative subjects who are searching for the hypothesis in order to "help" the researcher verify it. The fact that this design often makes use of records that are kept for other purposes and that subjects may not have to be tested directly at all or, if they are, are tested in an institutional setting such as a school or hospital where such testing is routine also contributes to the findings' freedom from reactive influence.

The typical application of this design also rules out statistical regression effects. If the two groups are selected on the basis of extreme standing on some characteristic, they are both selected in the same way, to be as comparable as possible. Therefore, any regression effect will contribute equally to $O_1$ and $O_2$. Furthermore, any special identity of the groups that might be related to the behavior being studied is likely to be established through a variety of long-term characteristics (there is certainly no direct prior testing) so that regression is not to be expected.

Finally, we need to say a word about the two blanks in Table 5-1. As was pointed out already in our discussion of Designs P-1 and P-2, and is equally true of Design P-3, the research problems to which all of these designs are most likely to be applied are phenomena that occur in the real world, and the questions toward which these preexperimental studies are usually directed are very practical ones and are therefore focused very narrowly on specific cases. When one wishes to determine the cause of a particular war or the effects of a particular social program, there is little need to be able to generalize the findings. Although it may be interesting to speculate about the relationship between X and O in similar cases, the main interest is in the case being studied. And because it was studied in its natural context, subject to all of the forces that ordinarily affect its "behavior," one can be fairly confident that the findings will be applicable.

## CONCLUSIONS

The Preexperimental Designs are primarily the province of lay people and researchers in the "less scientific" (we will eventually clear up that myth) disciplines. We have seen along the way that there are good reasons for their infrequent use in formal tests of scientific hypotheses. Table 5-1 shows these reasons very clearly. I have had to invent many of the examples in this chapter because examples are rare among published research studies in the behavioral sciences. Studies that employ these designs produce equivocal findings. And there are, as we will see, better designs that can usually replace them.

This, however, does not mean that they are not used. Even Design P-1 is used on occasion. In fact, as a way of reviewing our discussion of the three preexperimental designs, we will examine one of the rare examples of the use of Design P-1 in a very important and typically very sophisticated area of inquiry. Then we will consider how the meaning of the findings would be different if the same problem were attacked using Designs P-2 and P-3 in turn. But first, the problem.

Over the past several years, there have been many incidents in which people have been exposed to stored industrial wastes and, as a result, have faced serious health hazards. One of the worst of these occurred in a neighborhood in the city of Niagara Falls, New York, known as the Love Canal. The residents of this neighborhood learned that their homes and their children's elementary school were built over the wastes buried by a local chemical manufacturer. Then claims of health problems related to that chemical dump began to surface. The residents and local officials began to appeal to the federal government for aid.

In an attempt to evaluate the long-term effects on the basic health of Love Canal residents, the government financed a research study to determine whether these people had suffered chromosome damage. Pieces of broken chromosomes can recombine in new ways which can ultimately produce structural abnormalities (birth defects) in succeeding generations. Tissue samples were taken from 35 adults who met certain criteria. None had been exposed to dangerous chemicals or to radiation on their jobs, and none had recently had a viral infection. All these conditions are believed to cause chromosome breakage themselves, which then might have been mistaken for the effects of the Love Canal chemical wastes.

This study found that 11 of the 35 tissue samples that were examined contained broken chromosomes. The residents and many others who learned of these findings concluded that this was evidence that living in Love Canal had produced serious health problems. But there are some real problems in evaluating the results of this Design P-1 study in which X represents exposure to chemical wastes and O represents the assessment of chromosome breakage. We will consider only the most serious ones.

There is no way of knowing that these 11 people had not had the same chromosome breakage all along, even before being exposed to the hazards at Love Canal. In other words, group composition effects might be responsible for the observed damage rather than the chemical wastes. Their socioeconomic or ethnic backgrounds, the region in which they lived (chemicals or no), or some other background characteristic they shared could have been responsible. Or how do we know that any sample of Americans of similar ages, sexes, races, and medical history would not contain as many or even more individuals with broken chromosomes?

It is also possible that the person responsible for evaluating the tissue samples from the 35 people studied was influenced by the expectation that a high rate of chromosome breakage must have occurred. In other words, observer bias may have contributed to, or contaminated, the findings. This would depend, of course, on the extent to which the microscopic examination of the tissue samples left room for judgment on the part of the researcher who examined them. But because we have already seen examples of how subtle and unexpected this kind of bias can be, the possibility cannot be discounted easily.

Finally, it is possible that some factor other than the exposure to the buried chemical wastes at Love Canal might have been responsible for the amount of chromosome breakage that was observed. The criteria by which the research sample was selected seem to have ruled out some possible causes—exposure to chemical or radiation hazards and to viral infections. But many others are possible. One which might have affected a large number of those studied is psychological stress. By the time this test was conducted, they had not only been exposed to the chemical wastes for many years, but they had been aware of that exposure and its possible harmful effects for a period of years as well. Their lives had been disrupted all that time. They had been interviewed, written about, filmed, seen by millions on national television, and most important, frightened about what had happened to them and what might happen in the future to them and their children. One could hypothesize that these experiences alone must have had damaging effects on their health. Unless there is evidence that rules it out, chromosome damage could be included among those suspected effects.

What if the question of chromosome damage from exposure to Love Canal had been tested using Design P-2 instead? This would require that medical records containing the appropriate information—some way of assessing chromosome damage before exposure to the potential hazards of Love Canal—be available for the individuals being studied. If that information were available, it could be used to rule out two of the three threats to the validity of the findings just considered.

First, we could certainly find out if the 11 members of the sample who were found to have broken chromosomes had that condition before their exposure. Second, we could give the two tissue samples for each individual before and after, or at least give comparable records from those two time periods, without labeling which was which, to an observer for an assessment of chromosome breakage. This procedure would prevent any bias caused by the observer's expectations about the effect of exposure to Love Canal from contaminating the research findings. It would also guard against the possibility that the laboratory procedures in which the slides showing broken chromosomes were prepared could themselves have resulted in chromosome breakage (this is known by researchers in the field to actually happen). The slides could also be mixed to assure that pre- and postexposure samples were equally likely to be judged by any observer, at any time of day, week or year, or under any other possible set of conditions which might influence the judgments about them.

The pretest in Design P-2 would not do anything to eliminate the threat that extraneous events—events other than Love Canal to which the sample were exposed—might have caused the observed frequency of chromosome breakage. There would be ample time and opportunity. On the other hand, in this particular study, it would not have its usual drawback of influencing the postexposure measurement.

It would be even more feasible to carry this study out using Design P-3. Tissue samples from Love Canal residents could be compared with samples from some similar group of individuals who lived elsewhere, preferably some place similar in most respects but fairly certain to be free from the same kind of contamination. For example, a sample of residents could be chosen from a similar neighborhood in a different part of Niagara Falls. The study could ensure that they were of similar ages, sexes, races, medical backgrounds. In addition, they could be assumed to share with the residents of Love Canal many regional peculiarities of water supply, diet, climate, or prevailing pollution from automobiles or industry.

Again, two of the three threats to internal validity to which the

Design P-1 findings were vulnerable could be avoided (although not the same two as in Design P-2). The possibility that the chromosome breakage observed in residents of Love Canal was due to some extraneous event, and not the chemical dump itself, is ruled out to the extent that the comparison group members are subject to exposure to the same extraneous events. Residents of a nearby neighborhood would live in very similar environments, but they would not have been subjected to the same stress as being Love Canal residents. However, another comparison group might be found that was similar in that respect. For instance, local firemen and their families or others exposed to very stressful conditions over extended periods of time could help rule out the effects of this suspected extraneous event. And the design could be extended even further by adding additional comparison groups to help rule out others.

The problem of observer bias could be overcome in the same way as it was in the Design P-2 example. Again, there would be two samples of tissues to be compared. Simple precautions could ensure that they were evaluated under equivalent conditions by observers who were unaware of which group a particular sample came from, if not the research hypothesis itself.

However, the findings of this Design P-3 study would be vulnerable to the threat of group composition effects. No matter how much care is taken to match the Love Canal residents with the other group or groups to which they are compared, there is always the possibility that they differ in some respect other than residence at Love Canal that could be a cause of chromosome breakage. The more that is known about the possible causes of breakage and the more closely the groups can be matched on them, the smaller this threat becomes. But it cannot be eliminated completely.

Now it is time to sum up what we have learned from our examination of the three preexperimental research designs. The basic question in any research study concerns the effects of a suspected causal event on some behavior. The bare minimum requirement for an answer to that question is a set of measurements of that behavior at some point in time after the occurrence of the event. But our assessment of Design P-1 shows clearly that one set of measurements is not enough. Even if we know what the behavior is after the event takes place, we do not know that it was caused by the event. As is the case in any research study, the ultimate question of validity becomes the question of whether something other than X could have been responsible for the values of the measurements which are taken.

Designs P-2 and P-3 show, in two very different ways, that the problem of attributing causality to the event being studied can be solved only by comparing the behavior following it with behavior that takes place under some different set of conditions. These two possibilities are measurements of the same behavior taken before the event takes place and measurements of the same behavior in a different sample that was never exposed to the event. And the results of those different additional measurements are virtually the opposite of one another.

The addition of a pre-X set of measurements in Design P-2 eliminates group composition and sample attrition as potential threats to validity, but, at the same time, introduces pretesting effects and statistical regression effects as potential threats. Introducing measurements on a nonequivalent comparison group in Design P-3 eliminates extraneous events, observer effects, and statistical regression, compared to Design P-1, and introduces no new threats.

A direct comparison of Designs P-2 and P-3 also shows the different advantages of each means of comparison. Design P-2 is superior with respect to group composition effects and the effects of sample attrition. Design P-3 has the advantage when it comes to extraneous events, observer effects, the effects of pretesting, and statistical regression effects. Although these designs are not very useful themselves, they introduce both the two different sources of comparison data (pre-X and no-X measures) and the important general principle that each of the different methods of determining causality has its special advantages and disadvantages.

There is also an important principle to be learned from a comparison of the threats to the external validity of the three preexperimental designs. Although Designs P-2 and P-3 are both clearly superior to P-1 in the internal validity of their findings, they are actually somewhat inferior in external validity. This penalty is often associated with the acquisition of comparison measurements. The reactivity of the research process, in particular, is often increased as more information is sought, which in turn forces greater intervention into the cause-and-effect relationship being investigated.

Finally, despite all the criticism leveled against these preexperimental designs, they are valuable in several ways. First, they serve an important pedagogical function for us as students of research methods. They show us what can go wrong in drawing conclusions from observations of behavior and instances of what can be done about it. Second, they remain the only ways of attacking some important questions about behavior, and it is important to know just what kinds of answers they provide. Finally, they serve as a starting point for programmatic research into questions that can be attacked with some of the better methods we will be considering later. The study of the effects of group discussions of death may not have answered the question to which it was addressed in any definite way, but it does provide a starting point in the process of achieving a definitive answer. This relatively easy study made more complex and costly studies more likely because it showed a possible relationship worth pursuing at greater lengths. Preexperimental studies often serve as a first step, building interest in and shaping a question for better investigations in the future.

## REFERENCES

Evans, R. M. A group discussion of death with college students: Its effect on anxiety. Unpublished manuscript. Charleston, S.C.: The College of Charleston, 1979.

Maddi, S. R. The victimization of Dora. *Psychology Today,* 1974, *8*(4), 90–94; 99–100.

Shippee, G. Community energy planning and policy-making: A psychological analysis of energy policy-makers. Paper presented to Environmental Design Research Association, Charleston, S.C., 1980.

## SUGGESTED ACTIVITIES

### Study Questions

1. What are the most serious flaws in the One-Shot Case Study? How could the threats to validity of its research findings be eliminated by adding comparison groups or measures to the design? What legitimate uses exist for the One-Shot Case Study design in its original form?
2. Also answer each of the questions above for the One-Group Pretest-Posttest and Static-Group Comparison designs.

### Exercise

Look for examples of preexperimental tests of hypotheses. History books are good places to look. Can you find cases of conflicting explanations for historical events which demonstrate the difficulties of using Design P-1?

The daily newspaper is also a good place to look. Can you find examples of politicians from different parties or representatives of conflicting interest groups drawing very different conclusions from the same information about economic developments or international situations?

Cast each of your examples into the form of a research design. Which design best describes the analysis you found? What are the threats to internal validity which call conclusions about each case into question, or which account for conflicting conclusions by different analysts?

Assess the external validity of each of your examples. Do your cases show that preexperimental studies are relatively free of threats to external validity?

What can you think of adding to, or subtracting from, the preexperimental designs you found that would make it easier to draw valid conclusions about the events in question? Try going through the most serious threats to validity one at a time and thinking about how each could be eliminated. This is good mental exercise in preparation for reading the next chapter.

# Chapter 6
# True Experimental Designs

## INTRODUCTION

During the past 100 years or so, psychologists have been investigating the incredible variety of causes of human behavior—from events that take place in the brain to relationships between parents and their children. In this chapter, we will evaluate the research designs that have been used in the vast majority of those investigations. It may surprise you to learn that such an enormous amount of research can be described in terms of these three designs we will discuss. If it does, prepare yourself for an even bigger shock. In reality, these three designs have so much in common that they could be thought of as one basic design with some minor variations. And not only are they the basis for most psychological research, but also the basic principles that underlie them were adapted from research methods used in the physical sciences. Starting from the common philosophical base of logical positivism, physical scientists as well as psychologists in many different areas of specialization have adopted one basic way of doing their research.

Because these designs have enjoyed such great acceptance for so long, one would suspect that they must be very powerful ways of testing scientific hypotheses, including questions about behavior. And in many ways they are. The very important criteria of internal validity that we discussed at such length in Chapter 3 are satisfied quite well by these designs, although recent analyses of research methods in psychology have pointed out that this requires a little more care than was previously recognized. In this chapter, we will see how each of the threats to internal validity, one by one, can be eliminated through the careful use of a *true experimental design.*

We will also see, however, that the true experimental designs, as they have traditionally been used in psychology, have serious limitations. The ways in which these designs have been used, and the methods that have been designed to minimize potential threats to internal validity themselves, lower the external validity of the results of true experiments. These designs make it more difficult to generalize what is found in any particular experiment to other settings in which the behavior in question takes place, including those in which it occurs naturally. Why, then, have these designs been used so widely for so long? They were used first in the physical sciences where external validity was not a serious problem. Ball bearings behaved similarly in the laboratory and outside. Psychologists were misled by the success of physical scientists and adopted their research designs without very much sensitivity to external validity problems. More recently, they have been recognized as very serious problems that must be considered carefully in any thorough assessment of the true experimental designs.

We should not embark on this discussion without a note of optimism, however. The problems of external validity caused by the traditional use of true experimental designs can be dealt with successfully—not always easily or with complete success, but there are solutions. In fact, the entire following chapter is devoted to considering some of them.

## TWO TRUE EXPERIMENTAL DESIGNS AND AN EXAMPLE OF THEIR USE

One way to begin to understand the real character of these designs is to look at a concrete example of their use. Our example comes from a segment of the research literature of social psychology that was very active in the 1940s and 1950s—the study of attitude change or persuasion. These studies investigated a wide variety of factors which help to determine the effect of a persuasive message on the attitudes of those exposed to it. When do television advertisements, political speeches, sermons, and all the other persuasive communications

aimed daily at people succeed in convincing those with contrary attitudes to change in the direction being advocated? Or, from the more
practical viewpoint of those who plan and deliver such messages,
what kind of approach would be most effective in converting the sin-
ner to religion or the Ivory Snow user to Oxydol? How do the nature
of the speaker, the contents of the message, and the identity of the
target combine to determine the final effect?

If this example strikes you as being overly simple, there is a reason for it. The designs we will consider from now on are really general frameworks within which many specific variations are possible.
We begin with "bare bones" versions that would rarely be used in
actual research. This will simplify our introduction to the diagrams
used to represent the designs, and our initial discussion of their properties, without losing any essential information. Later in the chapter,
we discuss examples that show how the basic designs have been elaborated to be more useful in testing hypotheses. At the end of the
chapter, we will discuss more generally and at greater length the
ways in which the basic designs can be extended.

In its most general form, every one of the attitude change studies
consisted of exposing different groups of subjects to different messages and assessing the effects of those messages on a particular attitude that they held. One way is by using True Experimental Design
1 (E-1), the Pretest-Posttest Control Group Design, which is diagrammed as follows:

$$G_1 \quad R \quad O_1 \quad X \quad O_2$$
$$G_2 \quad R \quad O_3 \quad (C) \quad O_4$$

Let us consider how this design would be used to test the hypothesis
that "It is possible to increase the favorability of people's attitudes
toward the proposition that Vitamin C is a cure for cancer by exposing them to a written communication from a reputable source that
advocates that proposition." The first step would be to draw at random two groups of subjects ($G_1$ and $G_2$) from a pool of available subjects. It is not unusual for students taking introductory psychology
to be required to devote some of their time to research conducted
by professors or advanced students in the Psychology Department.
The required number of students could be contacted from the class
lists for arranging appointments for the study. Or announcements
could be circulated in class or posted on a bulletin board, including
times for appointments, so that students who were free then could
sign up to participate. In colleges and universities where students
taking Introductory Psychology are not required to participate as research subjects, they are sometimes offered extra credit toward their
grade in that course if they participate, or researchers whose projects

are well funded (or particularly difficult or time consuming) may offer to pay subjects money for their time; students might even be solicited to contribute their time to researchers without any promise of compensation.

No matter how they are induced to participate, the group of subjects that is available for the study would be randomly divided into two groups for executing Design E-1. Both groups would first be administered some measuring instrument for assessing their attitudes toward some particular "object"—let us say, for the purposes of our discussion, that it is a questionnaire to measure subjects' attitudes toward the use of Vitamin C as a cure for cancer. Several items would have to be written that, together, would provide a reliable measure of subjects' attitudes toward this controversial, scientific/political issue at the outset of the study. For example, subjects might be asked how strongly they agree with several statements such as, "Vitamin C is an effective therapeutic agent in the treatment of cancer." The subjects' responses summed across all the items would provide the pretest scores $O_1$ and $O_3$ in the diagram.

The pretest instrument would typically be administered to groups of subjects at the beginning of an experimental session they all attended together. It would usually follow some preliminary instructions designed to draw their attention away from the true purpose of the study. They might be told, for example, that the questionnaire was part of a campuswide public opinion survey. Then, when later in the same session they were asked to evaluate the "logic" of an essay, the experimenter would claim that the activity, including the essay, had nothing to do with the questionnaire they had completed earlier.

Subjects in each group of the research design ($G_1$ and $G_2$) would be given an essay to read and evaluate. For $G_1$ that essay would be a convincing defense of the position that Vitamin C is a cure for cancer. For $G_2$ it would be an essay of approximately the same length which also took a strong position on a complex issue. However, it would be unrelated to the Vitamin C–cancer issue, perhaps dealing with women's rights or nuclear power or faith healing. Following their examination of the essays, all subjects would be given another questionnaire, again asking them to express their attitudes toward the possible link between Vitamin C and cancer. It might contain items similar to those in the pretest questionnaire worded slightly differently. Their scores on this second questionnaire would provide the posttest measures, $O_2$ and $O_4$, for the two groups in the study.

When they finished filling out the second questionnaire, the experiment itself would be over. In most cases, however, a "debriefing" session would follow. Subjects would be asked questions about their perceptions of the experiment, especially its purposes. At the very end they would be told the true purpose of the experiment, the hypothesis that was being tested, the reasons for their deceptive instructions, and their questions would be answered. If future sessions were planned to complete the experiment, subjects would also be asked not to discuss what they had learned with their classmates for some specified period of time.

The outcome of this Design E-1 experiment could be assessed in various ways. In general, they fall into two categories. One option would be to first compare $O_1$ with $O_3$. If there were no statistically significant difference between the pretest scores (initial attitudes of the two groups), a simple comparison of their posttest scores ($O_2$ versus $O_4$) would reveal whether the pro-Vitamin C essay influenced the subjects in $G_1$ to be more favorable toward the therapeutic value of Vitamin C. If there were a difference in initial attitudes, a number of statistical techniques make it possible to take that into account when comparing the posttest scores of $G_1$ ($O_2$) and $G_2$ ($O_4$). They have the effect of adjusting subjects' posttest scores on the basis of their pretest scores in order to remove the initial inequality in their attitudes.

Another alternative would be to begin with a form of statistical analysis that utilized both pretest and posttest scores. Although there are highly technical debates about the statistical appropriateness of these techniques, it is possible to calculate change or gain scores for each group of subjects ($G_1$ and $G_2$) separately by subtracting $O_1$ from $O_2$ or $O_3$ from $O_4$ for each individual subject. Then a simple comparison can be made between those remainders. Or a "repeated-measures" analysis can be performed that treats the pretest and posttest occasions as two levels of a variable, both of which are administered to every subject.

Without going into the technicalities very deeply, it is worth pointing out that there are several reasons for using Design E-1, all of which center on the statistical value of pretest scores in evaluating the outcome of the study (the effects of X). In general, they all boil down to one essential point—they make the comparison of the two groups for the effect of the independent variable (X) more precise. All psychological research, especially that conducted with human subjects, must contend with the problem of variability. Subjects are different from one another before the research study begins, and their reactions to the identical experiences during the study will vary accordingly. When we want to compare the behavior of two groups of subjects who have been through two different experiences, the fact that the individuals within each group respond differently, even though they have all had the same experiences, makes the picture fuzzy. This is why it helps to have a pretest measurement that indicates at least one of the ways subjects differ from one another, so that these differences can be subtracted, in a sense, from the subjects' reactions to X. Then each subject's reaction is measured against a baseline of their own individual backgrounds rather than giving the false impression that the effects of X are unpredictable (more about this subject later).

Let's look very briefly at an alternative way of testing the same hypothesis in the same kind of laboratory setting, using Design E-2—The Posttest-Only Control Group Design represented by the following diagram:

$$G_1 \quad R \qquad X \qquad O_1$$
$$G_2 \quad R \qquad \qquad O_2$$

This experiment would be very similar to the one we have already described except, as its label implies, that subjects would receive no pretest. Their attitudes toward the Vitamin C–cancer issue are measured only after they have been exposed to one of the essays. There is the same selection and random assignment procedure, the same instructions (except for the pretest), the same essays, and the same posttest and debriefing procedures. In this case, the alternative means for evaluating the hypothesis are far less complicated. All that is possible is comparing $O_1$ with $O_2$, the attitudes expressed by the subjects after they have read the essays. If the hypothesis is correct, whatever statistical test is chosen should reveal that $O_1$ is significantly different from $O_2$ in the direction that indicates that subjects in $G_1$ are more convinced of the therapeutic value of Vitamin C than are subjects in $G_2$.

## THE FOUR WS—THE SOURCE OF "EXPERIMENTAL CONTROL"

The lengthy description of the actual "mechanics" of staging an attitude change experiment was written for a specific purpose. It was intended to emphasize the point that experimental designs are normally used in ways that give the researcher considerable control over the entire sequence of events taking place during the experiment. (Our expectations–performance study described in Chapter 1 is another example.) Experiments are often described as being "staged," and the researcher has the same kind of practical control over what happens as the director of a film or play has on the set or stage. Moreover, it is really this "directorial control," perhaps even more than the so-called control groups included in the research design itself, which provides the true experiment with its favored position as the research design of choice in psychology and other sciences. The researcher can control WHO will be exposed to X and who will not, WHEN X will occur, WHERE X will occur, and of WHAT X will consist. The researcher's control over these four Ws is made possible largely because the experiment is conducted in a very special kind of setting, which resembles in many ways the theater stage and the film set. It is a place that is isolated from the ongoing events of the world—a place in which researchers can choose who will act, when the action will begin, the script that they will follow, and the scenery and props that will surround and provide the context for their actions. This special place is known as "the laboratory," and it has been used so widely that the true experiments are often referred to as "laboratory experiments."

Let us look closely at exactly what contributions are made to the validity of the findings of true experiments by the directorial control the researcher can exercise in his or her laboratory. The term "laboratory" often conjures up images that are somewhat misleading with respect to the present discussion. If you imagine Dr. Frankenstein's laboratory or the laboratories of biochemists or medical researchers you have seen on *Nova,* or even the chemistry laboratory at your own college or university, your images are characterized largely by the esoteric technical equipment that those laboratories contain. Psychological laboratories, by contrast, are often simple rooms containing only tables and chairs or student desks (although some of them contain a fair amount of electronic equipment and the like). It is important to keep in mind that what makes them laboratories, like other scientific laboratories, is that they are the sites of experiments. And their principal contribution to those experiments is providing *experimental isolation.* They shut out the outside world and, in doing so, ensure that the events taking place during the experiment are those that the researcher has chosen and planned.

The first of our Ws refers to selecting the subjects who participate in an experiment. It is crucially important that the groups of subjects who are compared be equivalent to one another at the outset. Because the total number of subjects used in an experiment is divided randomly into the number of groups to be compared, we can be confident that the subjects in those groups, on the average, do not differ from one another in any background characteristic, whether related to the behavior being studied or not. Thus the researcher's ability to determine which subjects are exposed to which conditions, that is, to randomly assign subjects to be exposed to X or not, rules out several potential threats to internal validity. If a difference is observed between the behavior of subjects exposed to X and those not exposed (whatever analysis a particular form of true experiment requires, this is its basic object), it cannot be explained by preexisting differences between those groups of subjects. Random assignment rules out the possibility of group composition effects (threat 3). In a similar way, the interaction between group composition and temporal effects (threat 4) is eliminated as a rival hypothesis for the observed effects of X. Because the process of random assignment makes it likely that the groups are composed of equivalent subjects, any temporal effects that might be expected to occur in those organisms would be equally likely to occur to subjects in both groups. Similarly, any characteristic of the subjects which would make them vulnerable to the effects of extraneous events would be shared by the equivalent groups being compared. Finally, if the subjects are selected on the basis of their extreme scores on some test or on any measure of their behavior, the equivalence of the groups chosen by random assignment ensures that any statistical regression effects (threat 8) that occur will affect the groups equally. Thus random assignment of subjects to the groups whose behavior is compared in a true experiment rules out three potential threats to internal validity. This is reflected in Table 6-1 by the pluses in columns 3, 4, and 8 for all three true experimental designs. It is even more generally the case for every true experiment.

The ability of a researcher to schedule an experiment WHEN he or she wants also has some advantages for the interpretation of the findings. It should be clear from the description of the attitude change experiment that it could be carried out at any time of the day, week, or year. This arbitrary scheduling of an experiment reduces the likelihood that coincidental extraneous events will also affect the behavior in question. In contrast, a naturally occurring event has its own schedule, beyond the control of anyone who might want to study its effects. Any behavior that follows might be caused by that event or by other events that usually take place around the same time, including the behavior's own causes. There is another advantage to having control over when the experiment takes place and over the timing of the events that take place within it—the experiences provided for the subjects and the measurements of their behavior. Many experiments can thus be conducted within a single, fairly brief period of time. Brevity in itself makes several of the threats to internal validity—extraneous events, temporal effects, and sample attrition—less likely to influence the findings. There is simply not much time for any of them to occur. Thus control over WHEN X takes place rules out Threat 1, extraneous events, and can eliminate Threats 2 and 7 as well.

Perhaps the most important aspect of the researcher's directorial control, however, is the freedom to choose the location in which the experiment will take place. In most cases, the laboratory is cho-

**Table 6-1** VALIDITY SCORECARD: TRUE EXPERIMENTAL DESIGNS

| | INTERNAL VALIDITY | | | | | | | | EXTERNAL VALIDITY | | | |
|---|---|---|---|---|---|---|---|---|---|---|---|---|
| | EXTRANEOUS EVENTS | TEMPORAL EFFECTS | GROUP COMPOSITION EFFECTS | TEMPORAL X GROUP COMPOSITION EFFECTS | OBSERVER EFFECTS | EFFECTS OF PRETESTING | EFFECTS OF SAMPLE ATTRITION | STATISTICAL REGRESSION EFFECTS | NONREPRESENTATIVE SAMPLING | REACTIVITY OF THE RESEARCH CONTEXT | NONREPRESENTATIVE RESEARCH CONTEXT | LACK OF ECOLOGICAL VALIDITY |
| E-1: PRETEST-POSTTEST CONTROL GROUP DESIGN<br>$G_1$ R $O_1$ X $O_2$<br>$G_2$ R $O_3$ $O_4$ | + | + | + | + | + | + | + | + | − | − | − | ? |
| E-2: POSTTEST-ONLY CONTROL GROUP DESIGN<br>$G_1$ R X $O_1$<br>$G_2$ R $O_2$ | + | + | + | + | + | + | + | + | − | − | ? | ? |
| E-3: SOLOMON FOUR-GROUP DESIGN<br>$G_1$ R $O_1$ X $O_2$<br>$G_2$ R $O_3$ $O_4$<br>$G_3$ R X $O_5$<br>$G_4$ R $O_6$ | + | + | + | + | + | + | + | + | − | − | − | ? |

SOURCE: D. T. Campbell and J. C. Stanley. "Experimental and quasi-experimental designs for research in educational research." *Review of Educational Research*, 1966, p. 56. Copyright 1966, American Educational Research Association, Washington, D.C.

sen, and for some compelling reasons. Its greatest virtue is that it provides the researcher with freedom from interference by extraneous events that might affect the behavior being studied. World events, family quarrels, traffic noise, and most other unwanted influences go unnoticed in the laboratory. We have referred to this freedom from extraneous events as "experimental isolation." Thus having the experiment take place there greatly enhances the internal validity of its findings.

However, there are some extraneous influences that even the laboratory does not rule out, at least not automatically. These are extraneous events, temporal effects, and observer effects that can threaten the validity of the findings of psychological experiments even in the laboratory. They have not been recognized as clearly in the past as some of the other, perhaps more obvious, forms of these threats to validity. It is important to point out that these problems are not caused by the laboratory setting. In fact, when they do occur there they can be solved more easily than elsewhere. Let us now look at each one of these problems and the solutions that the laboratory context makes possible. We will continue to use our attitude change experiment to provide a context for this discussion.

Because two groups of subjects are required for that experiment in either Design E-1 or Design E-2, it would be possible to complete the experiment in two sessions. All the subjects in one session could be given the essay designed to alter the attitude being studied (Vitamin C and cancer). All the subjects in the other session could be given the "irrelevant" essay. That does seem like the easiest arrangement. However, extraneous events that take place in only one of the sessions are capable of affecting the comparison of the final attitudes in the two groups. Suppose a subject in the relevant-essay group started to cry while reading the essay because it reminded him or her of a close friend who was a victim of cancer. He or she might even blurt something out spontaneously to explain the outburst to the other subjects in the room. If this experience had any effect on the way some or all the subjects in that group answered the posttest questionnaire, it would be responsible for a difference between the two groups (because subjects in the other group presumably had not experienced this) which could be mistaken for an effect of the essay itself. Or imagine that during the session in which subjects are exposed to the irrelevant essay a brief, violent thunderstorm occurs. This might distract some of the subjects in that group, or even make them a little worried or a little depressed. That could affect their questionnaire responses in a way that, in the comparison with those of the other group who saw only sunshine and blue skies, could also result in a misleading interpretation of the research results, assuming them to be effects of the relevant essay.

A more subtle, but perhaps more likely, extraneous event which could intrude during this experiment is the experimenter-expectancy effect. If the person who conducted each of the separate sessions, whether the same person or two different people, was aware of the effect that the essay given to subjects in that particular session was supposed (hypothesized) to have on the subjects' attitudes, that expectancy could possibly be communicated from that experimenter to those subjects and it could have effects on their behavior that could be mistaken for effects of the essays. Even a subtle difference in the tone of the experimenter's voice while reading the instructions to the subjects might constitute an extraneous event that could affect the subjects' behavior.

In order to prevent any of these extraneous events, or others, from jeopardizing the validity of the findings of an experiment, one can simply mix together in each of the experimental sessions equal numbers of subjects exposed to all the different conditions being compared in the experiment. This solution could be implemented in the attitude change experiment by stapling the instructions, questionnaires, and essay together in the proper order in a booklet for each subject. In this way, subjects in the same room could be given different instructions, questionnaires, or essays without each other's knowledge and without affecting each other's behavior. If half the subjects in a single session are reading one of the essays and half are reading the other, any extraneous event that occurs will affect both conditions of the experiment equally and thus not affect the interpretation of the effects of the two essays on subjects' attitudes. Where adopting such a solution is not possible, because the experiment requires procedures that cannot be reduced to ink and paper and distributed to subjects privately, the subjects can be tested individually, with those under different conditions in the experiment distributed randomly across the available time periods to eliminate the possibility that any extraneous events could occur coincidentally when subjects under one condition were being tested. Experimenters would, of course, have to be kept ignorant of the hypothesis or out of direct contact with subjects.

Conducting the experiment in two separate sessions poses similar problems for the operation of temporal effects. If the sessions are conducted at different times of day, when potential subjects' levels of hunger or fatigue might differ, or different days of the week when students might be faced with different pressures in their classes, the effects of those influences could conceivably be mistaken for effects of the essays subjects are given to read. These problems can also be solved by mixing subjects within sessions or testing them individually across a broad sample of times. Then, temporal effects that do occur will affect subjects in the different comparison groups equally and therefore have no effect on the comparison between groups that constitutes the results of the experiment.

The extraneous events and temporal effects just discussed are sometimes referred to as "intrasession history." If they differ between conditions of the experiment, their effects can be mistaken for the effects of X. Although they are difficult to eliminate completely, even in the isolated laboratory setting, they can be prevented from coinciding with the different conditions of the experiment and thus eliminated as threats to the internal validity of its findings. Although the laboratory is not as isolated as some believe, with some care it can be made identical for subjects in all the comparison groups in an experiment.

Observer effects are a third potential threat to the internal validity of experimental findings that is a close relative to the two just discussed. If the behavior of all the subjects in each condition in an experiment is evaluated by a separate observer, or by the same observer on separate occasions, it is possible that the behavior of the different groups will be judged by different standards. Let us imagine, for example, that subjects' reactions to essays in an attitude change experiment were evaluated in interviews. If all the subjects exposed to one essay were interviewed by one person and all those who read the other essay were interviewed by a different person, any difference in the way the interviews were conducted could affect subjects' responses and thus invalidate the comparison between the two essays. Similarly, the same interviewer could be in different moods on two separate occasions. If subjects under one condition were interviewed on the first occasion and those under the other condition on the second, an invalid comparison of the effects of the two essays might result. If an interviewer were aware of which essay a subject had read, the interview procedure might be biased toward eliciting the responses that essay was expected to produce. All these possibilities are much more threatening when the evaluated behavior of subjects in an experiment permits an observer to exert a subjective influence. If subjects respond by pushing a button that transmits their response to a computer, where it is stored automatically, no observer effects are possible, except for errors that might be made eventually in copying subjects' scores or treating them mathematically. These operations can be influenced by knowledge of the experimental hypothesis, but evidence suggests that such errors are infrequent and small.

Where subjects' behavior is judged subjectively, observer effects can be averted as differences in intrasession history are eliminated. If each observer (preferably unaware of the hypothesis) on each occasion were to judge the behavior of equal numbers of subjects from each experimental condition, any effects of the traits or moods of the observers would affect equally the scores of subjects in all the conditions. There would then be no danger of such an effect being mistaken for the effect of X. This solution is implemented most easily by recording subjects' behavior on film or tape. Then judgments can be scheduled in whatever order is required.

As we pointed out earlier, the solutions to these problems are facilitated by the researcher's ability to schedule subjects when and where desired. Thus, the subtle problems that can occur in the laboratory can be dealt with more effectively because they do take place in a setting in which the researcher can exercise so much control over events.

The final aspect of the researcher's control is over WHAT happens to the subjects in an experiment. The researcher creates the causal event whose effects on some behavior are to be measured. It may consist of instructions—words intended to make the subjects believe they will do badly at a task or that someone likes them. Or it may consist of events—something a confederate of the researcher says or does to the subjects, or the results of their performance on some task. Or it may consist of one or more props that the researcher has placed in the laboratory strategically—an extremely attractive person or a machine that gives the experimenter a shock and threatens to do the same to the subject. Whatever it is, it is presented by the researcher in the specific form believed to be best suited to test the hypothesis. And it can be withheld just as efficiently from subjects who are not supposed to be exposed to it.

All this maximizes the possibility that any difference that is observed between the behavior of subjects in the different groups compared in an experiment is due to just the one event that differs between the experiences they have in the experiment. The likelihood of any extraneous event occurring to subjects in just one group is minimized because of the high degree of control over what exists and what happens in the laboratory. This control has other advantages as well. It makes it possible to provide a detailed description of precisely what words, events, or props are used to create the causal event in the laboratory. Those who read the results of the experiment, and others who might want to repeat it, can thus be reasonably certain of what happened. Events that occur naturally cannot be described as accurately and can never recur in precisely the same form. Yet another advantage of controlling what happens so completely is that the events that are created can be varied in a precise, quantitative manner. Rats' levels of motivation can be varied by testing the animals at different intervals after they are fed. Human subjects' familiarity with words they are memorizing can be manipulated by choosing words which occur with known frequencies in written English. One group of subjects' motivation or familiarity can be made twice that of another group, or 40% as great or whatever. The relationship between motivation and maze learning or between familiarity and ease of memorization can be established over a series of evenly spaced points. Natural events, like a worker's desire to do well on the job, or the familiarity of school subjects to students, cannot be ordered as easily or as precisely.

## FITTING A SHIP INTO A GLASS BOTTLE

For all the preceding reasons, researchers in psychology have consistently favored experimental research designs and laboratory settings when constructing tests of their hypotheses. This preference has led them to overcome many obstacles. Many events are recognized as important causes of human behavior which are not created easily in a psychological laboratory. Also many forms of human behavior occur very infrequently, which are performed by only a very few actors who are unlikely to be found in a researcher's pool of introductory psychology students. Yet many of these events and behaviors have been studied in experiments conducted in the laboratory setting by ingenious researchers committed to testing their hypotheses in that form.

How does one test the hypothesis that pathological depression is caused by a person's exposure to insoluble problems? How can events that take place over such an extended period and that have so much significance for those who experience them be created in an experiment? How can a researcher cause normal subjects to become mentally ill during their break between afternoon classes and dinner? Martin Seligman has studied depression by administering a series of strong, inescapable electric shocks to dogs. When they are faced later with the normally easy task of avoiding electric shocks by jumping a barrier when presented with a signal that regularly precedes the shock, these dogs fail to respond, suffering the shock instead. Dogs that did not receive the initial series of inescapable shocks learn quickly to jump to safety. In this way, the hypothesized causes and effects of depression in human beings are studied by creating an animal "analogue." This strategy has also been used to study neurotic behavior by exposing rats to a task in which a correct response requires the animal to discriminate between two stimuli that are too similar to distinguish. The animals become indecisive, unable to make any response and display signs of emotional excitement which resemble the anxiety of a neurotic human being.

What about the hypothesis that violence in our prisons is less a consequence of the character of guards and prisoners than of the roles they play in the corrections system? How can the effects of roles be observed independent of the kinds of persons who play them? Philip Zimbardo recruited Stanford University students for a two-week-long experiment to answer this question (Zimbardo, Haney, Banks, and Jaffe, 1973). They were brought to the basement of the Psychology Department building where laboratory rooms had been converted to resemble a prison—mostly by installing bars to replace the usual doors and windows. Half the subjects, who were picked up by local police before beginning the experiment, were randomly assigned the role of guard and half the role of prisoner. Both equivalent groups received uniforms. The guards wore mirror sunglasses and the prisoners stockings to simulate shaved heads. Guards were called "Sir" and the prisoners were referred to by numbers rather than names. In all these ways and more, the experimental setting was arranged to resemble a real prison. Within a few days, the behavior of both groups of students had started to resemble the inhabitants of real prisons—both the withdrawal and subservience of the prisoners and the arrogance and brutality of the guards. Long before the experiment was due to be completed, the frightened researchers, who were playing the roles of prison administrators, called the whole thing off. Zimbardo's approach is known as a simulation and has been used to study international relations, business decisions, and many other problems that occur naturally in complex environments in which experiments could not be conducted.

So powerful is the lure of being able to compare equivalent groups of subjects who have had different experiences—the heart of the true experiment—that researchers have even adapted that method to studying how personality traits affect people's behavior. Let us say that someone wanted to test the hypothesis that people with high self-esteem would be more capable of becoming acquainted with a stranger than those with low esteem. One way of going about it would start by testing the self-esteem of a large pool of prospective subjects with a standardized questionnaire. Then two groups who got contrasting scores could be put into the same kind of meeting with a stranger. That, however, would not be an experiment because the subjects were not randomly assigned to the comparison groups, and it would be unclear whether any difference in their behavior was caused by the difference in self-esteem or by some other attribute that varies together with self-esteem (physical attractiveness would be one likely suspect).

In order to test the same kind of hypothesis using a true experimental design, researchers have exposed two randomly assigned groups of subjects to an experience designed to produce a difference in their levels of self-esteem. After both groups take an important aptitude test, one can be told they have failed and the other that they have excelled in their performance. In this case, any difference between the two groups in a subsequent get-acquainted session with a stranger could be only due to a difference in their feelings about themselves produced by the arranged success and failure on the aptitude test. Even personality can be studied experimentally, it seems.

There are important causes of behavior that cannot be fitted into a true experimental design, such as sex and age. But it should be clear from the examples described above that they are few and far between. And, in fact, ingenious lines of reasoning have utilized hormones to simulate some of the differences between males and females, and techniques like role playing in which subjects assume roles they do not perform by virtue of their natural attributes (see Chapter 7) to adapt the true experimental designs to almost every hypothesis imaginable. If a three-masted sailing ship can be put into an empty wine bottle, why not?

## KNOWING THE SCORE

We should have enough background information to evaluate our first two true experimental designs, E-1 and E-2, on each of the potential threats to validity. Because they are so similar both in the operations they require and in the rival hypotheses they do and do not rule out, we will evaluate them both at the same time. Remember, these are the designs we are discussing:

| | | E-1 | | | | | E-2 | | |
|---|---|---|---|---|---|---|---|---|---|
| $G_1$ | R | $O_1$ | X | $O_2$ | $G_1$ | R | X | $O_1$ |
| $G_2$ | R | $O_3$ | | $O_4$ | $G_2$ | R | | $O_2$ |

You can follow along with Table 6-1 as you read the rest of this section.

## INTERNAL VALIDITY

### Extraneous Events

All the groups compared in the experiment are subject to exposure to the same events if intrasession history is controlled. Both the brief duration of most experiments and the isolation provided by the laboratory setting contribute to eliminating this alternative explanation for any observed differences in behavior between $G_1$ and $G_2$.

## Temporal Effects

Again, equating the groups for intrasession history, which is facili- tated by the brevity and isolated setting of most experiments, rules out temporal effects as a plausible alternative to X for explaining any differences between $G_1$ and $G_2$. Both extraneous events and tempo- ral effects that take place outside the experimental session—such as historical events or the aging process—would affect both groups in the same way and thus leave the comparison between them unaf- fected.

## Group Composition Effects

The possibility that any observed difference between the behavior of $G_1$ and $G_2$ was the result of some initial (pre-X) difference between the two groups of subjects is ruled out by the process of random as- signment of subjects to the groups, although always within limits cho- sen by the researcher. Whatever statistical test is applied to the measures of behavior that are obtained in the experiment, the level of statistical significance that is chosen determines the probability that an unequal distribution of some attribute between the two groups (sampling error) was responsible for the difference found be- tween their behavior. If one is willing to settle for 95% certainty, random assignment eliminates this threat to validity.

## Interaction of Temporal and Group Composition Effects

Random assignment of subjects to the two groups also rids both de- signs of the possibility that the behavior of the groups might be influ- enced differently by temporal effects, again by ensuring that the groups are equivalent at the outset. Any changes in the subjects' be- havior caused solely by the passage of time should be the same in both groups and therefore should not affect the comparison between them.

## Observer Effects

If the behaviors of the two groups are measured objectively, by elec- tronic instruments or responses on standardized paper-and-pencil in- struments (questionnaires and self-rating scales), there is very little likelihood that any observer error would produce an illusory differ- ence between them. Errors in tabulating scores or computing statis- tics from them tend to be quite small, even if done by experimenters who know the hypothesis and expect certain differences to emerge.

If the assessment of subjects' behavior consists of judgments by observers, care must be taken to ensure that similar standards are applied to both groups—by the same judges, or equivalent (random)
samples of judges, who are unaware of the hypothesis and who work
during equivalent periods of time. This is very feasible in experiments in which scheduling is at the discretion of the researcher, and
in which permanent records can be made of subjects' brief samples
of behavior and then assigned to observers anonymously in small
(therefore less recognizable) pieces, and in any order desired.

## Effects of Pretesting

Both designs rule out the possibility that the effects of a pretest will
be confused with the effects of X. In Design E-2, there is no pretest
at all. In the great majority of cases, this is the best way of eliminating
pretesting as a threat to internal validity, especially because the pretest ordinarily has little or no value in an experiment. In Design E-1,
the effects of pretesting on subjects' behavior that can threaten the
internal validity of research findings are taken into account when
comparing the behavior of the two (equivalent) groups. Both the effects of X and the behavior that occurs in the absence of X are observed in pretested subjects.

## Effects of Sample Attrition

This is another potential threat to internal validity that is averted in
many cases by completing an experiment within a single brief session. Even when an experiment is not that compact, subjects are usually known to the experimenter by name. This in itself makes it more
likely that they will fulfill their commitments. It also enables the experimenter to follow up on those who do not. In both these ways,
sample attrition is probably minimized.

At the very least, attrition in any experiment is likely to be noticed. The experimenter will be aware of how many subjects are lost,
their personal identities, and the groups in the experiment to which
they belonged. This can go a long way toward assuring that selective
attrition is not mistaken for an effect of X. Design E-1 has a special
advantage in this respect. The pretest scores that it provides can be
used to determine whether subjects who are lost are different from
those who remain (making the sample less representative) or
whether different kinds of subjects are lost from the groups being
compared (making the comparison of posttest scores one between
nonequivalent groups).

Despite this generally rosy picture, attrition problems can sneak
into experimental designs. The examples which follow illustrate two

of them. First, experiments are sometimes conducted in field (natural) settings in which attrition can be more difficult to assess. Consider a hypothetical experiment to test the hypothesis that passersby will help a man in trouble more often if he appears to be a respectable citizen than if he appears to be a derelict. The victim could be a male confederate of the experimenter who is instructed to walk down an uncrowded sidewalk, select an approaching passerby at random, and then fall down, pretending to be unable to get back up. If suspicious citizens in an urban area are likely to cross the street to avoid a derelict, the subjects who encounter the derelict and the "respectable" person in the experiment might be selected, unknowingly, from nonequivalent groups of passersby. It is conceivable that this could cause the derelict to be helped more often, but only because those who get near enough to him to be subjects are less suspicious, not because he is a derelict.

Subtle attrition problems can also be encountered in laboratory experiments. The following is an example from my own experience as an experimenter. I asked subjects to watch videotapes of several brief interviews and to record their impressions of each interviewee by selecting the 10 traits that best described each one from a list of 24 traits. I had hypothesized that they would form different impressions of male and female interviewees (in specific ways we do not have to be concerned with here). A student helped me by scoring the subjects' answer sheets and tabulating the results. Subjects got numerical scores for each interviewee they responded to. One day, while I was going over the results, I noticed that one subject had received precisely the same score for each interviewee she rated. This seemed so unlikely that I dug out her original rating sheets to find out if they had been scored correctly. I found that she described each person she saw on the tape by choosing the first 10 adjectives on the list of 24. She was apparently one of a special kind of dropout—a kind that stays in the experiment physically but passively withdraws from it mentally. The effect of what she did was to remove her judgments from the comparison I was trying to make because her "judgments" of men and women were identical. If subjects drop out like this selectively, because one part of an experiment is unpleasant for a particular kind of person, the comparison that is finally made will not validly reflect the effect of the events presented to subjects because it will be made between nonequivalent groups. In a case like this, the experimenter may never know.

## Statistical Regression Effects

Even if subjects are selected for one of these experimental designs from a pool of individuals who receive extreme scores on some measure, the fact that they are assigned at random to the group that receives X and the group that does not assures that any regression effects will occur equally in the two groups. Thus, as we have seen in other cases in which random assignment means that effects occur in both groups, the comparison between them will not be affected—an observed difference between the groups could not be caused by statistical regression.

## EXTERNAL VALIDITY

In our evaluation of the status of threats to the external validity of the results of true experiments, the distinction between the structure of a research design and the procedures by which it is implemented will become more important than ever. Hopefully, this brief introduction will serve to jog our memories and sharpen our thinking about this important concept.

The frequent use of animals and freshman psychology students as subjects in experiments is quite separate from the structure of the research designs themselves. The generalizability of experimental findings is often compromised because subjects are chosen for their easy availability rather than for their representativeness. In a similar vein, it is often more convenient for a researcher to assess subjects' behavior by administering a questionnaire or self-rating scales that make it easy for them to hide behaviors or feelings they would rather not make public than to use a measure that would be less likely to reflect the reactive nature of a laboratory setting—say, recording their actual behavior and having independent observers rate their mood or their actions toward another person, or something of that sort.

There is no need to go into any more specifics at this point. Remember that the following discussion is based on the typical uses of experimental designs as well as their structure. In Chapter 7, we will consider some of the exceptions and their effects on the external validity of experimental findings.

### Nonrepresentative Sampling

Most psychological experiments are carried out in laboratories, where it is easier for the researcher to exercise all the necessary forms of control discussed above. Most of the researchers and their laboratories are located on college and university campuses. Under those circumstances, it is more convenient to use subjects who are located nearby and who are willing to participate. That is largely why the vast majority of psychological experiments have utilized college students who volunteer under some sort of pressure from their in-structors, and laboratory animals, as subjects.

Of course, experiments can be carried out in more natural set-tings that are populated by people who are more representative of humanity as a whole, but they rarely are. Even in social–psychological research, where the use of field settings has probably been the most extensive, only a small proportion of the studies being done is conducted outside the laboratory. There is also a strong pre-cedent for establishing laboratories outside the walls of academia and recruiting subjects form the general population. Social psychologist Stanley Milgram's research in several different areas has provided several outstanding examples of the use of men and women of almost all ages and walks of life, recruited via newspaper advertisements in cities around the world. Unfortunately, very few researchers have followed his lead.

The extent to which researchers' choices of subjects for their experiment are dictated by convenience is also revealed by the fact that only a minority of published psychological research studies use women as subjects (Greenglass and Stewart, 1973). They may be ex-cluded because of some sort of sexist bias or to avoid cluttering up experimental findings with sex differences. Or this may be just an-other indication of how few researchers have considered the repre-sentativeness of their subject samples important enough to warrant the extra effort that adequate recruiting requires. Whatever the reasons, it seems clear that the powerful true experimental re-search designs have provided information about the behavior of an extremely limited and arbitrary segment of the total spectrum of living things.

Is it true, then, that psychologists can claim knowledge of only the behavior of college student volunteers, rats, and pigeons? The extent of the problem of generalizing across species and groups of people depends on whom you ask as well as on the particular behav-ior you ask about. A great deal of the criticism that has been aimed at the restricted nature of samples of experimental subjects has come from practitioners—those whose job it is to apply psychological knowledge. Because they usually have a specific target population in mind, such as neurotic people, any difference between that group and the sample of subjects tested in an experiment whose findings are relevant to their problem is readily apparent. Researchers, on the other hand, tend to be interested in theories that are stated in such general terms that they imply that the behavior of all living or-ganisms follows the same basic rule.

It also seems clear that some hypotheses deal with very funda-mental relationships between causes and behaviors that might exist in the same form across a wide variety of organisms, whereas others deal with more superficial relationships that could be expected to vary across species as well as within species. It is quite different to use rats as subjects in an experiment concerning the role of the hypothalmus in the regulation of eating than to use rats to study neurosis. Similarly, the results of an experiment concerning the relationship of the meaningfulness of verbal material to memory that utilized only college student subjects might generalize more successfully than the results of a simulation experiment about the effects of the levels of nations' armaments on the solutions to international conflicts that used only college students.

Logically, generalizing is always dangerous. We only know what we have seen—not what we might see—even if there are similarities between the two. But because we must generalize we need to recognize that the problem varies in its severity. In other words, we must take into account the plausibility of the threat that the findings of an experiment pertain only to the specific group of subjects on whose behavior they are based. This depends both on the use to which the findings are to be put and the nature of the behavior on which they bear.

### Reactivity in the Research Setting

Human subjects in laboratory experiments know that they are the objects of study. They might also suspect that the particular behavior being studied and the significance that the researcher attaches to it have not been revealed to them. Consequently, it is likely that those subjects would feel self-conscious and that their behavior would be inhibited by this procedure we call the experiment. That is what we mean when we say that the laboratory is a reactive setting for research. Many fear that reactivity places severe limits on the generalizability of experimental findings to the spontaneous behavior of people in their natural environments.

We have already seen several examples of the dangers that reactivity poses. Subjects seek to discover the researcher's hypothesis. Based on their own perceptions of what is expected of them, subjects may cooperate, or they may attempt to frustrate the researcher. Or they may act to present an image of themselves that they can feel proud of—that they feel others will approve of. Everyone wants to be smart, fair, and well liked. No one wants to fail or to seem prejudiced or to seem strange. Whatever effects reactivity might produce all have one thing in common, however. They cause the behavior that is observed in an experiment to differ from the behavior that would be observed under the same conditions, in response to the same events, in nonreactive settings, especially the real settings in which people live.

There are ways in which researchers can combat these problems. Inside the laboratory, subjects can be convinced of a false view of the experiment that distracts their attention from the behavior in which the researcher is actually interested. Their behavior can be assessed in ways that minimize the extent to which they can misrepresent how they feel and what they think. At the very least, researchers can avoid asking their subjects direct questions about their feelings and thoughts. Finally, the use of laboratory animals, although it poses other serious questions, avoids the problem of reactivity in experiments.

An alternative to these modifications of the laboratory setting is the investigation of behavior outside the laboratory. Field experiments are one way of doing this. Making use of valuable data about natural behavior is another—one that we will explore at great length in Chapter 7. But whether or not one seeks to combat reactivity and the limitations it imposes on the generalizability of experimental findings inside the laboratory, or by leaving the laboratory, it must be pointed out that the true experimental designs have been used most often in highly reactive settings. Their great advantage in ensuring the internal validity of their findings can only be achieved where the researcher can exercise a high degree of control over the participants and the events that take place around them. Reductions in reactivity are likely to be achieved at the cost of that control and some of the internal validity to which it contributes.

## Nonrepresentative Research Context

In order to fit the events specified in a hypothesis into the restrictive confines of a laboratory, they need to be altered, sometimes quite drastically. Events that cannot be reproduced in their natural forms inside the laboratory because they are too "big," take too long, or would not be believable out of context are recreated in the form of simple experimental tasks, games, and sundry activities. In many cases, early investigators' inventions have been adopted as a standard operating procedure by succeeding researchers. This practice saves the time that new inventions would require and also makes the findings of different experiments easier to compare. Preexisting measures of subjects' behavior, especially self-report instruments like questionnaires, checklists, and rating scales, offer similar advantages and are also made use of very liberally. Both these kinds of standardization, however, share a serious danger for the generalizability of experimental findings. They pose the likelihood that those findings would be obtained only when the standard instructions, apparatus, task, and/or questionnaire are used. In such a case, the implications of the much more general hypothesis that any version of the event would affect any manifestation of the behavior can be quite misleading. And, again, using such findings in an applied setting in which the real events and behaviors take place can be quite risky.

The obvious alternative to standardizing (to using the same arbitrary operational definitions in every test of the hypothesis) is intentional diversification. If many different versions of the causal event produce consistent effects on many different manifestations of the behavior in question, there is more reason to be confident that the effect is not limited to the particular, even peculiar, ways in which the event and the behavior were represented in an experiment. And although generalizing an effect to contexts in which it has not been investigated directly is inherently dangerous, the risk is lessened when it has been shown that minor variations in the form of the event and in the way the behavior is measured do not alter the relationship between the two.

Every operational definition is an attempt to capture the essence of a causal event or behavior. The particular instructions, props, and measurement techniques which are chosen arbitrarily to make up an actual experiment are just some of the innumerable possible combinations that could be used to test the same hypothesis. Each of these combinations has two different properties. First, it represents the actual elements of the hypothesis—the events and behaviors whose relationship is being studied. Second, it does that in a particular way. The observed relationship can reflect both of these. To the extent that it reflects the relationship between the actual events and behaviors, it should occur in every possible experiment. To the extent that it reflects a particular set of methods used to study the hypothesis, it will vary from one experiment to another. Thus it is very important that the research context be representative—that the relationship could be expected to occur in other contexts as well as in a particular one in which it has been studied. However, the arbitrariness of the laboratory settings in which most experiments are performed makes this unlikely, especially if they are standardized.

## Lack of Ecological Validity

Perhaps even more damaging than the fact that experiments are likely to be conducted in reactive and nonrepresentative contexts, with nonrepresentative samples, is the fact that the setting and its participants are often chosen without any consideration for the context in which the cause and the behavior concerned occur in nature.

More than anything, the laboratory context tends to be a stripped-down version of its real counterpart. One reason is that it is impossible to create the richness of the real context on the bare stage of the laboratory. Perhaps even more important is the conviction shared by most researchers that the hypothesized effects can be seen more clearly without the clutter of causal events and behaviors other than those specified in the hypothesis.

Although we have been over much of the ground before, another example might help us understand the problem even better. I have chosen one from the area of social–psychological research in which I have been working for the past several years, because I know it so well and because I feel it is a representative example. One problem that has been investigated in many experiments is whether people are able to tell what others are feeling by observing their facial expressions. In a large number of those experiments, subjects whose facial expressions were being studied were seated alone in a room where they were shown a series of 35-mm slides chosen for their emotional content—automobile accident scenes, explicit sexual scenes, and others. Subjects were led to believe that the purpose was to study their physiological reactions, and electrodes were attached to their bodies throughout the session. However, the main purpose was to record their facial expressions, which was accomplished by a hidden camera. Then the live TV picture or the film or videotape record of the facial expressions that coincided with each slide was shown to another subject or group of subjects who had to judge which type of slide was being viewed while their facial expressions occurred. These judges either saw the slides themselves or were given a verbal description of each category.

This procedure was adopted by many researchers because it has many of the virtues that true experimental designs emphasize. The recorded facial expressions can have been caused only by the slides presented to the subjects; there is nothing else for the subjects to react to in the empty laboratory. Also, the subjects have no reason to disguise their feelings about the scenes shown in the slides because they do not know that their behavior is being observed. Those who judge the facial expressions have a very unambiguous task because the antecedents of those expressions are so clear—the slides. And the experimenter can tell so easily which slide (and nothing else) produced which expression and whether judgments of that expression are correct or not.

Although this research context clearly reduces ambiguity, and thereby increases internal validity, it also differs in several potentially important ways from the context in which this process of nonverbal response to an event and the communication of that response to others takes place under normal conditions in people's everyday lives. In that natural context, people react to events in the presence of other people; in fact, often the "event" is another person or what someone else says or does. When people react under those conditions, they do care what others make of their reactions. And they often feel that they want to communicate their reactions to the people around them—to share their happiness or grief or to let others know where they stand (or, at least, where they would like others to think they stand). In addition, facial expressions during social interaction often include facial movements that accompany speech, such as those required to produce the sounds and to regulate the conversation, especially taking turns speaking. In short, the facial expressions that people normally try to interpret are different in several ways from those studied in the laboratory context described earlier. Real facial expressions do not have single, unambiguous causes.

There is an important difference on the other end of the communication process as well. When one is faced with the task of determining what another person is feeling from his or her facial expressions in a natural situation, one often has the advantage of an additional source of information that the judges in the laboratory setting are denied. Very often one can see the cause of the expression. Being there with the person in a natural setting provides a judge with access to the same events that person is reacting to. Common sense would tell us, and research has shown, that this kind of information is very influential in judgments about other people's feelings. If a facial expression follows a joke, it is more likely to be judged as a sign of happiness than if the same expression followed an insult. That people cover up hurt feelings with smiles we all know. But we also know that very few people feel happy about being insulted, even if they smile.

This analysis of the laboratory and the natural versions of the nonverbal communication process is just one example of a problem which is too common in psychological research. And this sort of thing is especially likely to happen when some complex behavioral sequence is fit into the rigid boundaries of a laboratory experiment. Experimental designs encourage researchers to oversimplify the relationships they study for the purpose of making what causes what as clear as possible. But in doing so they may end up studying a different causal relationship than the real one they are interested in. Their findings, in other words, lack ecological validity. They do not tell us very much about what happens outside the laboratory, and can even mislead us about the very different natural relationship they claim to represent.

Perhaps we can wrap up this particular presentation of this issue best with a concrete example from the kind of research on nonverbal communication described above. Some early experiments of that sort concentrated on differences among subjects in the ease with which their facial expressions could be categorized by judges. Some people's expressions were easy to judge and others' were much more difficult. A popular explanation for this finding assumed that people differ in the extent to which they learn, as they are growing up, to hide their feelings from others. Thus it was assumed that the subjects who were hard to judge were stonyfaced, inscrutable individuals.

I wanted to test that idea directly by devising a method for measuring the sheer amount of facial expression by each subject. When I discussed my plans with someone who had done some of this research himself, I found out that there was not enough facial expression in the typical laboratory situation to measure. This is certainly consistent with the analysis of the laboratory context made above. It is also consistent with the findings of a recent study of the facial expressions of spectators at a hockey game. It was found that very few facial expressions occurred when spectators faced the ice, where the exciting events in the game were taking place. Instead, facial expressions were limited mostly to times when spectators faced each other. When no one else is around or can see one's face, most of the functional value of facial expression is lost and so little of it occurs. Apparently, people respond more to the people around them than to the events which occur—except, of course, in experiments in which no people are around them. Removing the social context to reduce ambiguity may also have the effect of eliminating the behavior an experiment was designed to study.

By the way, I finally did a study in which subjects' facial expressions were recorded during an interview. This provided lots of facial expressions to measure. But there was no relationship at all between the amount of a subject's facial expression and the difficulty judges had in determining what kind of interview question was being answered. It had to be the type of expression that was important, perhaps whether it was being controlled or not. In fact, amount of expression was tied most closely to whether the subject was a woman or man—and although men were much less expressive, they were not really harder to judge, at least in that particular study.

## A DIME'S WORTH OF DIFFERENCE—AT LEAST

Up to this point, everything we have said about true experimental designs applies about equally to Designs E-1 and E-2. But do not be misled into concluding that there is no difference between them. The difference in the structure of the two designs—the inclusion of a pretest in E-1 but not in E-2—does make one important difference in the validity of the findings produced by them. In Design E-1, the pretest may influence subjects' responses to the causal event.

Subjects may respond differently to X because they have been alerted or sensitized by the pretest to the meaning of X. They may be made aware of the relevance of X for the particular behavior that was measured by the pretest. For example, in the attitude change experiments we discussed earlier, asking subjects questions about their attitudes toward the powers of Vitamin C just before they are presented with an argument supporting its effectiveness might lead them to perceive and to respond to that argument differently than if they had not just been asked. They might see it as an attempt to influence them even if the experimenter claimed otherwise. If pretesting could have such an effect, it would be difficult to tell whether the essay produced any observed difference between pretest and posttest scores in the group exposed to it. That might be true only because subjects were pretested before being exposed to the essay— and that could be a very important distinction. If the pretest made the subjects aware that the purpose of exposing them to the essay was to study how it affected their own attitudes toward the issue it addressed, then the attitudes they expressed on the posttest might be affected by the kinds of strategies associated with the subject role discussed earlier. For example, they might claim to be more favorable than they really are toward the issue if they want to cooperate, or less favorable if they want to frustrate the researcher's efforts. In any case, their behavior in response to the essay would be different from the behavior of people only exposed to the essay but not given a pretest and therefore not as aware of the essay's purpose. Thus this potential effect of pretesting is a threat to the external validity of experimental findings produced by Design E-1. Findings cannot be generalized from the pretested subjects in the experiment to unpretested subjects—that is, most people outside the experiment. Of course, Design E-2 is free of this potential problem because it contains no pretest.

Fortunately, there is a way to determine whether a pretest does sensitize subjects to the event to follow and, in the process, to determine the effect of that event over and above the effect of the pretest. That way is Design E-3, which looks like this:

$$
\begin{array}{llllll}
G_1 & R & O_1 & X & O_2 \\
G_2 & R & O_3 & & O_4 \\
G_3 & R & & X & O_5 \\
G_4 & R & & & O_6
\end{array}
$$

It is called the Solomon Four-Group Design, because it was introduced by a researcher named Solomon and because it utilizes four groups of subjects.

The structure of Design E-3 is simple—it is only Designs E-1 and E-2 added together. But its function is impressive. By allowing a comparison of the effects of X when it is and when it is not preceded by a pretest, it allows a pretest to be used when that is desirable (we discussed those reasons earlier) without jeopardizing the generalizability of the experimental findings. This is done by comparing $O_2$ with $O_5$. If they are different, then clearly X has different effects when it follows a pretest than if it does not. In such a case, at least, Design E-3 does show the effects of X on both pretested and unpretested subjects. These effects can then be generalized to the appropriate, similar cases.

Let us look at an example of the use of Design E-3 that shows both how pretest sensitization effects can occur and how they can be ruled out as a threat to external validity. Our example is the attitude change experiment conducted by Ralph Rosnow and Jerry M. Suls, which we considered for a different reason in Chapter 3. It actually consisted of two Design E-3 experiments, which provide yet another interesting contrast—one that demonstrates that some of our earlier speculations about the role of demand characteristics in experiments were quite accurate.

Rosnow and Suls's two experiments were conducted with two different kinds of subjects. The volunteers they requested from introductory psychology classes became the subjects in one experiment. The nonvolunteers who were later contacted individually were asked to participate without making them aware of the connection with the earlier request for volunteers. They became the subjects in the second experiment.

Aside from the fact that the sample in one experiment consisted of volunteers and the sample in the other consisted of nonvolunteers, both experiments proceeded in exactly the same way. The sample was divided randomly into four groups. Two were given attitude pretests ($G_1$ and $G_2$) and two were not ($G_3$ and $G_4$). Two were given a written argument related to that attitude ($G_1$ and $G_3$) and two were not ($G_2$ and $G_4$).

In both experiments, the amount of attitude change produced by the persuasive communication was different for pretested ($O_2$ versus $O_4$) and unpretested ($O_5$ versus $O_6$) subjects. But the difference was in opposite directions for volunteers and nonvolunteers. Volunteers who were pretested showed more attitude change than volunteers who were not pretested. The pretested nonvolunteers, however, showed less attitude change than the unpretested non-volunteers. If one assumes that the pretest made subjects aware that the purpose of the communication was to convince them to change their attitudes toward the position it advocated, the results of both experiments can be explained quite readily.

The volunteers had shown, by their response to the initial appeal for their help, that they wanted to cooperate with the researcher. When they knew, because of the pretest, that the researcher was trying to change their attitudes, they indicated on the posttest that they had changed considerably. The nonvolunteer subjects were uncooperative from the beginning, and used the knowledge of the purpose of the experiment that they gained from the pretest to resist the arguments presented to them. The more modest degree of attitude change toward the position advocated by the persuasive communication which was exhibited by the unpretested volunteers and nonvolunteers reflected the effects of the arguments on subjects who were not set (by a pretest) to acquiesce or to resist.

The results of Rosnow and Suls's experiments also show one more general value of Design E-3. When a researcher wants to use a pretest in an experiment, for whatever reason, but recognizes its danger, Design E-3 is a safer course to follow than Design E-1. Of course, it is also more work—twice as many subjects, more questionnaires, more data to analyze, and so on. However, if the researcher plans a series of experiments on the same general problem—trying out different kinds of communications or attitudes, for example—doing the first experiment with Design E-3 can justify doing the remainder with the simpler Design E-1. If the first (Design E-3) experiment shows no pretest sensitization effect—if, in other words, the effect of X is the same on both pretested and unpretested subjects—then future experiments can be performed using Design E-1. This design leaves open the possibility of a pretest sensitization effect; however, if there is evidence that the effect does not actually occur, it loses its plausibility as a limitation on the generalizability of the experimental findings.

## WHAT IS NO-X ANYWAY? (OR EVEN X, FOR THAT MATTER)

All three true experimental designs we have studied in this chapter involve comparisons between subjects who have been exposed to some event that is suspected of influencing some behavior and subjects who have not been exposed to that event. Although this might seem like an easy comparison to arrange, it is not always. To see why, we begin with an example—an experiment from the area of physiological psychology.

This experiment was designed to test the hypothesis that a particular area of the brain is influential in regulating eating behavior (e.g., Hetherington and Ranson, 1940). One approach to demonstrating this effect involves destroying brain tissue in the suspected area and then observing the eating behavior of the animals afterward. In one well-known version of this kind of experiment, rats are anesthetized, their skulls are opened surgically, and a very thin wire that is insulated except for its tip is inserted into their brains until the tip reaches the point in which the suspected eating control center—the ventromedial hypothalamus (VMH)—is located. Then an electric current is passed through the wire that destroys only the brain cells in the region of its uninsulated tip. After the rats recover from the surgery, their eating behavior is monitored while they are fed all they want to eat. What is observed is a very different kind of eating behavior from that of the normal rat of the same species. The destruction of the VMH—also called lesions—is followed by a very marked pattern of overeating, overweight, and underactivity known as hyperphagia.

But to which animals are the ones who have sustained VMH lesions to be compared? What if they were compared to their littermates (siblings) who simply spend the period of their surgery and recuperation idly in their cage? This is a no-treatment group in the most literal sense, but there are problems in comparing it with the lesioned group. It could be argued that the hyperphagia syndrome was produced not by the lesions in the VMH—the conclusion that proponents of the hypothesis would want to draw that the VMH acts as a "satiety" center that inhibits eating when the organism's needs have been met—but by some other aspect of the surgical procedure which produced the lesions. The shock of surgery and the scars it leaves behind, both physical and psychological, may have been responsible instead. Because the hypothesis specifies that the VMH lesion is alone the cause of eating irregularity, these other differences between the groups create a problem.

The solution that has been adopted in experiments on hyperphagia, as well as other studies of brain lesions, is called a "sham surgery" procedure. Animals that receive lesions are compared with littermates that go through the same surgical procedure except for the destruction of brain tissue itself (the passage of electric current into the brain). There are two ways of stating the advantages of using this kind of comparison group over the alternative use of animals who have had nothing done to them. First, the sham surgery treatment assures that the only difference between the two groups of animals is the lesion—all other experiences are common to both. Thus any difference in their subsequent behavior must be due to the lesions created in one group but absent in the other. Another way of thinking about this same argument is that the sham surgery treatment clarifies just what part of the VMH lesion treatment has caused the hyperphagia. In other words, it tells us more about what X really is. It is not the surgical procedure or trauma itself, but the loss of a particular kind of brain tissue.

This problem of equating comparison groups in all possible ways except for the specific causal event dealt with by the experimental hypothesis applies much more generally than only to experiments about brain lesions. The attitude change experiments is another example. If subjects in one group received a message intended to change their attitudes toward Vitamin C, whereas those in the other group just sat for an equivalent period of time, it would be more difficult to account for any differences that emerged between the two groups. If the group that received the message showed more favorable attitudes toward Vitamin C after reading it than the group that just sat, it would be possible to argue that the content of the message was not necessarily responsible for the difference in attitudes. It could be that reading about any controversial issue would make subjects who were skeptical of Vitamin C aware that there are always two sides and thus get them to take less extreme positions themselves. Thus a better comparison might be between two groups in which both read persuasive messages—one a message relevant to the attitude being measured, Vitamin C in our example, and one irrelevant to it. Unfortunately, it is not always easy to determine what the most appropriate comparison would be. Should the comparison message be about nuclear power—an issue that also has health ramifications—or would a more different controversial issue like politicization of the Olympic Games be better? Whatever an experimenter's decision is, it seems clear that understanding that these sort of comparison problems exist is just a first step toward solving them.

## MORE ABOUT X

Because the causal event in any experiment is a complex event that represents the real event addressed in the hypothesis in an indirect or abstract way, it is always difficult to determine exactly what is responsible for any observed behavioral effect. Yet there are certainly good reasons to want to do so. It is obviously important to be sure that the event created in the laboratory is truly closely related to the real event it is intended to represent. It is also important to know what part of the whole complex of words, apparatus, and actions making up the event which is presented to the subjects really causes the difference in their behavior—the "active ingredient" in it, so to speak.

Choosing the right comparison or no-X treatment is one way of accomplishing this. The fewer the differences are between it and the causal event of interest (X), the fewer will be the possible alternative causes of any difference in the behavior they produce—in other words, the closer that the experiment comes to pinpointing the specific cause.

The issue of standardization of experimental procedures is important here again. Every operational definition of a hypothesized causal event consists of two parts. The essence of that event, which may have the capacity to alter the behavior being studied, is one; we are calling this the active ingredient of X. The other one consists of the specific procedures that are used to convey that active ingredient; this we call the vehicle for X. Any experience could be conveyed to subjects by a variety of different vehicles. The specific words and actions of the experimenter, the size and style of the type used in the questionnaires, the size of the laboratory room, and the innumerable other details that go into an experimental treatment are usually chosen arbitrarily because they are convenient or esthetically pleasing or because they seem in the opinion of one person or another to be the right things to do. They are also irrelevant to the hypothesis, which deals with what happens, not how it happens. But they are not necessarily irrelevant to the subjects. They could affect their behavior. To the extent they do, any conclusion about the effect of X as described in the hypothesis would be misleading. We do not truly know what parts of the subjects' total experience—X as presented in the particular experiment—are responsible for the observed effects on their behavior.

If the presentation of X is standardized across the variety of experiments in which the event in question is being studied, the possibility that the behavioral effects observed were caused by some irrelevant aspect of the vehicle for X rather than by its essence becomes even more dangerous. First, a large number of experimental findings are in doubt. Second, every time the effects of that X are observed, the same specific irrelevant vehicle for X is present. If, instead, a different means of presenting X to subjects were used in every experiment, and X still had its predicted effects consistently across the whole series, two benefits would accrue. First, as we described earlier, the generalizability of the findings would be greater. But we would also know more about what the essence of X really was; only the parts of X that were common to all the experiments in the series would be possible candidates for the essence of X. All the various irrelevant aspects of the different vehicles for X would clearly not be possible causes for the behaviors predicted following X, because their presence or absence would have been shown to make no difference in those behaviors.

Finally, there is yet another way—in addition to careful matching of comparison groups and diversification of the means of producing X—to define an experimental treatment more precisely. It is called the *manipulation check* and its function is to monitor the effects of X on the subjects in an experiment. One of the best examples of a manipulation check is the brain lesion research we discussed earlier. Although the surgical procedures are very precise, researchers cannot be sure that the brain tissue is precisely that which they intend. After the behavioral measures of the animals' eating after surgery are completed, the rats are sacrificed and their brains are examined directly to determine exactly the location of the lesion that was produced. Only if it falls exactly in the VMH region does an animal qualify, after the fact, for the experimental treatment group.

There are similar problems in determining the precise effect of X in other areas of research as well. For example, in a social–psychological experiment to test the hypothesis that individuals who have low self-esteem are more easily persuaded to change their attitudes, subjects may be deceived into thinking that they have failed a test. The experimenter's intention is that this rigged failure experience temporarily lowers subjects' self-esteem. Even if it has the predicted effect on their behavior, however, one still could not be sure that their increased persuasibility was due to lowered self-esteem. Let us imagine that the subjects' success or failure on the rigged test was followed by a message designed to persuade them that capital punishment is effective in deterring violent crime. Someone might argue that the test failure caused the subjects to be angry, not the intended effect of making them doubt their self-worth, and that their response to the message simply expressed that anger, directed toward the criminals as a target of opportunity presented to them at that time.

How can one distinguish between these competing hypotheses? Was it lowered self-esteem or anger? One method is to ask subjects to rate their feelings, or mood, after the test results are given and before they read the persuasive message. They can be given a list of adjectives that includes angry and unsure, and their choices could resolve the issue. On the other hand, people may not be able to report their feelings accurately, and the rating instrument would interfere with the flow of the experimental procedure from test to results to message to attitude measurement. If the subjects were videotaped throughout the procedure, judges could be asked to rate their mood from their facial expressions. A concrete example of this less reactive and probably more accurate technique is presented in Chapter 7.

This discussion was not intended to provide solutions to even a representative sample of manipulation check problems. It simply points out that the events presented to subjects are recreations of the events specified in the experimental hypothesis. Their intended essence is the creation of some state in the subjects, some belief or expectation, the challenge of some special kind of task or problem, and so on. In order to see whether this intention is fulfilled successfully, one can usually design some sort of manipulation check to provide at least a partial answer. And the high degree of control provided by an experiment makes this safeguard easier to apply.

## EXTENSIONS OF TRUE EXPERIMENTAL DESIGNS

In an effort to understand the basic properties of true experimental designs, we have dealt with them in their simplest forms—one randomly selected group of subjects exposed to the causal event being investigated and another randomly selected group not exposed to it. If you go through your textbooks or psychological journals looking for published experiments that fit the diagrams of designs E-1, E-2, and E-3 in this chapter, you will find very few. If you try to use any of those diagrams as a model for an experiment to test some hypothesis you are interested in, you will probably find it difficult. In most cases, these true experimental designs are used in more complex forms than we have considered in this chapter.

In order to bridge the gap between the "textbook" and real versions of the true experimental designs, we will undertake a brief discussion of three ways in which the basic designs diagrammed in Table 6-1 can be extended to fit research hypotheses better. When you try later to apply what you learn here to all the areas of psychology you study, these should give you a head start to understanding all the different kinds of extensions which have been used.

### Multiple Levels of X

Very few real experiments compare the presence and the absence of an event. In fact, it is so rare that we have already had to use experiments that compare different versions of a causal event as examples in this chapter. Most true experiments, which are designed to investigate the effect of one particular event on one kind of behavior, compare more or less of that event rather than its presence in some form with its complete absence (nothing or a completely different kind of event). In some cases, this is because it is difficult to know what the complete absence of an event would mean. Consider the example of an experiment to test the effect of motivation on learning. We will use one of the many experiments of this kind that was done with rats that were required to run through a complicated maze to reach a food reward at the end. The animals' level of motivation was varied by testing them at varying intervals after they were fed. Thus an experiment might have compared several randomly selected groups of animals who were tested 0 (immediately after eating), 4, 8, 12, and 24 hours after being fed. But it would not be fair to say that the "zero hours of deprivation" group were not motivated—only that the greater the motivation (food deprivation), within this range, the better the animals' performance in the maze. What would no deprivation mean, anyway? As full as after Thanksgiving dinner? That is a tougher question than the experiment itself was intended to answer.

There are other good reasons for comparing a number of levels of X rather than just its presence and absence. One is that it permits us to examine the shape of the relationship between X and the behavior we are interested in. One of the most famous examples of this point is the relationship between motivation and performance. In an experiment published in 1957, Broadhurst investigated one specific example of that relationship. He tested rats on a discrimination task that required them to choose one of two routes to escape from an underwater maze. The routes were marked by lights of different intensities, randomly alternated between the alleys on the rats, left and right. One light was 15 times as bright as the other.

The rats' motivation was varied by detaining them for various lengths of time in the underwater entrance to this simple maze. Five levels of air deprivation were used—0, 2, 4, 6, and 8 seconds.

Animals had to choose either the bright or the dim light in order to find the route that led to an area in which they could first stick their heads above water and eventually leave the water entirely. Each animal was tested 10 times per day for 10 successive days.

The design for this experiment could be diagrammed as follows (X stands for the manipulation of air deprivation and O for the number of correct responses summed over all 100 trials, each with subscripts identifying the level of motivation by the number of seconds of air deprivation):

$$
\begin{array}{cccc}
G_1 & R & X_0 & O_0 \\
G_2 & R & X_2 & O_2 \\
G_3 & R & X_4 & O_4 \\
G_4 & R & X_6 & O_6 \\
G_5 & R & X_8 & O_8 \\
\end{array}
$$

Although there are five groups instead of two, this is still Design E-2. All the strengths and weaknesses of that design apply equally to interpreting the findings of this experiment. But the fact that Broadhurst included so many levels of X is significant in itself, as is evident in his findings. The best level of performance, about 80% correct, was observed in rats deprived of air for 2 seconds. At all other levels of deprivation, the animals chose correctly on about 70% of the trials, except for the group deprived for 8 seconds, which was down almost to 65%. In other words, the relationship between motivation and performance was nonlinear. Motivation did make a difference, but there was a complex difference in which both high and low levels were associated with relatively poor performance, and the animals performed best when their motivation was at a moderate level. In cases like this one, in which every increase in X does not simply produce a corresponding increase in O, comparing a strong dose of X with none at all could be very misleading. For example, if Broadhurst had compared just two groups of rats, one of which was deprived of air for 6 seconds and another which was not deprived at all, he would have found no difference in performance, and might have concluded, wrongly, that there was no relationship between air deprivation and discrimination accuracy.

The lesson to be learned here is that X and O can be related without their relationship necessarily being a simple linear one. And there are even types of relationships other than the simple linear one and the "U-shaped" relationship found by Broadhurst. It can be important to some hypotheses whether a curve is positively or negatively accelerated, that is, whether the increase in O is greater or smaller at higher values of X than at lower levels. Whatever the case, the more levels of X that are compared, the more information there is about the exact form of the relationship. And the number of levels that are compared does not determine, or alter, the nature of the experimental design.

## More Than One X (Multivariate Designs)

Another important way of extending an experimental design is by studying more than one causal event at the same time. We have already been introduced to this possibility in our discussion of the concept of interaction in Chapter 2. In that discussion, recall that an experiment that includes two causal factors at the same time can provide much more information than two separate experiments, each of which tests the effects of one of those factors. (Review it if necessary.) We will discuss it again only very briefly in the context of a single example—Broadhurst's experiment.

The truth is that Broadhurst investigated not only the effect of motivation on underwater maze performance, but also another potential influence. The part of his experiment that I described consisted of the five groups of rats that worked on the discrimination problem in which one light was 15 times as bright as the other. There were also five groups that worked on an easier problem, where one light was 60 times as bright as the other, and a third set of five groups that worked on an even easier problem, where the ratio of intensities was 300 to 1.

Thus, in addition to studying the effects of motivation level (length of air deprivation) on performance, Broadhurst also studied the effect of task difficulty. All possible combinations of the five levels of motivation and three levels of task difficulty were represented—15 separate groups of subjects in all. This is called a *factorial experiment*. This version of design E-2—and this is still the same design, no matter how it looks, because the essential features, random assignment and posttest only, are the same—would be diagrammed thus:

$$
\begin{array}{ccccc}
G_1 & R & X_0 & Y_{15} & O_1 \\
G_2 & R & X_0 & Y_{60} & O_2 \\
G_3 & R & X_0 & Y_{300} & O_3 \\
G_4 & R & X_2 & Y_{15} & O_4 \\
G_5 & R & X_2 & Y_{60} & O_5 \\
G_6 & R & X_2 & Y_{300} & O_6 \\
G_7 & R & X_4 & Y_{15} & O_7 \\
G_8 & R & X_4 & Y_{60} & O_8 \\
G_9 & R & X_4 & Y_{300} & O_9 \\
G_{10} & R & X_6 & Y_{15} & O_{10} \\
G_{11} & R & X_6 & Y_{60} & O_{11} \\
G_{12} & R & X_6 & Y_{300} & O_{12} \\
G_{13} & R & X_8 & Y_{15} & O_{13} \\
G_{14} & R & X_8 & Y_{60} & O_{14} \\
G_{15} & R & X_8 & Y_{300} & O_{15} \\
\end{array}
$$

Of course, this design can be broken back down into the equivalents of two separate experiments—one on the effects of task difficulty and one on the effects of level of motivation. To determine the effects of task difficulty alone, you could add up all five groups that performed the easiest task ($Y_{300}$—the 300 to one ratio of light intensities), all five that worked on the moderately difficult task ($Y_{60}$), and, finally, all five that were faced with the most difficult one ($Y_{15}$). When Broadhurst compared those three, he found that the rats did best on the easiest one (86% correct), worst on the most difficult (72%), and in between on the moderately difficult version (83%). No great surprise there!

However, a comparison of the five levels of motivation, combined for all three tasks, is somewhat surprising. There was very little difference. The rats that were deprived of air for 2 seconds (all three groups combined) did only slightly better (83% correct) than the others (about 80% for each). This is too small a difference to be sure it was not due to accidental inequality among the different groups of rats. The reason for the lack of difference is that the effect of the level of air deprivation depended on the level of task difficulty. We have already seen the results for the difficult task. Performance was best when the level of motivation was moderate (about 80%), and worst when it was high or low (70% or less). Performance on the easiest task improves slightly as the level of motivation increases, up to 4 seconds of air deprivation (84 to 88%); then it stays about the same at 6 and 8 seconds of deprivation. The results for the moderately difficult task were in between—a slight peak at 2 seconds (up to almost 85% from 81% at 0 seconds) and no decline at 4, 6, or 8 seconds (about 83% at each).

This information is the real contribution of a factorial experiment that includes more than one causal factor. The fact that the effect of one causal factor varies with the particular level of the other could not be learned from two separate single-factor experiments in which the effects of different levels of X (motivation) can be observed at only one level of Y (one task in this case).

## Blocking Subjects in a Factorial "Experiment"

A third way of extending the true experimental designs also involves adding a second factor. In this case, however, the additional factor is not another suspected cause of the behavior being studied. It is a measure of some characteristic of the subjects that is expected to interact with the causal factor being studied. In other words, subjects are grouped on the basis of some stable characteristic they possess, an ability or personality trait or social group membership, in order to determine whether the effect of X varies across the groups of subjects.

This procedure is sometimes referred to as "blocking" the subjects on whatever characteristic is chosen as the basis for grouping them. It is also known as a treatment-by-levels design, because the effect of a treatment, X, is investigated at various levels of the subject characteristic. Whatever it is called, this design has been used fairly widely by psychologists who have a long tradition of trying to compare different groups of people—from Galton's studies of individual differences through Binet's measurement of intelligence and Freud's and so many others' personality typologies to the current study of personality traits.

Blocking is used frequently in research which tests some procedure or program which has potential practical application. Teaching techniques, management training procedures, incentive systems for workers, and psychotherapeutic regimens are a few examples. In cases like these, it is often suspected that the advantage of one technique or procedure over another will depend upon the nature of the individuals to whom it is applied. A "back-to-basics" approach to educational curriculum may benefit the average or poor student more than the bright one. A more structured set of work rules may produce better results for workers who feel that lines of authority should be drawn very clearly than for their more egalitarian colleagues. Behavior therapy may produce better results among clients with phobias than among those who are depressed.

In all these cases, and similar ones, it would be misleading to compare the treatments of interest in a random sample of all neurotics, workers, students, or executives. As we saw in Broadhurst's study and in other examples as well, if the relationship of X to some behavior varies with some additional condition, its overall effect may be very misleading. It may appear to have no effect at all until its effects are examined with separate values of that condition. Some would say that its different effects in those different conditions cancel each other out. Even if they do not, it can still be true that the differences in the effects of X in those different conditions are important. If a teaching technique works much better for one kind of student than another, there would be practical reasons for finding that out. An educator who is aware of that fact could be selective in applying the technique, conserving scarce resources or looking for something that would work better for other groups of students. This cannot be done if the effects of the technique are studied only in a random sample of all students.

Let us look at one concrete example of such an "experiment" (the quotation marks will be explained soon). It was performed to compare the effects of two different teaching styles on students' performance in an introductory psychology course (Domino, 1971)—a subject which I am sure is close to all our hearts. The teaching styles differed in the amount of structure and direction imposed by the instructor.

In one case, the instructor made specific assignments, required attendance, and used class periods to present material which had been carefully outlined in advance. In the other case, students were given choices among a variety of assignments, attendance was optional, and students were encouraged to express their views in class and thereby to contribute toward determining its direction. When it came to predicting which style of teaching would be more effective, Domino recognized that it might depend on the characteristics of the individual student. He used students' scores on a personality test that had been administered to the entire freshman class to choose two contrasting groups from students in introductory psychology.

One group's scores indicated that they strove to meet standards set for them by others—the "achievement through conformance," or Ac group. The contrasting group expressed a desire to learn independently and an attraction to intellectual complexity—the "achievement through independence," or Ai group. Domino predicted and found that the more structured and less structured teaching styles were equally effective overall, but that the Ac students did better when the course was more structured, whereas the Ai students did better when it was less structured. This illustrates the value of examining the effect of X separately in different types of subjects. It indicates much more precisely how X affects the behavior involved, especially when some characteristic of the subjects is suspected correctly of determining their responses to X. Intelligence, gender, and personality traits have been popular bases for blocking subjects in psychological research. Of course, it should be clear to you by now that comparing subjects of different types is not an experimental procedure (hence the quotation marks used earlier).

Subjects cannot be assigned randomly to be independent or conforming, male or female, or highly intelligent or less intelligent. The best way to think of the design of this kind of study—now that we understand why it is not really an experiment—is as a series of experiments, each done with a particular kind of subject. Although the results would be treated the same statistically as the results of a factorial true experiment in which both causal factors were manipulated, the two studies mean very different things. If there is evidence of an interaction between X and the characteristic on which subjects are blocked, that means that those experiments did not all turn out the same. In Domino's study, in fact, the experiment with Ai subjects revealed the opposite effect of X as that with Ac subjects. The increased precision that this extension of a true experimental design makes necessary is often gained at no cost at all to the researcher.

As was true in the Domino study, the measurements on which blocking is based are often available from existing sources. In this case they were obtained from a questionnaire that was a routine part of students' orientation program. In a study comparing different teaching techniques (assuming it could be carried out as an experiment), school records of students' past grades might be used. Psychotherapy clients could be grouped on the basis of routine diagnostic test scores in order to compare the effects of different therapeutic techniques. And so on. In any case, the comparison of the various treatments within each group of subjects is still an experiment. If all those groups were combined, we would be left with one large experiment carried out on a single, representative sample of subjects.

## Extensions and External Validity

Specific knowledge is gained from each of the extensions of true experimental designs we examined: more information about the shape of relationship between X and O, the complex way different causal factors combine to determine behavior, and the way different kinds of subjects respond to X. But, in addition, they all have something important in common. In its own way, each extension adds to the external validity of experimental findings. We learn whether the effect of X can be generalized to different values or levels of X, to different levels of another condition that also affects the behavior in question, or to different kinds of subjects. We have already discussed the external validity problems associated with true experimental designs. We have also discussed ways in which series of experiments can incorporate a diversity of procedures in an effort to broaden the generalizability of their findings. In Chapter 7 other ways of increasing the generalizability of experimental findings will be considered. But here, we have seen how a single experiment can be extended, in some cases at very little increase in cost of time or effort, in order to make the conclusions drawn from its findings more broadly applicable. By building more different comparisons into the experiment itself, we can at least reduce the likelihood that its findings will be restricted to a very narrow range of situations similar to the experiment—or, in other words, that the conditions represented in the experiment will be a very peculiar subset of those under which the behavior can be influenced by X. Given the artificiality of most experimental settings, any gain in this area is very welcome.

## ETHICS IN EXPERIMENTAL RESEARCH

From the beginnings of its history as a science, as we have pointed out before, psychological research has relied on the experimental method. Practitioners of that method have believed that human subjects in experiments must be kept ignorant of the research's purposes to ensure that their responses to the conditions created by the experimenter will be natural. Otherwise, it has usually been argued, those conditions are likely to have very little impact on subjects, who will be more concerned with acting as they are expected to. As we've already seen, experimenters have usually solved this problem, and created the events their subjects would respond to, through the use of deception. This involves some combination of misleading or incomplete instructions, theatrical events and props, and hidden means of assessing those aspects of subjects' behavior specified in the hypothesis.

In the next chapter, we will evaluate some of the prevailing assumptions about the necessity of those deceptions and look at some alternatives to them. But for now let us consider only whether the researchers who use them are behaving responsibly and ethically, and whether the subjects to whom they are administered are harmed by them. If the answers to those questions are unsatisfactory, what can be done to improve the situation?

A debate on these issues has been continuing for some time in psychology—at least 30 years. It has been carried on for the most part by social psychologists, the foremost practitioners of deception (or, at least, the most conspicuous ones). Although some concerned scholars have persisted in raising these questions, for most the issue has flared up from time to time, fueled by highly publicized cases of deception that have elicited widespread criticism. We might do well to start with some of those for illustrative purposes.

Probably the best known example is the obedience research of Stanley Milgram which we looked at in Chapter 2 (Milgram, 1963). As you probably already know, Milgram deceived subjects into believing that they were participating in a human learning experiment. They believed they were punishing another subject's errors on the learning task with successively higher levels of electric shock. The deeper a subject became involved, as the session continued and the level of shock (and the "victim's" complaints) increased, the greater was the anxiety that the subject felt. Apparently, Milgram's subjects became very deeply involved in conflicts over whether to obey the experimenter or to act in the interests of the unfortunate "learner." In fact, Milgram cited extreme examples of his subjects' tension, including tremors, perspiration, and stuttering, to convince most of the readers that the deceptions were successful, that subjects believed the "play" was real, and that his findings could be trusted (we have already seen the possible flaw in that reasoning).

A more recent example, which is approaching Milgram's studies in its notoriety, is a study by West, Gunn, and Chernicky (1975). That study tried to examine the motives which underlay the infamous Watergate break-in by recruiting college students to assist in burglarizing an advertising company. A private investigator offered money, government approval (government approval included immunity from prosecution), or none of those incentives while he was explaining his elaborate plans for stealing documents from the company's office. Although the main focus of this study was on the reasons people do what they do, in the course of the study, some of the subjects agreed to commit an illegal act.

Both the Milgram and the West, Gunn, and Chernicky studies provoked considerable discussion about the possible harm done to subjects as a consequence of deception in experiments. Other psychologists wrote articles analyzing the ethnical issues involved, or letters to journal editors protesting or defending the researchers involved. But these two experiments are not basically very different from any others, probably just a little more interesting. It is common practice to deceive subjects into believing that they are doing things they would ordinarily be ashamed of, such as conforming, or hurting someone else, or cheating, or revealing sensitive information about themselves. Many of these subjects feel very anxious in the false situations experimenters create. Some may think less of themselves afterward than they did before, or they may be more skeptical of other people's motives afterward, or they may even be more pessimistic about their futures.

Most researchers accept the fact that subjects can be harmed, at least temporarily, by their experiences in such experiments. Even before criticism, or even ethical analysis, reached a very high level, researchers themselves had taken steps to safeguard their subjects. Most laboratory experiments were followed by debriefing sessions in which the need for deception was explained to subjects, their behavior was placed in the reassuring context of the behavior of all the other subjects who had been tested, and they were generally reassured and befriended by the experimenter. Milgram even used mental health professionals to screen potential subjects for special vulnerability and then had them interview actual subjects after the obedience experiment session was over, probing for evidence of serious harm. Some of his subjects were even followed up months afterward to guard against delayed, long-term effects.

Most of the analysts of psychological experiments (who have, incidentally, come from inside the profession) have suggested procedures similar to the course of action that many researchers have followed voluntarily for some time. Some have suggested that such procedures should be aimed at returning subjects to the state they were in before the experiment began. Subjects should not feel any more anxiety, their self-esteem should be at least as high as before, and their trust in others should be restored. Some research evidence even suggests that these goals can be attained. Unfortunately, much of it comes from studies in which subjects are asked directly how they feel and what they believe. If the subjects do not tell the truth, because they think the experimenter does not want to know it, the adverse effects of deception may not be uncovered.

An example of how this can happen can be found in the experience of a friend of mine. To study the effects of failure and resulting lowered self-esteem, he gave a group of student nurses a (supposed) test to show how well they got along with people. Half were chosen at random to "fail" the test. Then their behavior was observed in a standardized situation that was compared with the behavior of those who passed the test. Afterward, as part of the debriefing, my friend talked to each of his subjects, explaining that the test was not what he had claimed it to be and that their scores were not what he had told them they were. One young woman smiled and nodded like all the rest as he talked, then got up to leave. Just before she closed the door of the interview room, however, she said something like, "I'm glad I was in your experiment. And I'm grateful that you tried to spare my feelings. Now I've learned that I'm not the kind of person who should be a nurse. Thank you." My friend managed to drag her back into the room and, finally, he thought, convinced her that the experiment was a lie and the debriefing was the truth. After that experience, however, he wondered how many other subjects had felt the same way but had not said anything. He decided to put a sealed envelope containing a truthful description of the experiment on the table where subjects could see it during the entire experiment. Then, during the debriefing he would ask them to open it and read the truth that had been there before they ever saw the "test" or heard their results.

The real moral of this story is that undoing the effects of an experiment is not easy. Researchers who use deception seem to me to be much too optimistic, on the whole, about the results of their efforts. It is not easy for subjects to figure out which conflicting statement is the lie and which is the truth. Claiming to be telling the truth may not work if one has already admitted to being a liar. And subjects may not admit their true feelings to an experimenter when they realize that they are playing a game that permits and even encourages deception.

It has also been argued that even if researchers' efforts fail to completely undo the harm that has been caused to subjects, the remaining negative effects can be balanced by the ultimate value of the research findings. Frankly, it is difficult to imagine how this could be done. It would involve some very risky predictions before the research had even begun about the residual effects on subjects, as well as about the uses to which findings (if any) could be put by other researchers or by those who need to solve practical problems (some of which might not even exist yet). However, some simpler steps have been suggested. Some critics have pointed to what they perceive as frivolous motives on the part of some researchers (Ring,

1967; Rubin, 1970). In some cases, elaborate deceptions seem to be aimed more at impressing other researchers with their own cleverness and with the humorous and extreme behaviors that they can elicit from unsuspecting subjects than with the importance of the questions they might help to answer. It has also been observed, at least half-seriously, that too much of the risk to which subjects are put is unnecessary because the researchers are not competent enough to produce useful findings anyway (Steiner, 1972). Some means of restricting access to subjects to only those investigators who have proven they can produce findings of value should certainly improve the balance between harm and good (even if we cannot specify precisely what that is).

Recently, pressures toward protecting subjects have been brought to bear on psychological research from outside. The federal government has been the source of most of these. New analyses of the ethical problems have incorporated the views of people who are not behavioral researchers themselves, and thus have much less of a personal stake in preserving the researchers' domain. Legal views have also begun to be applied. The result of introducing both of these new perspectives has caused a very different view of the researcher–subject relationship. For one thing, it seems to have been more obvious to these outsiders that research subjects are very vulnerable to the pressures imposed by researchers. Their freedom is limited once they agree to participate. Ironically, researchers should have been even more sensitive to this fact, given their knowledge of the research findings like Milgram's. In fact, the use of college student subjects is partly due to their limited freedom to decline participation in the first place. In many cases, the researcher has formal power over the subject—professor over student, industrial psychologist/executive over worker, school psychologist over pupil, and so on.

With this point of view that is more sympathetic to the plight of the subject, one would expect different suggestions about protecting subjects' rights. And that is precisely what has occurred. Commissions have been formed in researchers' professional societies at the instigation of government agencies. Moreover, these commissions have been constrained to operate under guidelines formulated in part, at least, by officials whose views have been influenced by the input of ordinary citizens, who are closer relatives of subjects than of researchers, and lawyers. Under those ground rules, stressing the rights of subjects, two suggestions have emerged for policies governing the use of human subjects. The first is a review of research proposals by committees composed of scholars and lay people to evaluate potential hazards to subjects. All federally funded research has to undergo such review, and many universities and other institutions in which research takes place have begun to subject other research proposals to the same procedures. Second, it has been recommended that subjects ordinarily be used only after they have given their "informed consent." In other words, potential subjects would have to agree voluntarily to participate, and only after they were given enough information about the research to evaluate the potential harm and benefit for themselves.

By and large, researchers have argued against and resisted the implementation of these suggested policies. The traditional view that subjects must be kept ignorant still prevails. Spokespersons like Aronson (e.g., 1980) argue that deception constitutes a major part of the researcher's skill, and that debriefing can remedy any short-term (and necessary) harm to subjects if it is skillfully done. They imply, further, that such policies, especially the need to get informed consent, would have a chilling effect on behavioral research if they were implemented. (Although a milder variation of informed consent, called forewarning, has been used to a limited degree and appears promising.) In any case, at this point we have, except for federally funded studies, only proposed policies which are still being debated very hotly. Most research safeguards subjects' rights only through the consciences and good judgment of researchers and the occasional pressures of journal editors and others who have influence over them. This situation is likely to change only when government pressures become irresistible, or when methodological problems with deception become so widely recognized that effective alternatives are developed to replace it.

This discussion has focused exclusively on laboratory research with human subjects. That is certainly where most researchers' and critics' interest has been directed and, therefore, where the issues and arguments have been drawn most clearly. There are, however, other problems as well. Research with animal subjects is one. Animal subjects are often punished, painfully altered surgically, or disposed of after they have outlived their usefulness to researchers. Many people object to these practices, especially when the animal species involved are also kept as pets or seem extremely humanlike, such as dogs and monkeys. The federal government does enforce guidelines for the clean and healthful maintenance of laboratory animals, although this may be motivated more by a concern for people's safety than the animals'. In addition, there are laws and professional groups' codes of ethics for the "humane" treatment of animals, although these standards rule out very little of the cruelty that is seen as necessary for the research to be carried on. Animals are to be killed with drugs, for example, but there is no prohibition against killing them.

A special kind of ethical problem is also raised in experiments which are conducted to evaluate the effects of medical and psychological therapies. When applicants to a clinic are divided randomly into those who will receive immediate treatment and those who will be placed on a waiting list as a no-treatment comparison group—or when children are divided randomly into those who will receive an experimental vaccine and those who will receive a placebo injection—some individuals are deprived of the opportunity to receive a potentially valuable service so that the service can be evaluated in a rigorous scientific manner. Their lives are being affected in very important ways to fit the plans of the researcher. This has usually been justified by the great value of the information gained from such research. At the time, however, no one is sure just how much sacrifice the subjects' participation undergoes because the value of the treatment is indeterminate. Also, in many of these cases there is not enough treatment available for all who need it. Under those circumstances, it is difficult to conceive of a more ethical procedure than the lottery that is created by the random assignment of subjects to treatment and no-treatment groups.

But the picture can get even cloudier. In 1976, Schulz published an experiment that showed that a group of institutionalized elderly people benefited physically and psychologically by receiving for two months predictable and controllable visits from college undergraduates as compared with those who received randomly scheduled visits or none at all. However, two to three years after the original two-month study was over, Schulz and Hanusa (1978) found that these same elderly people were worse off than those who had been visited randomly or not at all during the study. It seems that the contrast between the end of the visits and the control over their lives and the well-being that resulted from those visits caused them to feel even worse than they had before the original study began. This unexpected result of the well-intentioned intervention into these elderly people's lives shows both how dangerous research can be for subjects and how difficult it can be to predict the dangers.

Research with human subjects that is conducted in field settings poses some very difficult ethical problems. We will deal with some of these in the chapter on quasi-experimental research designs. But experiments in the field in which researchers actively intervene in subjects' lives pose special problems all their own.

Both the existing remedies, careful debriefing and the proposed safeguard of informed consent, are very difficult to apply in field settings. Pedestrians, drivers, shoppers, and workers move through a field experiment too quickly to be informed and to give their consent beforehand or to be debriefed afterward. And because they are not aware that an experiment is taking place, they are deprived of the opportunity to defend themselves against unwanted scrutiny that laboratory subjects have. The methodological advantages of field experiments, which are discussed at length in the next chapter, make these ethical problems especially painful to consider. We can only hope that this and other difficult problems of reconciling the fair and ethical treatment of subjects with the need to understand behavior through scientific research can be solved more adequately in the future than their present state suggests. Some researchers have argued that research subjects are not exposed to greater risks in experiments than in their everyday lives. We all face pressures to conform and obey, embarrassing moments, temptations, and the like every day. But does the researcher have a right to add to them? Or to invade what little privacy any of us has left by observing our reactions?

## REFERENCES

Aronson, E. *The social animal,* third edition. San Francisco: Freeman, 1980.

Broadhurst, P. L. Emotionality and the Yerkes-Dodson law. *Journal of Experimental Psychology,* 1957, *54,* 345–352.

Domino, G. Interactive effects of achievement orientation and teaching style on academic achievement. *Journal of Educational Psychology,* 1971, *62,* 427–431.

Greenglass, E. R., & Stewart, M. The under-representation of women in social psychological research. *Ontario Psychologist,* 1973, *5*(2), 21–29.

Hetherington, A. W., & Ranson, S. W. The spontaneous activity and food intake of rats with hypothalamic lesions. *American Journal of Physiology,* 1940, *136,* 609–617.

Ring, K. Experimental social psychology: Some sober questions about some frivolous values. *Journal of Experimental Social Psychology,* 1967, *3,* 113–123.

Rubin, Z. Jokers wild in the lab. *Psychology Today,* 1970, *4*(7), 18–24.

Schulz, R. The effect of control and predictability on the psychological and physical well-being of the institutionalized aged. *Journal of Personality and Social Psychology,* 1976, *33,* 563–573.

Schulz, R., & Hanusa, B. H. Long-term effects of control and predictability-enhancing interventions. *Journal of Personality and Social Psychology,* 1978, *36,* 1194–1201.

Steiner, I. D. The evils of research: Or what my mother didn't tell me about the sins of academia. *American Psychologist,* 1972, *27,* 766–768.

West, S. G., Gunn, S. P., & Chernicky, P. Ubiquitous Watergate: An attributional analysis. *Journal of Personality and Social Psychology,* 1975, *32,* 55–65.

Zimbardo, P. G., Haney, C., Banks, W. C., & Jaffe, D. A Pirandellian prison: The mind is a formidable jailer. *New York Times Magazine,* April 8, 1973, pp. 38–60.

## SUGGESTED ACTIVITIES

### Study Questions

1. Why do true experimental research designs succeed so well, in general, at eliminating threats to internal validity? What are the most troublesome exceptions to that success? How can each of those problems be overcome?
2. Why do true experimental designs fail so badly, in general, at eliminating threats to external validity? Do you see the relationship between the reasons for their failures and the reasons for their successes? How does the purpose of a true experiment affect the seriousness of its deficiencies in external validity?

### Exercise

Find examples of true experiments. Psychology journals are filled with them. Choose six or so that deal with a variety of subjects, such as learning, social behavior, and physiological systems. How could you tell that a research study was an experiment?

Diagram each experiment. Can you fit it into one of the types discussed in this chapter? If not, try to describe it and even to name it yourself.

Evaluate each experiment using the Validity Scorecard. How many of the minuses and question marks could have been turned into pluses if the experiment had been done differently? What specific steps would you suggest to someone who planned to test the same hypothesis again to improve the validity of their findings over the original?

# Chapter 7
# Enhancing the External Validity of Experimental Research Methods

## INTRODUCTION

In Chapter 6, our analysis of experimental research methods pointed out rather clearly their vulnerability to threats to external validity. Twenty years ago such a critical analysis of these methods might have been considered surprising, if not heretical, by many experimental psychologists. However, over that period of time, the increasingly widespread application of experimental research designs to human subjects, and, particularly, the growth of laboratory research in social psychology, have made their limitations more and more obvious. Those developments have engendered a growing, increasingly vigorous debate through which the criteria for external validity have gained a more equal status to those for internal validity. Although much of that debate has dealt with the ethical implications of using deceptive experimental methods on human subjects, a question already considered in Chapter 6, it has slowly begun to face up to their potential methodological inadequacies as well.

At the heart of the methodological issue is the question of reactivity. It is not that the other aspects of external validity are less im-

portant in any absolute sense. The generalizability of research findings beyond specific groups of subjects and research settings is obviously a very important consideration. But some degree of specificity
is inevitable and reactivity seems to be more intrinsically involved
in the nature of experimental research with human subjects, and it
is this issue that has captured the lion's share of attention.

To recapitulate very briefly some of our discussion in Chapter
3, a basic prerequisite of the laboratory experiment is that the subjects be kept unaware of the purposes of the experiment. If the subjects knew what the experimenter expected them to do, their
behavior could not be assumed to be a spontaneous or natural reaction to the conditions to which they were exposed. Traditionally, experimenters have attempted to divert subjects' attention from the
true purposes of their experiments by giving them verbal instructions that misrepresented the purposes of the experiment and their
role in it. This "cover story" was often supported by props, both physical objects and other people playing parts written by the experimenter.

It is widely known that psychological experiments misrepresent
the truth, especially among the college students who usually serve
as subjects in them. And the presence of the experimenter makes
her or him a potential source of cues that might help unlock the mystery for the subject. Furthermore, the experimenter often treats subjects coldly, as objects of observation, and directs their performance
in an authoritarian manner. For all of these reasons, one must consider the possibility that experimental subjects, especially if they are
adult human beings of normal intelligence, will become sensitized
to the evaluative implications of the laboratory situation. It will probably be clear to them that they have been "put on the spot." Even
if they are unable to find out the experimenter's hypothesis, or the
particular aspects of their behavior in which the experimenter is interested, they are likely to feel self-conscious and to be aware of the
potential dangers of self-revelation that the experiment holds for
them. As a result, the effects of the intended experimental treatments may be confounded with the effects of the subjects' motives
for self-protection and mastery of the experiment.

At times, the debate over the effects of reactivity on the validity
of laboratory findings has produced more rhetoric than anything
else. Many critics of traditional experimentation have been satisfied
to attack its findings aggressively, without offering anything in the
way of constructive alternatives. Many of their targets have responded defensively, doing little more than denying the problems
that were raised. Fortunately, however, some good has finally begun
to come from all this. Many researchers have been led to a critical

reexamination of the traditional experiment. This has been especially true of social psychologists, who are among the greatest suffer-
ers and, ironically, among the best equipped to analyze laboratory
subjects' behavior.

That work has produced several promising new ways of doing
experimental research with human subjects that are less vulnerable
to attack on the grounds of reactivity. The rest of this chapter will
be devoted to a sample of these, but first a few preliminary points
need to be made. In our evaluation of the experimental research designs in Chapter 6, we made a summary judgment about the vulnerability of each method to each of the threats to validity. In fact, that
approach is used throughout this book. It may seem strange, then,
for us to begin discussing how the threat of reactive arrangements
can be lessened through using these innovative techniques. The
truth is that we have oversimplified the question for the sake of clarity. Any research design can be implemented in a variety of ways,
and its vulnerability to any particular threat to validity varies accordingly. To some extent, each design is at the mercy of its users. But
our overall judgments have to reflect the average difficulty that each
design presents in the ways in which it is typically used. In the present case, we were forced to acknowledge the comparative difficulty
of doing externally valid experiments.

The point also needs to be made that the techniques we are
about to describe are not sure cures for the ills of experimental research designs. As will become clear in our discussion of them, none
erases all doubt about the operation of reactive arrangements. But
each is valuable in suggesting a way of applying these very important
designs, with all their very real advantages, more effectively than
they have been applied in the past. Hopefully, we will see further
efforts to solve these problems even more effectively. Finally, we
have chosen to distinguish here between reactive measures of dependent variables and reactive manipulations of independent variables. Thus, our discussion will be divided into these two categories.

## OVERCOMING REACTIVITY IN MEASURING THE DEPENDENT VARIABLE

Frequently, the effects of experimental treatments on human subjects are assessed in a way that makes those subjects very aware of
which aspect of their behavior the experimenter is interested in.
They may suspect that the full significance of that behavior has not
been explained truthfully to them, and they may be apprehensive
about what it might reveal about them, either as individuals or as
subjects who are expected to be representative of all people. Conse-

quently, they may try to control that behavior, to avert the possibility of appearing inadequate or undesirable, and/or to create a favorable impression of themselves. To the extent that subjects engage in such tactics, the true effects of the experimental treatments will not be reflected in the data. Any behavior that subjects suspect to be the goal or target of the experimenter's inquiry is subject to manipulation in ways that they feel is to their advantage or to the benefit of the experimenter and his or her research.

How are experimenters to avoid such distortion of their data? We consider two possibilities in detail. The first is a technique called the *bogus pipeline* which seeks to encourage subjects to respond honestly by tricking them into believing that the experimenter has a foolproof way of assessing their true private feelings. The second utilizes aspects of the subjects' behavior with which they are unconcerned, or which they find difficult to control, or both. The great advantage of each of these techniques is that it does not rely on subjects' honesty.

## DECEPTIVE "LIE DETECTION": THE BOGUS PIPELINE

Suppose that you wanted to study racial stereotypes. Past studies have shown that white Americans hold a stereotyped view of black Americans. They believe most, if not all, blacks to be alike. They also believe that the characteristics that blacks share are less favorable than their own. For example, a 1933 study by Katz and Braly found that a large majority of a sample of white male college students agreed that "Negroes" were superstitious and lazy and that "Americans" (whites presumably) were intelligent and industrious.

You may suspect that those findings are archaic, that people's ideas surely must have changed since then. White Americans must be more deeply committed to equality today, especially those who are college students. They cannot still believe that all blacks or all whites are alike, or that whites are superior as a group. It may even be difficult for you to believe that they ever did. Maybe it is about time that someone set the record straight by showing that at least the young, educated white Americans of today do not still believe that all blacks are lazy and all whites intelligent. But don't they? There does still seem to be strong resistance to the integration of American society, at times even among educated young people. Blacks and whites still live apart in many ways. Perhaps there is a real question of whether those stereotypes have been abandoned.

As a matter of fact, the Katz and Braly study was repeated not too long ago, at the same university, and the findings were different. In 1969, Karlins, Coffman, and Walters reported that far smaller percentages of Princeton students still agreed that blacks and whites possess the traditional sets of stereotyped traits. Thus the stereotypes really have been abandoned, at least by many. Or have they? Is it possible that young, educated white Americans are merely more reluctant to admit to believing in the stereotypes than 40 years ago?

The difficulty in choosing between these two alternative explanations for the Karlins's findings is caused, largely, by the method they used to measure their subjects' beliefs. Is it reasonable to simply ask subjects to check off, on a very long list, those traits that they believe are characteristic of blacks or whites? What are the implications, in present-day America, of believing that any racial or ethnic group is homogeneous? Worse yet, what does it mean if someone believes that blacks are lazy and whites are industrious? In many segments of American society, such racist beliefs are openly discouraged; and "openly" is a key word. Even if people hold such beliefs privately, they are not expected to air them in public. Beyond that, it is important to many of us to believe that we ourselves are not racists. Regardless of what our true perceptions of some other group of people may be, we feel better about ourselves when we express our belief in equality and in the importance of treating each person as an individual.

Thus, if we simply ask people about their beliefs on such a sensitive topic, it may be unwise to put very much trust in their answers. But what if they thought that we had a way of finding out what their true private feelings were? What if we connected them to a very complex-looking array of electronic apparatus which we described as a new and highly sophisticated lie detector? What if they believed that it could reveal not only the intensity of their feelings, as current lie detectors are limited to doing, but the direction of those feelings as well? Would they tell us the truth if they thought that we would find out eventually anyway, and perhaps find out that they were hypocrites in the process? And would that truth be different from what they would report voluntarily?

Two social psychologists, E. E. Jones and Harold Sigall, devised just such a method for assessing people's beliefs. They called it the *bogus pipeline.* It involves deceitfully convincing subjects that they are attached to a machine that can detect their true feelings, and then asking them to predict the machine's readings. Subjects are asked to think about a statement about a person, group, issue, and so on, while connected to the machine. Then they are asked to indicate verbally how they feel about that statement. They are told that this tests how closely they are in touch with their true feelings, which presumably the machine has already recorded. If they have been convinced that the machine can do what it is claimed to do, then they would be forced to answer truthfully. A discrepancy between the "infallible" machine's readings and their verbal statements might imply that they have been less than honest in reporting their true feelings. (There is no sense trying to misrepresent yourself to someone who already has a direct pipeline to the truth about you. One thing that is surely worse than being known to have dishonorable thoughts is to be caught in a lie about them.)

A study by Sigall and Page (1971) illustrates the use of the bogus pipeline and, at the same time, sheds some light on the true status of racial stereotypes among white college students about 1970. They called their version of the bogus machine an electromyograph (EMG). In addition to being connected by skin electrodes to the EMG—an impressive-looking array of electronic gear—their subjects were asked to grip a steering wheel on which a pointer was mounted. Behind the wheel was a dial that was divided by seven scale markings and labeled "agree" at one end and "disagree" at the other. The subjects were told that the EMG would measure their true feelings by detecting otherwise unobservable muscle movements. It would be able to estimate the amount and direction they would have to turn the wheel to have the pointer reflect their true feelings on the dial, although the wheel and pointer would actually be locked in place, centered on the dial, as they held it in their hands.

To demonstrate the EMG's effectiveness, they were asked to think about several statements that they had rated earlier in private. Because those ratings were chosen to be of trivial importance to them, they could be trusted to have responded honestly. And, as far as the subjects knew, the experimenter had not seen their ratings, but the readings they saw on the EMG's dial were identical to their own ratings. Actually, those ratings had been copied secretly so that the EMG readings could be rigged to appear accurate. When they were asked afterward, subjects seemed to be convinced of the accuracy of the bogus pipeline by the total performance with which it had been presented—the electronic gear, the experimenter's description of its powers, and its apparent success in duplicating their earlier ratings.

At that point, the subjects were asked to predict the EMG's estimates of their reactions to the appropriateness of a list of adjectives as describing the personal characteristics of "Americans" or "Negroes." Each of the 22 adjectives was presented. As they thought about how much they agreed or disagreed whether each one did or did not describe Americans or Negroes, the EMG was supposed to be informing the experimenter of how they felt. The dial of the EMG had been covered up so that they could not see it, but the experimenter could. By having to predict its readings, they were presumably forced to tell how they really felt, insofar as they were able to do so. After all, the experimenter would find out when he saw the EMG readings.

Would subjects' expressions of their feelings about the characteristics of blacks and whites be any different under these conditions from what they would be if they simply told them to an experimenter who had no foolproof electronic means of checking on their truthfulness? In order to answer this question, Sigall and Page tested equivalent groups of subjects, randomly chosen from the same group of students, without the EMG. These subjects were simply asked to turn the steering wheel, which had been unlocked, until its pointer reached the scale marking that reflected their beliefs about the extent to which each adjective described Americans or Negroes. Thus they responded under much the same conditions as Katz and Braly's or Karlins's subjects had on questionnaires. As far as they knew, they were free to volunteer whatever information about their true feelings they wanted. Although the experimenter had urged them to answer truthfully, they had the ultimate responsibility for deciding what they would put on the public record about themselves.

These two procedures produced very different pictures of white, "liberal" college students' beliefs about the personal characteristics of blacks and whites. When subjects were connected to the bogus pipeline, their responses indicated a much stronger belief in the superiority of whites over blacks than when they responded without fear of contradiction by the EMG. If one accepts the bogus pipeline ratings as more honest and freer from the distortion that might be caused by subjects' apprehension about revealing themselves to be bigoted, it would appear that the greatest change in white college students' racial attitudes over the past 30 years may not be so much the abandonment of stereotypes as the development of a greater concern with appearing to have abandoned them.

Although the bogus pipeline has shown itself to be a promising new technique for measuring subjects' private feelings, its value may be even greater in demonstrating the concern with self-protection that subjects in any psychological experiment can be expected to have. Especially in those cases in which subjects are asked to reveal information about themselves that might adversely affect the evaluations that others, or even they, might make of them, they can try to influence those evaluations in a way that enhances their self-images. If they are permitted to do so, if such biased responses are accepted at face value, then the research findings may be of little use. They may even obscure the truth. To the extent that any procedure, including the bogus pipeline, prevents this sort of bias, its use can greatly increase the validity of research findings.

## INCONSPICUOUS "LIE DETECTION": THE NONVERBAL PIPELINE

Despite its demonstrated potential, there are two rather serious drawbacks to the use of the bogus pipeline procedure. The first is its high cost, especially in laboratory time. The scenario that is used to deceive subjects into believing that they are connected to a real pipeline is more complex and time consuming than many of the experimental treatments whose effects the pipeline might be used to assess. It may very well also require more equipment and involve both the experimenter and the subject more intensively than all the rest of an experiment in which it is used. Thus, the use of the bogus pipeline would make any experiment much more difficult to perform in a purely mechanical sense. Of course, difficulty is not a devastating criticism of a technique that could enhance the validity of research findings. Although difficulty may be an important determinant of the amount of research that gets done, quality is certainly much more important than quantity.

The unwieldiness of the technique is also cause for another kind of concern. One usually thinks of reactive measurement as risking biased estimates of behavior because it makes subjects aware of the particular aspect of their behavior being evaluated. Although the bogus pipeline promises to reduce that bias, it may engender an even more acute awareness of outside scrutiny than traditional procedures such as self-report questionnaires. It is positively coercive in the way it puts the subject on the spot, almost a kind of "third degree." This raises a question about the ethics of using it, because it may be very stressful for some subjects; it also raises a methodological question.

Many experimental treatments are designed to produce a particular cognitive or emotional state in the subjects exposed to them, such as thoughts or feelings about themselves, or of someone else who is present, or of a task they are working on. This state is often induced by lengthy instructions or by a drama which is created in the laboratory for the subject's benefit. But it is conceivable that the effect of a subsequent exposure to the bogus pipeline procedure could overwhelm the effect of that prior induction. By the time that the subjects are asked for their predictions of the pipeline's readings, they may have forgotten much of what the experiment depends on them keeping in mind, or they may be in a different emotional state from the one the experimental treatment put them in. Although the bogus pipeline procedure may succeed in convincing them of the need for truthful self-disclosure, by the time it does so the conditions whose effects were to be studied may have dissipated to the point in which their impact is immeasurably small. In short, the measurement procedure may sacrifice one of the greatest advantages of doing research in the laboratory—the absence of extraneous events which might detract from the effects of the experimental treatments.

Fortunately, there may be an alternative to the bogus pipeline that is also capable of producing accurate representations of subjects' private feelings without assaulting their privacy as savagely or dominating the experimental setting as obtrusively. This alternative is emerging from the contemporary study of nonverbal behavior. Many nonverbal behaviors are as much under our voluntary control as our verbal behavior is. Perhaps the most prominent example is facial expression. It is no more difficult, it would seem, to smile when we are afraid so that we hide our fear from others than it is to say "Glad to see you again" to someone whose company we find very boring. And there is no reason to believe that it would be any more difficult to do this in a psychological laboratory than in any other social situation. People who are on guard to protect their own as well as others' conceptions of what they are like can control some of their nonverbal behavior for that purpose. However, there are also nonverbal behaviors that are less susceptible to conscious control. These include behaviors whose information value is not recognized by the actor and which, therefore, seem to require no control. Posture and foot and leg movements are examples. There are behaviors over which it is physically difficult to exercise control for all but the specially trained. Tone of voice belongs to this category.

In an experimental situation that arouses feelings in subjects that they would prefer not to make apparent to the experimenter, or perhaps even to recognize in themselves, nonverbal behaviors that are relatively free of their control might provide more accurate information than more reactive alternatives like questionnaire responses. Furthermore, this source of information can be utilized without obtrusive observation or great expertise on the part of the experimenter. The potential of such an approach is illustrated in a study by Shirley Weitz (1972). Consistent with our example of the use of the bogus pipeline, her study was concerned with how trustworthy were verbal expressions of racial attitudes. But instead of comparing verbal reports with those expressed under the pressure of the bogus pipeline, she compared them with subjects' attitudes indicated by their tone of voice.

Weitz solicited 80 white male volunteers from Harvard summer school classes by distributing handbills on the campus and writing letters to students individually. Each volunteer was told that during the study he would be working on some unidentified task together with a fellow student. But first the two were to undergo, separately, some preliminary testing in preparation for that performance. In fact, the experiment consisted of a single session at which only one subject and the experimenter were present. The subject was exposed to a fictitious partner, who was described as male and as either black or white. Thinking he was eavesdropping over an intercom, the subject heard a tape recording in which a second experimenter was speaking to his partner in a nearby room. This procedure, the instructions and the recording, was designed to manipulate the subject's perceptions of the color of his partner, and to make the partner's presence and the promised encounter between them seem more realistic.

In preparation for that promised meeting, the subject had to do two things. One was to fill out questionnaires that asked, among other things, for his impressions of his prospective partner and for his preferences for various details of their forthcoming collaboration. The other was to rehearse and then later to read to the partner over the intercom a paragraph of instructions. The identification of the partner as black or white happened between the rehearsal and the actual delivery of those instructions, both of which were tape recorded without the subject's knowledge.

Weitz ended up with three pieces of information about each of her subjects. The first two came from the questionnaires. The subjects had indicated how friendly they felt toward their as-yet unmet colleague, and how long and intimately they were willing to work with him. The third came from the tape recordings. These were given to an independent panel of students who rated the friendliness expressed toward the intended recipient by each subject's tone of voice. Weitz compared ratings between the rehearsal, before the subject knew anything about his partner, and the actual delivery, after the partner's color had been revealed. In this way, the natural friendliness of each subject's voice could be used in evaluating how friendly he sounded the second time when he knew his partner's color and thought he was speaking directly to him.

In computing the relationships among these three sets of observations, Weitz made an interesting and potentially valuable discovery. She found that when the partner was black, the amount of intimacy that subjects indicated they were willing to accept by their choice of tasks on which to collaborate, and the number of sessions in which they were willing to participate with him, were both negatively related to their stated attitudes toward him. In other words, those who claimed to feel friendliest toward their black partners were the most reluctant to commit themselves to intimate or lengthy relationships with them. But the friendliness of their tone of voice was positively related to both of those choices. The friendlier they sounded as they spoke to him (remember that they all said exactly the same thing), the greater the intimacy and duration of partnership they chose. Finally, the amount of friendliness they expressed verbally was negatively related to the amount that others judged they had expressed in their tone of voice. Those who said they felt warmest sounded coldest. In contrast, when the partner was white all three measures were consistent with each other.

Weitz saw her findings as a reflection of what she called "repressed affect." In a society that condemns racism, and especially in a liberal college community which condemns it strongly, those who have the strongest racist feelings are least likely to admit them. In fact, in an attempt to hide those feelings they may even "bend over backward" and claim to feel very friendly toward a black person. However, when they can privately control the amount of actual contact they will have with that person, they choose to limit it as much as they can (presumably, it would have been inappropriate for Weitz's subjects to choose the least intimacy and the shortest contact they could). When they speak to the person, their tone of voice involuntarily reflects their true feelings.

Beyond their intrinsic value, these findings also demonstrate how behaviors such as tone of voice can be more trustworthy indicators of subjects' private feelings than their verbal statements. It would seem that many kinds of studies could make use of this fact. Whenever subjects' private feelings are important data, getting them to talk to another person aloud would permit a similar analysis of their tone of voice with that which Weitz used for her subjects. Even if the subjects were allowed to say different things, fairly simple techniques are available for removing the content from tape-recorded speech while leaving intact the speaker's tone of voice and all the information it may hold about the speaker's true feelings.

## OVERCOMING REACTIVITY IN MANIPULATING THE INDEPENDENT VARIABLE

For many years, researchers have relied on cover stories, deceptive instructions, and dramatic staging to create almost every conceivable experience for their subjects. Almost any variable can be studied in this way. Unlimited forms and variations can be created at will, with a convincing story and a few physical props or experimental confederates to back it up. Subjects can be deceived into believing that they are doing well or poorly, that someone in a nearby room is having an epileptic seizure, that they are admired or despised by an attractive or unattractive stranger, or whatever the experiment requires.

More recently, researchers have begun to question the effectiveness of these procedures. Do subjects believe what they are told? Do they respond naïvely to the conditions the experimenter intends to create, or do they reinterpret the events to which they are exposed to suit themselves? Can their behavior be accepted as truly reflecting the effects of the conditions the experiment was designed to study, or is it as deceptive an act as the experimenter's?

Questions like these indicate the concern that has been expressed about the continued use of the traditional laboratory methods for doing experiments. The experiment can be a powerful research tool, but it is quite vulnerable to subjects' attempts to protect their identities. Rather than abandon the experimental methods, or merely suffer suspicion about the validity of their findings, many researchers have begun to consider ways of adapting or modifying them to reduce their reactivity. In this section, we will sample three recent examples. The first is role playing, a technique which some have proposed be substituted for deception in the laboratory experiment. The second is field research, the transfer of experimentation from the laboratory to natural settings. Finally, we will consider a unique attempt to blend the laboratory with the field, thus creating a promising new setting for the experiment.

Because of limited space, we restrict our discussion to these few examples. As usual, we want to make clear that this is not intended as an exhaustive or even a representative sampling. It will serve, however, to convey some of the excitement and innovation which is currently being generated in the search for improved ways of using the experimental methods.

## ROLE PLAYING AS AN ALTERNATIVE TO DECEPTION

Throughout a 20-year-long debate over the use of deception, one alternative procedure has been suggested over and over again, and rejected just as often. That alternative is *role playing*. Its proponents have attacked the use of deception on ethical as well as methodological grounds. Its opponents, the supporters of deception, have dismissed it for logical as well as for empirical reasons. Both sides have been guilty of illogic and misrepresentation at times. We will try to present a brief review of that sometimes very elliptical debate, as well as some recent evidence which we feel adds considerably to our understanding of the true potential of role playing.

The objections to deception and claims for role playing are bound together almost inextricably. The proponents of role playing have stated the objections to deception most clearly. First, they have criticized it as unethical for the simple reason that subjects are exposed to dangerous psychological conditions without the opportunity to make an informed choice. Subjects are lied to about the purposes of the research in which they are participating, about the meanings of the events that occur during the experiment, about the quality of their own performance, and often about all these things and more. Almost every attempt to formulate a canon of ethics for psychological research with human subjects has included the precept that subjects should be allowed to decide freely whether or not they wish to participate in a given experiment after being fully informed about what it will entail. It seems clear that deception will never be able to meet that fundamental ethical test.

Role playing is claimed to be more honest. Subjects are asked to imagine that certain events are occurring or have occurred, rather than being deceived into thinking that they actually have, or to produce specified thoughts or feelings, rather than being manipulated into having them. They may be aided by physical props or by suggestions of past experiences on which they might draw. They are also made to feel that they are more collaborators than tools of the experimenter, by providing their own unique inputs into the experiment and having a large measure of control over and responsibility for producing the data upon which the experiment depends. In short, it is claimed that deceived subjects are manipulated, lied to, and made very aware that they are being observed by the experimenter. Role-playing subjects seem to be granted more autonomy, more dignity, and more equal status with the experimenter.

More importantly, for the purposes of our present discussion, this dichotomy is claimed to have important methodological implications. Deceived subjects, it is argued, can only redeem their low status and forced ignorance by uncovering, to their own satisfaction at least, the true purpose of the experiment, including the experimenter's hypothesis. They typically have available to them considerable information, such as the experimental instructions, the nonverbal and other incidental behavior of the experimenter, apparatus present in the laboratory, the task or questionnaire to which they have to respond, and information from previous subjects in the same or other experiments. Once they have decided, on the basis of all this, what the experiment is "really" all about, which may or may not be accurate from the experimenter's point of view, any number of actions may follow. They may try to fulfill an experimenter's expectations in order to advance what appears to them to be the interests of science, or to defeat an experimenter who they feel has treated them badly, or to portray themselves as competent or worthwhile. In any case, they may not respond to the experimental treatment in the naïve way that the experimenter intended and, consequently, their behavior will not provide the basis for a fair test of the experimental hypothesis. Role-playing subjects, on the other hand, are assumed to be more satisfied with their treatment and thus more likely to try to do what the experimenter asks of them. As a result, it is easier for the experimenter to produce the condition necessary for a fair test of the hypothesis and to observe the behavior which those conditions can truly be expected to produce.

The opponents of role playing argue that if deception is carried out well, subjects are thoroughly convinced by it. They are not suspicious, but believe the cover story and respond to the experimental treatment as the experimenter intends. The experiment has a strong impact on them, they become deeply involved in the contrived situation created for their benefit, and they respond to it spontaneously, naturally, as they would respond to the same situation when it occurred in the normal course of their lives. Role-playing subjects, on the other hand, can behave naturally only insofar as their imagination permits them to predict their behavior under the conditions that they have been asked to create for themselves. They know the situation is not real and cannot respond with the same spontaneity and involvement as if it were. As a result, their behavior is not representative of what would be produced by the natural conditions that the experiment is designed to investigate.

Those are the basic arguments that have been used. In essence, each procedure, deception and role playing, has been claimed to be reactive and to produce invalid findings by some and to be nonreactive and to produce natural, spontaneous behavior by others. Both sides have argued vigorously, even sarcastically at times. Unfortunately, they have made only token efforts at settling the issue with facts. And when they have, they have called on very different sources of proof.

The proponents of deception have implied, for a start, that virtually the entire discipline of social psychology owes its existence to using that method. We would not know what we presently know about behavior, what countless experimental findings have shown us, had it not been for deception. Also, the proponents point out that there is very little direct evidence that subjects actually do become suspicious of deception. In postexperimental interviews which probe carefully for suspicion, subjects rarely say that they disbelieved the cover story. There is even less evidence that subjects are able to uncover the experimenter's true intent. And in those rare cases in which suspicion has been uncovered, the behavior of the suspicious subjects has not been found to differ from the behavior of the unsuspicious ones.

Neither of these arguments is very damaging to the case for role playing. First, if deception is a reactive method, then our vast knowledge of behavior based on its use may be worth far less than it appears to be. If subjects in past deception experiments were not responding to the conditions intended, their behavior should not be interpreted as supporting the hypotheses being tested (or suggested after the fact). In that case, one can argue, deception may have produced a body of knowledge about subjects' motives rather than about natural behavior.

The findings of postexperimental probes into subjects' motives are at least as suspect. Suppose that a subject did suspect that an experimenter's instructions had misrepresented the truth, and that subject had responded instead to some privately structured reality. How likely would he or she be to admit that fact to that experimenter afterward? Asking a subject about his or her motives may constitute the most reactive assessment of all. It depends on a subject's willingness to admit dishonest behavior and to accuse the experimenter of dishonesty at the same time. Such a procedure is likely to underestimate greatly the true incidence of suspicion. One might even go so far as to speculate that the reason that the behavior of subjects who admit suspicion is similar to the behavior of those who deny suspicion is that all the subjects were actually equally suspicious, but some were simply unwilling to admit it.

Two other lines of evidence, however, are claimed by the supporters of deception for discrediting role playing as a fruitless exercise by comparison. First, it has been shown that subjects are often unable to predict what they would do under imaginary conditions. The most widely quoted example comes from Milgram's experiments on obedience in which deceived subjects seem to have delivered what they thought were strong, even dangerous electric shocks to fellow subjects at the experimenter's urging. Similar individuals to whom the experimental conditions were only described predicted that they would disobey the experimenter and refuse to risk harm to others. It follows that if we studied obedience (or, by implication, any other interesting social–psychological phenomenon) by using role playing, we would be more likely to find out what people would like to think they would do in the situation we described to them than what would actually happen in the real situation.

More evidence is available from several direct comparisons that have been made between deception and role playing. In each case, an experiment was carried out in two identical versions except that one used deception and the other used role playing to accomplish the experimental manipulation. These comparisons have shown that although the findings produced by the two procedures sometimes coincide, they also sometimes differ. On the basis of this evidence, it has been argued that without knowing in advance which result would obtain in other experiments, we cannot simply substitute role playing for deception. And because doing all experiments both ways would perpetuate the use of deception anyway, there seems to be no good way of verifying the effectiveness of role playing.

Both of these forms of evidence against role playing are based on myths which have somehow survived decades of learned debate. The first myth is that predicting one's behavior in a hypothetical situation is role playing. Actually, role playing consists of imagining conditions, with whatever aid an experimenter can provide, to which one then makes a real response, not a prediction. Suppose that a researcher wants to study the effect of mood on subjects' responses to a specific situation. Role playing could be used by asking subjects to imagine that they felt sad or angry or happy (the experimenter might vividly describe a common situation which would create the mood in question and ask subjects to imagine that they were in it) and then put them into the situation in question and observe their reactions. Thus, subjects would not simply be asked to predict what they would do if they were angry and in that situation.

The second myth is that experimental findings produced by deception provide a standard against which role-playing findings can be compared. But if deception is, as its detractors argue, vulnerable to efforts made by subjects to satisfy motives that have nothing to do with the conditions the experimenter is trying to study, and if role playing is more likely to produce valid findings by virtue of its relative freedom from such reactive conditions, then one would not expect their outcomes to coincide. We cannot know, solely on the basis of those comparisons, which findings are valid and should be used as a standard for judging the other findings. Despite the apparent decisiveness of directly comparing the two procedures, what is clearly needed is an independent source of evidence. We will suggest one shortly.

The role-playing forces have typically failed to support their case with research evidence. This may be responsible, in part, for their failure to gain much support. The use of role playing has not been very widespread, despite the growing dissatisfaction with the use of deception, both on ethical and methodological grounds. We will consider two sources of supportive evidence that have been overlooked. The first is a body of research generated by a variety of role playing which is known as *simulation*.

Simulation is a technique which is used typically to test groups of subjects. It consists of creating a physical environment and a set of rules to govern the participants' behavior which together constitute a facsimile of an important natural behavior setting. One popular use of simulation has been for the study of international relations. Subjects are given the task of making decisions like those made by real national leaders, based on sources of information like those used by such leaders. The role-playing task consists of assuming the positions, responsibilities, and motivations of those leaders. This kind of simulation has been used to study the effects of specific conditions, recreated in the information provided to the subjects, on decision makers' tendencies to respond peacefully or aggressively to military crises. It has also been used to study the effects of economic and other conditions on the relations among nations.

Simulation has also been used to study more basic psychological processes, as exemplified by the experiment conducted by Philip Zimbardo and his colleagues at Stanford University, which we looked at earlier. They recruited 24 male Stanford undergraduates for a two-week-long study of prison life. The experimenters functioned as prison administrators, and the subjects were randomly divided into equal groups of prisoners and guards. The inmate population numbered 12 and the guards were divided into three shifts of four men each. The basement of a building at Stanford was transformed into a mock prison by installing bars on the doors of the rooms to serve as cells. An attempt was made to create an environment of rules and physical conditions which captured some of the essential features of prison life. Prisoners were "arrested" without warning by the local police department to begin the study, uniforms were provided for guards and prisoners, arriving prisoners underwent a body search and delousing, there were rigid, authoritarian rules governing virtually every physical and social aspect of the prisoners' lives, and solitary confinement was used as punishment for violations of those rules.

Although the Stanford "prison" obviously differed in many ways from real prisons, it proved to be a very good functional simulation. It elicited very realistic behaviors from the subjects who populated it, and even from the experimenters who had created it. The "prisoners" defied their jailers at first. The "guards" responded repressively and even brutally, to the point of using physical force against them. Soon, the prisoners' behavior became passive and withdrawn, and several even developed such severe psychosomatic symptoms that they had to be released from the study as early as the second day to receive professional care. Even the experimenters eventually found themselves believing a prison rumor that the released prisoners were planning to return, with help, to free those they had left behind. After only six days, such extreme psychological changes had taken place in all the participants that the study had to be aborted. They had played their roles too well.

Some have argued that the evidence provided by simulations like Zimbardo's is anecdotal compared to the "hard" data collected in a laboratory experiment. As in the case of deception, the fact that a procedure yields interesting observations about behavior does not justify its use. But how would you go about trying to create prisoners and guards through the use of deception? In any case, more precise evidence, and perhaps a truer indication of the potential value of role playing as a substitute for deception, is provided by experiments that have used role playing to manipulate independent variables in the same way that deception has traditionally been used. An experiment performed by a former student of mine, William Neely, is a good example of this approach (Neely, 1975).

Neely wanted to test the hypothesis that the amount of eye contact between two people engaged in a cooperative relationship would be greater if they liked one another, whereas the amount of eye contact in a competitive relationship would be greater between two people who disliked one another. To do this, he needed to create liking and disliking between strangers who were randomly paired. Deception has been used for this purpose in the past. For example, subjects can be given flattering and unflattering evaluations that they are told come from one another but which actually originate with the experimenter. Such a procedure, however, requires that the contact between the subjects be limited to prevent them from finding out how the other one really feels. And Neely felt that such a procedure might not be very convincing anyway. He chose instead to ask his subjects to role-play liking or disliking—"to act as if you really liked one another or really disliked one another"—because the study was concerned with the effect it would have on a discussion that followed. That discussion was structured to be either cooperative or competitive.

The fact that the findings confirmed his hypothesis was rewarding, but, of course, it does not prove that the role-playing procedure was effective. However, he and I worked out a technique that was. We videotaped a sample of his subjects as they engaged in conversation with their partners who were off camera. Then we asked a separate group of subjects, who knew nothing about the experiment, to judge from silent videotape excerpts how much each subject appeared to like the person with whom they were talking. They agreed overwhelmingly that the subjects who were role-playing liking appeared to like their partners more than those who were role-playing disliking.

It may be immodest to say so, in light of my personal involvement, but this study seems to me to demonstrate two very important points that need to be made about the potential of role playing as a less reactive alternative to deception. First, it shows how role playing can be used as an alternative means of inducing in subjects a state whose effects an experimenter wishes to assess. The subjects did not role play or predict their behavior. The behavior in question, eye contact, was assessed directly as they performed it, in the same way as it would have been had liking and disliking been induced by deception (or been real). Second, it shows how the effectiveness of role playing can be assessed independently, through judgments of the appropriateness of the subjects' behavior in response to the instructions they were given. This kind of assessment, which falls under the general heading of a manipulation check, is as appropriate for deception inductions as for role playing. In fact, it is one meaningful way in which the two techniques might be compared. Its future use might shed some much-needed light on their relative merits.

To sum up, two recurring criticisms of role playing appear to lack logical foundation. First, role playing is not the same thing as asking subjects to predict their behavior. Rather, it asks them to help produce the conditions whose effects on their behavior are to be studied. The behavior itself is a response to the task assigned to them, such as a conversation, just as it is in deception or any other kind of experiments. Second, role playing, like deception or any other method, can and should be evaluated by some independent method, or manipulation check, and not by whether it produces statistically significant findings, or the same findings as some other method that has been selected arbitrarily as a criterion.

We do not mean to imply that role playing is perfect. Two very worrisome objections to its use have been raised only rarely in the past. First, it cannot be assumed to be completely nonreactive. Subjects may engage in the same kinds of self-protective behavior in response to role play as they have been suspected of doing in response to deception. Neither method can be demonstrated unequivocally to be nonreactive, given the difficulties in assessing subjects' true motives. Perhaps the use of techniques like the bogus pipeline or the assessment of voice quality can help solve this problem by uncovering those motives. In any case, the task of reducing reactivity by treating subjects more honestly and respectfully is complicated by the climate of suspicion created by the longstanding use of deception. Perhaps this process will prove reversible should deception ever be forsaken for more forthright methods. It should be pointed out, however, that role playing is only relatively more honest than deception. In the Neely study, for example, subjects were not informed in advance that their visual behavior was the target of the experimenter's observation. Full disclosure may be possible only in rare cases.

Second, another limitation in using the role-playing method lies in the conditions that subjects can reasonably be asked to role play.

Most of us are very familiar with liking and disliking. Other kinds of relationships or moods may be more difficult for subjects to imagine. Consequently, the outcome of role playing may not always be as rewarding as it was in the Neely experiment. But there does seem to be ample cause for alternatives such as role playing to be explored further and there is already reason to believe that that exploration may prove fruitful.

## RESEARCH OUTSIDE THE LABORATORY

The most energetically pursued alternative to the reactive arrangements of the psychological laboratory has been to move experimental research out into the real world. Research in natural settings is known as *field research* and can utilize many types of methods, including experimentation. Concerning reactivity, the field setting provides an attractive alternative to the laboratory. Subjects who are tested in their natural habitat, such as a city street or subway train, are unlikely to be aware that their behavior is being manipulated or observed. Consequently, their motives for self-protection are unlikely to be engaged beyond the usual ways in which people manage their everyday lives. Thus, the field setting offers an opportunity to study behavior that can be assumed to be spontaneous, without resorting to an implicit faith in the powers of experimenters to create reality for their subjects from a bare and threatening laboratory room.

It should be recognized, at the same time, that research in the field faces its own unique methodological problems. Compared with its laboratory cousin, the standardization of procedures from one subject to another is more difficult because of the limited control that a researcher can exercise over extraneous events in a natural setting. The sights and sounds of a city street, for example, change so rapidly that each passerby experiences a somewhat different environment. It is also more difficult to ensure the representativeness of the subjects in the research sample when anonymous passersby are tested. Finally, very serious reservations have been expressed over the ethics of field research. Subjects in the field may be manipulated without having given even the tacit permission that laboratory subjects do when they show up for an experiment. They have even less choice in the matter, or control over what the researcher may do to them, because they are unaware of his or her presence. And observation of their behavior without their awareness is claimed by some to constitute an invasion of their privacy, in spite of the fact that it is done in public places.

In order to compare the laboratory and field approaches, we

present two research problems that have been dealt with in both ways. They should serve to contrast the advantages and disadvantages of each. At the same time, our discussion will emphasize that the laboratory and the field settings are not mutually exclusive alternatives to one another.

## OBEDIENCE TO AUTHORITY

For our first example, we consider research on obedience to authority. The most widely publicized investigations of this phenomenon have been Stanley Milgram's laboratory experiments (Milgram, 1963). We begin by recounting Milgram's basic procedure very briefly. Paid volunteer subjects were assigned a role which appeared to require them to punish a fellow subject with electric shock for making errors on a learning task. In reality, the other subject was a confederate of the experimenter and was not actually shocked. But every effort was made to convince the real subjects that they were required to deliver an increasingly intense shock to their partner after each succeeding error. The subjects were exposed to simulated reactions of the partner, recorded on tape, which reflected the increase in intensity. The partner's complaints gradually increased until he appeared to be in great pain. If subjects expressed any reluctance to continue because of the partner's apparent distress, the experimenter urged them to go on for the sake of "the experiment."

Most subjects did obey the experimenter and gave as many shocks as were required. Almost all of them continued beyond the point in which the shocks appeared to be causing substantial pain to their partners. For Milgram, their behavior constituted evidence of the way in which the members of our society, if not every society, are taught to obey those who occupy positions of authority. We learn that the commands of such officials take precedence over our own feelings about what is right and wrong.

Milgram's research has been criticized very strongly on ethical grounds for deceiving subjects into performing such an objectionable act. But of more interest to us right now is its vulnerability to criticism on the grounds that it depended for its success upon successful deception in a psychological laboratory. By the time these experiments were carried out, considerable attention had already been paid to Orne's concept of demand characteristics and several other conceptions of subjects' self-defense strategies, which were considered in Chapter 3. Thus it is not surprising that Milgram's findings were greeted with some skepticism. Did his subjects really obey the experimenter in spite of the horrible cost to their partner? Or did they, perhaps, perceive the experimental situation differently from

what Milgram intended them to? Did the fact that they were participating in a psychological experiment change the meaning of their
behavior?

It was argued that Milgram's subjects may have obeyed as much
as they did because they were not convinced of the apparent consequences of their behavior. They may have believed (correctly, in
fact) that a Yale professor would not allow one Yale undergraduate
to inflict that much harm on another in his laboratory. Thus they may
have decided that the experimenter was "putting them on," as many
social psychologists have done to their subjects, and that their partners' reactions exaggerated the true risk of the shocks they were getting, if, in fact, they were getting any at all. In sum, they may have
felt safe in what they were doing because they believed that things
could not be what they appeared to be in a psychological experiment.

Milgram may have anticipated the possibility that others would
try to explain away his findings in this way. He went to great lengths
to describe how stressful the experiment appeared to be for his subjects. His anecdotal evidence that several became extremely upset,
apparently as a result of the conflict between their conscience and
the experimenter's demands, suggests that the situation was real for
them. Milgram also repeated the experiment outside Yale, in a
rented office in Bridgeport, Connecticut, with subjects from all walks
of life who were recruited through newspaper advertisements. In
this version, the experimenter was identified as an employee of a private, and not very prestigious, research company. None of this
seemed to make much difference in the amount of obedience observed in the subjects. Those at Bridgeport obeyed only slightly less
than those at Yale, despite the fact that they seemed to have much
less reason to respect or to trust the experimenter. Milgram concluded from both the stress he observed and the results of the Bridgeport study that reactivity was an improbable explanation for his
findings.

But reactivity is a difficult rival hypothesis to dismiss, because
its effects occur in the subjective world of the subject. Is Milgram correct or are his critics? Did his subjects see the experimenter as having
a legitimate right to demand their cooperation in the brutalization
of a fellow student, or did they believe that they were merely participating in a charade as coconspirators of the experimenter? One approach toward answering this question is to confront subjects with
the demands of authority in a natural setting. Here, they would have
no reason to play the role of a subject in an experiment.

A field experiment by Leonard Bickman (1971) did exactly that.
Passersby on a New York City street were confronted by a stranger

who ordered them to obey some request. The stranger, or experimenter, was a male, dressed in one of the three uniforms that were designed to represent increasing levels of authority: a sport jacket and tie (as a "civilian"); the white uniform of a milkman (complete with wire basket and empty milk bottles); and a private security guard's gray uniform (resembling a policeman's uniform, but with different insignia and no gun). And the order he gave to the subject was one of three which seem to require increasing levels of cooperation. In one case, as the subject approached, the experimenter stood on the sidewalk with a brown paper bag beside him on the pavement. When he had captured the subject's attention, the experimenter said, "Pick up this bag for me!" In the second condition, the experimenter stood on the sidewalk next to a row of cars at parking meters. Pointing to an assistant leaning against one of those cars, he told the subject, "This fellow is overparked at the meter but doesn't have any change. Give him a dime!" In the last, and seemingly most demanding case, the experimenter approached a subject waiting alone at a bus stop sign which read, "Bus Stop. No Standing," with the command, "Don't you know you have to stand on the other side of the pole. The sign says no standing."

Each of the three orders was followed by an explanation if the subject failed to obey immediately. In the case of the paper bag, the experimenter claimed to have a bad back. After his demand for a dime, the experimenter admitted that he had no change either. And at the bus stop, the improbable explanation for telling the subject to move was: "Then the bus won't stop here, it's a new law."

As you may have guessed already, the order to leave the bus stop was obeyed least frequently, and the request to pick up the bag most (in our presentation of the results, we are going to lump together obedience after the initial order and the obedience following any subsequent explanation). More importantly for our understanding of obedience to authority, the kind of uniform worn by the experimenter giving an order made a great difference in the frequency with which it was obeyed. In each case, the civilian was obeyed less often than the milkman who, in turn, was obeyed less often than the guard.

Despite the fact that they were given much less demanding orders, fewer of Bickman's subjects obeyed than Milgram's (about 50% overall). But it is very difficult to compare the two experiments directly, which is a reflection of a basic difference between laboratory and field research. It is inconceivable that passersby on a city sidewalk could be put into the kind of situation Milgram's subjects were. There is no time to create such a complex setting or to provide such varied response alternatives. Nor is it possible to create a very elaborate identity for the experimenter. The instantaneous contact with subjects to which one is limited in the field makes it necessary to rely on a simple set of cues which can be perceived very readily—in this case, the way in which the experimenter was dressed. But although Bickman's findings do not replicate Milgram's in any real sense, they do lend them some plausibility. They show that people who are apparently quite unaware that their behavior is being studied will defer to someone whom they identify as having been delegated a degree of formal authority. If a security guard, or even a milkman, has a right, by virtue of his "office," to expect obedience, a psychologist might also. (Imagine the power of someone identified as a General or a President or Der Fuhrer!) Taken together, the findings of these two experiments, Milgram's and Bickman's, are much more meaningful than either is alone because their designs complement one another. The major weakness of the field experiment, its lack of impact and of precision, is balanced by the high degree of impact and precision which can be attained in the laboratory. At the same time, the susceptibility of the behavior in the laboratory setting to distortion by demand characteristics is balanced by the comparative lack of reactivity in the field.

## THE FRUSTRATION–AGGRESSION HYPOTHESIS

The frustration–aggression hypothesis, which has been a popular subject of research since its introduction more than 35 years ago, provides the basis for our second laboratory–field comparison. At the risk of oversimplifying, the basic premise of the hypothesis is that when a person's attempt to achieve a goal (solve a problem, obtain some reward, etc.) is blocked, a likely, if not the primary, response is aggression. However, the likelihood of aggression, and the form that it takes, whether it is a direct attack against the frustrator, the intent to retaliate, or merely hostile feelings, will depend on several qualifying factors. One of these is the status of the frustrator. The higher the frustrator's status is, the less likely that a victim would react aggressively to the frustration, because the frustrator would have more power to punish that aggression. This idea has been tested in a laboratory experiment by Arthur Cohen (1955), and also in a field experiment by Anthony Doob and Alan Gross (1968). These two experiments show quite dramatically the range over which the reactivity of experimental arrangements can vary from the laboratory to the field. They also demonstrate once again how the findings of a reactive laboratory experiment and a nonreactive field experiment can complement one another.

Cohen recruited 60 female college students for the supposed

purpose of surveying opinions about campus life. Each subject was given written descriptions of 14 hypothetical cases in which one person frustrated another. The frustrator was identified as a person of higher status than, or authority over, the victim in half the cases. In the other half, the two actors were put into an equal status or peer relationship. The subjects' task was to predict how aggressively "people" would feel and act toward the frustrator, in each instance, should they be the victims. This third-person form of response was chosen as a less reactive alternative to asking subjects how aggressively they themselves would respond. Cohen felt that this would free them to project their own true, spontaneous feelings toward the frustrator into their judgments. Thus, he felt, they would be more likely to reveal what they themselves would do in those situations than if they were asked directly.

The subjects judged that a victim would be less likely to respond aggressively toward a higher-status frustrator than toward one of equal status. But does this mean that people are really less likely to respond aggressively when frustrated by someone in a position of authority over them? Or does it mean that only Cohen's subjects would be less likely themselves to do this? Cohen had taken some precautions, the misleading cover story describing the study as a survey rather than as a test of the frustration–aggression hypothesis, and the "projective" measure of the dependent variable. But it is still possible, as he himself pointed out in discussing his findings, that the subjects merely responded in the way they believed was most logical or in the way they believed the experimenter expected them to. They may not even have known how "people," or even they themselves, would actually behave in the situations described to them.

Cohen did claim that his findings might be valuable as a guide to future studies of a more behavioral nature. And they were. Twenty years later, his study was cited by Doob and Gross in the rationale for their field experiment. They set out to test the same hypothesis in a city street. Drivers were frustrated after they drove up behind the experimenter's automobile which stopped at a red light. After the light changed to green, the experimenter failed to drive on for a period of 12 seconds. And the intersection which had been chosen as the site for the experiment was too narrow for drivers to go around the "frustrator." Finally, the frustrating auto was either a shiny, almost-new luxury model or a weatherbeaten, old economy model.

In all, 82 subjects, more than two-thirds of them men, were frustrated by the driver of a car in front of their cars. They knew very little about that person other than the kind of car he drove. From what could be seen of the driver, it was apparent only that he was male and dressed either in a stylish plaid sport coat or in a rumpled khaki jacket, which was consistent with the condition of his car. The experimenters intended that half the subjects would be led to assume that they were being frustrated by someone of relatively high status and half by someone of relatively low status.

Whatever they assumed, the appearance of the frustrator did make a great difference in the subjects' willingness to use the form of aggression most readily available to automobile drivers, that is, horn honking. When the frustrator appeared to be of relatively low status, almost twice as many drivers honked at him, more than twice as many honked more than once, and those who honked waited less time before doing so.

Based on the criterion of reactivity, there seems little doubt that the Doob and Gross experiment provides more trustworthy evidence that aggression is a less likely response to frustration when the frustrator's status is high. Compared with the Cohen experiment, its findings depend less on subjects' willingness and ability to characterize their behavior truthfully. They are also less vulnerable to the effects of subjects' self-consciousness about being the objects of an experimenter's observations and their concern over the implications of their responses for their self-images.

It is possible to imagine shades of reactivity between these two examples. Subjects might be confronted in a laboratory with a confederate of the experimenter who frustrated their attempts to perform some task. That confederate might be identified and/or costumed to represent someone of either high or low status relative to the subjects. But would subjects respond naïvely and spontaneously in such a situation? Or might they suspect that the events had been staged by the experimenter and then tried to control their responses accordingly? Might they be less willing to display aggression for an experimental psychologist than they would be in other settings? Or more likely, if they felt that it was expected of them?

Perhaps the best strategy to test such an hypothesis is a multiplex one. One might first use questionnaires, as Cohen did, to see what potential subjects think they would do or what they are willing to admit to. Then a field experiment, like Doob and Gross's, could be used to check on the external validity of those reports. Laboratory experiments could test the effects of qualifying conditions, such as the importance of the task and the arbitrariness of the frustration, which would be difficult to reproduce in a natural setting. By combining the findings from methods having different strengths and weaknesses, it would be possible to cover all the methodological bases. Our knowledge of the phenomenon would thus not be limited by the deficiencies of any one procedure. No single method could accomplish as much by itself.

## A CONCLUDING STATEMENT ABOUT FIELD RESEARCH

The major advantage of field research is its lack of reactivity. People who are going about their everyday lives in public places are not burdened with the artificial concerns of subjects in the laboratory. They are not especially self-conscious or test-shy. Nor are they trying to fulfill or frustrate the experimenter's goals. For these reasons, their reactions to the events created by the experimenter are about as spontaneous and uncontrolled as behavior ever is. In this respect, the findings of field experiments have higher external validity than would those of laboratory experiments addressed to the same questions.

Field research also has its drawbacks. Events cannot be created in natural settings with the same flexibility as they can in the laboratory in which an experimenter can use words to produce almost any conceivable experience. And the occupants of a natural setting usually cannot be asked to submit to the same kinds of exhaustive interrogation, by questionnaire or by interview, that laboratory subjects seem to accept so easily. Thus the experimenter's sources of information are more limited. Furthermore, unplanned events in the field can produce effects that may obscure those being studied, especially if the researcher is insensitive to their occurrence. At the very least, one would have to expect to contend with greater variability in subjects' behavior in the constantly changing real world than in the relatively insulated environment of the laboratory. Finally, people's rights to privacy and freedom of action are more difficult to protect in the field than in the laboratory in which their status as subjects is clear to all concerned.

In summary, field research has enormous potential to overcome some of the weaknesses of laboratory methods. It may never prove to be a viable substitute, but it is already a valuable and even necessary complement.

## A "FIELD LABORATORY": THE BEST OF BOTH WORLDS?

Over the past decade, Stuart Cook has developed a technique that incorporates many of the advantages of research in the field without sacrificing as much of the control provided by the laboratory. Although we have already discussed this research in Chapter 3, it is important enough to the present discussion to be repeated. Essentially, what Cook has done is to move his laboratory into a more natural setting. He has created a setting that looks to all but the subjects much like a traditional social–psychological laboratory. To the subjects, it is the setting for a part-time job. In it, the experimenter has a measure of control over what happens to the subjects and a capability to monitor their behavior that approach those that are possible in a traditional laboratory. But, although the subjects' freedom is greatly restricted, it is a restriction like that encountered naturally at work or in school. The subjects are not made to feel like the focal point of a psychological inquiry. This should minimize their concern with experimenter expectations or the subject role. Subjects' motives should therefore be more representative of those that normally direct their behavior than would occur in a traditional laboratory setting.

Perhaps the best way of describing Cook's procedure is to consider a specific experiment in which he has used it (Cook, 1971). This experiment was designed to test the prediction that close and cooperative contact with blacks of equal status that took place in a supportive context would reduce prejudice in highly prejudiced whites. A bogus company solicited female college students on several predominantly white southern campuses. Handbills offered payment to women who were willing to take a 15-hour test battery twice, over two-week periods, several months apart. The purpose was ostensibly to determine the reliability of the battery, that is, whether people's scores remained constant over time. Actually, a measure of racial attitudes embedded in the battery was used to identify those women who were highly prejudiced against blacks. They were later contacted by individuals from a different local college and offered a part-time job. To avoid suspicion that there was a special interest in them as individuals, they were told that they had to complete a preliminary training program in order to qualify as employees.

After each woman who accepted the offer had passed her training, she was introduced to her job, the Railroad Game. She was told that it was being developed for eventual use as a management training device. She would be playing it for four weeks, five days a week, to provide information upon which modifications would be based. Two women were in charge of the testing laboratory, a white supervisor who was in her 30s and her younger black assistant. There were also two other players, both women college students who were ostensibly hired by the same procedure as the subject. Each day the three would play the game, which was patterned after the management of a railroad, for two 30–40-minute sessions. Between sessions they would take a lunch break in the laboratory.

Each subject's two playing partners were confederates of the experimenter. One was white and the other black. They cooperated with the experimenters to maximize the beneficial aspects of the contact between the prejudiced white subject and her black partner.

The confederates themselves got along well and they sometimes discussed race relations over lunch in a way that highlighted the damaging effects of prejudice and discrimination on blacks. The supervisor and her helper seemed to enjoy a friendly and cooperative and apparently equal-status working relationship.

The subjects' interactions with the other participants were monitored by two hidden observers. Their racial attitudes were reassessed one to three months after the game sessions had ended, as part of the test battery that they had previously agreed to retake and that they presumably did not connect with their job playing the Railroad Game. The change in their behavior toward the black confederate over four weeks of contact constituted one dependent measure, but the major one was the change in their racial attitudes between the two test batteries as compared with subjects whose initial scores were equally prejudiced but who had rejected the "job offer."

Cook's results showed that the experimental contact had reduced his subjects' prejudice dramatically, both in their face-to-face behavior toward their black coworker and in their expressed attitudes toward blacks in general. Our major interest, however, is in the method he used and, specifically, in its advantages over both traditional laboratory techniques and field research. Hiring subjects for off-campus jobs, rather than conscripting them from psychology classes, should have lessened the problem of reactivity. It must have been much less obvious to the subjects that they were being studied in a psychological experiment. Perhaps even more important, the major dependent variable, subjects' attitudes toward blacks, was measured in a way that minimized its connection with the experimental treatment. Thus, even if subjects had been suspicious of the contact experience, they might not have seen its relationship to the final test battery as far removed as the two events were in space, time, and every other way. Although field research is even less obtrusive, and even less likely to engage subjects' defenses, it generally does not permit the degree of control that Cook had in this study. In a natural setting in which a real job was being done by real people, it would be very difficult to control the nature of interracial contact or to know, in the final analysis, what caused any observed change in attitude or lack of it. It would also be more difficult to gain access to the subjects' behavior. Moreover, it would be more difficult to hide observers on a real job site or to ask real workers to take test batteries. These capabilities need to be built into the setting at the start.

The potential of Cook's approach, or one like it, seems very great indeed. It is flexible enough to accommodate a wide variety of experimental manipulations, and it provides the experimenter with considerable control over the subjects' experiences and access to their behavior. In those ways it preserves important advantages of laboratory experimentation. Its level of reactivity is low and could be reduced even further. If subjects could be selected at random, as would ordinarily be possible, the need for pretesting could be eliminated. People could be hired, through ads or employment agencies, for jobs that incorporated the desired experimental treatments. Dependent variables could be assessed directly through subjects' spontaneous behavior, as Cook did to a limited extent. The subjects' job performance itself might provide important data in some cases. The major drawback to Cook's approach is not methodological, but that its use is much more expensive, in time and material resources, than most field or laboratory methods. However, it may be worth every bit of its premium price. Important research questions deserve the best answers we can provide.

## CONCLUSION

The experimental methods have been the backbone of research in psychology, and for good reason. They have marked advantages over other approaches to answering scientific questions, as our evaluation of their internal validity in Chapter 6 should have made clear. But recently it has become more widely recognized that their use with human subjects in the traditional psychological laboratory poses serious methodological problems. Beginning with Orne's analysis of demand characteristics, more and more attention has been paid to the criteria of external validity. Because of that attention, the concern over the validity of the findings of laboratory experiments has grown.

As we pointed out in Chapter 3, the generalizability of findings from laboratory experiments can be enhanced greatly through using representative samples of subjects, posttest-only designs, and counterbalancing procedures in those cases in which more than one experimental treatment must be administered to a single group of subjects. But the assumption that subjects' behavior in the laboratory is representative of people's behavior in natural settings is more difficult to meet. Unfortunately, there are no simple formulas for eliminating subjects' suspicions, overcoming their inhibitions, or unlocking their most private feelings.

We have seen, however, that the growing interest in these problems has already spawned some promising solutions. The truthfulness of subjects' verbal reports can be enhanced by using the bogus pipeline technique. And more reliable indicators of subjects' private feelings, such as voice quality, can be used to circumvent the difficulties associated with verbal self-reports. Perhaps even more important, the problems caused by using deception to translate theoretical variables into experimental treatments can now be dealt with. In some cases, deception can be replaced by role playing. In others, experiments can be moved out of the laboratory to settings in the real world, or close to it. There, experimenters' intentions are less transparent and subjects' behavior is more likely to be genuinely responsive to the conditions of interest to the experimenter.

There is a potential for even greater progress in the future. As the interest in rehabilitating laboratory experimentation continues to grow, and new alternatives are explored, we should be able to expect the development of even better ways of doing experiments without their traditional reactive consequences. The problems of reactivity are not permanently locked into the experimental methods. The examples considered in this chapter demonstrate that experimental findings with high external validity can be produced while still retaining much of their traditional superiority in internal validity.

However, to be realistic we must point out that there are potent threats to continued progress. Many researchers have become deeply committed to their traditional laboratory methods. Suggestions of improvements in those methods are sometimes taken as personal attacks by individuals who hold powerful positions in the scientific establishment. Also, accepting the need for alternative nonreactive procedures implies significant alterations in the scientific life-styles of many experimental psychologists. These alternatives frequently take longer and are more difficult, and fewer experiments could be performed if the cost and the duration of each were increased. In many cases, a series of experiments, using a variety of procedures, would be required to solve the methodological problems raised by a particular research question, where a single experiment might have sufficed before.

These are formidable obstacles, but the survival of the experimental methods may depend on them being overcome. The questions that have been raised about the external validity of experimental findings will not simply go away. And science has a conservative tradition of rejecting findings that are tainted by such plausible doubts. To a large extent, the continued vitality of psychological research depends on continued progress toward adapting the experimental methods to eliminate such doubts. Without it, talented students may eventually turn away from psychological research as a potential direction for a career in science, and sophisticated consumers of research findings may begin to look elsewhere to fill their needs.

## REFERENCES

Bickman, L. Effect of different uniforms on obedience in field situation. Paper presented at the annual meeting of the American Psychological Association, 1971.

Cohen, A. R. Social norms, arbitrariness of frustration, and status of the agent of frustration in the frustration-aggression hypothesis. *Journal of Abnormal and Social Psychology,* 1955, *51,* 222–226.

Cook, S. W. The effect of unintended racial contact upon racial interaction and attitude change. Final report, Project No. 5-1320, Contract No. OEC-4-7-051320-0273. Washington, D.C.: U.S. Office of Education, Bureau of Research, August 1971. (Reported in L. S. Wrightsman, *Social psychology in the seventies.* Belmont, Cal.: Brooks/Cole, 1972. Pp 324–334.)

Doob, A.N., & Gross, A. E. Status of frustrator as an inhibitor of horn-honking responses. *Journal of Social Psychology,* 1968, *76,* 213–218.

Jones, E. E., & Sigall, J. The bogus pipeline: A new paradigm for measuring affect and attitudes. *Psychological Bulletin,* 1971, *76,* 349–364.

Karlins, M., Coffman, T. L., & Walters, G. On the fading of social stereotypes: Studies in three generation of college students. *Journal of Personality and Social Psychology,* 1969, *13,* 1–16.

Katz, D., & Braly, K. W. Racial prejudice and racial stereotypes. *Journal of Abnormal and Social Psychology,* 1933, *30,* 175–193.

Milgram, S. Behavioral study of obedience. *Journal of Abnormal and Social Psychology,* 1963, *67,* 371–378.

Neely, W. T. *Eye contact and interpersonal attraction in cooperative and competitive situations.* Unpublished doctoral dissertation, University of Maine, 1975.

Sigall, J., & Page, R. Current stereotypes: A little fading, a little faking. *Journal of Personality and Social Psychology,* 1971, *18,* 247–255.

Weitz, S. Attitude, voice, and behavior: Repressed affect model of interracial interaction. *Journal of Personality and Social Psychology,* 1972, *24,* 14–21.

Zimbardo, P. G., Haney, C., Banks, W. C., & Jaffe, D. A Pirandellian prison: The mind is a formidable jailer. *New York Times Magazine,* April 8, 1973, Pp. 38–60.

## SUGGESTED ACTIVITIES

### Study Questions and Exercise

1. How can the external validity of experimental research findings be improved by using less reactive measures of behavior? Give examples.

   Find examples of published experiments for which you can suggest alternative, less reactive measures of behavior that could be substituted for those actually used. Secondary sources such as social psychology textbooks should provide enough material to work with.

2. How does role playing work? What is the best evidence that it is a useful substitute for deception? How should more and even better evidence comparing the two be sought in the future?
3. In what ways are the results of field research easier to interpret than the results of laboratory research (you will find it easier to answer this question if you think about parallel studies testing the same general hypothesis in both ways)? In what ways are field research results more difficult to interpret?
4. In what sense did Cook combine the advantages of field and laboratory in his study of the effects of interracial contact? Can you find an example of a laboratory experiment for which you could suggest an alternative setting analogous to the one Cook devised—one which would enhance the external validity of the findings of the research?

# Chapter 8
# Quasi-Experimental
# Designs

## INTRODUCTION

Despite their obvious strengths, there are two serious limitations on the use of true experimental research designs in testing hypotheses about behavior. The first is a practical limitation. To test a hypothesis in a true experiment requires considerable intervention into the relationship between the suspected cause and the behavior of interest. As already seen, the researcher must be able to determine which subjects are exposed (or not exposed) to which events, at what times, and in which forms. As a result, the true experimental method is incapable of accommodating many important causes of behavior which occur unpredictably and exclusively in nature. If we limit our research to true experiments, we stand to lose many rich opportunities to study behavior as it is influenced by real and powerful events that are scheduled and shaped by forces we cannot control. Real events are important causes of behavior, but they cannot be scheduled or assigned to subjects at random.

In such cases, our only option, should we still wish to limit ourselves to true experimental research, is to recreate the events in question in a laboratory setting. As seen previously, behavioral researchers have been inspired by their commitment to true experimental research to great achievements in simulating or creating analogues for natural events in their laboratories. But this is where the second limitation of the true experiment becomes most apparent. It is methodological in nature—the limitation on the external validity or generalizability of the findings of true experiments. In experiments, there is considerable risk that the causal relationship will be distorted in the process of fitting it within the confines of the research design.

Considerable intervention or manipulation is necessary to fulfill the requirements of the true experimental designs while studying natural phenomena. Equivalent comparison groups must be created by random assignment of subjects to rule out preexisting differences among the members of the group. The events being studied must be scheduled arbitrarily to rule out the influence of coincidental extraneous events and temporal effects. And so on. These techniques threaten to alter the motives of the actors as they become aware of being studied. They also threaten to distort the context in which the action takes place as it is scaled down to meet these demands. To the extent that these distortions occur, the research findings lack generalizability beyond the unusual laboratory setting, and especially to the true occurrences of the phenomenon in nature that the experiment was intended to copy in the first place.

As these limitations of true experiments have come to be understood better in recent years, increasing attention has been paid to an alternative type of research design, the *quasi-experimental designs.* These require less manipulation of the phenomena being studied. This increases both the range of their application and the generalizability of the findings they produce. At the same time, it makes it more difficult to rule out extraneous influences on the behavior being studied. However, the balance between the strengths and weaknesses of the quasi-experimental designs is far more favorable than their detractors (the advocates of true experiments) have claimed. They promise to greatly enrich behavioral research as they become understood and used better in the future. One purpose of this chapter is to make that happen.

We begin by reviewing Chapter 5. Recall that we looked at two ways of improving the most primitive procedure for answering a question empirically, Design P-1, the one-shot case study. In Design P-2, the addition of a pre-X measure provided more time perspective. That made it possible to determine whether the behavior had been the same all along—a stable property of the subjects that had existed even before X came along (ruling out group composition as a competing explanation). In Design P-3, the addition of a comparison group helped rule out coincidental events and temporal trends by showing that a group exposed to them alone did not behave in the same way as the group that was also exposed to X.

Then, in Chapter 6, the true experimental designs showed us a powerful way to improve the internal validity of research findings, the use of random assignment to create equivalent comparison groups. But true experiments are possible only when the researcher has enough control over the who, where, when, and how of the events and subjects being studied to accomplish the random assignment of subjects to events. The steps which are necessary to gain such control often require researchers to compromise the generalizability of their findings.

Now we are dealing again primarily with events and subjects that either cannot be controlled because they are the products of natural forces or that should not be controlled because to do so requires that they be studied in a nonrepresentative context. But we will see in this chapter that the same basic methods whose potential we glimpsed in Chapter 5—comparisons over time and across non-equivalent groups—can be used in more sophisticated ways to produce very useful research findings.

Those better ways are the quasi-experimental designs. Their label implies that they are almost like (true) experimental designs. It also implies to some, for reasons already discussed, that they are almost as good. There will be considerably more about that later. For now, it is enough to say that neither comparison is quite as simple as it sounds.

We will consider the quasi-experimental designs in two groups, mostly for the sake of convenience. However, before we look at the first group, there is one issue we must discuss. As is true of every research design, the quasi-experimental designs all consist of some combination of Xs and Os—events that are suspected causes of behavior and measurements of that behavior. With the quasi-experimental designs, however, there are two ways in which a causal event can happen amid the measures that are made of the behavior in question. That event can occur either as a result of natural forces or at the instigation of the researcher. As seen in our previous discussion of the value of scheduling events being studied arbitrarily, this is bound to make a great difference in the interpretations that can be made of the research findings.

When the event occurs naturally, its causes are coincidental with other events that might affect the behavior it is credited with causing itself. When the researcher schedules the event, those coincidences are less problematic and causal inferences about the relationship be-

QUASI-EXPERIMENTAL DESIGNS  275

tween the event and the behavior are more trustworthy. That is why these two alternatives are sometimes called the "weak" and the "strong" versions of the quasi-experimental designs, respectively. But the researcher's control over the event is, as always, a two-edged sword. Because it is gained inevitably at the expense of changing the context in which the event occurs, it jeapordizes the generalizability of the research findings. We will examine examples of both versions of the designs, and the differences between them should be apparent. But it should also be apparent that they are not really strong and weak. They are different in several ways, some of which favor one way and some the other.

## SECTION I. QUASI-EXPERIMENTAL DESIGNS: COMPARISONS OVER TIME

The first group of quasi-experimental designs are those which utilize comparisons over time as the primary means of increasing the interpretability of their findings—QT Designs, for short. We have seen that gaining a better perspective of the way a behavior changes over time is advantageous. Experiments typically take place during very brief periods of time, permitting at best measuring the behavior just before and just after X occurs. And repeated measurements in the artificial settings in which most experiments take place can actually add as much to validity problems as they take away. Natural events take much longer to unfold, thus making a broader time perspective extremely important in assessing their effects. But natural events are not always predictable enough to permit the scheduling of measurements over sufficient spans of time in advance. As we will see, quasi-experimental designs can be devised to meet the requirements of these and many other research problems.

## DESIGN QT-1—THE SINGLE INTERRUPTED TIME SERIES DESIGN O O O OXO O O O

We start with a design that illustrates both advantages of gaining a broader time perspective on a causal event—behavior relationship and the complexity of interpreting events which take place over long periods of time. As a first step, consider the following questions which might be addressed by behavioral research.

> A detergent manufacturer makes a trivial change in its product, then markets it in a redesigned package featuring the words "New and Improved" prominently on its front panel. Does this marketing strategy cause the sales of the detergent to rise?

A new state law mandates the use of seatbelts by every automobile driver and passenger. Does that new policy result in a lower automobile accident fatality rate?

A factory owner introduces a four-day work week in his plant. Does this action cause the workers' productivity to increase?

The federal government mandates the mainstreaming of handicapped students in the public schools. What effect does that new policy have on students' academic achievement?

A life insurance company introduces a new competition among its agents that offers special bonuses for those who make the most sales in each office, state, and region. Does this additional incentive increase sales?

The U.S. Congress abolishes military conscription in favor of an "all-volunteer army." What effect does that change in policy have on the capabilities of our armed forces?

A hospital buys new equipment to permit continuous monitoring of its cardiac patients. Does this cause the desired increase in those patients' survival rate?

The answer to each of these questions depends on comparing the behavior (detergent sales, auto fatalities, etc.) before and after the hypothesized causal event (change in marketing strategy, state law, etc.) takes place. This is the same kind of question we considered in Chapter 5 in our discussion of Design P-2, the one-group pretest-posttest design. The most striking similarity is that only one sample or group is available to be studied. Unlike laboratory manipulations of independent variables, which can be given or withheld at will, the corporate and government policies described in the examples above must ordinarily be implemented over entire administrative units. Laws and work rules usually apply to whole states or countries or factories. They are usually implemented by people who feel they are good ideas that should be spread as far as possible. Even if they could be applied selectively, as a change in a product package might, to provide a valuable comparison, those who are responsible for the policies rarely think in those terms. And in many cases, their effects could be distorted by the knowledge of the citizens or workers affected that other people were governed by different rules for no apparent reason.

However, even though there is no comparison group, the availability of a pre-X assessment of the behavior being studied provides a valuable reference point. In Design QT-1, as in Design P-2, it rules out group composition and sample attrition as explanations for any pre-X to post-X difference that is observed.

Design P-2 is, however, otherwise quite unsatisfactory. It fails to rule out temporal trends, the effects of repeated measurement, and change in O due to statistical regression as explanations for a change between the single pre-X and the single post-X measure of behavior. Design QT-1, on the other hand, incorporates one kind of solution to all these problems.

The strength of the approach taken in Design QT-1 is as much a product of the settings in which the research takes place as of the planning skill of the researcher. Many institutional settings, including most corporations and governments, have elaborate built-in mechanisms for keeping constant track of their own activities as well as those outside their boundaries that are important to the functions they perform. Corporations keep records of the sales of their products and the performance of their workers. Governments keep records about almost everything imaginable through censuses, licensing and other control agencies, the Weather Service and too many other bodies to name. In addition, many private parties, such as polling and rating services, exist for the sole purpose of keeping records of events and behaviors someone thinks are important.

The availability of these running records, or archives, makes it possible to evaluate many causal events over extended periods by comparing long series of measures both before and after they take place. These measures are called *time series.* Together with the events which "interrupt" them, they are represented by the regular and symmetrical model in the diagram shown in the heading at the beginning of this section. Daily or weekly or monthly sales figures, police reports, medical records, stock market reports, and many other "statistics" make it possible to test hypotheses about many causal events in many settings in exactly this way. Of course, time series need not be perfectly regular or symmetrical in order to provide useful information.

The principal value of the time series form of analysis, especially in contrast to the findings produced by Design P-2, is illustrated in Figure 8-1. These are some of the possible outcomes of a time series analysis. They are presented in an idealized form, ignoring the irregularities that would show up in any actual example, merely to represent some interesting types of outcome. To begin with, it is important to recognize that the differences between measures $O_4$ and $O_5$ (the only ones which would be analyzed in Design P-2) are the same for every pattern in Figure 8-1, except for pattern D, which portrays a possible delayed effect of X (if that delay were anticipated, Design P-2 might then utilize $O_4$ and $O_6$ as its two measurement points). Yet, it is clear that some patterns containing this same pre-X to post-X difference clearly rule out the three alternative explanations for Design P-2 findings mentioned above. Patterns A and B could not be

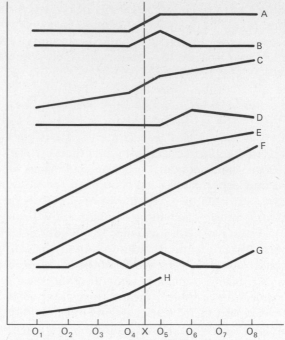

Figure 8-1. Idealized Models of some of the possible outcomes of time series research.

(After D. T. Campbell and J. C. Stanley "Experimental and quasi-experimental designs for research in educational research." *Review of Educational Research,* 1966, fig. 3, p. 38. Copyright 1966, American Educational Research Association, Washington, D.C.)

explained as the result of a temporal trend independent of X, nor as the result of the repeated measurements of O, nor as a statistical regression effect. All these extraneous influences would show up as changes in the $O_1$ to $O_4$ portion of the time series, not just between $O_4$ and $O_5$. Table 8-1 shows these strengths of Design QT-1 as $+$s where $-$s appear in the evaluation of Design P-2 in Table 8-1. Patterns F, G, and H in Figure 8-1 show how these extraneous influences on O that could produce misleading findings in a study using Design P-2 would show up in the extended sampling of measures of O provided by a time series design.

Design QT-1 is also less likely to mistake observer effects for an effect of X. Because it typically uses archival data which are collected automatically and independently of the researcher's interest in a specific hypothesis, it is less likely that different criteria will be applied to the behavior being studied after X than before. There are also ad-

**Table 8-1** VALIDITY SCORECARD: QUASI-EXPERIMENTAL RESEARCH DESIGNS I—COMPARISONS OVER TIME

| | INTERNAL VALIDITY | | | | | | | EXTERNAL VALIDITY | | | | |
|---|---|---|---|---|---|---|---|---|---|---|---|---|
| | EXTRANEOUS EVENTS | TEMPORAL EFFECTS | GROUP COMPOSITION EFFECTS | TEMPORAL X GROUP COMPOSITION EFFECTS | NONREPRESENTATIVE SAMPLING | REACTIVITY OF THE RESEARCH CONTEXT | NONREPRESENTATIVE RESEARCH CONTEXT | LACK OF ECOLOGICAL VALIDITY | OBSERVER EFFECTS | EFFECTS OF PRETESTING | EFFECTS OF SAMPLE ATTRITION | STATISTICAL REGRESSION EFFECTS |
| QT-1: TIME SERIES DESIGN<br>O O O OXO O O O | − | + | + | + | ? | + | + | + | ? | ? | + | + |
| QT-2: MULTIPLE TIME SERIES DESIGN<br>$G_1$ O O O OXO O O O<br>$G_2$ O O O OXO O O O | + | + | + | + | + | + | + | + | ? | ? | + | + |
| QT-3: EQUIVALENT TIME SAMPLES DESIGN<br>$X_1O$ $X_0O$ $X_1O$ $X_0O$ etc. | + | + | + | + | + | + | + | + | ? | ? | − | − |

SOURCE: D. T. Campbell and J. C. Stanley. "Experimental and quasi-experimental designs for research in educational research." *Review of Educational Research*, 1966. Copyright 1966, American Educational Research Association, Washington, D.C.

vantages to using of archival data for the external validity of time series findings. In the typical case in which the measurements of O do not directly touch the individuals whose behavior is being studied, there is no reason to fear that the results will be generalizable only to subjects who are tested repeatedly or who are self-consciously aware of being studied. It is also typical for time series analyses to be used in studies of policy evaluation such as in the examples discussed earlier. In evaluation studies like those, the researcher's interest is both practical and focused narrowly on the group being studied. The detergent manufacturer is interested only in its own product, and the federal government only in this nation. In such cases, questions of generalizability to other samples are secondary. In addition, the behaviors being studied occur in their natural context. There is no question about how X would affect them with all their other usual influences operating on them. This is precisely how any observed effect was produced, that is, in its representative and natural context. Time series analyses are usually applied to real behavior, as they are reflected in the most reliable, objective records which could be kept.

Having said all these favorable things about the time series design, we also need to point out that it could be applied in very different circumstances. Novel measurements of O could be applied directly and obtrusively to the subjects being studied. The measures used could focus on some peculiar, nonrepresentative aspect of the subjects' behavior. The observer could be aware of the hypothesis being studied and of the date of the occurrence of X. The behavior could take place in an unnatural context, even a psychological laboratory in which many of the customary influences on it were artificially removed. In such applications, observer bias would be a much more serious threat to the internal validity of the findings and their generalizability would be far more limited than in the cases described earlier.

Regardless how the time series design is used, the internal validity of its findings is subject to one serious threat which we have not considered. The typically long duration of policy changes raises the distinct possibility that extraneous events which occur at the same time as X could be responsible for any change in the series of measurements that occurs, however clearly, when X occurs or when its effects are expected. When the events and behavior are natural ones, this possibility is even greater. Any event causing X to occur, like a change in the economy or in existing technology or in the availability of oil, could also account for a change in the behavior being studied. Thus, extraneous events, and especially "third-variable" influences on X and O, are potential alternative explanations for time series findings.

As we have seen, the Single Interrupted Time Series Design is often used to evaluate the effects of a change in corporate or governmental policy. One example of that kind of research is a recent study by Luckey and Berman (1979). In Nebraska, in 1976, a new state law went into effect to regulate involuntary commitment to mental hospitals. Nebraska's previous commitment law had been ruled unconstitutional for failing to protect adequately the rights of mental patients. The new law was stricter, requiring a series of evaluations and hearings, four steps in all, which served as safeguards against the continued commitment of any citizen who was not dangerous or unable to care for himself or herself.

Like any new policy, specific effects were intended by those who wrote the new law. In this case, the number of involuntary admissions was expected to be reduced. Critics of the law even claimed that it would make it more difficult to provide treatment to those who needed it. Luckey and Berman undertook their study to determine empirically which of these claims was true or false, and to find out in a more general way how the new law worked.

Because commitment to a mental hospital and the treatment a patient receives there are matters of continuous public record, Luckey and Berman were able to use a time series analysis. A computerized statewide record system was instituted for the three state hospitals in Nebraska almost two years before the law took effect and records were available for an equal period following the change. These records were divided into three-week periods and totals for each period represented points in the time series. There were about 30 before and a similar number after X. Separate series were constructed for each of the possible effects of the new law in which Luckey and Berman had an interest. These included the number of admissions, the type of patients committed (place of residence, sex, age, diagnosis, etc.), and the length of treatment and likelihood of readmission after treatment. These series were analyzed using a statistical process known as multiple regression analysis, which is capable of determining whether an interruption in a time series (X) was associated with a change in the level of the series (how many or how much of whatever is being measured) or a change in its scope (the rate of increase or decrease over time of whatever is being measured).

Luckey and Berman found that introducing the new law did precede changes in several measures they examined. First, the number of involuntary admissions dropped significantly immediately after the law took effect. But it began to rise after a short time, reaching the old level again in about 18 months. Some of the characteristics of involuntary admission changed also. Women and people from the more rural counties of Nebraska accounted for most of the drop in involuntary admissions. Admissions from the most populous counties of the state actually increased at a faster rate after the new law took effect than they had been before. Finally, the average length of treatment for involuntary admissions decreased after the change in the law, but the number of patients who had to be readmitted increased.

One exercise that might be useful at this point is to look at two of the actual time series that were analyzed in this study, and espe-

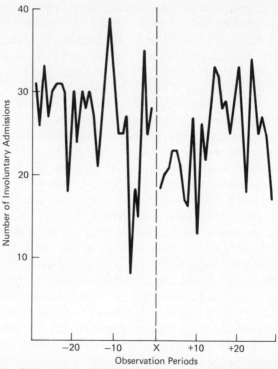

Figure 8-2. Time series representation of effects of change in Nebraska commitment law on number of involuntary admissions to state mental hospitals.
(After Luckey and Berman. "Effects of a new commitment law on involuntary admissions and service utilization patterns." *Law and Human Behavior,* Vol. 3. Plenum, New York, 1979, fig. 3, p. 158.)

cially to relate them to the patterns in Figure 8-1. Figure 8-2 shows the series for the number of involuntary admissions. Perhaps someone with a special skill for perceiving spatial relations could tell just by looking at that figure exactly what had happened during those three-and-a-half years. But I certainly could not. When the points in that series are entered into a multiple regression analysis, however, it turns out that the portion of the series which immediately follows the interruption by X is made up of smaller values than the portion before X, but that the rate of increase after X is greater than the rate of increase before, eventually returning the series to its original level. The variability in the series from one point to the next, undoubtedly reflecting all the other causes of commitments to mental hospitals which change with the week, month, and year, makes this very difficult to see with the naked eye.

The pattern of changes in committed patients' average length of stay in Nebraska's state mental hospitals, shown in Figure 8-3, is similarly difficult to interpret without using sophisticated statistical analysis. The casual observer might ask whether there is a general decline across the entire series of measures that is affected very little by the interruption in the middle. In fact, it might appear that the the length of stay time series in Figure 8-3 has about the same shape as pattern F, in Table 8-1, although the two patterns are in opposite directions to one another. Pattern F in Figure 8-1 is an example of a time series that shows that the change from before to after the suspected causal event is not caused by that event at all, being simply one step in a regular pattern of change, or temporal trend, which began long before X and continued along the same path long after. But the multiple regression analysis conducted by Luckey and Berman showed that there was actually a greater drop in the length of stay measure after the new law took effect than one would have expected from the pattern that existed before. The average length of stay of committed patients then leveled off somewhat, declining at a slower rate than it had before.

Whether the changes in the law caused any of these observable differences is not a matter that can be decided statistically. To decide that, we need to look at the possibility that plausible rival hypotheses exist for these particular time series findings. As already seen, the most serious contender for that position is some extraneous event that happened to coincide with the change in Nebraska's commitment law and that could reasonably be expected to have all the same effects that were hypothesized and found to follow the change in the law. If there were such an extraneous event, its detection would re-

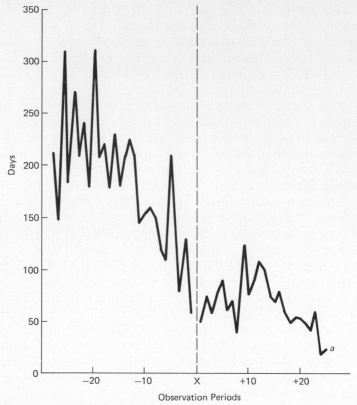

Figure 8-3.  Time series representation of effects of change in Nebraska commitment law on average length of stay in hospitals.

(After Luckey and Berman. "Effects of a new commitment law on involuntary admissions and service utilization patterns." *Law and Human Behavior,* Vol. 3. Plenum, New York, 1979, fig. 4, p. 158.)

quire considerable knowledge both of the mental health care system in general and the local conditions in Nebraska.

Although time series analysis does not rule out this possibility in the affirmative way a true experiment does, we are unlikely to find out as much about the effects of commitment laws in an experiment. It might be possible to simulate this phenomenon in a psychological laboratory, even with some of the same kinds of public officials who make these decisions in the real world. But the narrower generalizability of such findings would have to be weighed against the slight gain in certainty about the causal role of X. It is especially true in evaluation studies like Luckey and Berman's, which are intended to learn about one particular event in its particular context, and which take advantage of records that would have been kept in any event without disturbing the ongoing phenomenon by the process of studying it, that generalizability poses as little difficulty as imaginable of any research findings. In this particular case, the only apparent restrictions in attempting to apply the findings obtained would be to the public or state hospitals in Nebraska (involuntary admissions to private institutions might not follow the same pattern) and to the period of the middle 1970s that was studied (10 years later, other conditions might have changed so much that the 1976 law would have different effects).

The findings of the Luckey and Berman study are also instructive, beyond a methodological analysis, about the practical value of evaluation studies that utilize the time series and other quasi-experimental research designs. In both the public and the private sectors, policy changes will occur from time to time. They are based on policymakers' perceptions that reforms in existing policies are necessary to make a system function better. But policymakers' assumptions about the effects of their reforms are not always correct. The actual effects are not always those that were intended. Research is the only way to learn what really happens. That knowledge is extremely important for three reasons.

In the immediate context of a particular reform, it allows the "fine tuning" of important public policy. In the case of the Nebraska commitment law, there are suggestions in Luckey and Berman's findings that the desired reduction in the number of involuntary commitments did occur, but that it was only temporary. Luckey and Berman speculate that commitment boards were at first uncertain about how to implement the law, but that they eventually returned to doing things the same as they had previously, thus failing to implement the changes required by the new laws. In addition, there was some evidence that the reduction in committed patients' average length of stay had the unintended effect, anticipated by critics of the new law, of increasing the number of released patients who had to be readmitted for treatment. Thus, it seems that there may have been cases where the new law worked to the detriment of patients. The additional finding that the greatest drop in involuntary admissions occurred in the state's least populous counties was interpreted as an indication that the complex procedures required by the new law were beyond the resources of rural areas. There, patients who were intended under the law to be committed may not have been

because rural counties could not afford to follow the necessary procedures. These facts, and others, imply that those responsible for executing the law need to look further into the processes of commitment
and treatment of involuntary patients in Nebraska state hospitals to
determine what further changes need to be made in implementing
the law or in the law itself to better serve the intent of those who
passed it.

In a less specific way, studies like these tell us, especially the policymakers among us, more about what to expect from reforms in general. They demonstrate that assumptions are no substitute for facts
and that the procedures by which reforms are implemented can be
at least as important as the policies themselves. Finally, they can
even provide data which add to our basic knowledge about behavior.
Luckey and Berman's found, for example, that the temporary reduction in the number of involuntary admissions after the new law went
into effect was made up primarily of women patients. This may cor-
roborate the theories of several persons who have explored the process by which persons came to be labeled mentally ill and in need
of treatment. They have proposed that different criteria are applied
to women and to men. The provision in the Nebraska law that being
dangerous and unable to support oneself were the sole criteria for
commitment may have worked in women's favor because they are
perceived as less dangerous and are less likely to be in a position
where they are solely responsible for their own support. In the same
way as preexperimental studies, quasi-experimental studies can be
rich sources of hypotheses that might later be investigated in more
precise ways.

The use of time series designs to test theory-based hypotheses
about behavior is still quite rare. But a recent study by Simonton
(1975) provides an opportunity to see how they can be used in this
way and, at the same time, to learn something about the interesting
subject of creativity. Simonton was interested in how a creative person's work is affected by the surrounding cultural atmosphere.

Specifically, he hypothesized that creativity in the "discursive"
(writing) fields of science, philosophy, literature, and music composition was influenced by a variety of sociocultural factors, that is, the
state of the social institutions which form the context within which
the creative person works. To test his hypotheses, he chose to examine the works of creative individuals as they are recorded in the history of Western civilization. He used histories, anthologies, and
biographical dictionaries to catalog these works over a period of approximately 2500 years, from ancient Greece and Rome in 700 B.C.
until modern Europe at the beginning of the nineteenth century.

To construct a time series of measures, he divided this span into

20-year "generations." Simonton began in the first year of each century (1500, 1600, etc.) and included those creative persons who were about 40 years old at the generation's midpoint (1509–1510, 1609–1610, etc.). Thus Simonton dealt with groups of creative persons whose productive periods, between the ages of 30 and 50, fell during one of the fifths of a century. Their works were added together to produce one creativity score for the entire 20-year generation. Scores were derived which reflected the number of persons whom history shows were active during that period, the total number of works they produced, and their importance as reflected in the frequency with which later chroniclers of the period refer to them.

Along these time series, Simonton placed the variety of potential causal events he wished to study. Among the sociocultural factors he suspected of positively influencing creativity was the availability of role models for creative individuals. The more creative work going on during a potential creator's formative years—the two generations preceding the one in which a creator could be working productively—the more likely that person's own creative talents would be nurtured. Another hypothesized positive influence was the amount of cultural diversity in the artist's world. The existence of autonomous cultural groups, each vying for its share of influence over a country or continent, the greater is the pool of conflicting ideas and values toward whose resolution creative persons could direct their talents. Once these factors had coalesced into stable nations and alliances, the grist for the creator's mill would have dried up considerably. However, instability could also be viewed as a destructive force for the creative individual. When a stable government disintegrates into rival factions, with violent changes in authority through coups d'état and assassinations, the sense of personal control over one's life and the sense that the future is predictable from a rational analysis of the present are lost and the creative person's equanimity and productivity may be lost along with them.

The models of time series designs at the beginning of the chapter and in Figure 8-1 portray causal events as discrete occurrences. They happen at specific points in time. The causal influences of Simonton studies are, by contrast, continuous trends. Creativity is not present or absent in the world, but it is more or less common. Cultures are not diverse or homogeneous, but more or less toward one extreme or the other. Therefore, Simonton's analyses of his data were not comparisons between points before and after, but somewhat more complicated regression analyses. We will have to simplify the technical issues a little to look at his results. On the average, the amount of creativity in each of the 127 generations of creators he studied was related positively to the amount in the two preceding generations (presumably because more role models were available for developing creators). Creative productivity in any generation was also related positively to the degree of cultural diversity during the immediately preceding generation, when the creators, then aged 10–30, were developing their talents. But political instability during that developmental period was negatively related to creativity in the subsequent generation of creators in their productive periods.

As in all time series studies, however, difficult questions remain about the causal relationships among these three sociocultural factors and creativity. We do know that the curves change direction after certain events occur. This "time lag" between the supposed cause and effect is always the main reason for thinking we know which is which. After all, creativity in one generation certainly could not have affected events that took place in earlier generations. And Simonton showed that none of the sociocultural factors described above predicted creativity for its own generation, when the mature creators had already been formed by earlier experiences, as well as it did for later generations.

But changes are too frequent and other events too common to stop there. Extraneous events are, here as always, the greatest threat to the internal validity of time series findings. As Simonton himself asks, how can we be certain that economic conditions, or any of the other possibilities, could not have caused both the creativity in each generation and the sociocultural conditions which led up to it? How can we be sure that any third-variable cause would be apparent to us if it had, in fact, existed? Simonton tried to rule out some of the possibilities, using complex methods we do not have space to discuss here. We can say, however, that his efforts were not very reassuring. Extraneous events remain a serious threat to the validity of his findings.

The second serious threat to the internal validity of time series findings is one that Simonton handled much more successfully. As seen already, it is crucial to the analysis of time series data that observers apply the same criteria to all measures in the series, so that they are all comparable. This assures that differences along the series can be interpreted as the result of something other than observer bias. There is one form of potential observer bias to which historical analyses are especially vulnerable. Historians may overvalue the products of their own time. Simonton, in fact, found just such a recency bias in his data. The sources he used tended to give higher marks to creative persons during their own times than observers later in history would. He eliminated this source of bias by applying a statistical correction to the data. Thus the numbers he finally analyzed were comparable in this respect.

The most remarkable thing about Simonton's findings, however, is their external validity. They illustrate very clearly how advantageous the use of natural data can be to a theory-based study. There is, to begin with, very little problem in generalizing Simonton's findings about the relationships among sociocultural factors and discursive creativity to other samples. He studied almost the entire history of Western civilization. The public record condenses the behavior of many individuals over a very long time into a form that can be studiod, in oontraot with tho laboratory that oxplodoo tho briof ao tions of a few subjects into what often seems like too much information to comprehend.

There is also a difference between an archival study like Simonton's and the study of contemporaneous behavior that is more typical of psychological research, in the potential for reactive distortion of the behavior being studied. There is no way in which Simonton's research could have altered the actual creative behavior which took place through the centuries. There is no uncertainty about what happened that can be attributed to the close inspection that was made of it. But there is always the problem, in every research study, of the representativeness of a researcher's choice of measures of the phenomena being studied. This is kept to a minimum in archival studies where, to some extent, the choice is kept out of the researcher's hands. The people and events Simonton studied were real, in some sense beyond those studied in most psychological research. The countries, governments, revolutions, symphonies, and the people themselves were taken directly from the historical record, the clearest picture we have of all that happened. Moreover, they all existed in all the indescribable richness of context in which all real history takes place. And to ensure that his rendering was faithful to reality, Simonton checked his figures with those of other investigators who had used the same history. Thus, we can be reassured that independent observers testing different hypotheses interpreted the historical record similarly.

The ecological validity of Simonton's findings is also enhanced by the use of an archival time series. By relying on the seasoned judgments of experts, summed over thousands of years, one can be more certain that the works one is counting are really creative products and not just current fads that all future generations of scientists, philosophers, writers, and composers might laugh at or ignore. This is especially important in the study of creativity. Because it is such a rare behavior and one to which the researcher has so little access, many researchers have given "brain-teasing" problems to their undergraduate students and studied the conditions under which "creative" solutions emerge. The problem would remain the same if professors or any other group participated. The behavior would not be creativity in any real sense, when one considers that Simonton's data included the works of Michaelangelo, Galileo, Aristotle, and Bach. Thus, although the internal validity of Simonton's findings may have left something to be desired, one must admire the fact that they say something about a very important and real form of behavior. As we have seen, much the same could be said about a great deal of time series research.

## DESIGN QT-2—THE MULTIPLE TIME SERIES DESIGN

$$\begin{array}{ccccccccc} O & O & O & O & X & O & O & O & O \\ O & O & O & O & & O & O & O & O \end{array}$$

As we have seen, time series analysis can be a powerful way of answering questions about behavior, both practical and theoretical ones. It is especially appropriate under circumstances in which no comparison group is available, but a running record of the behavior of interest is available both before and after the occurrence of a suspected causal event. There are many occasions, however, when comparison groups are available. Then the time series analysis can be strengthened even further. Its principal failing, the possibility that the observed change in the behavior over the series of measurements is not caused by the hypothesized event, but by extraneous events that happen to coincide with it, can be remedied. This added strength can be provided by a comparison series of observations of another sample or group that is not exposed to the causal event in question, but that is exposed to all other possible influences on the behavior and for which the same running record or archive of behavioral measures is available. The result is a *multiple time series* analysis.

Consider one of the examples with which we began our discussion of the Single Interrupted Time Series Design. What if our hypothetical detergent manufacturer divided its market into two similar parts, and introduced the new product (new marketing ploy, actually) in one area while staying with the old one in the rest? This is actually a fairly common practice called test marketing. Both markets would be exposed to at least some of the extraneous events which could affect detergent sales, such as national economic conditions, season of the year, and competitors' policies (although they would not be quite equivalent because of residual regional differences). Thus a change in sales in the market where the new product was introduced could be compared against the sales record (time series) of the old product to determine whether it was caused by the intentional change in company policy or by one of those other influences on detergent sales. That is information the single time series cannot provide. A similar strategy could be used by the hypothetical insurance company, comparing the effect of its new bonus idea in some regions with its traditional practices in others. However, it would be more difficult for a government to pass new laws or institute new policies for selected areas of its jurisdiction and keep the old laws and policies in the rest. And even though a large corporation could institute a four-day workweek in some of its plants and not in others, if the workers communicated with one another, through their union representatives, for example, the comparison would be distorted by the knowledge that each group had of the other group and its different working conditions.

Where an additional time series is available for comparison, and where that comparison is not affected by people's feelings that they are in an experiment or that they are being treated differently for reasons they do not understand, it can be a valuable adjunct to a time series analysis. A recent study by Rindfuss, Reed, and St. John (1978) shows that very clearly. It also, like our second example of a single time series study, makes an important theoretical point about historical human behavior.

On May 17, 1954, the United States Supreme Court decided a landmark case. It ruled that state laws that established dual school systems, segregating black and white students into separate and supposedly equal schools, were unconstitutional. One can only imagine the impact that this ruling had on citizens in those states that maintained dual systems and also throughout this country and even the rest of the world.

Fortunately, the behavioral scientist can do more than imagine their effects. And one possible course of action is made possible by the extensive running records or archives of behavior to which we referred earlier. That is, in fact, where Rindfuss and his collegues investigated the effects of the *Brown* v. *Board of Education* ruling. More specifically, they went to data collected in the 1960 national census. There they found what they called a "fertility reaction." They found a decline in the birthrates of whites who lived in states that faced the need to desegregate their schools as a result of the Supreme Court's ruling. They went on to explain that decline as the result of decisions made by individual white families to stop trying to have children or to give up plans to try to have children by starting or continuing some form of birth control. We will look at that phenomenon piece by piece, even though it may detract from the drama

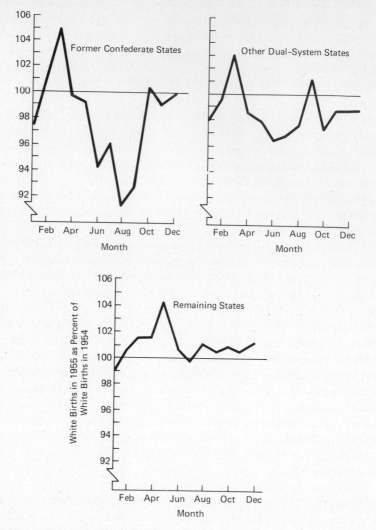

Figure 8-4.  Rindfuss and colleagues data broken down into separate time series.

of what they found, in order to make some important points about time series analyses.

We look first at what happened to the birthrate among white Southerners during 1955, the year following the Supreme Court's decision. The first panel in Figure 8-4 shows a time series of white births during that year. The number of births, however, is expressed as a percentage of the number in 1954, the previous year, to show increases and decreases rather than the actual numbers. And the points on the graph represent the births in only 11 states—the states that had dual school systems in 1954 and had previously belonged to the Confederacy during the Civil War. That curve shows clearly that for most of 1955 there were fewer births in white Southern families than in 1954. But does it show that the Supreme Court decision had anything to do with it?

Does it even show a real drop in the birthrate? When we discussed the possible outcomes of the single time series design and the portrayal of its possible outcomes in Figure 8-1, we pointed out that they were idealized models. However, this is an actual time series and, like our previous example, it shows how complex the analysis is. Two issues in particular come to mind. The first is how much of a drop below the previous year is worth talking about. The graph in Figure 8-4 makes the drop from April to October of 1955 look substantial. But of the 12 points connected by it, only 4 are very far below the 100% line—the points for June, July, August, and September. And the lowest point, the one for August, is still above 90% of the births for the corresponding month of the previous year. Is even that a substantial drop? Graphs can be very useful, but the choice of scale can influence the appearance of the data quite dramatically, making small fractions of difference appear quite large or large differences quite small. We cannot even use traditional statistics because each month's figure is a single point. If we separated them into the individual states they combined, a traditional statistical analysis would be possible. But even if the differences among the points were shown to be statistically significant, that would be difficult to interpret. Even statistical tests do not tell us whether a difference is large enough to be important, only whether it really exists or not.

A second issue in interpreting the time series in Figure 8-2 is the timing of the drop in birthrates among white families in former Confederate states. It is important in evaluating the effects of an event like the 1954 Supreme Court desegregation ruling to decide when a particular behavior should be affected by it. If white Southerners actually did change their plans as a consequence of the Supreme Court's decision, that change would presumably take place in the weeks following the decision as it became widely publicized and as they considered its implications. The outcome of that change in plans would not be apparent, however, until about nine months later, when those who did change their plans would not have had children that we would have expected had the decision not occurred. That would place the time of an expected decline in their birthrate no earlier than April 1955, the time when the decline actually did begin. A decline that began six months earlier could not have been attributed to the Supreme Court's action. Also, a decline that began six months later would be much more difficult to explain.

But Rindfuss and his colleagues found an even better way to support their interpretation. They compared the birthrate decline among whites living in former Confederate states with the fertility of whites in the rest of the country. And they divided the other 38 states including the District of Columbia (Alaska and Hawaii were not yet states at that time) into two groups. Seven of them had dual school systems at the time of the decision, but were not really Southern states (they included border states like Kentucky as well as the District of Columbia). The remaining 31 states did not have school segregation laws in 1954. Figure 8-5 shows the time series of birthrates during 1955 (all compared with the previous year) for all three of these groups of states. This comparison makes it clear that the drop in the birthrate among Southern whites was shown also, but to a lesser degree, among whites in non-Southern states that had dual school systems. Whites living in states that did not have dual systems, in contrast, showed a fairly consistent increase over the previous year. The contrast in patterns among these groups of states may be even clearer in Figure 8-4, where they are presented side-by-side. This suggests that the decline in fertility among Southern whites was not due to extraneous events such as an economic recession or the threat of war or any other event which had an impact on the nation as a whole. It is still possible that some local trend such as a poor market for some important Southern crop or a disastrous stretch of bad weather confined to the Southeastern region of the country could have produced these findings. But the position of the non-Confederate dual-system states, between the Confederate and non-dual-system states, makes these unlikely possibilities. It extends the area of the effect beyond one compact region, to the Midwest and Middle Atlantic states.

Another way of framing the same comparison is by categorizing states as having higher or lower white birthrates in 1955 than in 1954. Table 8-2 presents the results of such an analysis for the three groups of states defined above. Not only does it show the different patterns of fertility in the former Confederate and non-dual-system states, but it makes them easier to evaluate. The simple statistic known as Chi-squared can be computed from the numbers in Table 8-2. When I actually did the computations, the result showed that there was less than one chance in 100 that the variation in the splits between increases and decreases in white fertility in states in the three groups could have come about as the result of random fluctuation.

A further advantage of the form of comparison shown in Table 8-2 is that it facilitates an examination of white fertility in the individ-

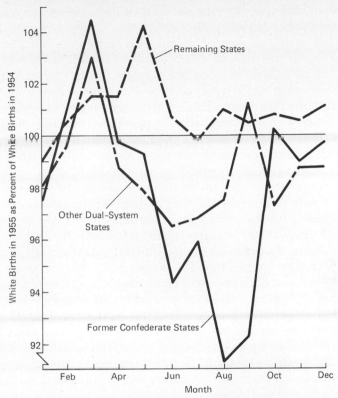

Figure 8-5. Multiple time series analysis of fertility reaction to Supreme Court decision in 1954 on *Brown* v. *Board of Education*.
(After R. R. Rindfuss, J. S. Reed, and C. St. John. "A fertility reaction to an historical event: Southern white birthrates and the 1954 desegregation ruling." *Science,* Vol. 201, July 14, 1978, fig. 2, p. 179. Copyright 1978 by the American Association for the Advancement of Science.)

ual states that are combined in the time series shown in Figure 8-5. The only two former Confederate states that did not show a decline in white fertility between 1954 and 1955 were Florida, whose population contains a relatively large number of immigrants from the North, and North Carolina, one of the most industrialized of the Southern states. Of the minority of nine non-dual-system states that did not show increases in white fertility between 1954 and 1955, several had relatively high levels of school segregation, including Pennsylvania and Indiana, and Kansas, which was one of the states in which the Supreme Court case had originated, but which did not have a dual school system mandated by law. Although the state-by-state analyses cannot be conclusive, they do lend some credibility to the conclusion that the changes in fertility were, in fact, caused by the Supreme Court's decision.

This study can also be useful in making one more important point. One of the ways in which Rindfuss and his colleagues helped us to compare their three groups of states was by converting the actual numbers of white births in 1955 into percentages of births during the previous year. This simple technique eliminates some extraneous events as alternative explanations for shifts in the time series. There is, for example, seasonal variation in fertility. If one were to predict more births in the summer and in early fall from some historical events, it would be misleading to claim confirmation for the hypothesis based on an increase in fertility from the winter and spring months to the summer and fall. That happens every year, regardless of what events take place beyond the seasonal change. The use of seasonally adjusted rates eliminates the changes caused by season and it does so for every state individually, so that the three groups of states are also made comparable in this respect. Even if the summer and fall increase in births might be greater in the Northeast than in regions with more moderate climates, state-by-state adjustment makes all regions comparable as their individual seasonal variations are eliminated.

In the terms we've been using, transforming data into rate measures can eliminate temporal trends like seasonal variation that could otherwise be mistaken for the effects of a hypothesized causal event. This is as true of single time series as it is of multiple time series analyses. If you have ever heard government economists trying to explain changes in inflation or unemployment or the gross national product, you may have noticed that the measures they use are always seasonally adjusted. This sort of transformation is a big help in understanding any series of measures over an extended period. In comparing of different time series, there is the added benefit of equating the

**Table 8-2** CHANGE IN WHITE FERTILITY IN THE UNITED STATES, 1955 VERSUS 1954

| STATE GROUP | NUMBER OF STATES WITH | |
| --- | --- | --- |
| | INCREASE | DECREASE |
| Former Confederate states | 2 | 9 |
| Other dual-system states | 3 | 4 |
| Remaining states | 22 | 9 |

SOURCE: R. R. Rindfuss, J. S. Reed, and C. St. John. "A fertility reaction to an historical event: Southern white birthrates and the 1954 desegregation ruling." *Science*, vol. 201, pp. 178–180, July 14, 1978. Copyright 1978 by the American Association for the Advancement of Science.

different series. In other words, the interaction of temporal trend with group composition—the fact that different groups may have unique trends that also may look like the effects of causal events—is also eliminated as an alternative explanation for the findings if rate measures are used rather than raw data.

Although we digress a little from our current discussion, it seems like the best time to point out the more general value of transforming raw data into rates or proportions. In studies of natural behavior, where everything else is not nearly as equal as in a laboratory experiment, the actual frequencies of behaviors observed or the actual measurements of the size or strength or speed of a behavior can be very misleading bases for comparisons from one group or time to another. A good example of not only the problem but also of how it can arise in the most common and routine contexts is in a newspaper article I read recently (Rigsbee, 1980). It was concerned with the problem of litter and possible solutions to it. A group of Youth Conservation Corps members took on the project of cleaning the litter from 2 miles of roads inside one of our national forests. One of their leaders, a science teacher, analyzed the 931 pounds of litter they gathered. He made the following observations. Of the 158 pounds of cans collected, only 17 pounds were aluminum. Of the 486 pounds of glass bottles collected, only 28 pounds were returnable. He concluded that people (travelers and campers presumably) are less likely to throw away things that have monetary value, and that if deposits were required on all such containers, the amount of litter along our roads would be greatly reduced. Although all that may be true, his data do not prove it. We do not know if only 17 of the 158 pounds of cans thrown away (about 11%) were aluminum because aluminum cans have value or because many more cans sold, especially by weight, are steel rather than aluminum. We do not know, either, whether more nonreturnable bottles are discarded (94% by weight) because they have no cash value or because many more nonreturnable bottles are sold than returnables. If the numbers of steel and aluminum cans were compared as proportions of the numbers sold, and if the numbers of returnable and nonreturnable bottles were compared as proportions of the numbers sold, the conclusions drawn from this informal study of litter would be a lot easier to interpret. It is a good lesson for those who do and read about behavioral research, which, it seems, includes just about everyone.

Given adequate attention to its potential problems, the multiple time series design can be a powerful tool for the evaluation of policy changes in our public and private institutions as well as for testing theories about behavior. It takes maximum advantage of the abundant records that are kept by our public and private social institutions and in which the effects of many important historical, political, economic, and other influences on human behavior can be reflected. A formal inspection of the strengths and weaknesses of the design in Table 8-1 bears out this favorable verbal description. The introduction of a comparison time series helps to rule out extraneous events, the single most serious threat to the internal validity of single time series findings. As a result, Design QT-2 receives perfect marks for internal validity. The single and multiple forms of time series analyses are comparable in their freedom from threats to external validity. When these designs are applied to archival data, unobtrusive and nonreactive measures of the behavior of broad spectra of people to important events which occur over extended periods in their natural contexts, research findings pose very few problems of generalizability. As was the case in Design QT-1, this is true especially of cases in which the design is used to evaluate changes of policy in particular factories or governmental jurisdictions for very practical purposes so that the researcher's interest is no broader than the samples and measures actually used in the research. In those cases, the question mark for nonrepresentativeness becomes a "$+$." When the design is used to test general hypotheses or theories about behavior, the same question mark becomes a "$-$," unless samples as large and representative as Simonton's can be studied.

## DESIGN QT-3—THE EQUIVALENT TIME SAMPLES DESIGN

$$X_1O \quad X_0O \quad X_1O \quad X_0 \quad \text{ETC.}$$

We now come to a design that is a bit of a contradiction. Although it is generally considered to be a quasi-experimental design, it is capable of producing findings that rival the findings of true experiments for internal validity. When the internal validity of its findings is threatened, it is often for the same reasons that apply to true experiments. And the findings of the Equivalent Time Samples Design often suffer from the same lack of generalizability as the findings of experimental designs.

Not only does this design act in many ways more like an experimental than a quasi-experimental design, but it also illustrates very clearly the way in which the same quasi-experimental (or any other) design can be applied in different ways that result in very different patterns of strengths and weaknesses in the validity of their findings. We referred already to so-called strong and weak versions of quasi-experimental designs. That contrast is nowhere else as great as it is here.

We start at the "strong" extreme. The Equivalent Time Samples Design has been used for what are generally considered some of the most scientifically powerful research studies in the history of psychology. They are studies of operant conditioning. In one of their most common and basic forms, a pigeon is the subject. Actually, three pigeons are often used, because one bird could behave abnormally or die during the course of a long study because of an undetected physical defect, and in order to be sure that a second one will be available as a check on the first, a third bird is tested as a backup.

The pigeons are tested in a soundproof chamber that contains two features that are significant to them. One is a translucent plexiglas circle mounted on one inner wall of the chamber. It is spring mounted so that it can be pushed back into the trigger of a microswitch. This makes it possible for any response that puts sufficient pressure on this "key" to set off a subsequent event via the capability of the microswitch. In these experiments, the subsequent event, the second significant feature, is usually the operation of a device called a feeder, which delivers a small quantity of grain whenever it is operated by the microswitch, which has in turn been activated by pressure on the key.

The most basic experiments of this type are designed to determine the effects of the grain on the pigeon's key-pecking behavior. Complex electrical circuits, which can include counters and timers, can be interposed between the key and the feeder to create a wide variety of patterns of relationship between the key-pecking response and the feeder's operation. In this way, varying numbers of responses or intervals of time between responses can be required before the feeder will operate and the pigeon will receive a ration of grain. The key-feeder circuitry is connected in turn to mechanical devices that constantly monitor their activity, thus automatically providing a complete record of what goes on during the study.

In the simplest form of operant conditioning study, there are three phases, during which the subject is exposed successively to three versions of the causal event. In the first phase, the feeder is simply disconnected. The rate at which the key-pecking response takes place, sometimes called the operant rate, is determined, while nothing happens after the response is made ($X_0$). Because the chamber is so unfamiliar to the pigeon, it is possible that no responses will be made. If that happens, the feeder can be connected and operated for a short time by an experimenter. Responses that approximate a key peck more and more closely, such as facing the key and then approaching it, are followed by the delivery of the measured amount of grain. After this "shaping" process succeeds in producing the first key peck, the second phase begins and each succeeding one is followed by the automatic operation of the feeder. After a sufficient record has been acquired, during this second phase of the study $(X_1)$, which usually requires many sessions over a period of weeks or months, the feeder is disconnected again and the pigeon's key pecking is monitored for another lengthy period ($X_0$ again). The design of this particular study could be diagrammed as follows: $X_0O$   $X_1O$ $X_0O$.

Most such studies show a very low rate of key pecking (if any) during the first or "baseline" phase, an increase in the rate of key pecking during the record or "reinforcement" phase, and a decline in the rate during the third or "extinction" phase. It is generally concluded from those results that the grain acts as a reinforcer because its delivery is followed by an increased rate of key pecking. That is, of course, a causal inference. But it is a difficult one to dispute, which an evaluation of the potential threats to the internal validity of the findings of such studies reveals very clearly.

The isolation from extraneous events of the chamber in which studies of operant conditioning takes place could hardly be more complete. Except for the brief shaping period, the apparatus ensures that the only events that occur are the mechanical and completely controllable ones programmed by the researcher. This isolation is strengthened by the limited capabilities of the pigeons used as subjects. Unlike human subjects, who may form their own individual hypotheses and interpretations of the events which occur around them, pigeons respond in a much more reflexive and uniform manner (which allows these studies to be virtually single-subject case studies).

Temporal trends are also unlikely to explain the findings. One reason for using pigeons in these studies is that their behavior is extremely consistent. They are tireless workers and they do not fill up on grain very easily. Spacing the studies over long periods of daily sessions also helps ensure that effects of momentary moods or fatigue or similar temporal trends (if pigeons showed any of them) are not mistaken for the effects of the grain reinforcer.

Because comparisons are made "within-subjects," of the same animal's behavior at different times, group composition effects and their interactions with temporal trends are ruled out as alternative explanations. And because the comparisons are based on purely mechanical records of the pigeons' behavior, observer effects would seem to be ruled out as well. And because the recording process is automatic, an inherent consequence of the pigeons' behavior, effects of repeated testing pose no threat. Finally, if any of the birds is lost during a study, it is for health reasons. Inspecting the records of the birds up to that point usually shows that they are indistinguishable from one another. Individual differences among pigeons are extremely small, which makes selective attrition extremely unlikely and statistical regression effects virtually impossible.

Thus the operant conditioning study utilizing Design QT-3 receives perfect marks for internal validity. There seems to be little room indeed for doubting that any changes in the rate of key pecking are caused solely by the presence and the absence of grain following that response. And this is why it has been said that Design QT-3 is based on an "experimental logic" that substitutes equivalent time samples for the equivalent comparison groups of experimental designs. But although it may be difficult to dispute the internal validity of these Design QT-3 findings, it is also difficult to generalize them. Although parallels can be drawn between the operant conditioning setting that consists of pigeons, keys, and grain and that of virtually every behavior that humans perform in the infinite variety of contexts of their lives, we saw in Chapter 3 that these parallels do not hold up very well to close scrutiny.

It would be a mistake to attribute the flawless internal validity of operant conditioning studies solely to their use of equivalent time samples designs. It is necessary to remember that the way a design is applied is crucially important to the way it functions. The choices of subject, task, and setting make a great difference in the interpretability of the resulting findings. That point could hardly be made better than by comparing the discussion of operant conditioning above with what follows immediately below. In 1930, Pitrim Sorokin set out to investigate a problem that was very similar to the operant conditioning study. But he studied human subjects in a very different kind of setting, and his findings must be interpreted accordingly.

Sorokin actually did a series of studies with a number of colleagues. All of them were aimed at determining the effects of different kinds of incentives, or "remunerations," on children's performance in a gamelike task. His subjects included preschoolchildren, kindergarten, and high school students. It is not exactly clear in Sorokin's paper, but it seems that they were all boys. Although the studies included a variety of procedures, we will only look at one representative example.

Preschoolchildren participated in this study in groups of two, three, or four. There were eight groups and 22 children altogether. In each group, a comparison was made between the same two incentive conditions. Toys or pennies were promised if the child "earned" them, either "individually," so that the child understood he would own them and be able to take them home with him, or "collectively," so that the group as a whole would receive them and they would be kept in the playroom (laboratory) where all the members of the group could play with them.

Each group participated in the study on two consecutive days. Each day, they worked on the same task twice. On the first day, the first session was conducted under collective remuneration and the second session, under individual. On the second day, the first session was under individual remuneration and the second under collective. Four of the groups worked at the task of carrying marbles from one location in the playroom to another. The other four had to fill cups with sand at one location and carry them to another. The tasks were chosen because they were difficult enough for incentive conditions to make some difference to the children and because the children's performance could be measured very objectively (by simply counting marbles or cups of sand). Each group worked at the same task for all four sessions. The length of session was constant for every group's four sessions, but it varied from group to group from about 1½ minutes to 3 minutes.

The results of this study are difficult to evaluate because Sorokin did not use statistics or even present the data in a form that could be analyzed statistically. It seems, however, that there was a noticeable tendency for the groups to work harder when remuneration was individual than when it was collective. All four of the marble-carrying groups showed that pattern, although the differences were as small as one marble. Only two of the four sand-carrying groups showed that pattern with fairly large differences, whereas one showed no difference and the fourth showed a one-cup-of-sand difference in the opposite direction.

Sorokin concluded from this study and the similar results of the other studies that were very similar that incentive conditions made a great difference in the children's performance, especially on tasks which required a minimum of intellectual activity. Furthermore, the findings of all the studies together indicated that incentive conditions that stress individual accomplishment, self-interest, and competition produce the highest levels of performance. Sorokin concluded that societies everywhere would benefit from an individualistic organization of their labor resources more than from a communistic one.

Leaving the issue of how widely his findings can be generalized until later, we need to ask first whether his comparison of individual and collective remuneration was a fair one. Let us go through the potential threats to its validity and see.

There is a substantial danger that the groups of children were exposed to extraneous events that escaped control of the intrasession history during the study. Although Sorokin points out that subjects were never informed of the purpose of the study directly, the experimenter, who was present during their performance, probably knew the hypothesis of the study and had sufficient opportunity to communicate it to them. Their cooperation with such a perceived demand may have been made more likely by the fact that the study was not carried out in the children's schools or other usual play locations, but in a novel setting that existed for the sole purpose of conducting psychological research—in other words, a reactive setting. The fact that the children were taken to this strange place may have alerted even the youngest of them to pay especially close attention to what was expected of them.

Because the order in which they worked at the tasks was the same for every group in the study, it is also possible that a temporal trend contributed to the observed differences. Because the tasks were probably not very stimulating, considerable fatigue and/or boredom may have built up through the course of each session. That alone could cause the second task performance in each session to be inferior to the first. And that could be even more pronounced on the second day than the first. If that were so, it could account for or at least figure in the small advantage of individual over collective remuneration.

Because each group performed under both incentive conditions, the differences observed by Sorokin could not have been group composition effects. Of course, that is one of the great strengths of the Equivalent Time Samples designs. For the same reason, no interaction between group composition and temporal trends could account for Sorokin's findings.

Observer effects, unfortunately, could have been responsible for some of the differences that were observed. If those who were responsible for rating the children's performance were aware of the incentive conditions under which they were performing and of the hypothesis, they could have applied different criteria under the different kinds of incentives, even unintentionally. If a group were in the middle of a "run" as time was about to run out, the strictness with which the observers enforced the time limit could have depended on the incentive condition. They might have been more inclined to give a group credit for a whole or even a partial marble or cup of sand (partial credit was given in some cases) when it was performing under an incentive condition that was "supposed" to make the boys want to try harder.

Pretesting is unlikely to have had any effect in this particular study because the tasks which the children performed were routine activities that any child would have had considerable experience with. The "tests" which measured their performance were simply part of the activities. Sample attrition was also ruled out, because no subjects were lost. As in most studies conducted in laboratories, especially those in which the subjects are under the close control of the experimenter, as children are by their teachers, fairly brief sessions leave little opportunity for attrition. Statistical regression could not have affected the scores of children who were not selected as members of extreme groups.

Even if the likely threats to internal validity (extraneous events, temporal and observer effects) did not contribute to the differences Sorokin reported—and if there really were differences between the incentive conditions—the findings of this study would be difficult to generalize. We already mentioned the fact that they were obtained in a reactive setting. And despite Sorokin's willingness to speculate about the performance of workers in economic systems which offer different kinds of incentives, the behavior of children less than six years old performing mindless tasks of fetch and carry seems to have much less far-reaching relevance, if it has any at all beyond children's play. Because children are usually willing to play without any extrinsic incentives, that is precious little relevance indeed.

The Sorokin studies illustrate that the use of Design QT-3 under laboratory conditions raise many of the same issues about the validity of its findings as do laboratory applications of experimental designs evaluated in Chapter 6. The problems can be overcome to a large extent by a researcher who is sensitive to these pitfalls of the laboratory (which Sorokin can hardly be expected to have been in 1930). However, the problems of generalizability, including nonrepresentative sampling, reactivity, nonrepresentative research context, and ecological validity, would remain to a large extent. The modern investigator might be more circumspect about the conclusions drawn from such findings, but they would not be generalized any more easily. In any event, we have certainly had a good look at the Doctor Jekyll and Mr. Hyde contradictions within the Equivalent Time Samples Design. Its "logic" of comparing different conditions which are studied within a single group of subjects compared across equivalent samples of time can produce findings as internally valid as a true experiment under certain conditions, and externally valid to boot. When the design is used with competent human subjects in a laboratory setting, it can exemplify the worst features of laboratory experiments without preserving any of their virtues.

The keys to the internal validity of Design QT-3 findings include, first of all, the transience or reversibility of the different versions of X being compared. Operant conditioning studies succeed because a pigeon's responses to a particular reinforcement condition are not affected by prior conditions. The same procedure has also been successful with special groups of human subjects. The term behavior modification is used to describe practical applications of operant conditioning procedures to patients in mental hospitals, institutionalized retarded persons, and "problem children" in schools, among others. These groups' behavior changes with the application of praise, attention, candy, money, and other reinforcers. And perhaps because their behavior functionally resembles that of animal subjects in operant conditioning studies more closely than does that of people who are functioning normally, the causal relationship between the reinforcer and the behavior that it follows seems just as clear.

In those applications, the problems of unintentional communication from experimenter to subject and reactivity of the research setting that were so troublesome in interpreting Sorokin's findings seem as benign as they did in the case of the conditioning study. But the best known example of how these problems can plague the user of the Equivalent Time Samples Design is a series of studies on job satisfaction among industrial workers carried out over 40 years ago in a factory owned by the Western Electric Company and located in Cicero, Illinois (Roethlisberger and Dickson, 1939). Over a period of 12 years, the researchers varied a large variety of work conditions, including heating, lighting, and length and timing of rest periods, to determine how workers' job satisfaction affected their job performance. They found that every change in working conditions produced an increase in workers' productivity. Finally, they just pretended to make changes and found that improved performance was more a function of the workers' perceptions that the studies were being carried out than the actual changes in their working conditions. It is very difficult to administer different variations of conditions to the same human subjects without engendering hypotheses about the purposes of the changes and the related response strategies which make it difficult to assume that comparisons reflect the operation of the conditions themselves.

One way of combating this problem, so that different treatments can be compared more satisfactorily within a single group or sample of human subjects, is to modify the Equivalent Time Samples Design. Usually, subjects perform a task during several time periods. The conditions under which they work are varied from time period to time period, so that their performance can be compared across those time periods to determine the effects of those conditions. The modification consists of varying the specific materials with which subjects work during different time periods. Comparisons of the subjects' performance with these different materials then become the focus of the study. The variation in materials, such as the differences between problems in a long math test, is much less likely to be noticeable than the variation in remuneration created by Sorokin or the variation in working conditions created in the well-known Hawthorne studies of industrial productivity (Roethlisberger and Dickson, 1939). As a result, the problems that plagued those studies can be lessened dramatically. The effects of different materials samples on subjects are transient, reversible, and nonreactive.

This variation in Design QT-3 is sometimes referred to as the Equivalent Materials Samples Design. It might be diagrammed as follows to indicate that the treatments actually consist of variations in the task materials:

$$(M_1X_1)O \qquad (M_0X_0)O \qquad (M_1X_1)O \qquad (M_0X_0)O \quad \text{etc.}$$

We refer to it as Design QT-3a for convenience. I think that it is best understood by an example, and I have chosen a recently completed study of my own to serve that purpose (Cherulnik, Way, Ames, and Hutto, 1981).

This was a study of interpersonal judgment, or forming impressions of other people. It was an attempt to find out whether, in one particular case, people could tell what other people were really like based on a very small sample of their behavior. There are aspects of our personality, or the consistencies in our behavior that make each of us a little different, which are actually directed toward other people. For example, the introvert avoids other people, but also tries to keep them away. On the other hand, the extravert seeks other people out and tries to bring them closer. The person who ranks high on a trait called Machiavellianism depends on an ability to influence other people—to be admired, believed, and followed by others—to reach personal goals. The person who is low in Machiavellianism, on the other hand, is more open and honest with others, seeking no strategic advantage in interactions with them—a perfect target for the Machiavellian individual.

In order for people to pursue strategies like introversion or extraversion, or high or low Machiavellianism, for them to be effective strategies for the people who use them, it would seem that other people would have to become aware of them. For example, for a person to pursue a Machiavellian strategy successfully, other people would have to perceive qualities like self-confidence, credibility, and competence. Thus we were looking for people to make accurate judgments in differentiating other people with different personalities. We chose Machiavellianism as our target personality trait, using a sample of 18 men categorized as either high or low, on the basis of a questionnaire typically used for that purpose. For each of those men, we used a 1-minute silent excerpt from a videotaped interview in which they had participated. The tape showed them from the perspective of the interviewer, sitting at a table, looking almost directly into the camera. The camera, which they did not see, was aimed over the interviewer's right shoulder and recorded only the interviewee.

The task for our one group of subjects was to look at each of the 1-minute excerpts and to judge after each one whether the person they had seen was high or low in Machiavellianism. They were given instructions which included capsule descriptions of high and low Machiavellian persons. Also included were corresponding lists of behaviors that research studies have shown to differentiate high and low Machiavellians and a brief description of one of those studies that contrasts the two types in a particularly sharp and illuminating way.

The series of videotape excerpts contained both high and low Machiavellian men mixed together in a random order. All the subjects watched a large television screen together in a partially darkened classroom. The comparison specified in the research hypothesis was between judgments of high and low Machiavellian excerpts. Across the entire group of 40 subjects, over 70% of the low Machiavellian excerpts were judged to be low Machiavellian and over 60% of the high Machiavellian excerpts were judged to be high Machiavellian. Statistical tests showed that judgments of both types were highly accurate, compared with the 50% accuracy one would expect if subjects merely guessed.

Thus it seems that our subjects' judgments were certainly affected by the actual traits of the persons they saw. Could any other explanation account for the differences we observed? A brief review of the list of threats to internal validity should be reassuring. The differences in the two kinds of judgments could not have been produced by extraneous events or temporal trends. They were observed in the same unselected group of subjects, from which none was lost along the way, totally objectively. This seems to rule out, in order, group composition, regression effects, selective attrition, and observer bias. As the scorecard for Design QT-3 in Table 8-1 indicates, internal validity is quite high.

By comparing the effects of different materials across equivalent time samples, this form of Design QT-3 preserves the same experimental logic and assures internal validity to the same degree as an operant conditioning study performed with Design QT-3. At the same time, and in the same way, the required degree of control to create equivalent materials samples (or equivalent time samples in Design QT-3 or equivalent comparison groups in true experiments) has its costs in external validity. Certainly some doubt exists about whether people generally make these sorts of judgments of others or whether they make them in quite the same way. Do people make such judgments without being asked? Can they judge individuals whom they meet in groups and who vary along many different dimensions as accurately as in a long series of isolated persons who differ in just one way? The degree of control made possible by the laboratory context is almost always acquired at the cost of realism and at the risk that the researcher's activities will be perceived by subjects as an intrusion into their lives.

## SECTION II. QUASI-EXPERIMENTAL DESIGNS: COMPARISONS ACROSS GROUPS

In cases in which subjects cannot be assigned at random to treatment and no-treatment groups, experiments are not possible. There are, however, methods of achieving a lesser degree of control that can be substituted for random assignment. We have seen already how multiple measurements over a period can provide a reliable basis for comparing different treatments. Equivalence of occasions, or near equivalence, can be substituted for equivalence of comparison groups.

Another useful substitute for the equivalent comparison groups of experiments is the *nonequivalent comparison group*. It is the one used in the group of quasi-experimental designs we are to consider. In some cases, it is possible to determine which subjects are to be exposed to the hypothesized causal event, but institutional policies require that existing groups like workers in a factory or students in a classroom be kept intact. All their members must be exposed to only one treatment. In other cases, interference with the institutional routine necessary to break the group up would be so obtrusive that an intolerable level of reactivity would result. In either case, the group's responses may be compared with those of other intact groups, receiving different treatments or no treatment. These comparison groups may be different in some way, but we will see that if they are chosen judiciously they can be valuable nonetheless.

## DESIGN QG-1—THE NONEQUIVALENT CONTROL GROUP DESIGN

$$G_1 \quad O_1 \quad \text{-----} \quad O_2$$
$$G_2 \quad O_3 \quad \quad \quad O_4$$

We saw one form of comparison across nonequivalent groups in Design P-3. That was not a very satisfactory arrangement. Because it was used to study naturally occurring events after the fact, it was impossible to determine if the comparison groups had been similar in the behavior being studied even before the suspected causal event had taken place.

The Time Series Design (QT-1) is a great improvement over Design P-3, taking advantage of the existence of a running record of recurring measurements of the behavior both before and after the occurrence of X. When the occurrence of X can be anticipated, or when it is created by the researcher, another kind of alternative to Design P-3 is available. It consists of comparing nonequivalent groups for whom a single pre-X measure of the behavior being studied is made. That is Design QG-1, The Nonequivalent Control Group Design. The availability of that single additional measure of O, overcoming the "static" nature of Design P-3, adds greatly to the interpretability of an observed difference between the groups being compared following X.

Design QG-1 is used frequently to compare the effects of alternative teaching techniques. Because it is administratively difficult and, as already stated, methodologically undesirable to break up existing classes, intact groups are often used. We will evaluate this design entirely in the context of an exciting recent study published by Lucker, Rosenfield, Sikes, and Aronson (1976). It is a perfect prototype of the way this design has been used most often, showing both its great potential and its deficiencies.

The Lucker study was a test of a proposal originally made by Aronson (1972) for facilitating the integration of students from different ethnic backgrounds into public school classrooms. Aronson saw the traditional classroom as a place where students competed against one another for the favor of the teacher. Each student's success depended on the failure of other students. Whether answering questions aloud in class or on examinations, a student's performance could stand out as exemplary only if other students' poor performance provided the necessary contrast. Consequently, students wished for each other's failures and resented each other's successes. The fact that the classroom routine was organized so that every student faced the teacher and interacted only with the teacher discouraged communication among students that might moderate that highly competitive relationship.

In an integrated classroom, the competitive atmosphere could have even more undesirable effects. Minority students were often the targets of unfavorable stereotypes and prejudices to begin with. They were also often inferior in traditional academic skills to white, middle-class students. In a competitive classroom, the minority students were likely to fail, reinforcing the stereotypes others held of them. And the more successful students might ridicule them, as failures are usually ridiculed (perhaps with added epithets that different ethnic groups often use for one another). Minority students might lose confidence in themselves, they might develop negative attitudes toward school, and they might resent the better students in their class whose success came at their expense. All these negative attitudes, in turn, might lower their performance even further.

Based on his analysis of the traditional classroom, Aronson proposed an alternative he called the "jigsaw" classroom. He reasoned that better attitudes among students and better performance by minority students would both follow from substituting cooperative, student-focused procedures for the traditional competitive, teacher-focused ones. In the jigsaw classroom, students would work in small groups of four to six. The materials for each lesson would be divided among them, so that each student had his or her unique part. Then each student in the group would teach that portion to the others.

All the children would take separate examinations and get individual grades, but according to Aronson's analysis, they would be interdependent during the crucial learning process. If one student in a jigsaw group failed to learn, all the members would suffer, even the brightest, because they would lack some of the information which that person alone had been given about the assignment. It would be to everyone's advantage to encourage the poorer student, to be friendly and supportive, to ask effective questions. Students could actually gain satisfaction from helping another student to succeed, often one from a different ethnic group.

Lucker set out to test one crucial aspect of Aronson's thesis. He hypothesized that the jigsaw method, because it would produce greater involvement of students in the learning process (including a role in teaching others) and improve children's attitudes toward each other and toward school (previous research had shown that already), would produce better academic performance in the students who participated in it. The test consisted of comparing the performance of two sets of fifth and sixth grade classrooms on a 2-week American history curriculum unit.

Four fifth- and two sixth-grade teachers volunteered to try the jigsaw method in their classrooms during this one period (40–45 minutes) a day. They were trained by the researchers to "foster cooperative learning." Their Austin, Texas, classes were integrated among Anglo (about 75%), Mexican-American (about 16%), and black (about 9%) students. The classes were split into groups of four to six students, all with similar ethnic diversity. Three fifth-grade and two sixth-grade classes were chosen by the researchers on the basis of three criteria. Their teachers were reported to be among the best in their schools, the mix of white, Mexican-American, and black students was similar (82%–10%–8%, actually) and their reading achievement scores were about equal. These classes were run in the traditional manner.

Both groups were given a test on the colonial America curriculum units before they began to study it. After the 2-week period, they were given a similar test. Both tests were drawn from the same large pool of true-false, multiple-choice, and matching questions—all objective items. The jigsaw and traditional classes received about the same average scores on the pretest, although the Anglo students scored higher than the minority students (they had higher reading scores also). But the jigsaw classrooms did better on the posttest, and there was no difference between Anglo and minority students overall. Further analyses showed that the jigsaw method affected the minority students the most. Anglo students performed about the same in the jigsaw and traditional classrooms (less than one percentage point difference, on the average), but minority students did much better in the jigsaw classroom (almost seven points). Their "gain" was responsible for the overall advantage of jigsaw classrooms, which did not seem to contain the minority of inferior students the traditional classes had.

Lucker felt he had proved Aronson's point. Most researchers whose findings are consistent with their hypotheses do feel that way. But we need to examine this study systematically for threats to the validity of their findings. This will also give us an opportunity to examine Table 8-3 for the overall scorecard for Design QG-1.

Because the nonequivalent comparison groups were tested simultaneously, they were both subject to exposure to any extraneous events that occur outside the classroom—in their schools, cities, and so on. The coincidental occurrence of a natural disaster, for example, during the 2-week period of the study would affect students in both jigsaw and traditional classrooms. But it is more difficult to keep extraneous events out of the classroom itself. The teachers in the jigsaw classrooms might have been excited about the "experiment" and communicated those feelings to their students, even without realizing it. For reasons other than the jigsaw method itself, students in those classes might have been more eager about that special class period each day. If care was not taken during the teacher training process to guard against revealing that minority students were expected to be special beneficiaries of the jigsaw method, teachers might have shown increased concern with them. That concern would be an extraneous event because it is not an integral part of the jigsaw method. Lucker pointed out that teachers do very little in the jigsaw classroom, but we know how subtly feelings can be communicated to subjects and we should be concerned about this problem. That is why Design QG-1 has received a question mark for the first potential threat to internal validity, that is, extraneous events. We should add that this is a difficult problem to overcome. Teachers cannot do something without being aware of it. Even if they were assigned, rather

**Table 8-3** VALIDITY SCORECARD: QUASI-EXPERIMENTAL RESEARCH DESIGNS II—COMPARISONS ACROSS GROUPS

| | INTERNAL VALIDITY | | | | | | | | EXTERNAL VALIDITY | | | |
|---|---|---|---|---|---|---|---|---|---|---|---|---|
| | EXTRANEOUS EVENTS | TEMPORAL EFFECTS | GROUP COMPOSITION EFFECTS | TEMPORAL X GROUP COMPOSITION EFFECTS | OBSERVER EFFECTS | EFFECTS OF PRETESTING | EFFECTS OF SAMPLE ATTRITION | STATISTICAL REGRESSION EFFECTS | NONREPRESENTATIVE SAMPLING | REACTIVITY OF THE RESEARCH CONTEXT | NONREPRESENTATIVE RESEARCH CONTEXT | LACK OF ECOLOGICAL VALIDITY |
| QG-1: NONEQUIVALENT COMPARISON GROUP DESIGN<br>$O_1$ X $O_2$<br>- - - - - -<br>$O_3$    $O_4$ | ? | + | + | − | + | + | + | ? | ? | ? | ? | + |
| QG-2: SEPARATE-SAMPLE PRETEST-POSTTEST DESIGN<br>R $O_1$ (X)<br>R   X $O_2$ | − | − | + | + | ? | + | − | + | + | + | + | + |
| QG-3: SEPARATE-SAMPLE PRETEST-POSTTEST COMPARISON GROUP DESIGN<br>     R $O_1$  (X)<br>$G_1$ R     X    $O_2$<br>     R $O_3$<br>$G_2$ R        $O_4$ | + | + | + | − | + | + | + | + | + | + | + | + |

SOURCE:  D. T. Campbell and J. C. Stanley. "Experimental and quasi-experimental designs for research in educational research." *Review of Educational Research*, 1966. Copyright 1966, American Educational Research Association, Washington, D.C.

than volunteering, they would have a special feeling about doing something new and different when supervising the jigsaw classroom. If they were not told why they were doing it, they would guess.

Temporal trends should not be a problem as long as the two comparison groups are studied simultaneously. It should be relatively easy to choose the same class period, especially when the same curriculum unit is being studied by both kinds of classes.

The availability of the pretest scores makes it possible to determine whether the comparison groups were alike in the behavior being studied before X occurred. Lucker not only showed that the two groups of classes had the same level of knowledge about colonial America, but also that their reading scores, a measure of their general academic ability, were the same.

However, matching students is not a guarantee that differences will not emerge because the two groups have not been equated by random assignment; thus the minus next to the fourth threat to validity. Assume for the moment that when teachers were asked to volunteer to try a new teaching method in their classes, those who felt their students were highly motivated and got along well with each other and themselves (the teachers), would be more likely to agree. This would not mean that the students could read better—that is the product of the four or five years they had already spent in school in addition to the time spent in their current classes. And it certainly would not mean that they would have more specific knowledge about a subject they had not studied yet, such as colonial America. But it could mean tht they would do better on any curriculum unit than other classes with less enthusiasm and poorer rapport, regardless how the material happened to be presented. Thus a different temporal trend (mastery of the material over time) could occur because the groups were different to begin with—not in the behavior being studied or in other characteristics on which the researchers thought to compare them, but in some way because they did not end up in the different status of jigsaw participants accidentally (by random assignment). Something (in this case, someone) put them there.

The problems inherent in comparing nonequivalent groups are crucial to interpreting the findings from all the designs in this section (QG-1, QG-2, and QG-3). An especially clear example of how they arise and of their effects is provided by a study published by Sanford and Hemphill in 1952. They participated in an effort to introduce a practical course in psychology into the curriculum of the United States Naval Academy at Annapolis. Fifteen hours of class, lecture, and discussion were organized around a specially prepared text which stressed such topics as drawing "logical" conclusions from observing people's behavior, leadership, and other material chosen more for its practical benefits to naval leaders than its importance in academic psychology. This course was given to the entire second (sophomore) class of 800 midshipmen. For the usual administrative reasons (all sophomores at Annapolis take exactly the same curriculum, for example), it could not be administered to only part of the group.

The purpose of the study was to evaluate the gains in practical knowledge about human behavior produced by this brief encounter with psychology. Its success hinged on the availability of a group who was comparable with the sophomores who took the course but who was not exposed to the special course. Sanford and Hemphill chose members of the junior class at Annapolis. Because they realized that these older students would be different, they used a sophisticated statistical procedure to match the two groups for the practical psychological knowledge they had when the course began. One hundred students were sampled from each of the two classes. They took a battery of tests designed to assess selected aspects of the knowledge that might be gained from the course, both before the course began in February and after it ended in May. The resulting four sets of scores were used in a regression (correlational) analysis. We use only one test from the battery, the Common Sense Test designed especially for this study, as an example, but it is typical of the others.

The regression analysis is based on the assumption that the relationship between the pretest and the posttest scores of the group who was not exposed to the treatment (the juniors who did not take the course) would be the same as the relationship between the scores in the other group (the sophomores who did take the course) if they had not been exposed either. Therefore, one can use this relationship found for the juniors to predict from the pretest scores of the sophomores what their posttest scores would have been if they had not actually taken the test. The difference between those predicted scores and their real scores must then be due to the course itself. In other words, what the sophomores knew after taking the course was compared (statistically) with the knowledge of the juniors who did not take the course and who knew only what they did at the beginning.

But there is a big problem in all this that Sanford and Hemphill apparently did not see (that might make the readers feel better if they did not understand exactly what they were trying to do). It becomes apparent when looking directly at the scores they obtained. Table 8-5 shows the scores for our example, the Common Sense Test. One might be able to see, first of all, what Sanford and Hemphill thought had happened. The sample of sophomores who took the psychology course scored 3.63 points higher, on the average, afterward than before. The juniors, on the other hand, actually scored 1.73

**Table 8-5** MEANS AND STANDARD DEVIATIONS OF SCORES ON COMMON SENSE TEST

|  | CONTROL GROUP[a] | | | EXPERIMENTAL GROUP[b] | | |
|---|---|---|---|---|---|---|
|  | MEAN | SD | N | MEAN | SD | N |
| Pretest | 17.64 | 6.74 | 100 | 14.57 | 7.68 | 100 |
| Posttest | 15.91 | 7.84 | 98 | 18.20 | 8.49 | 100 |

SOURCE: After Sanford and Hemphill, 1952.
[a]Juniors not exposed to psychology course.
[b]Sophomores exposed to psychology course.

points lower. Their reasoning was that if the sophomores had not taken the course they would have scored lower on the posttest, too. When you go through all the actual mechanics, one finds that the sophomores scored 4.48 points higher, on the average, on the Common Sense Test than they would have been expected to on the basis of the scores of juniors who did not take the course and scored as they did on the pretest.

There is other information in Table 8-5 that is useful in evaluating that argument. The juniors' pretest scores are three points higher, on the average, than the sophomores' pretest scores. Why, without having had the opportunity that the new psychology course was supposed to provide for gaining insight into human behavior, did the juniors know so much more than the sophomores? Perhaps, as the saying goes, they had grown a little older and a little wiser. But although the sophomore year seems to have been a fruitful period for learning about human behavior, the junior year does not. The second semester of that year produced no gain at all in "Common Sense" (the decrease may have been a result of repeated testing) among the sample of juniors. One explanation is simply that people mature faster earlier than later on. If the experiences students have at Annapolis lead inevitably to a better understanding of people, or the students grow older, assume positions of greater responsibility, and form more intense relationships with their fellow students, there should be a more rapid increase in maturity earlier in their careers. Students just out of high school and their parents' homes would learn considerably more than those at the end of three-and-a-half years at Annapolis, for example. Similarly, sophomores would learn more than juniors. If that is true, then Sanford and Hemphill's argument for comparing sophomores and juniors is not. We would not expect sophomores to gain the same amount of sophistication in three months as juniors, all other things being equal. Rather, we would expect them to gain more, even without a special psychology course, because the temporal trend in their social adjustment is steeper than that of the juniors. Unfortunately, we cannot tell how much of the

roughly four-and-a-half point greater gain this more rapid maturation accounts for—maybe all of it (the juniors' apparent gain over
when they were sophomores was about the same as the sophomores'
apparent gain from the course). But we can tell, from their own data,
that the increase in "Common Sense" which Sanford and Hemphill
attributed to the course they helped develop may have been caused
by an interaction between group composition and temporal trends
instead.

Now, back to the Lucker study of the jigsaw classroom. Neither
observer effects nor pretesting are likely explanations for a difference in the behavior of the two comparison groups. Both were given
the same objective tests (if they had been given essay tests, it would
have been possible for teachers who did not know what type of classroom a student had been in to score equal numbers of papers from
the two groups). And because both were tested twice, the effects of
the pretest on the posttest scores should have been the same for both.

Sample attrition is no problem. If students drop out between the
pretest and the posttest (a few students out of hundreds might be
out of school on the day of the posttest, as on any other day), their
pretest scores can be used to make sure that they are not atypical
of their group as a whole. If more jigsaw students (or traditional class
students) happened to drop out, the researchers would know that
and not mistake the jigsaw method for the real cause of a difference
in performance between the two groups.

Finally, for the threats to internal validity at least, we come to
the possibility that statistical regression effects could produce a difference between the two groups' behavior. Lucker did not select his
students for their extreme scores on the specific behavior he was
studying, or even for general academic skills (although he probably
selected an extreme group of teachers, a point we return to later).
But he did try to match the two groups of students—an understandable aim given that the nonequivalence of the two groups is a key
feature of this design. Under different circumstances, matching can
be responsible for a statistical regression artifact. Let us imagine that
we want to compare the effects of a group therapy on one group of
depressed patients with its effects on a group of "normal" persons.
We might hypothesize that the depressed patients would gain more
in feeling satisfied with their own personalities. But if they feel very
much less satisfied to begin with, it is not a fair comparison. Thus we
select a group of normals who have the same level of satisfaction as
the depressed patients and follow these two groups through the therapy. The normals, however, are really a very extreme subgroup of
normals, those who feel as bad about themselves as depressed pa-

tients do. Their scores on the test of self-concept are bound to increase just because of statistical regression. Thus the depressed patients will not seem to improve as much relative to the normals as they really have. Whenever we have to select only extreme individuals in one group to match that group to the other, we raise problems of statistical regression. Coupled with its limited value in making the two groups comparable, because of the possible interaction between group composition and temporal trends, this is another drawback to using matching in designs in which random assignment is impossible.

Conducting research in natural settings like schools is generally associated with better external validity. But the degree of intrusive control required to conduct studies like the jigsaw classroom evaluation, where it is necessary to introduce special procedures into the ongoing routine of the institution, has its costs in the generalizability of the research findings.

The representativeness of the groups of subjects studied in natural settings tends to be greater than in the laboratory. Given the restrictions on the ethnic diversity of the classes needed to test his hypothesis, Lucker studied a normal cross section of Austin fifth and sixth graders. But the need to pretest the subjects may have created groups of jigsaw- and traditional-classroom students who were more aware than is usual of the importance of the curriculum unit they studied; students are not usually tested on course material before they study it. Furthermore, the jigsaw method may have worked better with the students whose teachers volunteered their classes for the new procedure than it would work on unselected classes. If one wanted to adopt the procedure for normal use in a school, in place of the traditional classroom procedure, one's expectations for its success would have to be tempered accordingly.

The break in the school routine that the jigsaw method created in the Lucker study also makes the setting more reactive. The jigsaw students' other studies were conducted in the traditional manner, making the colonial America curriculum unit stand out as a special test, even if they did not know the hypothesis. In this sense, the research context was not representative of the context in which the jigsaw method would be used if it were adopted as a general substitute for traditional teaching methods. It was a novelty because of the contrast with the traditional class periods surrounding it—a break in a routine. If it were the routine itself, its benefits might not be as great, even if Aronson's assumptions about its inherent advantages were correct. Although it was conducted in the normal ecological context of students' own schools, classrooms, and teachers, and the normal testing procedures they were used to, introducing a special test into an ongoing institutional routine causes events to stand out, and perhaps to affect the behavior of those exposed to them, differently from what they would otherwise.

The Lucker study demonstrates some of the difficult problems in using Design QG-1 in an ongoing institutional setting. On the one hand, it seems desirable to evaluate an educational program in children's normal classrooms. To operate outside that framework, with an experimenter taking the place of a regular teacher, and with an experimental task rather than a part of the school curriculum, would create much greater problems of generalizability for the research findings than seen already in the Lucker study. The setting would be more reactive, the context less representative, and the findings would have far less ecological validity.

However, staying within the bounds of the institution has great costs of its own. One can do so only with the consent of administrators and teachers, which really means that they must volunteer their school districts, schools, and classes. Those willing to try out new programs, or even to have behavioral researchers evaluate what they normally do, must be suspected of being different from those whose schedules, administrative routines, or the like force them to decline reluctantly to cooperate with the researcher. They may perhaps be more progressive, or self-confident, or effective in what they do. We may not know how they differ, but because their behavior is different we must assume that they do differ. And the problems of controlling what goes on in the classroom (intrasession history) and of assuming that classes receiving a treatment (new program) are comparable to those not receiving it (those who continue with the traditional program), even if they are matched, and of generalizing any observed effects to nonvolunteered classrooms, naturally follow. Only if the comparison groups are recruited similarly can we be confident that they are truly comparable. Similarity of pretest scores is much more reassuring in that context.

In the end, though, comparability depends to a great extent on the kind of causal event being investigated. A teaching technique or a managerial style cannot simply be assigned to a teacher or a factory supervisor. Even if the institution were so authoritarian that they were forced to accept any assignment, their performance could not be trusted to do justice to the treatment being evaluated. If, on the other hand, the causal event were simply some content to be added to a course that seemed as if it belonged there, or a change in the duties of a supervisor that did not alter the basic method of supervision, assignment might very well be made to teachers or supervisors, or to schools or plants, at the researchers' discretion. It is even possible to assign units at random to the treatments to be compared, if those assignments are universally acceptable. The individuals within those units are still not equivalent, but if enough units can be tested and each unit contributes just one total or average score to the analysis, we have random assignment and a true experiment (Design E-2). The use of a pretest would still raise external validity problems, but we know from Chapter 6 that in a true experimental design pretests are unnecessary because the groups being compared are equated by the process of random assignment.

## DESIGN QG-2—THE SEPARATE-SAMPLE PRETEST-POSTTEST DESIGN

$$G_1 \quad R \quad O_1 \quad (X)$$
$$G_2 \quad R \quad \qquad X \quad O_2$$

There are cases in which a single group of people is exposed to a special kind of educational or training program designed to change their skills or attitudes or personalities. More often today than ever before, the designers of such a program or course, or the government agency or private institution that sponsored it, might want a formal evaluation of its effects. In order to find out if the program works as it is intended to, there would be a need for some measuring instrument capable of assessing the skill or attitude or personality dimension toward which the program is directed. This might be one of the thousands of existing psychological tests and research instruments, or one designed specifically for the particular program and the study to evaluate it. The research hypothesis would predict a specific change in the participants from what they were like before their participation, which would be reflected by a change in their score on the chosen instrument.

We have already reviewed several designs that could be used for such a study. The simplest would be Design P-2 (O  X  O), but that design has numerous shortcomings, not the least of which is that any change which might be observed between the pretest and the posttest could be attributed just as easily to the subjects having responded to the measuring instrument twice as to X. If a running record were available for the behavior or attitude or trait being studied, the problem of repeated testing could be solved by the analysis of a time series of measures. But it is uncommon for such a record to exist. Fortunately, ordinary people do not yet have such records on file. Another possibility would be to compare the program participants with some similar group that could provide an estimate of the effects of repeated testing alone if they were to receive the same tests at the same times but did not participate in the program. But if the program participants were selected because they had special positions or personal attributes which the program administrators value, and/or if they applied because they had some special needs or interests which the program promised to serve, finding a truly comparable group could be very difficult.

Design QG-2 provides one more way out of this dilemma. If only a single group is available, and the behavior in question can be assessed only just before the program and just after, the group might possibly be divided randomly into two halves, one of which can be administered only the pretest and the other only the posttest. Because random assignment assures that these two halves of the original group are equivalent, any difference between the pretest and the posttest scores would have to result from something that occurred during the time interval between the pretest and the posttest. And, because none of the subjects who took the posttest would have also taken the pretest, the experience with the test could not have resulted from any of those events.

One of our examples of the Single-Group Pretest-Posttest Design, P-2, shows very clearly how this design could be used. Recall the study of the government officials who participated in a workshop on energy problems. Instead of giving them all the attitude questionnaire as they arrived for the workshop, the researchers could have randomly determined ahead of time which half of the participants would receive it. If they feared that testing just half the group might arouse suspicions about their purposes, they could have given the other half some other similar questionnaire, or possibly even asked half the group half the questions they were interested in and the other half the other questions. If the two sets of questions were very different, answering one set before the workshop might not affect answers to the other set afterward. At the end of the workshop all the participants could be given another questionnaire. Each person would then receive the questions they did not answer the first time.

One of the few actual examples of the use of Design QG-2 (we will discuss the reasons for the scarcity later) is a study published in 1957 by Duncan, O'Brien, Murray, Davis, and Gilliland. They were actually more interested in the test they administered to their subjects than in the program that came in between, but the research design problems are the same. It was a test of "psychological misconceptions." One hundred items contained both true and false statements about animal and human behavior which the test's creators, J. W. Holley and C. E. Buxton (1950), had assembled. Respondents were asked to tell whether each statement was true or false and score one point each time they were correct. The statements included "Rats, cats, and dogs have the power to reason" (which, incidentally, was keyed as true) and "It is probable that man's instinct to fight is the fundamental cause of wars" (which, Lorenz notwithstanding, was keyed as false).

Duncan studied the 351 students enrolled in four introductory psychology classes at Northwestern University. During the first week of class, the instructors divided their classes in half down the middle of the room. One-half was excused and the other half was given the Holley and Buxton test. Eleven weeks later, all the students in the four classes took the same test. Thus the study added one element to the basic structure of Design QG-2, the posttest scores of the halves of the classes that were pretested. It turned out that the pretested group got the same posttest scores, on the average, as the group that had not been pretested, showing that in this case repeated testing had no effect. Incidentally, both groups received considerably higher scores (about 10 points on the average) after studying psychology for 11 weeks, than the pretested subjects had received before the course had started. We will see what that might mean as we review the threats to the internal and external validities of those findings one by one (see Table 8-3).

Both extraneous events and temporal trends are plausible rival hypotheses for the subjects' apparent gain in knowledge about behavior. There is no telling what other courses they took during the intervening 11 weeks, or what books they might have read on their own, or how much they could have learned from their day-to-day experiences as well. One might even say that the passage of time itself is bound to produce more knowledge by reading, conversations, television programs, and other sources of information encountered by a normally active person.

Because the pretest and the posttest halves of the single group exposed to X are equated by random assignment, neither the group composition effects nor the interaction of group composition with temporal trends can account for a difference between the pretest and the posttest. By the same logic as we used to analyze the randomly constituted groups in experimental designs, the pretest and posttest groups can be assumed to be identical (with the same reservations about sampling error and the probabilistic nature of statistical comparisons). They may be thought of, for this purpose, as the same group before and after X, as in any single-group design, thus making group composition no issue at all.

Observer bias seems unlikely to have affected the findings of the Duncan study, because the test was scored completely objectively. But care does need to be taken that the pretest and posttest measures of O are applied the same way. If there is any chance for observer judgments to affect subjects' scores, using different observers at the two different occasions, or the same observer scoring each set on a different occasion, or using any observer who can tell pretest from posttest and is familiar with the research hypothesis, or even enough of the details of the study to permit a guess about the hypothesis, the comparison can be biased. If the subjects' behavior can be recorded on paper or tape or film, the pretest and posttest measures can be mixed together randomly and scored anonymously in equal numbers by observers who are unfamiliar with the research hypothesis. This procedure assures their comparability.

As already noted, Design QG-2 eliminates any possible effects of repeated testing because no subject is tested more than once. Statistical regression effects are also eliminated by testing subjects only once. But sample attrition poses a difficult problem for this design. If the design is used to evaluate the effects of a lengthy program, it is likely that some individuals will be lost along the way. This loss could make the subgroup that receives the posttest different in some important respect from the subgroup that received the pretest. When the two groups are chosen initially, random assignment ensures that they are equivalent. But several weeks or months later, they may not be. If the dropouts are not representative of the groups as a whole (and they often are not), a difference between $O_1$ and $O_2$ can result simply from the absence of those individuals from the posttest group.

Because Design QG-2 is often applied to all the members of a large and heterogeneous group, placing no restrictions on participation, its findings may be generalized fairly widely. Of course, the representativeness of the sample varies from one study to another. The fact that the same subjects are not tested before and after X adds to the feeling of confidence that the findings do not just apply to individuals who experience X in light of a pretest. The lack of repeated testing also lessens the likelihood that the research setting will be reactive. However, reactivity also varies with the specific procedure. If the measures of O are unobtrusive, then reactivity will be low. If students in school are given the same kind of course examinations they are accustomed to taking, and especially if their scores count toward their grades, they are unlikely to be aware of any special investigation of their behavior or to tailor their responses to special perceived demands for their performance. Measuring the productivity of factory workers would be relatively nonreactive as well. On the other hand, if the subjects' normal routine is interrupted by the administration of some new test, reactivity will be higher and the generalizability of the findings beyond the research setting will be lower. The Duncan study would seem to fall somewhere in between.

Design QG-2 is applied most often in natural settings to study the effects of natural events. Even the behaviors studied, like the gain in knowledge shown on a test in a college course, is often an integral part of the setting. The findings of Separate-Sample Pretest-Posttest Design studies are relatively easy to generalize to other settings where events like X typically occur. They represent behavior in its typical, rich context of influences.

In summary, an inspection of the scorecard for Design QG-2 in Table 8-3 reveals great strengths in freedom from threats to external validity, but glaring weaknesses in freedom from threats to internal validity. The use of the design would appear to require a very difficult trade-off. But there is a way of improving the balance. We saw before that each of the designs represented in Tables 8-2 through 8-5 is really a skeleton aversion that can be, and usually is, fitted to actual research studies by adding more groups of subjects, versions of X, and measures of O. Now, for the first time, we look closely at how such additions can be tailored to solving particular validity problems. Campbell and Stanley (1963) have referred to this process as "patching up" research in order to rid it of some of its faults.

Without having labeled it as such, we already ran into one of those patches. Duncan added one simple element to the basic version of Design QG-2 diagrammed at the beginning of this section and in Table 8-3. Table 8-4 shows both the basic version of QG-2 and this very slightly elaborated one that we call QG-2a. It also shows the benefits conferred by the "patch" ($O_3$). Notice that Design QG-2 is vulnerable to the effects of sample attrition, whereas its sibling QG-2a is not. The fact that the pretested subgroup also receives the posttest makes it possible to evaluate sample attrition. The researcher can determine which of the pretested group has failed to survive the program being evaluated. Because both subgroups are equivalent, this also shows whether the posttest group can be expected to be representative of those who began the program and thus whether the comparison of the pretest and the posttest scores is likely to be influenced by selective attrition. Although Duncan did not actually make use of this feature, it is a simple way to correct one of the most obvious faults of the Separate-Sample Pretest-Posttest Design.

In order to look at some of the other possible ways of patching up Design QC2, we will switch to a hypothetical example of how this design could be and, in fact, would ordinarily be used. We mentioned earlier that there are very few actual examples of its use. Now is also the time to see why.

All over the country, civic groups sponsor many different kinds of summer programs for young people with special talents or needs. There are remedial programs for disadvantaged children who are doing poorly in school, enrichment programs to accelerate the prog-

**Table 8-4** VALIDITY SCORECARD: THE SEPARATE-SAMPLE PRETEST-POSTTEST DESIGN (QG-2) AND ITS PATCHED-UP VERSIONS (A, B, AND C)

| | INTERNAL VALIDITY | | | | | | | | EXTERNAL VALIDITY | | | |
|---|---|---|---|---|---|---|---|---|---|---|---|---|
| | EXTRANEOUS EVENTS | TEMPORAL EFFECTS | GROUP COMPOSITION EFFECTS | TEMPORAL X GROUP COMPOSITION EFFECTS | OBSERVER EFFECTS | EFFECTS OF PRETESTING | EFFECTS OF SAMPLE ATTRITION | STATISTICAL REGRESSION EFFECTS | NONREPRESENTATIVE SAMPLING | REACTIVITY OF THE RESEARCH CONTEXT | NONREPRESENTATIVE RESEARCH CONTEXT | LACK OF ECOLOGICAL VALIDITY |
| QG-2<br>R $O_1$ (X)<br>R    X   $O_2$ | − | − | + | + | ? | + | − | + | + | + | + | + |
| QG-2a<br>R $O_1$  X  $O_2$<br>R    X  $O_3$ | − | − | + | + | ? | + | + | + | + | + | + | + |
| QG-2b<br>R $O_1$ (X)<br>R    X  $O_2$<br>- - - - -<br>R    $O_3$ (X)<br>R       X  $O_4$ | + | − | + | + | ? | + | − | + | + | ? | + | + |
| QG-2c<br>R $O_1$  (X)<br>R $O_2$  (X)<br>R    X  $O_3$ | − | + | + | + | ? | + | − | + | + | ? | + | + |

SOURCE: D. T. Campbell and J. C. Stanley. "Experimental and quasi-experimental designs for research in educational research." *Review of Educational Research*, 1966. Copyright 1966, American Educational Research Association, Washington, D.C.

ress of children with especially high aptitudes, and citizenship programs for children who have shown leadership potential. Many of these programs share the goal of enhancing the participants' sense of self-worth, thereby increasing their self-confidence and their satisfaction with themselves as persons. Not only do the participants in these programs learn new facts and new skills, but they also live away from home (many of them for the first time) and meet strangers from a variety of different backgrounds. Thus they face new opportunities for growth in personal as well as in intellectual and other directions.

Let us focus on this latter goal of improving young people's personal adjustment. How would one evaluate the effectiveness of such a program in meeting that goal? One would first need some way of measuring adjustment. Many existing questionnaires could be used, depending on one's own thinking about exactly which attitudes toward the self are the most important. Design QG-2 is one likely way of going about comparing attitudes before the program and after. We said already that it is not actually used very much. That is because some researchers choose good alternatives such as Design QG-1. But it is also because many choose poor alternatives such as Design P-2; they are unaware of the difficulties in interpreting the findings from that design—principally, that a pre–post difference is just as likely to result from the repeated testing of the same subjects as from the program that comes in between pretest and posttest (unless the test is a rare one whose scores are unaffected by repeated administration, as Duncan found the Holley and Buxton test of psychological misconceptions to be).

If we use Design QG-2 and find that the students are better adjusted after their summer program than they were before—more satisfied with themselves, more confident, better able to get along with other people, or whatever—we might claim success for the program. But there are still three serious rival hypotheses to contend with.

First, it is possible that sample attrition resulted in the loss of some special group of participants during the program, accounting for the difference in scores between the pretested and posttested groups. If only a few students became homesick, or were unhappy enough with the program, or left because they could not get along with their roommates or any of the other participants, this might make the group tested at the end better adjusted, on the average, than the group tested at the beginning for an entirely different reason from the program itself.

Second, it is possible that some event other than the program itself that occurred between the pretest and the posttest caused the change in the students' feelings about themselves. Because they are all in roughly the same place, it is not all that unlikely that some extraneous event could affect enough of them to make a difference in the group's average score on the test. Let us say, for example, that a sizable number of the program participants, in their free time, went to an inspirational church service or lecture or film, or saw a TV program, that had a powerful effect on them. It would be difficult to argue that the program itself should be credited with the benefits the students derived from this incidental event.

The third possibility is that the difference between pretest and the posttest scores might reflect changes in the participants that occurred simply as a function of the time that passes between the tests. There are certainly ages during which young people experience profound periods of difficulty managing their personal lives. These are often followed by periods of rapid personal growth or improved adjustment. This is often called a process of maturing. If the program participants were at such an age, their improved adjustment could be, at least partly, a temporal trend which is independent of the program in which they happen to be participating at the time.

Each of these rival hypotheses can be eliminated by patching up QG-2 in an appropriate way. Table 8-4 shows these alternatives and their contributions. As we look at each of these variations in turn, we will see that the necessity for introducing each of the "controls" for these threats to internal validity varies depending on the hypothesis being tested and the procedures being used to test it. As seen previously, the choice of a design depends on the extent of the researcher's knowledge about the behavior being studied and the specific procedures being used to study it. For example, the Duncan study showed that the Holley and Buxton test is not affected by repeated testing, making Design P-2 a good and economical alternative to Design QG-2 in that particular case.

We have already seen that the effects of sample attrition can be dealt with through using the version of Design QG-2 labeled Design QG-2a. The simple addition of a posttest for the subgroups which received the pretest makes it possible to determine whether the subjects who remain at the end of a program are representative of the initial group. If there is little enough attrition, or if attrition is nonselective, then sample attrition can be ruled out as a possible cause of the pretest–posttest difference. In our example of a special summer program for schoolchildren, attrition is not very likely, making the use of Design QG-2a less critical. In a case like the Duncan study, the dropout rate may very well be large enough and the possibility that the students who were lost would be those with the least knowledge about behavior would be great enough to warrant the relatively simple precaution of posttesting all subjects.

The effects of extraneous events can also be ruled out by extending the basic Design QG-2. In some cases, it is possible to repeat the design while the program or course being evaluated is repeated. We call this extension Design QB-2b, and it can be diagrammed as:

$$
\begin{array}{llll}
R & O & (X) & \\
R & & X & O \\
\hline
R & & & O & (X) \\
R & & & & X & O
\end{array}
$$

The first two lines represent the first application of Design QG-2. The next two lines represent its application to the next cycle of the program (and, of course, more cycles could be studied, especially if they recur regularly one after the other and don't last too long). If the predicted pretest–posttest difference is observed in each cycle, the likelihood that some coincidental event is responsible is lessened considerably. How likely is it, after all, that two consecutive groups of students would be exposed to some sermon or lecture or film outside the program itself that had the effect predicted for the program? This procedure would be especially effective if the behavior being studied was likely to be influenced only by some very irregular event. For example, political attitudes could be changed by some international conflict (like Pearl Harbor) or domestic upheaval (like Watergate) which would be very unlikely to be repeated summer after summer or semester after semester. Students taking introductory psychology, on the other hand, might be likely to take some other course that could influence their knowledge about behavior (or their ability to reason about it) if their total curriculum were a very structured one that forced all the successive generations of students to take sociology or logic at the same time as they were taking psychology.

Temporal trends could be ruled out by a different extension of Design, QG-2. If the group were divided randomly into three (or more) groups, as the large numbers in the Duncan study could very easily have been, pretests could be administered at several intervals before the program or course actually began. This variation, which we call Design QG-2c, could be diagrammed as:

$$
\begin{array}{llll}
R & O_1 & (X) & \\
R & & O_2 & (X) \\
R & & & X & O_3
\end{array}
$$

If the behavior being studied really was changing over time, independent of X, there would be the same kind of difference between the different pretest groups as between the pretest and posttest scores. If the successive pretests were not different, the existence of a temporal trend could be ruled out. This could also be applied to a study of the effects of a summer educational program on adjustment by contacting and pretesting a randomly selected subgroup of the program participants during the latter part of the regular school year after they were selected for the program but before it actually began. If there were evidence that they were maturing "naturally" during the time period of the program, statistical tests could be used, which, in effect, subtracted this temporal trend from the change which occurred during the program in order to determine whether the program itself added anything to the trend. This variation would have been extremely useful in the Duncan study to chart the increasing sophistication among West Point cadets.

Table 8-5 shows how each of the patched-up versions of Design QG-2 can be used to correct for the weaknesses of that design that would be especially troublesome in a particular research study in which it might be used. It also shows that the external validity of those versions may be affected by the patching procedures as well. Both variations QG-2b and QG-2c may increase the reactivity of the research setting. In a single school or factory or similar setting, the repeated testing of different subgroups of individuals could alert those who were not tested that a particular behavior is being studied. Even though they themselves are not tested, it might not be possible to isolate them from the experiences and speculations of their classmates or fellow workers. Unless the measures of behavior used are the normal tests schoolchildren take, or the production records that every factory keeps continuously, the use of repeated waves of testing may jeopardize the external validity of the research findings.

## DESIGN QG-3—THE SEPARATE-SAMPLE PRETEST-POSTTEST COMPARISON GROUP DESIGN

$$
\begin{array}{llll}
G_1 & R & O_1 & (X) \\
G_2 & R & & X & O_2 \\
\hline
G_3 & R & O_3 \\
G_4 & R & & & O_4
\end{array}
$$

Our evaluation of Design QG-2 revealed some serious threats to internal validity. Perhaps the most pervasive of them, in light of the fact that the design is usually applied to evaluate long-term phenomena, is the possibility that influential events other than the treatment being studied could affect the subjects' behavior. One of the patched-up versions of QG-2 (version b) did address that problem, but it is not always a very practical solution. Few investigators relish the prospect of spending additional months, semesters, or even years to test successive waves of participants in a program. And, in fact, many programs that need to be evaluated do not recur with that kind of regularity. As our first example will show, Design QG-3 presents another alternative to preserve the strengths of Design QG-2, while adding to it greater freedom from the threat of extraneous events. We could have added it to our list of patched-up variations on Design QG-2, but it is important enough to deserve a place of its own (although, like QG-2, it has not been used very much yet). Besides, we are still trying to keep the chunks as small as we can.

Our discussion of Design QG-3 is based on a study published in 1950 by Star and Hughes. Their purpose was to evaluate an educational campaign conducted between September 1947 and March 1948 in Cincinnati, Ohio. Radio and newspaper advertisements (no TV then), public lectures, church discussion groups, and so on, were carried out to give the residents of Cincinnati more information about the activities of the United Nations. The national public opinion polling organization with which Star and Hughes worked surveyed two separate representative samples of over 700 Cincinnati residents before and after the campaign. The results of that (Design QG-2) study showed that respondents showed more interest in the activities of the U.N. after the campaign than before. However, the postcampaign sample also expressed greater pessimism about the possibility of resolving world tensions in a peaceful manner. Could both these differences have been caused by the information that was distributed about the U.N.?

Fortunately, Star and Hughes's organization was also assessing those two beliefs in nationwide polls at about the same time (September and March to be exact). And those polls, conducted with people who were not exposed to the special educational campaign in Cincinnati during those months, showed the same differences. It seems, then, that whatever events caused these changes to occur had happened on a much broader scale than the publicity campaign in Cincinnati. The most likely explanation is that the news during the latter part of 1947 and in early 1948 was dominated by the escalating "cold war" conflict between the United States and the Soviet Union. It seems likely that this extraneous event, not the publicity campaign, made people in Cincinnati and all over the country more conscious of the U.N. role and more pessimistic that its goal of keeping the peace would be attained (and the Korean War was, after all, just around the corner). We were alerted to that fact by the opportunity to compare what happened in Cincinnati with what had happened at the same time elsewhere. The addition of this kind of comparison is the essence of Design QG-3. The change in the social unit—city, factory, school, or whatever—which is exposed to X is measured against another unit, or units, which is comparable in the sense that it is exposed to possible extraneous influences on the behavior being studied.

A hypothetical example of the use of Design QG-3 will show how such a comparison can help rule out other threats to internal validity that cloud the interpretation of findings from Design QG-2. Table 8-3 shows quite clearly the relative advantages of QG-3 over QG-2. When a suitable comparison group is available, all the advantages of the separate patched-up versions of Design QG-2 can be gained at one time through using QG-3.

At the college where I taught, a small group of faculty members got together to offer a special program for incoming freshmen. They had attended a series of workshops in which experts from other schools around the country had demonstrated how the principles of intellectual development espoused by the Swiss psychologist/educator Jean Piaget could be used in the college classroom. The exercises that Piaget used to demonstrate different stages of intellectual development, and to train young people to use what he considered higher forms of intellectual reasoning were adopted as the basis for lesson plans in various academic subjects. Convinced that these procedures could improve their own teaching, my colleagues agreed among themselves to initiate a Freshman Abstract Reasoning (FAR) program at our college. First, they designed freshman-level courses in economics, sociology, mathematics, astronomy, and introduction to the library (their particular disciplines) along Piagetian lines. They then set about to recruit incoming freshmen to take at least three courses from this group in each of their first two semesters (the economics and astronomy courses each lasted two semesters).

The goal of the FAR program was to improve the abstract reasoning skills of college students. From the group of freshmen who applied to participate in it (and whose planned courses of study did not conflict with the courses being offered), a sample was admitted that represented as wide a spectrum of academic aptitude as possible. The students who were chosen represented all available levels of SAT scores. At the same time, a plan was formulated for evaluating the program to determine whether the expected gains in abstract reasoning skills were actually realized. Rather than describing their plan, which did not have the benefit of our knowledge of research designs, I will describe what they might have and we would have done (now you can feel superior to college professors, including some with doctoral degrees in the social sciences).

The obvious place to start is with the students who actually take part in the FAR program. A test of abstract reasoning has been devised by educators who have tried similar programs in the past. That test could be administered to a randomly chosen half of the FAR students at the beginning of the program ($O_1$) and to the remaining half at the end of the program ($O_2$). What we have so far is a Design QG-2 study. If the scores at the end are higher than those at the beginning, the difference must therefore be interpreted very cautiously. Design QG-2, after all, fails to eliminate several rival hypotheses for an observed $O_1$-$O_2$ difference.

It could be that any freshman curriculum would have produced the same gain in abstract reasoning skills. Perhaps it was not the FAR program at all (assuming the test had turned out that way) that was responsible, but the change from a high school regimen of teacher domination, objective tests, and rote memorizations to a college style which required independent studying, thinking, and writing. If that were true, the non-FAR courses these students took would have contributed as much to their abstract reasoning abilities as the FAR courses. Even extracurricular discussions with fellow students, defending philosophical, religious, and political positions that had been long taken for granted against people from different backgrounds who take different positions for granted, might have made an important contribution.

If all this were true, even the use of QG-2b would be of little help in separating the effects of this very global extraneous event, the students' exposure to college intellectual life, from the effects of the FAR program. For one thing, this would be a case in which Design QG-2b would be very difficult to use. Each wave of freshmen would take a whole year to go through the program, making the minimum duration of a Design QG-2b study two years in this case. Even worse, it would not do much good in separating the effects of the FAR program from the effects of college studies in general. Every wave of freshmen would be exposed to both; thus even if the gains were consistently high, wave after wave, the influence of extraneous events in the students' college experience would still be as good an explanation for increases in abstract reasoning skills as the FAR program (X) would.

Another alternative explanation for a gain in abstract reasoning test scores between $O_1$ and $O_2$ would be that the changes in reasoning skills were simply due to the passage of time. Piaget himself, the inspiration for the FAR program, has maintained that intellectual development is governed to a large degree by the process of biological maturation. It is true that freshmen in college are considerably beyond the point in age in which Piaget's theory stops, but that does not mean that the simple aggregation of experiences acquired by people in their late teens, especially an ambitious group who expressed an interest in improving their reasoning skills by applying to the FAR program, in an environment as rich in experiences as a college campus, could not have a measurable effect on abstract reasoning. It might be possible to check on this alternative explanation by modifying the research design to include an earlier wave of testing, that is, by using Design QG-2c.

If students could be chosen for the FAR program early enough—say in the spring of their senior years of high school when many decisions about college are made—the group could be divided randomly in thirds. One-third could be tested and then perhaps contacted individually through their high school guidance counselors. Four to six months later, the second third could be given the preprogram testing. The last third would be tested after the program. Then the difference between pretest and posttest could be compared against the difference between pretest and high school testing. Any gain produced by a temporal trend should show up in both comparisons, although the abbreviated time lapse between $O_1$ and $O_2$ would have to be taken into account or prorated for the differences between $O_1$ and $O_2$ and $O_2$ and $O_3$ to be compared meaningfully.

Administratively, this procedure might be difficult to carry out. Requiring such early decisions about the membership of the FAR group would restrict the number of students available for the program. Last minute changes in plans would make it difficult to anticipate the eventual final roster, probably requiring an initial overselection that could result in too few or too many students or a group who was less representative of the student body than desired. Even more problematic, there is no assurance that a temporal trend will be regular. Recall the time series patterns considered early in this chapter. The three points provided by Design QG-2c might still leave some doubt about the contribution of a temporal trend to an observed gain between the pre-FAR and post-FAR tests.

The other threats to the internal validity of Design QG-2 findings would be fairly easy to deal with in the hypothetical evaluation of the FAR program. It would be easy to posttest every participant, to use variation 2a of the Separate-Sample Pretest-Posttest Design—in other words, to check on the effects of sample attrition. The objective abstract reasoning test could be scored by assistants who did not know which of the individuals participating in the program had been pretested or posttested. However, rather than consider which patched-up version would be most feasible or which threat to validity was most serious, there is an alternative that can deal with all these problems at the same time, with far fewer practical headaches and even greater certainty of eliminating rival hypotheses. We could use Design QG-3.

With the assistance of the college registrar, it would be possible to identify freshmen students outside the FAR program who were taking similar courses. We would want people with equivalent course loads (not very much lighter or heavier) and people with similar interests (FAR participants, because of the courses they had to take to participate in the program, could not be students with strong mathematics or natural science interests). We would also want a group who were as representative of the wide range of scholastic aptitude in the college student body as a whole, as the FAR group was. If we were able to get a group of students outside the FAR program which met all these requirements and which was about as large as the FAR group, we could compare their gains in abstract reasoning skills over the same freshman year with those of the FAR group. In other words, we could use Design QG-3 rather than Design QG-2 to evaluate the FAR program. All that would be necessary would be to administer the abstract reasoning test to a randomly chosen half of non-FAR students at the same time early in the school year when half of the FAR group was pretested, and to the remaining half at the same time late in the school year when the other half of the FAR group was posttested. We could contact students individually, ourselves, or through their advisers, or the college counseling service, or however it would be easiest.

If we found a gain in abstract reasoning skills, measured by our test, in the group who participated in the FAR program but not in the comparison group of similar freshmen, we could be fairly confident that the two most serious rival hypotheses could not plausibly explain the difference. Both groups, FAR and non-FAR, would have experienced the same changes from high school to college teaching styles and learning environments; both groups would have gone through the same maturational processes. As long as the two groups are truly comparable in their exposure to extraneous events that might influence their abstract reasoning skills and in their vulnerability to influential temporal trends, those threats to validity are ruled out.

Of course, the pretest scores of the two groups could be used to determine whether they started out with equivalent abstract reasoning skills. Because the FAR students joined the program voluntarily, one might suspect they had more interest in abstract reasoning than students who did not apply. Unfortunately, this means that even if their skills were equivalent at the outset of the program, they might have been developing their skills at a faster rate during the progress of the program. Table 8-3 shows that the interaction between group composition effects and temporal trends is a problem in Design QG-3 because the groups that experience X and the groups that do not are not randomly constituted. At least, this problem could be reduced if a variation of the "waiting-list control" procedure used in psychotherapy outcome studies could be applied. If enough students applied for the FAR program, half from each ability level could be admitted at random and half told they would be admitted later when vacancies occurred. Then those on the waiting list could serve as the comparison group for those in the program, making the two groups more nearly equal in interest or motivation than groups of applicants and nonapplicants would be. Thus it seems that Design QG-3 offers a more workable and potentially more informative solution to the problem of evaluating the FAR program, or any similar research problem, than Design QG-2 or any of its variations. When a suitable comparison group is available, Design QG-3 would certainly seem to be the method of choice. Of course, where all students or writers or citizens must be exposed to a new program together, Q-3 cannot be used.

In fact, it is possible in some cases to extend Design QG-3, to patch it up in other words, to assure not only the validity of the findings which result but their representativeness as well. We will refer to this as version Design QG-3a and Table 8-6 shows how high its marks are on the Validity Scorecard. The diagram in Table 8-6 shows that Design QG-3a consists of several replications of the basic Design QG-3. If similar programs in different locations can be evaluated simultaneously, the possibility that an observed change could be produced by some special property of a particular group of participants that was associated with a unique temporal trend can be eliminated. In the case of the FAR program evaluation, it might be possible to coordinate the efforts of groups of faculty members who were conducting similar programs at different colleges so that samples of FAR students and non-FAR students could be compared within each institution and across the different institutions.

Perhaps even more important than the gain in internal validity that would result from such a large-scale evaluation would be the increase in confidence that the effects of such a program were not limited to a particular student body or institution or method of administering the program. If gains in reasoning skills could be shown to occur consistently in a variety of FAR-type programs in different settings, over and above any gains that might be observed in similar groups of students outside the programs, the demonstration of the value of abstract reasoning training would be even more impressive. This example also points out an interesting difference between the practical evaluation research to which quasi-experimental designs are often applied and experiments that are more often used to test theories. As we discussed in Chapter 6, one common objective

# Table 8-6 VALIDITY SCORECARD: DESIGNS QG-3 AND QG-3A

| | INTERNAL VALIDITY | | | | | | | | EXTERNAL VALIDITY | | | |
| | EXTRANEOUS EVENTS | TEMPORAL EFFECTS | GROUP COMPOSITION EFFECTS | TEMPORAL X GROUP COMPOSITION EFFECTS | OBSERVER EFFECTS | EFFECTS OF PRETESTING | EFFECTS OF SAMPLE ATTRITION | STATISTICAL REGRESSION EFFECTS | NONREPRESENTATIVE SAMPLING | REACTIVITY OF THE RESEARCH CONTEXT | NONREPRESENTATIVE RESEARCH CONTEXT | LACK OF ECOLOGICAL VALIDITY |
|---|---|---|---|---|---|---|---|---|---|---|---|---|
| QG-3 | + | + | + | − | + | + | + | + | + | + | + | + |
| QG-3a | + | + | + | + | + | + | + | + | + | + | + | + |

QG-3
$$R \quad O_1 \quad (X) \quad O_2$$
$$R \quad\quad\quad X \quad O_2$$
$$- - - -$$
$$R \quad O_3 \quad\quad O_4$$
$$R$$

QG-3a
$$R \quad O_1 \quad (X)$$
$$R \quad\quad\quad X \quad O_2$$
$$R' - - -$$
$$R \quad O_3 \quad (X)$$
$$R \quad\quad\quad X \quad O_4$$
$$R \quad O_5$$
$$R' - - -$$
$$R \quad O_6$$
$$R \quad O_7$$
$$R \quad O_8$$

SOURCE: D. T. Campbell and J. C. Stanley. "Experimental and quasi-experimental designs for research in educationa. research." *Review of Educational Research*, 1966, American Educational Research Association, Washington, D.C. Copyright 1966.

of true experiments is to isolate the exact component of a treatment that affects a particular behavior. Comparison groups can be designed to rule out irrelevant aspects of the administration of a treatment and to identify the "active ingredient" that is ultimately responsible for making it work as it does. In evaluation studies, it is impossible to separate the administration of a treatment from its functional components (and it makes less sense to try). When a program is used in a natural setting, all its "irrelevant" aspects will always be present as it functions. Whatever practical value the program might have needs to be evaluated in the total context in which it has to be administered. It is more impressive to know that the program functions effectively in a wide variety of forms and contexts than to know which of its facets are relevant and which are not, or how each facet influences behavior independent of all the others. The practical goals and theoretical goals each has its own special methodological requirements.

This is also a good time to reinforce the point that the research designs we have been evaluating are only idealized models. Many variations on each of them can be used to suit the requirements of the great variety of specific hypotheses about behavior. This can be seen in a recent study by Baum and Valins (1977). They tested an environmental psychological hypothesis about the effects of the design of interior building spaces on occupants' behavior. They compared several aspects of the behavior of college students who lived in two different kinds of dormitories. One group lived in "dorms" that followed a "corridor" design. Pairs of students occupied double rooms, 16 or 17 of which were arrayed on both sides of a long corridor. Along the same corridor was one large communal bathroom that all 32 or 34 residents of that floor shared. At one end of each corridor was one lounge area that they all also shared. The other group of students lived in "suite"-design dorms. Four or six students occupied self-contained modules of two or three bedrooms plus bathroom and lounge. Each module was separated from a connecting corridor by a door. Floors of suites contained about the same number of residents (34) as floors in the corridor-style dorms. More important, both dormitory designs provided the same total amount of living space (bedroom plus bathroom plus lounge) per student (120 square feet in the corridor dorm and 118 in the suite dorm).

We will limit our discussion to two of the more important comparisons that Baum and Valins made between the two groups. Questionnaires distributed during the spring semester of the students' year's residence in the dorms showed that a sample of corridor-design residents perceived their environments as more crowded than did a sample of suite-dorm residents, despite the actual similarity of their living space. Additional samples of corridor- and suite-dorm residents were recruited individually to participate in a "psychological experiment." When they arrived for their appointments, they were asked to fill out a questionnaire in an adjoining waiting room while the arrangements for the experiment were being completed. When they entered the waiting room, they saw a row of chair desks. Near one end of the row was another student, a stranger to them, quietly working on a questionnaire. This waiting-room situation actually was the experiment for which the student had been recruited. A hidden observer kept a record of whether the students looked at the stranger in the room, whether they said anything by way of greeting the stranger, and how close they chose to sit to him. Corridor-room residents were less likely to look at or talk to the stranger, and they sat farther away from him, on the average, than did suite-dorm residents. Baum and Valins explained these, and a number of related findings, as the result of students' lack of control over their interaction with others in corridor dorms. Their design, they argued, made it necessary to interact constantly with strangers (in the halls, bathroom, etc.), reduced the students' privacy, and discouraged forming friendships among students who lived there.

That much of the study could be diagrammed as follows: X represents the "treatment" of living in the dorm for about six months. O represents the questionnaire measures of perceived crowding in the dorm, or the response to the stranger in the "waiting room."

$$G_1 \quad X_c \quad O_c$$
$$\overline{\phantom{G_1 \quad X_c \quad O_c}}$$
$$G_2 \quad X_s \quad O_s$$

The subscripts c and s represent corridor and suite. You undoubtedly recognize this as a variation of the Static-Group Comparison Design (P-3). The two groups were not assigned to dorms at random, but by the usual procedures colleges use to assign housing to students. Some students may prefer a particular dorm because of its design or location, or because they have friends there. There may be provisions for students with more seniority to be assigned to newer or better-located dorms. Or housing might be assigned on a first-come first-served basis. It is possible that residents of corridor and suite dorms were different kinds of people (different interests, differences in seniority or promptness in applying for housing, or whatever) before their experience in those dorms began. For that reason, Baum and Valins sought some kind of evidence that could rule out the effects of group composition as a cause of the differences in belief and behavior they had found between the two groups. It was too late to pretest their subjects, which would not have been the best solution anyway. Repeated testing would certainly have caused problems in their study. Baum and Valins decided to test the following year's residents of the same dorms before their classes started and before their experience in the dorms could have had much of an effect on them. They found none of the differences between these samples of corridor- and suite-dorm residents that they had found earlier between samples with six month's experience in the dorms, even though group composition differences should have been about the same (assuming the rules for room assignment had not been changed in the interim). In one way, this procedure is even better than a pretest that could have been administered the previous year. It is less likely that the experiences of the pretest and posttest samples could have influenced each other.

The four groups Baum and Valins tested—corridor-dorm residents before and after exposure, and suite-dorm residents before and after exposure—do not conform exactly to the Design QG-3 model, because the before and the after groups were not randomly chosen from the same larger group. However, if the students assigned to a particular type of dorm in two successive years are equivalent groups, it is functionally the same design. It might still be best to diagram it the way it really is (the dashed lines between the before and after groups in the same type of dorm are fainter because the differences are probably smaller):

$$
\begin{array}{llll}
G_1 & & X_c & O_c \\
\text{- - - - - - - - - -} \\
G_3 & O_c & (X_c) \\
\text{- - - - - - - - - - - - - -} \\
G_2 & & X_s & O_s \\
\text{- - - - - - - - -} \\
G_4 & O_s & (X_s)
\end{array}
$$

Baum and Valins also worried about the possibility that the particular student body and campus setting, at the State University of New York at Stony Brook, with which they worked might have set into motion the interpersonal processes they later measured. Did the particular rules of housing assignment (and the groups of students they placed in the comparison dorms), the particular social climate or student body of that university produce an effect which would not have occurred under different conditions? Again, the match is not perfect, but we are discussing something very similar to the interaction between temporal trends and group composition effects, the principal weakness of Design QG-3 (see Table 8-6). To overcome this limitation, they repeated their research on a different campus, that of Trinity College. Although the dorm designs were not exactly the same there, they compared the two dorms which had analogous properties, larger versus small groups of students sharing the same facilities. And they got the same results.

The final form of the Baum and Valins research, then, is similar to Design QG-3a, something similar to this:

$$G_1 \qquad\qquad X_c \quad O_c$$

$$G_3 \qquad O_c \quad (X_c)$$

$$G_5 \qquad\qquad X_{c'} \quad O_c$$

$$G_7 \qquad O_c \quad (X_{c'})$$

$$G_2 \qquad\qquad X_s \quad O_s$$

$$G_4 \qquad O_s \quad (X_s)$$

$$G_6 \qquad\qquad X_{s'} \quad O_s$$

$$G_8 \qquad O_s \quad (X_{s'})$$

As in the diagram following Design QG-3 above, $G_1$ and $G_3$ are the pre- and postcorridor groups and $G_2$ and $G_4$ are the pre- and postsuite groups, all at Stony Brook, $G_5$ and $G_7$ are the pre- and postcorridor groups and $G_6$ and $G_8$ are the pre- and postsuite groups, all at Trinity (the primes on these lines indicate that the dorm designs, or treatments, were not exactly the same on the two campuses). All in all, the study leaves very little room for alternative interpretations of its findings.

## ETHICS IN QUASI-EXPERIMENTAL RESEARCH

When quasi-experimental research studies involve direct contact with human subjects—the direct manipulation of the events to which they are exposed and the direct examination of their behavior—they raise many of the same ethical issues as experimental studies. We have already reviewed many of those problems and some of the possible solutions to them.

There is, however, one additional point that needs to be made here. The vast majority of experiments take place in the laboratory. Subjects who are recruited for those experiments can usually, to some degree at least, decide for themselves whether to participate (although we have seen how voluntarism can limit the external validity of research findings). Moreover, most experiments take place in institutions where some degree of protection is provided for the subjects. At the very least, colleges and hospitals are staffed by professionals who recognize threats to subjects, are aware of ethical issues and guidelines, and communicate with one another about their work.

By contrast, many quasi-experimental studies are conducted in schools, factories, and other institutions where the people have less freedom to decline participation and fewer safeguards to protect them. In these settings, schoolchildren, workers, and patients are under formal constraints to be cooperative. They are accustomed to following orders. They all have bosses, and both parties usually recognize the right of the bosses to exercise control over their charges. Therefore, in many quasi-experimental studies the researcher's treatment of subjects is likely to meet less resistance and the subjects' rights may be less likely to be respected. For those reasons, even more vigilance is demanded in these settings than in the laboratory.

But the more typical quasi-experimental studies, which make use of archival data, raise some special issues of their own. The principal threat to the subjects whose behavior is examined in quasi-experimental studies is the invasion of their privacy. The measures that are analyzed come mostly from public records that are anonymous. The census is conducted by legal mandate and responses to public opinion polls are given voluntarily. Moreover, such records are kept for purposes other than research and by people other than researchers, and the people represented in them are not identified by name. It seems, then, that their use poses no ethical dilemma for behavioral researchers. There are also, however, public records such as tax rolls and license records that do identify individuals by name. Although they are open to the public, they are usually available in limited locations such as government offices at limited times such as regular business hours. If they were to be distributed more widely, it might affect the lives of the individuals involved, thus presenting unusual risks. Although this is done quite regularly by journalists and others, it usually affects very limited numbers of people, and only those who are of special interest to the public. Most researchers take the precaution of reporting data only in aggregated form (totals or averages) while preserving the anonymity of the people involved. This would certainly seem to be the preferable procedure on ethical grounds.

In general, there are far fewer ethical problems in quasi-experimental research by virtue of its minimal interference with individual subjects' lives. There are, however, some difficult exceptions. When corporations and even, to some extent, governments institute their policies, they are, in effect, exercising control over their employees' and citizens' lives. Their goals in setting those policies may be to make corporate and governmental bureaucratic structures function better, but, it must be asked, to whose benefit? Is it the workers or the citizens who gain, or the administrator who has jurisdiction over some part of their lives? One of the most serious ethical dilemmas faced by the researcher who helps evaluate public policy, then, is concerned not with the treatment of subjects during the research itself, but with the uses to which the research findings might be put. It is rare that the researcher's clients are laborers, or mental patients, or convicts, or even the average taxpayer. Where the goals of the evaluation study are clearly in everyone's best interest, evaluation research is an ethical paradise for the researcher. It harbors few possibilities for harm and offers great opportunities for good in instituting effective policy. Everyone wants peace and health. But in the majority of cases in which the beneficiaries of successful policy are less clear, it is an ethical quagmire. If the therapists and managers and government bureaucrats decide on both the policies and the criteria by which they are evaluated, by virtue of their control over the purse strings and thereby the evaluators, successful policy may no longer be an unmitigated boon. It can mean more efficient control over people's lives or preserving the status quo of economic and social inequality. The applied researcher needs to wrestle more vigorously with the question of whom to serve and how.

## CONCLUSION

During the course of this very long chapter, we have been exposed to a great variety of research designs most researchers have seen very rarely, if at all, in our study of the findings of behavioral research. It may help, at this point, to repeat some of the reasons for devoting so much time and energy to them.

Most important, quasi-experimental research designs can be used to answer questions to which true experimental designs cannot be applied. Many important causes of behavior cannot be created by researchers, except in the most artificial simulated form. These designs also permit the behavioral researcher to take advantage of many important sources of information about the causes of behavior that exist independently of the researchers' efforts. These archival records offer important evidence about many powerful causes of behavior. They also offer many practical benefits. Policies that are set by government officials, corporate boards, and educational administrators, among others, can be evaluated using these methods, often with little or no intrusion into the institutions being studied. Most institutions keep records for their own purposes that can supply the necessary data.

However, quasi-experimental designs offer even more than ways of testing hypotheses that true experiments do not fit and of evaluating institutional policies. They provide information about the relationships between events and behavior that can be generalized more broadly than can the findings of true experiments. Quasi-experiments can be carried out in settings that are populated by more representative groups of subjects than can be brought to the laboratory. They can also be conducted less obtrusively, with less threat that the behavior being studied will be altered by the reactivity of the study itself. And they can be applied to behavior that occurs in the natural context of all its other influences, thus providing a more realistic picture of the effects of the particular cause being studied and a picture that is less likely to change radically when minor aspects of the context change.

These gains in external validity are made at some cost to internal validity, but we have seen that these costs are not as great as those committed to experimental methods may believe. In fact, there are substitutes for the control group (equivalent comparison group) logic of experiments that are so good that little difference in internal validity can be detected. Quasi-experimental designs QT-2, QT-3, and QG-3a score about as high on internal validity as the true experimental designs, with QG-3a scoring much higher on external validity.

Perhaps the most important reason for our extended consideration of the quasi-experimental designs, however, is, anomalously, their relative obscurity. As I put together the materials from which I wrote this chapter, I found it very difficult to find recent examples of published behavior research that utilized these designs. In some cases, there was virtually none and I had to rely more on hypothetical examples than I would have liked. One reason for this, of course, is that most published research is experimental. But there are, today more than ever, many researchers and professional journals committed to applied behavioral research and problems that do not lend themselves very easily to experimentation. Unfortunately, their efforts tend to be confined to much less powerful research methods than the quasi-experimental designs we have been learning about. A very interesting article by Cummings, Molloy, and Glen (1977) points up the problem quite well. They surveyed 58 published studies of the effects of working conditions on workers' behavior. Each of the studies was diagrammed and evaluated using much the same procedure as in this book. The vast majority of those studies used preexperimental methods with the same glaring weaknesses we discussed in Chapter 5.

There promises to be continued growth in applied research fields such as industrial/organizational psychology, environmental psychology, and medical psychology. In addition, there is likely to be increased use of archival data to supplement experimental methods in testing theoretical hypotheses about behavior. Let us hope that the researchers engaged in those endeavors become better acquainted with the quasi-experimental designs for research so that their findings will have the greatest possible value for psychology and for society as a whole.

## REFERENCES

Aronson, E. *The social animal.* San Francisco: Freeman, 1972.

Baum, A., & Valins, S. *Architecture and social behavior: Psychological studies in social density.* Hillsdale, N.J.: Erlbaum, 1977.

Cherulnik, P.D., Way, J. H., Ames, S., & Hutto, D. Impressions of high and low Machiavellian men. *Journal of Personality,* 1981, *49,* 388–400.

Cummings, T. G., Molloy, E. S., & Glen, R. A methodological critique of fifty-eight selected work experiments. *Human Relations,* 1977, *30,* 675–708.

Duncan, C. P., O'Brien, R. B., Murray, D. C., Davis, L., & Gilliland, A. R. Some information about a test of psychological misconceptions. *The Journal of General Psychology,* 1957, *56,* 257–260.

Holley, J. W., & Buxton, C. E. A factorial study of beliefs. *Educational and Psychological Measurement,* 1950, *10,* 400–410.

Lucker, G. W., Rosenfield, D., Sikes, J., & Aronson, E. Performance in the interdependent classroom: A field study. *American Educational Research Journal,* 1976, *13,* 115–123.

Luckey, J. W., & Berman, J. J. Effects of a new commitment law on involuntary admissions and service utilization patterns. *Law and Human Behavior,* Vol. 3. New York: Plenum, 1979. pp. 149–161.

Rigsbee, F. Litter—forest cleanup shows recycling pays off. *The Evening Post* (Charleston, S.C.), June 23, 1980, pp. 1-B–2-B.

Rindfuss, R. R., Reed, J. S., & St. John, C. A fertility reaction to a historical event: Southern white birthrates and the 1954 desegregation ruling. *Science,* 1978, *201* (14 July), 178–180.

Roethlisberger, F. J., & Dickson, W. V. *Management and the worker.* Cambridge, Mass.: Harvard, 1939.

Sanford, F. H., & Hemphill, J. K. An evaluation of a brief course in psychology at the U.S. Naval Academy. *Educational and Psychological Measurement,* 1952, *12,* 194–216.

Simonton, D. Sociocultural context of individual creativity: A transhistorical time-series analysis. *Journal of Personality and Social Psychology,* 1975, *32,* 1119–1133.

Sorokin, P. An experimental study of efficiency of work under various specified conditions. *American Journal of Sociology,* 1930, *35,* 765–782.

Star, S. A., & Hughes, H. M. Report on an educational campaign: The Cincinnati plan for the United Nations. *American Journal of Sociology,* 1950, *55,* 389–400.

## SUGGESTED ACTIVITIES

### Study Questions

1. Under what conditions are quasi-experimental designs used? Why couldn't true experimental designs be substituted for them under the same conditions?
2. What are the major advantages and disadvantages of quasi-experimental designs relative to true experimental designs?
3. Is there really a trade-off between internal and external validity? Does a gain in one automatically come at the cost of a loss in the other?
4. Given a choice of any research design to investigate an important hypothesis, which would you choose and why?

### Exercise

Examples of published research utilizing quasi-experimental designs are not easy to find. But looking for them can be an educational experience in itself.

Can you guess by now what kinds of professional journals would be the best ones to look in? Applied research is more likely to require quasi-experimental designs. Why? Journals that publish research done in schools, factories, and other applied settings are the best sources for finding quasi-experiments—those in the areas of educational, industrial/organizational, and clinical psychology, for example.

Sample a few studies from journals in each of a few areas. Just pick articles whose titles interest you. Then describe the research design used in each study, with the usual symbols. Can you identify the type of research design—preexperimental, true experimental, or quasi-experimental—in each case? In those cases in which the designs are not quasi-experimental, can you explain why? Were there good reasons for choosing another type of design? Might some quasi-experimental design have provided more valid findings? Which one? In what ways would it have been better?

Evaluate the validity of each of the designs you sampled using the Validity Scorecard. Do the results bear out the arguments you read in this chapter? If not, can you explain the discrepancies? How would you suggest improving each of the designs in order to eliminate additional threats to validity?

# Chapter 9
# Adding up the Score

## INTRODUCTION

We have learned a great deal in these hundreds of pages—about the language of behavioral research, studies which have been done to test hypotheses about behavior, and others which might be done, and a system for evaluating the adequacy of research findings. There have been thousands of bits and pieces of information along the way—names, places, ideas, and facts; and hundreds of thousands of words. At the time, each bit or piece assumes an equal importance as we try to understand it. But the time has come to step back and take a broader look at the ground we have covered, the forest which is made up of all those trees. Undoubtedly, you have already formed some sort of global impression yourself. Now I'm going to give you mine.

The largest part of this book has been focused on the faults of the various alternative ways of doing behavioral research. We have found fault even where most have assumed that there is great strength. But the purpose of this inquisition has not been to devalue behavioral research, or even its findings. The more we know about the true strengths and weaknesses of research findings, the more valuable they are to us. Critical analysis is the only way we can choose correctly among the conflicting findings that methodological imperfection is bound to produce. We can expect to build a successful science of behavior only out of knowledge, not out of ignorance. All the academic disciplines depend upon debate, adversary confrontation, and the clash of ideas to discover the truth they are after. The discovery of fault should not make any of us pessimistic. Instead, we should see it as further progress toward the truth.

## TRUE AND QUASI-EXPERIMENTS: INTERNAL AND EXTERNAL VALIDITY

There are two general approaches to the study of behavior. True experimental research designs tend to be applied in laboratory settings in which randomly assigned groups of subjects, usually college students, rats, or pigeons, can be exposed to a suspected influence on behavior or not, at the choice of the experimenter. The high degree of control that the researcher can exercise over the events taking place in the laboratory makes it possible to achieve findings that are very high in internal validity. But the artificiality of the laboratory setting and the subjects' direct interaction with the experimenter bring the generalizability of those findings into serious question.

Quasi-experimental research designs tend to be applied to behavior that occurs in natural settings, such as the normal activities of students in their schools and workers in their factories. Researchers can exercise very little control over the events taking place there, often making it very difficult to pinpoint the exact cause of observed variations in behavior. However, the unobtrusiveness of such studies, and the rich, natural context of the behavior being studied, make the findings more broadly generalizable and more real.

Based on this kind of thinking, many analysts of the research process have written of a choice between true experiments and quasi-experiments, based on a trade-off between internal and external validity. But we have seen that both kinds of research designs can be implemented in various ways. Experiments can be performed in less reactive field settings in which more representative samples of subjects can be observed in natural surroundings where they are much less aware of the assessment of their behavior. And, although it is logically not possible to generalize beyond the context in which a research finding is produced to all other contexts, even the most artificial laboratory simulation will generalize to some. On the other side, the availability of an archival running record of behavior, and of nonequivalent comparison groups, can be utilized to rule out most threats to internal validity in quasi-experiments.

Furthermore, laboratory experiments, especially those that utilize human subjects, have their own buried weaknesses when it comes to internal validity. And the quasi-experimental designs can require so much intervention in the ongoing settings to which they are applied as to severely restrict the generalizability of their findings.

## DISCOUNTING RESEARCH FINDINGS

A less simplistic view is clearly indicated. First of all, all research findings must be suspected of being flawed. This, however, does not mean that they have no value. One who knows the relative strengths and weaknesses of the different research designs, as they are applied to different behaviors in different contexts, can place just as much confidence in a given finding as it deserves. Just as the banker calculates the charges for a loan on the basis of the risks that it will not be repaid, the researcher and the consumer must discount research findings by the potential threats to their validity. But it is never possible to rule out all alternative explanations. It is always a question of which rival hypotheses exist, not whether there are any. It is not as easy as some would have us believe to assign priorities to the different threats to validity. Traditionally, threats to internal validity have taken precedence in behavioral research. Hence there is the dominant use of animal laboratory experiments to test hypotheses about behavior. But it has become clear to most students of behavior by now that relationships between causal events and behavior that hold only in the artificial context in which they are discovered have very little value. There is an increasing interest in applying research findings to solving practical problems. This comes both from an increasing commitment on the researchers' part and from pressure that is being exerted by governmental and private sources of research funds.

There are, however, other concerns as well. For example, note than in 1969, Chris Argyris pointed out that several of the most influential social psychological theories are based on "findings from the experimental laboratory" which do not "reflect the noncontrived world." This view, which strikes home harder at most researchers than the concern over the applied value of their findings, has become more and more widespread over the intervening years. But if all research findings are flawed, and if the flaws in external validity that tend to afflict experimental findings more are as serious as the flaws in internal validity that tend to afflict quasi-experimental findings more, how is one to choose the appropriate research design, or the best ones among a body of conflicting research findings? We would argue that one need not choose among them at all. The more appropriate course of action is to combine methods and findings based on what is known about the strengths and weaknesses of each.

## COMBINING EXPERIMENTAL AND QUASI-EXPERIMENTAL DESIGNS FOR RESEARCH

A recent paper by Cohen, Evans, Krantz, and Stokols (1980) illustrates one way in which experiments and quasi-experiments can be used together. For many years, a large body of research findings has been accumulating on the effects of noise on behavior. Researchers found that exposure to loud noise, especially when it is unpredictable and uncontrollable, can cause increases in physiological arousal, interference with task performance, and feelings of lack of control or helplessness. These findings, however, have come almost exclusively from laboratory experiments. Cohen and his colleagues wanted to find out whether they would generalize to a natural setting. They chose the elementary school. More specifically, they set out to determine whether the children who were attending the four noisiest elementary schools in the air corridor of Los Angeles International Airport would show the same physiological, cognitive, and motivational ill effects as had been found in the previous laboratory research. They compared them with students of similar social and ethnic background who were attending schools that were not affected by aircraft noise. Where there were preexisting differences between the two groups, they used statistical "controls" in making comparisons to avoid extraneous group composition effects.

The results of this study are especially interesting in the way they compare with the prior laboratory findings. Children in noisy schools had higher blood pressure than those in quiet schools. This finding is consistent with the laboratory findings, although it is not evidence of increased arousal upon direct exposure to noise, because blood pressure measures were obtained in a quiet laboratory just outside the school buildings. More children from noisy schools failed to complete a "moderately difficult" puzzle and were more likely to have given up before reaching the time limit as compared with children from quiet schools. Again, these findings are similar to laboratory findings of interference with task performance, although they, too, were observed in a quiet environment rather than upon direct exposure to noise. Both the blood pressure and task performance/helplessness findings may be considered aftereffects of the children's exposure to noise during their days in school.

Although the Cohen study thus provides some confirmation for earlier laboratory findings, and evidence that those earlier findings do generalize to an important natural setting, the overall picture is not all that clear. Despite their higher blood pressure readings, children in noisy schools were no different in their ratios of weight to height ("ponderosity"), which is one measure of their state of health. And their rates of absenteeism from school were actually significantly lower than those of children in quiet schools, another indication that their health had not suffered from the noise. Moreover, despite their poorer performance and perseverance on a laboratory task presented to them outside the school, school records showed that the scores of the children in noisy schools on standardized reading and math tests were no lower than those of students in quiet schools. It seems that the noise had not hurt their ongoing academic achievement. Both their overall health and achievement data might be considered inconsistent with the implications of laboratory findings on the effects of noise.

That should come as little surprise considering the differences in context between the laboratory and the schools. Children in noisy schools are exposed over very much longer periods of time which may permit a degree or kind of adaptation to noise that cannot be expected to occur in the brief duration of a laboratory experiment. Although the findings of the Cohen study are a mixed bag of consistency and inconsistency with laboratory findings, it seems fair to say that they demonstrate the value of checking out laboratory findings in natural settings before trying to apply them there. If schools are to be moved away from sources of noise such as airports, it will not be because the research evidence indicates that their students' health or academic performance suffers from the noise; at least, not yet. Despite the vast amount of laboratory data available, the Cohen quasi-experimental study is a pioneering effort to determine the behavioral effects of noise in the real world. Much more evidence is needed before any firm conclusions can be drawn. And many other areas of research that have similarly been confined to laboratory settings need to be moved into natural settings through using quasi-experimental designs before they are used as the basis for practical interventions in education or industry or any other arena.

This is just one example of the ways in which causal events, which are shown to affect behavior in the rarefied context of the laboratory, may turn out to interact with characteristics of the more varied people and places in which the behavior occurs in nature. It is precisely this possibility that can be checked out in attempts to verify experimental findings by retesting hypotheses in nonexperimental studies.

It is just as important, in principle, for nonexperimental findings to be verified in experiments that narrow down the range of potential causal events. Experiments in highly controlled laboratory settings offer the valuable advantage of isolating very precisely that component of a complex causal event that is crucial to the variation in observed behavior. At this time, however, the use of nonexperimental means of testing hypotheses about behavior is still quite limited. Not only do experiments still dominate the behavioral research literature, but relatively few of the few existing nonexperimental studies are tests of theoretical hypotheses. Most of these studies are evaluations of unique programs or events that have little interest to those not directly involved. Therefore, the use of experiments to check out nonexperimental findings with potentially serious shortcomings in internal validity remains largely for the future.

## OVERLAPPING EXPERIMENTAL AND NONEXPERIMENTAL RESEARCH DESIGNS

The value of checking out the findings produced by one kind of research design by retesting the hypothesis with another kind of design is beyond question. But there is an even more ambitious approach to the problem of compensating for the weakness of one kind of research design with the strength of another. In many cases, it is impossible to test a hypothesis in a single study that is free from serious threats to validity. Each of the appropriate designs has its own unique weaknesses in internal or external validity. But all these designs can be combined into a research program. A series of studies utilizing a variety of flawed research designs can succeed in eliminating all potential threats to validity. If the studies yield consistent findings and if each potential threat to validity is ruled out by at least one of the research designs employed, then the findings of the entire research program together can be argued to provide a perfectly valid test of the hypothesis. Although each of the individual findings may permit a rival hypothesis to have equal status, one is left with a choice between explaining all the findings with the hypothesis that was tested or using a different rival hypothesis to explain the (identical) findings of each separate study. Such a choice can be made on the basis of the scientific principle of parsimony—the single hypothesis is preferred. Thus, when research designs have complementary strengths and weaknesses, their combination can be effective in ruling out all threats to validity.

The effort required by such a research program is warranted only by an important hypothesis. One very important hypothesis that has been the target of an extensive research program utilizing a wide variety of research designs is the relationship between diet and health. Considerable scientific effort has been devoted to the search for a possible link between the concentration of cholesterol in the blood and the development of cardiovascular disease. This is a very complex question in several different ways. For example, the amount of cholesterol in the fats we eat seems to be less important in determining the level of cholesterol in our blood than are the other components of those fats. Furthermore, a very imperfect relationship exists between the amount of fat we eat and the amount that can be measured in our blood. Apparently genetic factors and other individual differences such as body weight and level of physical activity enter into the equation. Given all that we do not know, both scientist and lay person, this is still a good example of using varied research designs in the programmatic test of an important hypothesis. We will just have to oversimplify and be very selective in order to avoid getting mired too deeply in all the real complexities of this issue.

We will consider three very different ways of testing the relationship between serum cholesterol (the concentration in the blood) and cardiovascular disease (atherosclerosis, coronary artery disease, stroke, etc.). The first is known as epidemiological research. In this approach, a wide-ranging sample of the population is surveyed for the disease to identify the characteristics that differentiate between those who have it and those who do not. These are known as risk factors. Among the risk factors in cardiovascular disease are being male, a positive family history of the disease, hypertension, obesity, diabetes, cigarette smoking, physical inactivity—and high levels of serum cholesterol. But if we know that individuals whose blood contains high concentrations of cholesterol are more likely to suffer from cardiovascular disease, how much do we really know? Perhaps serum cholesterol is a result of cardiovascular disease, rather than the cause. Even more likely is the possibility that a genetic predisposition, perhaps one associated with a person's ethnic background, causes both the disease (perhaps through such mechanisms as hypertension) and the high levels of cholesterol (perhaps through a combination of diet and metabolic factors which cause a relatively large proportion of the fat ingested to be deposited in the bloodstream). In the terms we have been learning throughout this book, epidemiological research is pre-experimental in nature. Our Design P-3 is a good way of representing it. The suspected causal event is the level of serum cholesterol and the "behavior" is cardiovascular disease. But the groups being compared, those having high and low cholesterol levels, are not equivalent. There are numerous ways in which they might be different other than in the concentrations of cholesterol in their bloodstreams. Any of these differences could conceivably be a cause of the differences in their rates of cardiovascular disease, especially when one considers the wide variety of potential causes. Thus, group composition effects are the most serious threat to the validity of epidemiological findings.

A second approach is to feed different amounts of fats to randomly constituted, thus equivalent, groups of subjects. This can produce high levels of serum cholesterol in laboratory animals whose relatively short life spans would permit observing changes in cardiovascular structure. This kind of study would be a true experiment, such as Design E-2. One could then be quite certain that any differences in the development of cardiovascular disease between groups in which different levels of serum cholesterol were created were not influenced by any other factors operating within the experiment. Such a finding would have, in other words, very impressive internal validity. Its relevance to the relationship between diet cholesterol and cardiovascular disease in humans, however, is not so clear. For example, the pattern of causes of cardiovascular disease in humans is different from the pattern in other species. Even if the disease can occur naturally in those species, it is unlikely to be caused by cigarette smoking, high-fat diet, or physical inactivity. In addition, the influence of a factor produced in the laboratory might be quite different from the influence of that same factor in the context in which it normally occurs. We do not know if the levels of serum cholesterol that can be produced artificially through feeding programs (or by drugs) are comparable with those that diet, heredity, and the other influences produce naturally. We also do not know if the effects of serum cholesterol alone are comparable with those of serum cholesterol in combination with all the other causes that operate in the natural setting in which people develop cardiovascular disease. The findings of such a study, in other words, would have very low external validity. They would be very difficult to generalize to the human problem they are intended to help clarify.

A third research approach to testing the same hypothesis about cholesterol and cardiovascular disease utilizes a quasi-experimental design. Middle-aged men who have suffered heart attacks are randomly assigned to different prescribed diets that are designed to lower the serum cholesterol of some but not others. Over the succeeding months and years, records are kept of the incidence of new heart attacks in the various groups as well as their survival rates (age and other influences being equal). This sounds like a true experiment, but, as we saw in Chapter 8, assigning human subjects different diets is likely to produce other differences in them as well that cause the compared groups to not remain equivalent to one another even if they were originally assigned their diets at random. They may sleep differently, exercise differently, or feel differently about themselves and their futures. Therefore, even if the incidence of disease and the rate of mortality show differences between the groups, the fact that the research design resembles our Design QG-1 means that an interaction of group composition with the trends caused by the subjects' activities during the course of the study could be responsible, rather than the differences between the diets themselves.

We have seen, so far, how three very different kinds of research designs—preexperimental, experimental, and quasi-experimental— could be used to investigate the relationship between serum cholesterol and cardiovascular disease. The validity of the findings of each of the individual studies would have a serious limitation. The epidemiological finding that people with higher cholesterol levels are more likely to suffer from cardiovascular disease might be explained as the result of preexisting differences between groups with different cholesterol levels—a group composition artifact. The experimental finding that rats in which higher levels of serum cholesterol are created by special feeding programs are more likely to develop cardiovascular disease is very difficult to generalize to the much more complex context of the relationship between cholesterol and disease in humans. Finally, the fact that heart-attack victims placed on different diets have different rates of subsequent attacks and mortality could be explained alternatively by changes in activities triggered by the assigned diets, which, in turn, influence other risk factors for the disease. However, by the principle of parsimony defined earlier, a consistent pattern of findings across all three types of studies would be explained better by the research hypothesis— that high levels of serum cholesterol cause cardiovascular disease— than by the three separate alternative hypotheses of group composition differences, the different temporal trends among the groups, and the differences between the animal analogues and the natural development of the disease in humans. (For accuracy, it needs to be pointed out here that, unfortunately, the actual findings of the research on the effects of serum cholesterol are not perfectly consistent.)

This argument could be extended into an even more general form. If a hypothesis is verified by a program of research studies that utilizes a variety of designs that permit different alternative explanations of their findings, it can be argued that each rival hypothesis that is ruled out by at least one of the studies is a less plausible explanation than the research hypothesis. If no rival hypothesis can be entertained as an explanation for more than one of the individual findings, the research hypothesis should be accepted as the best available explanation for the total body of findings produced by the research program. Table 9-1 shows how this could be done for the research

**Table 9-1** OVERLAPPING RESEARCH DESIGNS IN TESTING THE RELATIONSHIP BETWEEN CHOLESTEROL AND CARDIOVASCULAR DISEASE

| THREATS TO VALIDITY | EPIDEMIOLOGICAL STUDY DESIGN P-3 | EXPERIMENT DESIGN E-2 | QUASI-EXPERIMENT DESIGN QG-1 | CUMULATIVE PROGRAM OF RESEARCH |
|---|---|---|---|---|
| 1. Extraneous events | + | + | ? | + |
| 2. Temporal effects | − | + | + | + |
| 3. Group composition effects | − | + | + | + |
| 4. Temporal X group composition effects | − | + | − | + |
| 5. Observer effects | + | + | + | + |
| 6. Effects of repeated testing | + | + | + | + |
| 7. Effects of sample attrition | − | + | + | + |
| 8. Statistical regression effects | + | + | ? | + |
| 9. Nonrepresentative sampling | − | − | ? | ? |
| 10. Reactivity in the research setting | ? | − | ? | ? |
| 11. Nonrepresentative research context | O | ? | ? | ? |
| 12. Lack of ecological validity | O | ? | + | + |

program on cholesterol and cardiovascular disease. Note that in the last column, labeled "Cumulative Program of Research," there is a plus sign for each threat to validity that is ruled out by at least one of the three individual research designs in the preceding columns. Thus the strengths of one design overlap or cover up for the weaknesses in another. Imperfect individual designs can thus be combined into very strong programs of research.

## COMBINING THE FINDINGS OF INDEPENDENT RESEARCH STUDIES

The goal of combining studies with complementary strengths and weaknesses into research programs may be furthered by the recent work of Robert Rosenthal and some of his colleagues (e.g., Rosenthal, 1978). They have been advocating a new statistical approach to summarizing the findings of independent but related studies, at least with respect to the statistical criterion of sampling error. Traditionally, research findings have been summarized verbally. The findings of a single study are either statistically "significant" or "nonsignificant." Thus the findings of a study can either be said to support the hypothesis or not. A series of studies is produces "consistent" or "inconsistent" findings. In the first case, of a single study, scientists have accepted a totally arbitrary convention that they will take no greater risk of a finding produced by sampling error than 1 chance in 20. In the second case of a series of studies, there is no convention at all. Are 7 significant findings out of 10 related studies a consistent pattern? Or do we need 8? Or would 6 be enough?

Rosenthal and his colleagues have been arguing for extending the use of statistics from the data of a single study to the findings of a series of studies. This would provide two different kinds of benefits. First, it would lend a more precise, mathematical tone to the description of the findings of a research program. Numbers would communicate more clearly than words how strongly the whole pattern of findings supports the hypothesis. Second, it would permit some use to be made of findings which are not strong enough to meet the arbitrary .05 level criterion. The results of a single study that just fails to meet that dichotomous criterion may, in fact, be too uncertain a basis for judgments about a hypothesis. (Although it still seems reasonable to ask, "Why not .06, or even .07"?.) But if several studies testing the same hypothesis come that close, it can be shown that their combined findings do lend "significant" support to the hypothesis. Rosenthal (1979) has also pointed out that a shift to reporting the findings of a series of studies in this way would not only guarantee that all findings would be used. It would also rule out the possibility that most tests of a hypothesis could fail to produce statistically acceptable support but not be reported for that reason, whereas the few "successful" studies reported made the hypothesis look much more viable than it really was.

## QUASI-EXPERIMENTAL DESIGNS ARE ESSENTIAL

Since their development began, quasi-experimental designs have been advocated as a last resort, to be used only when true experiments are not possible. Even their strongest supporters advocated this limited role for them. It was clear that they were superior to pre-experimental research or to no research at all, but because internal validity was the primary criterion for scientific research findings, experiments were the preferred means for producing them, Many hold to that view to the present day, but I am going to dispute it over the next few pages. (Even at the risk of repeating some of what I have already said earlier, I feel it is that important.) I wish to make it clear, however, that I am not advocating an end to experiments (not that they are in any danger, given their powerful advocates and predominance in behavioral research)—just a new beginning for quasi-experimental research. It is much more important to the science of human behavior and to society than it has been given credit for.

No science of behavior can survive indefinitely without tackling the forms of human behavior that matter most to all of us. The most violent forms of aggression—Lizzie Borden, Jack the Ripper, and all their modern counterparts. The most passionate forms of affection—any pair of new and enthusiastic lovers. A poker player bluffing for a $10,000 pot, or the quarterback in the Super Bowl, or the corporate executive betting on her future by initialing a memo. The family who have lost a loved one. The hero who jumps into a flooded river to save a drowning child. The soldier crawling through a hail of bullets and artillery shells. In short, the ultimate thrills and threats which people can face during their lives.

Some behavioral scientists believe that the feelings and behaviors that take place naturally under those extreme (but not all that rare) circumstances can be studied in the laboratory. Aronson (1976) argues that deception that is clever enough, the experiment that is good-enough theater, can produce a realistic approximation of any situation a person might encounter in real life. Others simulate international conflict, life-threatening emergencies, and even erotic experiences in their laboratories. But no one dies in laboratory wars, or experiences orgasm as a subject whose response to hard-core pornography is being studied, or gets blitzed by the Pittsburgh Steelers. It is not, however, that strong feelings cannot be aroused in research

subjects. Milgram appears to have been able to do that in his studies
of obedience. But many specific feelings that need to be studied because they are important parts of human behavior cannot be. And
the few exceptions like Milgram's research raise very serious ethical
questions that would be compounded if the experimentalist were really as omnipotent as Aronson would have us believe.

If we rely exclusively on experiments where events must be created for subjects at an arbitrary place and at an arbitrary time (where
and when they do not occur naturally), and where the act of studying
the subjects' responses is obtrusive and even threatening to them,
theories about behavior will always have to skirt the edges of many
of the most important and most interesting forms of behavior. It is
only by studying these forms as they occur in nature, through the
use of nonexperimental research designs and archival records, that
we can hope to get to the heart of the matter (pardon the pun). Of
course, even in these cases, experiments would serve as an invaluable
adjunct to refine theories by sorting out the complex processes that
occur in nature into their components, separating the effective influences on behavior from their inert vehicles. Again, we are not advocating an end to experimentation, just an end to its exclusive use.
And those causal factors that are isolated in experiments, where
close, precise measurement is applied and most or all natural context
has been stripped away, are much more interesting if there is evidence that they are also influential in behavior that occurs outside
the laboratory. Then we can feel confident that we are not merely
constructing elaborate theories about causes of behavior that have
trivial effects when other causes are operating alongside them. External validity is as important to theory as it is to application.

That brings us to the role of quasi-experimental research in serving the needs of society. Whatever one's political philosophy might
be, it is undoubtedly clear that governments at all levels are responsible for providing crucial services to us all. These include public education at all levels, management of important natural resources,
protection from natural hazards, from industrial pollution, and from
each other—and too many more to list anywhere. If these essential
services which consume so much of our national wealth are to fulfill
their assigned functions, they must be implemented, as Campbell
(1969) has put it, experimentally. There must be objective evaluations of their effectiveness. Campbell points out that those who administer programs in government (and the same is likely to hold in
the private sector) may resist such evaluation for fear of being
blamed for evidence of failure.

But if administrators can be held accountable for finding good
solutions rather than for a particular solution, this situation may be

changed. In any case, there is a great need to resist choosing programs on the basis of rhetoric or the personal appeal of their advocates. The needy whom government tries to help, the taxpayers who finance social programs, and the workers and owners of the industries that suffer from low productivity and the inability to adjust to changing market conditions, and all citizens who depend on the judicial system and on the economic policies of government bureaucrats and private bankers—all of us—must demand that policy be governed by its successes or failures. Policies that succeed should be kept. Those that fail should be replaced by alternatives, which are, in turn, evaluated. If such evaluations are to become an integral part of program administration (as the laws establishing government programs are already beginning to mandate), behavioral scientists must develop the means to carry them out. Quasi-experimental research designs are precisely those means. There are rare cases in which new policies can be implemented by randomly assigning a new program to half of a large number of groups (schools, cities, states, factories, etc.), or introduced by stages so that the groups receiving the program first and those waiting their turn are chosen at random, or begun as a pilot project in a randomly chosen sample of groups. In those cases, an evaluation may take the form of a true experiment. But in the vast majority of cases an entire governmental or corporate unit is affected by a change in policy. Then, research designs like the time series, multiple time series, Separate-Sample Pretest-Posttest, and other quasi-experimental designs must be used. These designs, and hopefully future improvements on them, are essential to the kind of objective process for selecting effective programs upon which the future success of our society, economic and social, depends.

The increased attention to, and use of, quasi-experimental research designs will also serve the important function of promoting cooperation among the many diverse disciplines which are engaged in the study of behavior. One of the important lessons to be learned in considering nonexperimental research is that the study of human behavior is much broader than the traditional laboratory science of pscyhology. Historians, political scientists, economists, lawyers, sociologists, anthropologists, and others are also students of human behavior. For a long time, cooperation between psychologists and members of these other disciplines has been blocked by a difference in jargon and academic affiliation. Only psychologists were accustomed to bringing behavior into the laboratory for study, modifying it to fit the scientific apparatus which was housed there, and clinging to the snobbish identification with the methods of the natural sciences (even though, as we have seen, they work out quite differently when applied to the subject matter of behavior). As the value of quasi-experimental designs becomes more widely recognized, behavioral scientists of all types will find themselves working in more similar ways, studying more similar questions, and seeing more possibilities for cooperation. This will bring closer to all of us the possibility of a comprehensive science of behavior that will broaden the scope and the empirical foundations of our theories of behavior as well as the resources that we can bring to bear on the problems of our society that, whether they are called crime, inflation, or education, have causes and effects that so often turn out to be in our behavior.

## JUST A BEGINNING

All that we have learned so far is just a starting point. The first century or so of scientific research into behavior has taught us, more than anything else, how elusive a target we are after. A complete understanding of the problems of assessing the validity of research findings is still far off. The truth we have discovered so far is in need of much more refinement in the future. And we have not even considered many of the issues that are crucial to the development of a reliable science of behavior. There are many other skills which the study of behavior demands—in the areas of statistics, neuroanatomy and physiology, biochemistry, and so many other fields that are essential to understanding behavior. But we should not be discouraged by what needs to be learned. No science has an end point at which its work is done. Our successors on this earth will be as busy as we are. And that is all to the good.

## REFERENCES

Argyris, C. The incompleteness of social psychological theory: Examples from small group, cognitive consistency, and attribution research. *American Psychologist*, 1969, *24*, 893–907.

Aronson, E. *The social animal*, second edition. San Francisco: Freeman, 1976.

Campbell, D. T. Reforms as experiments. *American Psychologist*, 1969, *24*, 409–429.

Cohen, S., Evans, G. W., Krantz, D. S., & Stokols, D. Physiological, motivational, and cognitive effects of aircraft noise on children: Moving from the laboratory to the field. *American Psychologist*, 1980, *35*, 231–243.

Rosenthal, R. Combining the results of independent studies. *Psychological Bulletin*, 1978, *85*, 185–193.

Rosenthal, R. The "file drawer problem" and tolerance for null results. *Psychological Bulletin*, 1979, *86*, 638–641.

# Glossary

**archival data.** Records of behavior that are used as a source of data in a research study, although they were kept originally for some other purpose.

**artifact.** An observed effect on the behavior being studied that was not caused solely by the operation of the independent variable.

**blind experimenter.** A person conducting a research study who is unaware of the hypothesis being tested.

**bogus pipeline.** A technique that attempts to reduce distortion in behavioral measures by convincing subjects that the experimenter has a foolproof way of assessing their true private feelings.

**conceptual hypothesis.** A general notion that some factor is a cause of a particular behavior.

**confounding.** The influence of an unintended causal factor that makes it impossible to determine the separate effect of the independent variable.

**control.** The process of preventing the influence of extraneous variables on the behavior being studied.

**control treatment.** Events to which research subjects are exposed to provide a basis for comparison of the effects of the independent variable.

**data.** Observations of behavior that has occurred under the conditions specified in the hypothesis.

**dependent variable.** The measure of behavior utilized in order to assess the effects of variations in the independent variable.

**dissimulation.** The effect of an extraneous variable that creates the hypothesized differences in behavior.

**ecological validity.** The extent to which research results represent the effect that occurs when the behavior is subjected to the influence of the causal event in a natural setting.

**equivalent groups.** Groups of subjects that have been constituted through a process of random assignment from one original group and therefore share the same characteristics.

**evidence.** Observations made in the course of a research study that form the basis for conclusions about the effects of a hypothesized causal event.

**experimental isolation.** The elimination of the effects of extraneous variables by conducting research in a setting that shields subjects from events other than those created by the researcher.

**experimental manipulation.** A procedure used to create the variations of the hypothesized causal event that are studied in research (in contrast to those that might occur naturally).

**experimental mortality (sample attrition).** The nonrandom loss of subjects from the groups that are being compared in a research study.

**experimental treatments.** The specific variations of the independent variable which are studied in research.

**experimenter.** The person who does the actual work of performing a study (meeting subjects, giving them instructions, etc.).

**external validity.** The extent to which research results can be expected to hold true beyond the specific setting in which they were obtained.

**extraneous events.** Events other than the independent variable that affect the dependent variable, and thus prevent the true effects of the independent variable from being determined.

**extraneous variable.** Any causal factor irrelevant to the hypothesis being tested that affects the behavior being studied at the same time as the independent variable.

**factorial experiment.** An experimental research design that evaluates the effect of more than one causal event simultaneously.

**field research.** Research conducted in natural settings.

**field studies.** Research that investigates the effects of naturally-occurring events on behavior in a natural context.

**finding.** Conclusion that is drawn from the results of a research study.

**group composition effects.** Extraneous effects on the behavior being observed that are covered by preexisting differences among the groups of subjects being compared.

**hypothesis.** A statement about the cause of some phenomenon upon which a research study is based.

**independent variable.** A particular set of causal conditions whose effect the researcher seeks to observe.

**interaction.** The effects of a causal condition whose impact on the observed behavior varies across different levels of some other specified causal condition.

**interaction of temporal and group composition effects.** The error introduced when temporal (or maturational) effects differ among treatment groups because of preexisting differences among those groups.

**internal validity.** The extent to which the observed values of the dependent variable are free from the influence of extraneous variables operating within the temporal and spatial confines of the research setting.

**invalid finding.** A conclusion that attributes the obtained results of a research study to a factor other than their true cause.

**main effect.** The effect of a causal condition that remains unchanged across varying levels of other specified causal conditions.

**manipulation check.** A method used to assess the degree to which an experimental treatment produced the intended effects on the subjects.

**masking.** The effect of an extraneous variable without which the independent variable would be observed to have the hypothesized effect.

**maturation (temporal effects).** Changes in the dependent variable that are bound to occur during the time span of the investigation as a result of some characteristic that the subjects or phenomena possess naturally.

**multiple time series.** The addition to a time series of a comparison series of observations of another group that is not exposed to the causal event in question.

**nonequivalent comparison group.** An intact group used to assess the effect of exposure to a hypothesized causal event when random assignment is not feasible.

**nonrepresentative sampling.** The use of research subjects whose characteristics limit the generalizability of the research results.

**observer effects.** The error introduced in the acquisition of data when those data do not reflect the application of the same standard of measurement to all groups being compared.

**plausible rival hypothesis.** A rival hypothesis that is supported by existing research data or theory.

**practice effect.** Changes that occur in subjects' scores on a measure of behavior that are attributable to previous exposure to that measure.

**preexperimental designs.** Research plans that either lack appropriate comparison groups or sufficient observations over time to assess the effects of the independent variable.

**pretesting.** The direct administration, before exposure to the independent variable, of an instrument that will later be used to measure the dependent variable.

**quasi-experimental designs.** Research plans based on comparisons of single groups of subjects over time, or comparisons among groups that were not constituted by random assignment.

**reactivity.** The use of procedures that make subjects aware that they are being studied and thus limit the generalizability of the research results.

**regression toward the mean (statistical regression).** The error introduced by the fact that, on the average, extreme scorers tend to score less extremely, or closer to the overall group mean on successive testings.

**research context.** The time and place in which a research study is conducted.

**research design.** The plan that specifies the comparisons to be made in the research study, including the method of assigning subjects and the sequences of events to which subjects are to be exposed.

**research hypothesis.** The hypothesis actually tested in a research study in which specific representations have been chosen for the causal factor and behavior of the conceptual hypothesis.

**research setting.** The specific procedures employed to carry out a research study, including instruments, physical setting, and so on.

**result.** Observations made in the course of a research study.

**retrospective attrition.** Nonrandom loss or absence of observations from records of past behavior.

**rival hypothesis.** An explanation other than the original research hypothesis that accounts for the results of a study and cannot be ruled out.

**role playing.** A way of manipulating an independent variable in which subjects respond to imagined events or situations rather than deceptive ones.

**sample attrition (experimental mortality).** The nonrandom loss of subjects from the groups that are being compared in a research study.

**sampling error.** Differences between groups of subjects that exist in spite of the fact that subjects have been randomly assigned.

**sensitization.** The effect of a pretest that alerts the subject to the research hypothesis and/or that aspect of his or her behavior that is of interest to the researcher.

**simulation.** A means of recreating an important natural setting for behavior by physical props and instructions that represent its essential properties to subjects.

**sociohistorical context.** The time in history and the culture that surround a research study.

**statistical regression (regression toward the mean).** The error introduced by the fact that, on the average, extreme scorers tend to score less extremely, or closer to the overall group mean, on successive testings.

**study.** A general term used to refer to any research, regardless of the methods it employs.

**subjects.** The organisms whose behavior is observed in a research study.

**temporal effects (maturation).** Changes in the dependent variable that are bound to occur during the time span of the investigation as a result of some characteristic that the subjects or phenomena possess naturally.

**true experimental designs.** Those research strategies in which the researcher controls which subjects are exposed to which events, at what times, in which forms.

**threats to external validity.** Features of a research study that restrict the generalizability of its findings.

**threats to internal validity.** Extraneous influences on the dependent variable that are produced within the temporal and spatial confines of the research setting.

**time series.** A series of measures extending over a long period of time, both before and after the occurrence of a hypothesized causal event.

**true experimental design.** A research plan based on comparisons among equivalent groups of subjects created by random assignment.

**valid finding.** A conclusion which attributes the obtained results of a study to their true cause.

**validity.** The extent to which research results reflect accurately the effects of the hypothesized causal event.

**Validity Scorecard.** A device for judging a research design against all the criteria for validity.

# Author Index

# Subject Index

and sample attrition, 196, 206–207
Solomon four-group design, 216ff
and statistical regression effects, 196, 207
and temporal effects, 196, 198, 199, 205
and threats to external validity, 208ff, 230, 239ff
and threats to internal validity, 204ff
True scores, 70

Undifferentiated random sample, 77

Valid finding, 7–9, 12, 364
Validity, 3, 16ff, 364
  discriminant validity, 44, 47
  ecological validity, 117, 126, 134, 361

external validity, 21, 22, 82, 85ff
  threats to external validity, 22, 82ff
internal validity, 21, 22
  threats to internal validity, 21, 22, 26ff, 134
internal versus external validity, 134ff
Validity scorecard, 142, 146, 364
Variable, 8, 9, 22, 56, 148
  blocks variable, 56
  dependent variable, 8, 148
  extraneous variable, 9, 22
  independent variable, 8, 148
  levels variable, 56

Waiting-list control procedure, 49

Yerkes-Dodson Law, 110